Antisemitic Myths

Antisemitic Myths

A HISTORICAL AND CONTEMPORARY ANTHOLOGY

EDITED BY

Marvin Perry and Frederick M. Schweitzer

Indiana University Press

BLOOMINGTON AND INDIANAPOLIS

This book is a publication of

Indiana University Press
601 North Morton Street
Bloomington, IN 47404-3797 USA

http://iupress.indiana.edu

Telephone orders   800-842-6796
Fax orders   812-855-7931
Orders by e-mail   iuporder@indiana.edu

The paper used in this publication meets the minimum requirements of American
National Standard for Information Sciences—Permanence of Paper for Printed Library
Materials, ANSI Z39.48-1984.

Manufactured in the United States of America

Library of Congress Cataloging-in-Publication Data

Antisemitic myths : a historical and contemporary anthology / edited by Marvin Perry
and Frederick M. Schweitzer.
p.   cm.
Includes bibliographical references and index.
ISBN-13: 978-0-253-34984-2 (cloth)
ISBN-13: 978-0-253-21950-3 (pbk.)
1. Antisemitism—History—Sources. 2. Antisemitism—History. I. Perry, Marvin.
II. Schweitzer, Frederick M.
DS145.A633 2007
305.892′4—dc22

2007023453

1 2 3 4 5   13 12 11 10 09 08

CONTENTS

PART 3. CONTEMPORARY

PREFACE

In a previous collaboration we published *Antisemitism: Myth and Hate from Antiquity to the Present* (2002), which focused on historic and contemporary myths about Jews that have made antisemitism both a lethal force and a case study in the persistence, power, and danger of the irrational in human affairs. Over the centuries, many people believed and propagated bizarre myths that demonized and dehumanized the Jewish people. No matter how absurd and inconsistent, these myths, which saw the Jews as the source of all evil, attracted myriad believers, even among the educated, and provoked and justified persecution, expulsion, and massacre. Even after the Holocaust, these myths continue to circulate, particularly in the Muslim world, which has enthusiastically embraced medieval Christian, modern European, and Nazi antisemitic myths. The Nazi years demonstrated the failure both of the Western humanist and Christian traditions; neither provided an effective defense against genocide. And adherents of both traditions embraced, at times with obscene enthusiasm, Nazi racial doctrines that buttressed extermination. The documents in this anthology illustrate the character and evolution of those antisemitic myths that ultimately culminated in the Holocaust and continue to threaten Jews today. In tracing these antisemitic tracts, one descends into the murky world of the irrational, over which reason exercises a very limited influence. That these tales were widely believed illustrates Freud's conviction that reason is a puny instrument in comparison with the volcanic strength of non-rational impulses, and that these impulses deflect people into destructive behavior and make political life precarious. Nazism demonstrated that antisemitism threatened not only Jews but also the core values of Western civilization. At a time when bashing Israel often crosses the line into antisemitism, it is imperative that this truism be remembered.

The ninety-some documents that make up this volume are a representative selection from the vast corpus of primary source material available to the modern student of antisemitism. Every century of the Common Era and many lands and societies added their litany to this lethal ideology, which has been called "the longest hatred." What must strike anyone who peruses much of that huge reservoir of loathing and condemnation—as the reader will find in analyzing the ninety documents presented here—is the unique intensity of Judaeophobia, the irrational fear of the Jews, the fanatical conviction that drives antisemitic authors, and the ostensibly limitless allegations of Jewish evildoing and superhuman capacity for crime and destruction. These allegations—rooted in myth and the fear, hatred, and fanaticism they evoked—provided the intellectual and psychological motivation and justification for Nazi mass murderers and those who assisted them throughout conquered Europe. Had not antisemites for decades been urging an ultimate reckoning to free the world of the perpetual menace of Jewry? Well before the Nazis came to power, radical antisemites in many European lands did not regard the dispossession, expulsion, or even annihilation of Jewry as unthinkable. That such virulent hatred, at once viscerally felt and ideologically grounded, persists today must be obvious to anyone who reads the signs of the times. And one sign of the times may be the enactment by the United States Congress of the Global Anti-Semitism Review Act of 2004, the publication of the mandated "Report on Global Anti-Semitism, July 1, 2003-December 15, 2004" in 2005, and the appointment by the secretary of state of a Special Envoy for Monitoring and Combating Anti-Semitism in 2006. It is our hope that readers of our work will master its lessons.

Having completed this volume, we have special pleasure in acknowledging those who helped make it possible. We wish to thank Manhattan College colleagues Professor Robert Kramer for his translation of Hitler's 1920 speech, Dr. Eleanor T. Ostrau for her translation of *Civiltà Cattolica* material, Dr. Jeff Horn for his translation of the editorial from *La Croix*, Dr. Joseph Castora for his translation of Origen, and Tatyana Gourov, a former student, for her translation of the "Letter of the Attorney General to Investigate Jews" that was provided to us by Dr. Ilya A. Altman, Vice-President of the Russian Holocaust Foundation in Moscow. In addition, we are indebted to Shlomo Daskal, a graduate student in the Department of Arab Language and Literature at the Hebrew University of Jerusalem, for his translation of Sayyid Qutb; to David G. Littman of the Association for World Education in Geneva for his insightful guidance on questions concerning the United Nations and providing documentary material difficult to acquire; and to Richard S. Levy of the University of Illinois at Chicago for all his help over many years.

Librarians and libraries have greatly facilitated our researches. Most especially, the O'Malley-Hayes Library of Manhattan College and its librarians; in particular we thank Brother Thomas O'Connor, FSC, Ph.D., for indispensable assistance in tracking manuscripts and archival material, and John Gormley for procuring a long list of interlibrary loans. We also acknowledge the wonderful assistance of Eleanor Yadin and her colleagues at the Dorot Jewish Division of the New York Public Library; the Walsh Library of Fordham University and its Sidney Rosenblatt Holocaust Collection at Lincoln Center; the Ryan Library of Iona College; the Research Department of the Anti-Defamation League in New York City; the Jacob H. Schiff Library of the Jewish Theological Seminary of America; Butler Library of Columbia University; the library of Union Theological Seminary; the National Archives in Washington; and the British Library in London.

For reviewing portions of the book, criticism, bibliographical suggestions, and various forms of assistance, we thank Manhattan colleagues Professors

Joan Cammarata, Brother Patrick Horner, FSC, Claire Nolte, and Mark Taylor. On specific topics we have had the benefit of expert guidance from Professor Emeritus Henry Feingold of Baruch College and the City University of New York; Dr. Eugene Fisher, Director of the Secretariat for Ecumenical and Inter-religious Affairs of the National Conference of Catholic Bishops; Rabbi Steven Franklin of Riverdale Temple; Dr. Zev Garber of Los Angeles Valley College; Dr. Steven Jacobs of the University of Alabama at Tuscaloosa; Dr. John T. Pawlikowski, O. S. P., of the Catholic Theological Union of Chicago; Michael G. Rapp of Xavier University in Cincinnati; Professor William D. Rubinstein of the University of Wales, Aberystwyth; Professor Emeritus John Weiss of Lehman College and the City University of New York; and Mark Weitzman of the New York Wiesenthal Center. For some critical references, our thanks go to the renowned historian Bernard Lewis of Princeton and to Ms. Esther Web-man of the Stephen Roth Institute at Tel Aviv University. Professor Robert S. Wistrich of the Hebrew University of Jerusalem provided invaluable guidance on Muslim antisemitism. Professor Omer Bartov of Brown University assisted us royally in questions concerning antisemitism in Russia and Ukraine and obtained Professor Amir Weiner's aid in establishing the strange publication history of *The Black Book* by Ilya Ehrenburg and Vasily Grossman. It is a plea-sure once again to acknowledge our indebtedness to the numerous scholars and writers whose works we have drawn on, those who are cited in the endnotes as well as the many not mentioned. We wish to acknowledge the professional staff at Indiana University Press for their commitment to our project: Janet Rabinowitch, Director of the press and our Sponsoring Editor; Anne Teillard-Clemmer, Assistant Sponsoring Editor; Miki Bird, Managing Editor; Brian Herrmann, Project Editor; and Matt Williamson, Senior Artist and Book De-signer. We especially wish to commend Sarah Brown for her meticulous edit-ing of the manuscript. We also wish to express our gratitude to Neill Bogan for compiling the index. Finally, we note with great sadness the passing of a dear friend, Sister Rose Thering, O. P., whose study of Catholic religious education was fundamental in inducing the Second Vatican Council to formulate *Nostra Aetate* and who remained an intrepid fighter against antisemitism, genocidal ideologies, apathy, and Holocaust denial.

* * *

Marvin Perry wishes to thank Phyllis Perry, his wife of more than fifty years, for supporting unreservedly his commitment to this project and for providing the warm companionship that facilitated its completion. He is grateful to Houghton Mifflin Company for permission to use some of his material from previously published works, particularly *An Intellectual History of Modern Europe* (1993), *Sources of the Western Tradition* (6th ed., 2006), and *Western Civilization; Ideas, Politics, and Society* (8th ed., 2007). His thanks also to Peter Lang for permission to use passages from his article in *Jewish-Christian Encounters over the Centuries: Symbiosis, Prejudice, Holocaust, Dialogue* (1994), co-edited with Frederick M. Schweitzer; and to Palgrave Macmillan for allowing him to use some of his material from *Antisemitism: Myth and Hate from Antiquity to the Present* (2002; paperback, 2005), also co-authored with Frederick M. Schweitzer.

Frederick M. Schweitzer wants above all to avow his wife Jacqueline's tender-loving care, sustained encouragement, and great interest in all his work, and her dauntlessly buoyant spirit despite the afflictions that the passing years mete out to us. But the relentlessly passing years also bring us great pleasure and satisfaction in our children and grandchildren. A salute also to Manhattan College, his professional home for nearly fifty years, which from the start was generous with summer grants, sabbaticals, travel funds, and the like, but equally with the intangible support and encouragement for his initially somewhat eccentric commitment to Jewish history and Catholic-Jewish relations. It continues to be a remarkable venture for him and Manhattan together in breaking free of inherited stereotypes and the bondage of age-old antipathy. With the founding in 1996 of the college's Holocaust Resource Center, the relationship has taken on a new energy and direction.

ACKNOWLEDGMENTS

Saint John Chrysostom, *Discourses against Judaizing Christians*, reprinted by permission of The Catholic University of America Press from *The Fathers of the Church*, edited by Paul W. Harkins, vol. 68, copyright © 1979.

Sebastián de Horozco, "Ritual Murder" at La Guardia, Spain, reprinted by permission of Manchester University Press from *The Jews in Western Europe 1400-1600*, edited by John Edwards, copyright © 1994.

Rabbi Avigdor Kara of Prague, "All the Afflictions," reprinted by permission of Yale University Press from *Gentile Tales: The Narrative Assault on Late Medieval Jews* by Miri Rubin, copyright © 1999 by Miri Rubin.

The Passau Host Desecration of 1478, reprinted by permission of Hebrew Union College Press from *The Jew in the Medieval World, A Source Book: 315-1791* by Jacob R. Marcus, copyright © 1938 Union of American Hebrew Congregations.

Jacob von Königshofen, "If they [the Jews] had been poor and if the feudal lords had not been in debt to them, they would not have been burnt," reprinted by permission of Hebrew Union College Press from *The Jew in the Medieval World, A Source Book: 315-1791* by Jacob R. Marcus, copyright © 1938 Union of American Hebrew Congregations.

The Royal Edict of 1492, "throw the . . . Jews out of our kingdoms," reprinted by permission of Manchester University Press from *The Jews in Western Europe 1400-1600*, edited by John Edwards, copyright © 1994. Damião de Gois, *Expulsion, Forced Conversion, and Massacre*, reprinted by permission of Manchester University Press from *The Jews in Western Europe 1400-1600*, edited by John Edwards, copyright © 1994.

Martin Luther, *On the Jews and their Lies*, from *Luther's Works*, vol. 47: *Christian in Society IV*, edited by Franklin Sherman, copyright © 1971 by Fortress Press. All rights reserved. Used by permission of Augsburg Fortress.

Johann Andreas Eisenmenger, *Judaism Exposed*, reprinted by permission of Richard S. Levy, Department of History, University of Illinois at Chicago, from Richard S. Levy, ed., *Antisemitism in the Modern World: An Anthology of Texts*, copyright © 1991 by D. C. Heath.

"A Children's Story Perpetuates the Myth of Ritual Murder," *Andreas of Rin*, reprinted by permission of The Edwin Mellen Press from *Anti-Jewish Prejudices in German-Catholic Sermons* by Walter Zwi Bacharach, copyright © 1993 by The Edwin Mellen Press.

Karl Marx, "The Jewish Question," reprinted by permission of Philosophical Library from *Karl Marx: A World Without Jews*, edited by Dagobert D. Runes, copyright © 1959 by Philosophical Press, Inc.

Édouard-Adolphe Drumont, *Jewish France*, reprinted from Marvin Perry et al., eds., *Sources of the Western Tradition*, Sixth Edition, Vol. 2, Copyright © 2006 by Houghton Mifflin Company. Used by permission.

La Libre Parole, 1894, "The Jewish Judas," excerpted by permission of Rutgers University Press from *The Dreyfus Case: A Documentary History*, edited by Louis L. Snyder, © 1973.

"An Anti-Dreyfus Poster, 1898" and "Anti-Dreyfusard Reflections of a Small Businessman of Caen, 1898" from *The Anti-Semitic Moment: A Tour of France in 1898* by Pierre Birnbaum, translated by Jane Marie Todd. Translation copyright © 2003 by Jane Marie Todd. Reprinted by permission of Hill and Wang, a division of Farrar, Straus and Giroux, LLC.

Richard Wagner, "Judaism in Music," reprinted by permission of Peter Owen Publishers from *Richard Wagner: Stories and Essays*, edited by Charles Osborne, copyright © 1973.

Hermann Ahlwardt, "The Jews versus the Germans," reprinted by permission of the American Jewish Committee from *Rehearsal for Destruction: A Study of Political Anti-Semitism in Imperial Germany* by Paul W. Massing, Studies in Prejudice Series, copyright © 1949.

Theodor Fritsch, "The Antisemitic Catechism & The Antisemitic Ten Commandments," reprinted by permission of the American Jewish Committee from *Rehearsal for Destruction: A Study of Political Anti-Semitism in Imperial Germany* by Paul W. Massing, Studies in Prejudice Series, copyright © 1949.

Konstantin von Gebsattel, The Jewish Threat, 1913, reprinted by permission of John C. G. Röhl from *From Bismarck to Hitler: The Problem of Continuity in German History*, edited by J. C. G. Röhl, copyright © 1970.

Theodor Herzl, *The Jewish State*, reprinted by permission of the American Zionist Movement from *The Jewish State: An Attempt at a Modern Solution of the Jewish Question* by Theodor Herzl, copyright © 1946.

"The Kishinev Pogrom, Easter 1903," reprinted from Marvin Perry et al., eds., *Sources of the Western Tradition*, Sixth Edition, Vol. 2, Copyright © 2006 by Houghton Mifflin Company. Used by permission.

"A Ritual Murder Trial in the 20th Century: The Beilis Case: International Protests," reprinted from Cecil Roth, *The Ritual Murder Libel: The Report by Cardinal Lorenzo Ganganelli*, copyright © 1935 by Woburn Press.

Hans Knodn, "The Solution of the Jewish Question," reprinted by permission of Oxford University Press from "Hostages of 'World Jewry': On the Origin of the Idea of Genocide in German History" by Herbert A. Strauss, *Holocaust and Genocide Studies: An International Journal*, Vol. 3, copyright © 1988; permission conveyed through Copyright Clearance Center, Inc.

Adolf Hitler, *Mein Kampf*, reprinted by permission of Houghton Mifflin Company from Marvin Perry et al., eds., *Sources of the Western Tradition: From the Renaissance to the Present*, Vol. 2, Fifth Edition, copyright © 2003 by Houghton Mifflin Company. Used with permission.

Jakob Graf, "How We Can Learn to Recognize a Person's Race," reprinted by permission of the University of Wisconsin Press from *Nazi Culture: Intellectual, Cultural and Social Life in the Third Reich*, edited by George L. Mosse, translated by Salvator Attansio et al., copyright © 1966.

Johannes Stark, "The Jewish spirit has little aptitude for creative activity in the sciences," reprinted by permission of the University of Wisconsin Press from *Nazi Culture: Intellectual, Cultural and Social Life in the Third Reich*, edited by George L. Mosse, translated by Salvator Attansio et al., copyright © 1966.

Julius Streicher, "Jewish Murder Plan against Gentile Humanity Exposed: The Murderous People," reprinted by permission of Randall L. Bytwerk from *Julius Streicher: The Man Who Persuaded a Nation to Hate Jews* by Randall L. Bytwerk, copyright © 1983.

Julius Streicher, "The Pan-Jewish Worldwide Attack: Secret Plans against Germany Revealed: The Jewish World Conference," reprinted by permission of Randall L. Bytwerk from German Propaganda Archive, www.calvin.edu/academic/cas/gpa/ds6.htm, copyright © 1999.

Joseph Goebbels, *"The Jews are to Blame,"* reprinted by permission of Randall L. Bytwerk from German Propaganda Archive, www.calvin.edu/academic/cas/gpa, copyright © 1998.

"It is on the issue of genocide. . . . " reprinted by permission of Cornell University Press from *Germany's War and the Holocaust: Disputed Histories* by Omer Bartov, copyright © 2003.

"Anyone who has ever looked at the face of a red commissar. . . . " and "Every officer must be filled with the conviction. . . . " reproduced with permission of Palgrave Macmillan from *The Eastern Front, 1941-45: German Troops and the Barbarisation of Warfare* by Omer Bartov, copyright © 1986.

"Since 22 June the German Volk is in the midst. . . . " and "It has become increasingly clear to us this summer. . . . " and "I have received the 'Stürmer'. . . . " are reprinted by permission of Oxford University Press, Inc., from *Hitler's Army: Soldiers, Nazis, and War in the Third Reich* by Omer Bartov, copyright © 1992.

Chaim A. Kaplan, *Scroll of Agony: The Warsaw Diary of Chaim A. Kaplan*, reprinted with the permission of Scribner, an imprint of Simon & Schuster Adult Publishing Group, from *Scroll of Agony* edited by Abraham I. Katsh. Copyright © 1965 by Abraham I. Katsh. All rights reserved.

Y. Pfeffer, The Concentration Camp Routine: Daily Brutalization and Humiliation, reprinted by permission of Franklin Watts, an imprint of Scholastic Library Publishing, Inc. from *A History of the Holocaust* by Yehuda Bauer, copyright © 1982. All rights reserved.

Terrence Des Pres, Degradation by "Excremental Assault," reprinted by permission of Oxford University Press from *The Survivor: An Anatomy of Life in the Death Camps* by Terrence Des Pres, copyright © 1976.

Rudolf Höss, Commandant of Auschwitz, On the Necessity to Murder Jewish Children, reprinted by permission of Routledge Publishing from *The "Final Solution" in the Extermination Camps and the Aftermath, The Holocaust:*

Selected Documents in Eighteen Volumes, edited by John Mendelsohn and Donald S. Detwiler, Vol. 12, copyright © 1982, permission conveyed through Copyright Clearance Center, Inc.

Evangelical Church of Germany Council, *Stuttgart Declaration of Guilt*; and Synod of the Evangelical Church in Germany, *Statement on the Jewish Question, Berlin-Weissensee*, reprinted by permission of Indiana University Press from *A Church Divided: German Protestants Confront the Nazi Past* by Matthew D. Hockenos, copyright © 2004 by Indiana University Press, Bloomington & Indianapolis.

The Church Council of the Evangelical Lutheran Church in America, *Declaration on Lutheran-Jewish Relations*, reprinted from www.jcrelations.com by permission of Franklin Sherman, Department for Ecumenical Affairs, Evangelical Lutheran Church in America.

Ruth Okuneva, "Anti-Semitic Notions: Strange Analogies," reprinted from Theodore Freedman, ed., *Anti-Semitism in the Soviet Union: Its Roots and Consequences* by permission of the Anti-Defamation League, copyright © 1984 by the Anti-Defamation League. All rights reserved.

Judicial Proceedings against Members of the Jewish Anti-Fascist Committee, reprinted by permission of Yale University Press from Joshua Rubenstein and Vladimir P. Naumov, eds., *Stalin's Secret Pogrom: The Postwar Inquisition of the Jewish Anti-Fascist Committee*, Copyright © 2001.

"The Doctors' Plot: 'beasts in the guise of physicians'," reprinted from Theodore Freedman, ed., *Anti-Semitism in the Soviet Union: Its Roots and Consequences* by permission of the Anti-Defamation League, copyright © 1984 by the Anti-Defamation League. All rights reserved.

Ingo Hasselbach, *Führer-Ex: Memoirs of a Former Neo-Nazi*, reprinted from *Führer-Ex* by Ingo Hasselbach, copyright © 1996 by Ingo Hasselbach. Used by permission of Random House, Inc.

William L. Pierce, *The Turner Diaries*, reprinted by arrangement with Barricade Books from Andrew Macdonald (pseud.) *The Turner Diaries*, Second Edition, copyright © 1996.

The Canard of Ritual Murder in Cincinnati, "All Christian Parents: The Safety of Your Children is at Stake!" reprinted by permission of *The New York Times* from Jacob Rader Marcus, ed., *The Jew in the American World, A Source Book*. Copyright © 1996 by *The New York Times Co.*

Raphael S. Ezekiel, *The Racist Mind*, reprinted from *The Racist Mind: Portraits of American Neo-Nazis and Klansmen* by Raphael S. Ezekiel, copyright © 1995 by Raphael S. Ezekiel. Used by permission of Viking Penguin, a division of Penguin Group (USA) Inc.

The Historical Research Department of the Nation of Islam, *The Secret Relationship Between Blacks and Jews*, excerpted by permission of the Historical Research Department from *The Secret Relationship Between Blacks and Jews*, Vol. 1, copyright © 1991 by Latimer Associates. All rights reserved.

Khallid Abdul Muhammed, ". . . You're from the Synagogue of Satan," reprinted from *The New York Times* by permission of the Anti-Defamation

League. Copyright © 1994 by the Anti-Defamation League. All rights reserved.

Henry Louis Gates, Jr., *"Black Demagogues and Pseudo-Scholars,"* reprinted by permission of *The New York Times* from Henry Louis Gates, Jr., "Black Demagogues and Pseudo-Scholars," Copyright © 1992 by *The New York Times Co.*

Arab Theologians on Jews and Israel, excerpted from *Arab Theologians on Jews and Israel; Extracts from the Proceedings of the Fourth Conference of the Academy of Islamic Research* edited by D. F. Green, (pseud. of David G. Littman and Yehoshafat Harkabi), excerpted by permission of David G. Littman. Third edition, 1976.

Egyptian Soldiers' Handbook, *Our Faith—Our Way to Victory,* reprinted from *Arab Theologians on Jews and Israel; Extracts from the Proceedings of the Fourth Conference of the Academy of Islamic Research,* edited by D. F. Green (pseud. of David G. Littman and Yehoshafat Harkabi), by permission of David G. Littman. Third edition, 1976.

"Covenant of the Islamic Resistance Movement," Hamas, Gaza, reprinted from *Selected Translations and Analysis* (Simon Wiesenthal Center, Fall 1988).

Fiamma Nirenstein, "Observations: How Suicide Bombers are Made," reprinted from *Commentary,* September 2001, by permission of Fiamma Nirenstein and *Commentary;* all rights reserved.

Hassan Sweilem, "The Jewish Personality and the Israeli Actions," copyright © 2000, and "Jews Use Teenagers' Blood for 'Purim' Pastries," copyright © 2002, reprinted from www.memri.org by permission of the Washington-based Middle East Media Research Institute (MEMRI).

INTRODUCTION

Many historians regard the Holocaust as a seminal event of the twentieth century. The murder of six million innocents, including 1.5 million children, by a regime that thought it was doing humanity a service by cleansing Europe of a wicked race unworthy of life, showed that even in an age of sophisticated science the human mind remains susceptible to mythical modes of thought. The Nazi assault on reason and freedom, the core ideals of modern Western civilization, demonstrated anew our civilization's precariousness. This assault would forever cast doubt on the Enlightenment's conception of human goodness, secular rationality, and the progress of civilization through advances in science and technology. Auschwitz, Treblinka, Sobibor, and the other death factories represent the triumph of human irrationality over reason—the surrender of the mind to a bizarre racial mythology that provided metaphysical and pseudo-scientific justification for mass murder. The death camps—embodying "The Theory and Practice of Hell" in the title of a famous work by a survivor—also represent the ultimate perversion of reason, a calculating reason used to manufacture and organize lies and disseminate beliefs in a structured system with its own inner logic, and to employ sophisticated technology and administrative techniques to destroy human beings spiritually and physically. Science and technology—together with bureaucratic efficiency—made mass extermination possible. The eighteenth-century thinkers, who valued reason as a great human achievement, had not foreseen the destructive power unleashed by its perversion. Historian Omer Bartov poses this disturbing question about the failure of reason and the Western humanist tradition:

> What was it that induced Nobel Prize-winning scientists, internationally respected legal scholars, physicians known throughout the world for their research into the human body and their desire to ameliorate the lot of humanity, to become not merely opportunist accomplices, but in many ways the initiators and promoters of this attempt to subject the human race to a vast surgical operation by means of mass extermination? What was there (or is there) in our culture that made the concept of transforming humanity by means of eugenic and racial cleansing seem so practical and rational?[1]

The Nazi regime that made the annihilation of European Jewry a cardinal policy and many of its collaborators in several European lands who participated in the murderous process regarded Jews as the source of all evil, human demons that conspired to ruin Germany and dominate the planet. In their worldview, rooted in myth, fantasy, and delusion, Jews were a lower and racially defective species of life, but immensely powerful and dangerous. Exterminating them would prevent defilement of Aryan blood and the corruption of European culture and would rescue humanity from its Jewish overlords. A Jewish physician-inmate at Auschwitz asked one of the Nazi doctors who selected Jews for the gas chambers how he could reconcile mass murder with his Hippocratic oath. His reply demonstrates the demonological antisemitism and distorted idealism that inspired Nazi executioners: "Of course I am a doctor and I want to preserve life. And out of respect for human life I would remove a gangrenous appendix from a diseased body. The Jew is the gangrenous appendix in the body of mankind."[2] Nazi propaganda spread this kind of fantasy in order to promote hatred of Jews throughout Europe. Even after World War II and the systematic slaughter of two-thirds of the Jewish population of Europe, Jew-hatred, fueled by classic antisemitic myths, persisted tenaciously in many areas. In post-Holocaust Poland, rumors that Jews had tortured and murdered a Polish boy for a religious ritual triggered a pogrom in Kielce and its environs that took the lives of eighty Holocaust survivors. In the first years after 1945 some fifteen hundred Jews were murdered by Poles, and at a provincial meeting of the Polish Peasants Party in August 1945 a speaker "put out a resolution that Jews [in addition to Germans] should also be expelled from Poland, and he also remarked that Hitler ought to be thanked for destroying the Jews (tumultuous ovation and applause)" by the thousand party delegates and activists.[3]

The documents in this anthology illustrate many myths about Jews that have made antisemitism such a persistent, lethal force in European history and are now generating potential genocidal developments in the Muslim world. The documents in part 1, "Medieval and Early Modern," illustrate Christian demonization of the Jews that culminated in persecution, expulsion, and massacre. Scholars have long emphasized that two thousand years of Christian anti-Judaism, which denigrated Jews as pure evil, as an eternally criminal people, prepared many Europeans to subscribe to Nazi racist myths and to participate in, endorse, or remain indifferent to Hitler's Final Solution. To be sure, traditional Christian anti-Judaism, which condemned Jews for their religion and rejection of Christ and normally welcomed Jewish converts, contrasts with Nazism, which saw Jews as a racially inferior and dangerous subspecies of humanity who could never escape the curse of their genes. Nevertheless, because the image of the Jew as irredeemably evil—"Christ-killers," "children of the Devil," "agents of Satan," ritual murderers—and a menace to Christianity was preached and broadly held for centuries, Europeans were receptive to Nazi antisemitism. James Carroll, a Catholic writer and former priest, summarizes the relationship between Christian and Nazi attitudes toward the Jews:

Auschwitz, when seen in the links of causality, reveals that the hatred of Jews has been . . . a central action of Christian history, reaching to the core of Christian character. . . . Because the hatred of Jews had been made holy, it became lethal. . . . However modern Nazism was, it planted its roots in the soil of age-old Church attitudes and a nearly unbroken chain of Church-sponsored acts of Jew-hatred. However pagan Nazism was, it drew its sustenance from groundwater poisoned by the Church's most solemnly held ideology—its *theology*.[4]

Part 2, "Modern," focuses on the intimate relationship between antisemitism and modern nationalism, the dominant spiritual force in late nineteenth- and early twentieth-century Europe. Nationalists regarded Jews as an alien organism that threatened the nation. In their twisted logic, they spoke of a Jewish conspiracy to dominate their people, rule the world, destroy Christianity, corrupt culture, and exploit humanity as slaves. Often their antisemitic rhetoric was augmented with racist theories that had become popular during the nineteenth century. Several documents in this section cover the emergence of racial thought and its culmination in Nazism and the Holocaust.

Part 3, "Contemporary," covers several topics: improved Catholic-Jewish relations and the efforts of Christian churches to confront their antisemitic past; the continuity of antisemitism in the Soviet Union and post-communist Russia; the lingering appeal of Nazi racial myths; the propagation of lethal antisemitism in the Arab-Muslim world; and two recently manufactured myths, Holocaust denial and the Jews as the principal force behind the slave trade.

The Arab-Israeli conflict has again made antisemitism intellectually and socially acceptable in Europe. Many Europeans, perhaps to ease their conscience regarding their forebears' behavior during the Nazi years, villainize Israeli Jews in their dealings with Palestinians as no better, or worse, than Nazis. Whereas in the past antisemitism was generally a bulwark of the Right and remains entrenched in the radical Right today, significant circles on the Left have adopted the language and imagery of antisemitism in order to delegitimize Israel. Viewing themselves as irrevocably antiracist, anti-imperialist, and defenders of oppressed non-Westerners, New Left intellectuals see Israel and Zionism as "reactionary" and "illegitimate," as a racist, colonizing, and militaristic force that has to be overcome. They see the Palestinians as "progressive," as victims, and as freedom fighters, including organizations that sponsor suicide bombers; and the Jews, who have lost their victim status, are oppressors, today's Nazis. To them the very idea of the Jews recreating a state in their ancient homeland is anathema, and they would welcome its disappearance as a boon to humanity. Often the Left's thinking is infused with hatred of America, which they demonize as wickedly imperialist, exploitatively capitalist, and a selfish promoter of globalization.

But it is the Arab-Muslim world that is now the epicenter of antisemitism, and it is the explosion of antisemitism in these lands that is the theme of the concluding section of part 3. Jew-hatred is disseminated in Arabic translations of classic antisemitic literature, principally the infamous forgery the *Protocols of the Learned Elders of Zion* and Hitler's *Mein Kampf*, both of which circulate widely and can be purchased everywhere; in the writings and lectures of intellectuals and government officials; in the sermons and tracts of theologians; in the textbooks and teaching in schools; and in the editorials and reports in the mass media. In October 2005 Iran's fundamentalist president Mahmoud Ahmadinejad proclaimed anew the necessity "to wipe Israel off the map" and condemned peace efforts between Arabs and Israel as a diversion from the "Crusader Wars" between Islam and "World Arrogance." He dismisses the Holocaust as a "myth" and "fairy tale" fabricated by Europeans to justify creating a Jewish state (a "Jewish camp" that became a "tumor," he declaims) to the harm of Islam.[5] At about the same time a professor proclaimed on Tehran TV that the Jews are "the source of all corrupt traits in humanity; Hitler had therefore been perfectly justified in gassing and burning them; if anything, he should be blamed for letting some of them survive."[6] Thus, like much Holocaust denial, the Iranian president and the Iranian professor argue simultaneously that the Holocaust occurred and was absolutely right, and that it never happened. In 2006, Ahmadinejad sponsored two vile events in Iran: a cartoon contest mocking the Holocaust and a conference to "debate" whether the Holocaust actually occurred. The conference was attended by neo-Nazis and antisemites from many lands; speaker after speaker insisted that the Jews invented lies about gas chambers and mass executions in order to wrest money from Germany and deceive the world into giving them Palestinian land.

Employing Goebbels-like big-lie techniques, Islamic propagandists incriminate Jews/Israelis for infecting Arab children with AIDS and supplying poisoned chewing gum to Palestinian children and accuse them, not Al-Qaeda, for launching the terror attacks on 9/11. Some Muslim authorities immediately blamed Israel for the bombings of the London transport system in July 2005. In July 2006 the speaker of the Iraqi Parliament, Mahmoud al-Mashhadani—who earlier had been jailed by American forces for terrorist connections, but was released and praised by the American government for his superior leadership qualities, moral courage, and rejection of political violence—blamed the insurgency and sectarian violence in his country on the Jews: "Some people say 'we saw you beheading, kidnapping, and killing. In the end we even started kidnapping women who are our honor.' These acts are not the work of Iraqis. I am sure that he who does this is a Jew and the son of a Jew."[7] In September 2006 the Arab-Muslim media, angered over a remark by Pope Benedict XVI quoting a medieval text critical of Islam, accused "international Zionism" of seeking to convert Christianity to Judaism and of inflaming hostilities between Islam and Christianity. Shiel Hassan Nasrallah, the leader of Hezbollah, reportedly said in 2000, "Anyone who reads the Qur'an . . . sees what acts of madness and slaughter the Jews carried out throughout history. . . . [T]hey are a cancer which is liable to spread at any moment. . . . The Jews invented the legend of Nazi atrocities . . . but we [are supposed to] forget the massacres they committed against us which are documented and proven." The same terrorist said in 2002, "If the Jews all gather in Israel, it will save us the trouble of going after them worldwide."[8] Such aberrations are not confined to Islamist extremists. The great bulk of this vicious piffle emanates from government-controlled media and publishing houses closely affiliated with Arab regimes. As Robert Wistrich observes,

> The Jews are portrayed in Arab cartoons as demons and murderers, as a hateful, loathsome people to be feared and avoided. They are invariably seen as the origin of all evil and corruption, authors of a dark, unrelenting conspiracy to infiltrate and destroy Muslim society in order eventually to take over the world. The most common visual distortion of the Jew is to portray him as a stooped, dark, bearded man wearing a black robe, with a long crooked nose and a devilish appearance—the kind of hideous stereotype familiar from the classic Nazi propaganda rag, *Der Stürmer.* Judaism itself is presented as a sinister, immoral religion, based on cabals and blood rituals, while Zionists are systematically equated with or identified as criminal racists or Nazis. The aim is not simply to morally delegitimize Israel as a Jewish state and a national entity in the Middle East, but to dehumanize Judaism and the Jewish people as such. No objective observer remotely familiar with this cascade of hate currently attaining new heights of defamation can doubt that it is profoundly and totally anti-Semitic.[9]

Much of the content of Islamic antisemitism repeats traditional Christian, modern European, and Nazi myths regarding Jews that culminated in the Holocaust. In 1928, Salo Wittmayer Baron, author of a highly regarded multivolume history of the Jews, warned against the "lachrymose" interpretation of Jewish history prior to the French Revolution as all woe and martyrdom.[10] He argued persuasively, without ignoring pogroms and expulsions, that the Jewish community not only survived but in many cases flourished. In the Middle Ages, he said, Jews were better off than the great mass of peasants and between incidents of persecution they developed a rich intellectual life and a sustained piety and spiritual quest. Baron also judged positively—though he regretted the decline of communal autonomy and the inroads of assimilation—the Enlightenment and democratic revolutions that brought Jews emancipation from the ghettos and citizenship, making possible the great achievements of European Jewry by the first decades of the twentieth century. Baron did not anticipate—no one did—the Holocaust a mere decade later. In retrospect, Baron underestimated the enduring power of antisemitic myths, nearly two millennia in the making, and the deep-seated hatred and fear of the Jews that induced people in many European lands to participate willingly in the Final Solution. These same myths, fears, and hatreds, as this book lays out, are now an integral part of the worldview of much of the Muslim world.

A painful lesson of the twentieth century is that ideologies spewing Jew-hatred threaten not only Jews but also the core values if not the existence of Western civilization. This maxim now applies to Islamists or jihadists, militant Muslims who reject features of the modern world—including secularism, religious tolerance, and democracy, historically liberal values with which Jews

have been intimately linked—and aspire to resuscitate the medieval past: a politically united Muslim community in which everyone conforms to a "pure"
Islam, mosque and state are fused as one, and the *Shar'ia*, religious law, is strin-
gently enforced. Islamism is rooted in a semi-mythical past, seeking to restore
the Caliphate—what the Muslim historian and religious thinker Mohamed
Talbi condemns as "ideological necrophilia"[11]—but is also modern in its adoption of Western imports, most notably totalitarianism, antisemitism, and
technology, including weaponry of every sort. Since 1945 many Muslims—
travelers, students, businessmen, engineers, intellectuals, government officials,
military officers, and others—sojourned in the Western world, often for pro-
longed periods, absorbing some or much of its culture. Exemplifying what
Paul Berman calls "the hyphenated personality of modern life" with one foot
in the Muslim East, one in the modern West, many of the Islamist terrorists
are Western educated and middle class who have adopted some of the worst features of the Western civilization they aim to injure or destroy, including antisemitism and the totalitarian vision of a future utopia achieved through terror
and repression.[12] Like totalitarian communism and Nazism before it, Islamism,
with its global reach and cadres of fanatical believers committed to destroying the infidel, now constitutes a serious threat not only to Jews but to Western
civilization.

In 2002 the authors published *Antisemitism: Myth and Hate from Antiquity
to the Present*. We would like to conclude this introduction with a passage from
our earlier work that reflects strongly our approach and sentiments:

> Antisemitism has very little to do with the actual behavior of Jews or the con-
> straints of their highly ethical religion—indeed, antisemites usually are to-
> tally ignorant of the rich tradition of rabbinical writings that discuss, often
> wisely and insightfully, biblical themes and Jewish law—but is rooted in delu-
> sional perceptions that are accepted as authoritative and passed on and embel-
> lished from generation to generation. As such, antisemitism affords a striking
> example of the perennial appeal, power, and danger of mythical thinking—
> of elevating to the level of objective truth beliefs that have little or no basis in
> fact but provide all-encompassing, emotionally satisfying explanations of life
> and history. In the period from the late nineteenth century through World
> War II, the widespread belief in the myth of the world Jewish conspiracy
> demonstrates that even highly educated, intelligent people can be moved and
> unified by baseless myths that provide gratifyingly simple explanations and
> resolutions for the complexities of the modern world. Democratic society is
> continually threatened by such an abandonment of reason and regression to
> mythical modes of thought and behavior.[13]

Finally, a word of caution. While most of the documents in our anthology
depict Jewish-Gentile relations at their worst—defamation, persecution, expulsion, massacre—there are important examples of European and American
Christians and secularists raising their voice against the mistreatment of Jews
and denouncing the antisemitic myths and lies that culminated in and sanctioned this persecution. Unfortunately, space limitations prevented us from

developing this significant theme more fully. These same limitations also compelled us to drop several selections that would have enhanced the anthology.

NOTES

1. Omer Bartov, *Germany's War & the Holocaust: Disputed Histories* (Ithaca: Cornell University Press, 2003), 136.

2. Quoted in Robert Jay Lifton, *The Nazi Doctors: Medical Killing and the Psychology of Genocide* (New York: Basic Books, 1986), 16.

3. Quoted in Jan T. Gross, *Fear: Anti-Semitism in Poland after Auschwitz, an Essay in Historical Interpretation* (New York: Random House, 2006), 226; the resolution was not voted upon. Antisemitic explosions occurred in Poland in 1958 and 1968.

4. James Carroll, *Constantine's Sword: The Church and the Jews, A History* (Boston: Houghton Mifflin, 2001), 22.

5. *The New York Times*, Jan. 2, 2006, A6; Simon Wiesenthal Center, *Response*, 27 (Spring 2006): 2-4.

6. Paraphrased in Walter Laqueur, *The Changing Face of Antisemitism* (New York: Oxford University Press, 2006), 140

7. Quoted in Paul Krugman, "March of Folly," *The New York Times*, July 17, 2006, A17.

8. Quoted in op-ed piece by Marvin Hier and Abraham Cooper, *Florida Sun-Sentinel*, Aug. 23, 2006.

9. Robert S. Wistrich, *Muslim Anti-Semitism: A Clear and Present Danger* (New York: American Jewish Committee, 2002), 4-5.

10. Salo W. Baron, "Ghetto and Emancipation," *Menorah Journal*, 14 (June 1928): 515-526.

11. Quoted in Ronald L. Nettler, "Mohamed Talbi's Ideas on Islam and Politics," in *Islam and Modernity*, ed. John Cooper et al. (London: Tauris, 1998), 153.

12. Paul Berman, *Terror and Liberalism* (New York: Norton, 2003), 106.

13. Marvin Perry and Frederick M. Schweitzer, *Antisemitism: Myth and Hate from Antiquity to the Present* (2002; paperback, New York: Palgrave Macmillan, 2005), 3.

Antisemitic Myths

PART ONE

Medieval and Early Modern

The Hebrews and the Greeks are the principal sources of Western civilization. The Greeks are the founders of philosophical and scientific thought; from the Hebrews we derive the idea of monotheism, codes of morality, and the principle of social justice. In the ancient world the Hebrew view of God as one, eternal, omnipotent, the source of all in the universe, and the shaper of the moral laws that govern human beings marked a profound break with Near Eastern religious thought. In contrast to pagan gods, who were indifferent to human beings, Yahweh was attentive to human needs and made ethical demands on his people. The new conception of God made possible a new awareness of the individual. In God's plan for the universe, human beings were the highest creation, subordinate only to God. Of all his creations, only they had been given the freedom to choose between righteousness and wickedness, between "life and good, and death and evil" (Deuteronomy 30:15). But having the power to choose freely, men and women must bear the responsibility for their choices. The Jews came to interpret the belief that man was created in God's image to mean that each human being has a divine spark in him or her, giving every person a unique dignity that cannot be taken away. The great value and dignity that westerners give to the individual derives in part from the ancient Hebrews, who held that men and women were created in God's image and possess free will and a conscience answerable to God. Inherited by Christianity, these ideals are at the core of the Western tradition.

Jewish history was marked by the emergence of spiritually inspired individuals known as the prophets, who felt compelled to speak out and act as God's messengers. In attacking oppression, cruelty, greed, and exploitation of the poor, the classical prophets added a new dimension to Israel's religious development. Amos, a prophet of the mid-eighth century BCE, denounced the pomp of the heartless rich and the hypocrisy of pious Jews who worshipped God in the prescribed manner but neglected their social obligations to their neighbors, and he demanded justice. To live unjustly, to mistreat one's neighbors, to act without compassion—these actions violated God's Law and endangered the social order. In holding out the hope that life on earth could be improved, that poverty and injustice need not be accepted as part of an unalterable natural order, the prophets helped shape a social conscience that has become part of the Western outlook.

Numerous links connect early Christianity and Judaism. Jesus himself and his earliest followers, including the twelve apostles, were Jews who were faithful to Jewish law. Jesus's message was first spread in synagogues throughout the Roman Empire. Early Christianity's affirmation of the preciousness of the human being, created in God's image, its belief that God rules history, its awareness of human sinfulness, its call for repentance, and its appeal to God for forgiveness are all rooted in Judaism. Also rooted in Judaism are the moral norms proclaimed by Jesus in the Sermon on the Mount and on other occasions. For example, "Do not do unto others what you would not want others to do unto you"—an extension of the Golden Rule "Love thy neighbor as thyself" (Leviticus 19:18)—was the maxim of the Jewish sage Hillel, an older contemporary of Jesus, who founded a religious academy that lasted into the fourth century. Christianity inherited the great value that the Torah gives to charity. Jesus's use of parables to convey his teachings, the concept of the messiah, respect for the Sabbath, and congregational worship also stem from Judaism. The Christian invocation of God as a "merciful Father" derives from Jewish prayer. And, of course, Christians view the Hebrew scriptures as God's word. The historical Jesus cannot be understood apart from his Jewish background, and his followers appealed to the Hebrew scriptures in order to demonstrate the validity of their beliefs. For these reasons, we talk of a Judeo-Christian tradition as an essential component of Western civilization.

Over the centuries, however, Christians forgot or devalued this relationship to Judaism. And some thinkers began to show hostility toward Judaism and Jews that had tragic consequences in later centuries. Several factors fueled this anti-Judaism: resentment against Jews for their refusal to embrace Jesus; the polemics of the Jewish establishment against the followers of Jesus; the role in Jesus's death ascribed to Jews by the New Testament; bitterness against those Christians who Judaized, that is, continued to observe Jewish festivals and the Jewish Sabbath, regard the synagogue as holy, and practice circumcision; and anger that Judaism remained a vital religion, for this undermined the conviction that Christianity was the fulfillment of Judaism and the one true faith. What made Christian anti-Judaism particularly ominous was the effort of patristic theologians (Church Fathers, third through seventh centuries) to demonize the Jewish people. The myth emerged that the Jews, murderers of the incarnate God who embodied all that was good, were a cursed people, children of the devil, whose suffering was intended by God.

Medieval Christians also showed hatred for Jews—a visibly alien group in a society dominated by the Christian worldview. The First Crusade, 1095–1099, was a turning point for medieval Jews. Until then there were few instances of organized violence against Jewish communities. If we are warring against God's enemies in the Holy Land, reasoned zealous crusaders, it is incumbent upon us to annihilate the Lord's enemies who are living in our midst. In 1096 bands of crusaders, proclaiming that they were seeking revenge against "Christ-killers," massacred Jews in French and German towns and cities. The marauding crusaders were often aided by townspeople eager to seize Jewish property. In the city of Mainz more than a thousand Jews lost their lives in the course of the bloodshed that punctuated the First Crusade. Some, in an act of martyrdom, chose to kill themselves and their children rather than submit to forced baptism or face a crueler death at the hands of the crusaders. The malevolent hatred of Jews unleashed during the First Crusade triggered other massacres, at times fomented by the clergy.

In the mind of medieval Christians the crime of deicide—the killing of God—eternally stained the Jews as a criminal people; medieval Christians saw Jews as dangerous infidels rejected by God and deserving of eternal punishment. Christian theologians taught that though they were to endure to the end-time, Jews were to live in ignominious subjection to Christian authority. It was just such a view that led town magistrates and princes periodically to confiscate Jewish property, at times after burning the helpless victims alive in a public spectacle. The flames of hatred were fanned by the absurd allegation that Jews, made bloodthirsty by the spilling of Christ's blood, tortured and murdered Christians, particularly children, to obtain blood for ritual purposes. Although rejected by several popes as baseless, this blood libel was widely believed by the credulous masses and incited numerous riots that led to the torture, burning alive, pillaging of property, and expulsion of countless Jews.

The role of Jews as moneylenders also provoked animosity against them. Jews were increasingly excluded from foreign trade—where they had been pioneers—and most professions, and they were barred from merchant and artisan guilds and in most areas from landholding as well. Hence virtually the only means of livelihood open to them was moneylending—in reality an important activity in an expanding economy.

The policy of the Church toward the Jews was that they should not be harmed—since by their suffering and degradation they were destined to testify to the end of time to the truth of Christianity—and several medieval popes sought to protect Jewish life and property from wanton violence. Yet the Church also wanted Jews to live in humiliation, a fitting punishment for the arch-crime of deicide and continued refusal to embrace Christianity as well as to bear witness to the triumph of the Church. Thus, the Fourth Lateran Council (1215) barred Jews from public office (reiterating imperial decrees of the fourth century), ordered them to remain out of sight during Christian festivals, and required them to wear a distinguishing hat or badge on their clothing, a symbol of their degradation. Christian art, literature, and religious instruction depicted the Jews in a derogatory manner, often identifying them with Satan, who was very real and terrifying to medieval Christians. Such people deserved no mercy, reasoned medieval Christians. Indeed, nothing was too bad for them. Because Jews were seen as evil allies of Satan engaged in a diabolical plot against God and Christendom, Jew-baiting was regarded as an expression of Christian virtue, a message routinely spread by preachers.

The twelfth century also saw relentless attacks on the great body of Jewish biblical commentary and interpretation, the Talmud (see note 1, page 53), as a heretical and subversive work, "not of God but of earth"; under papal direction, the Talmud was confiscated and burnt, and Jews were forcibly subjected to conversionist assaults by Dominican and Franciscan preachers—on the grounds that Judaism was Talmudic, had ceased to be biblical, and therefore must no longer be tolerated. The Jews' expulsion from England in 1290 inaugurated the series of massacres, forced conversions, expropriations, and expulsions that left Western Europe virtually emptied of Jews by the end of the Middle Ages. Jews were hated and feared— and punished—as the source of every danger and catastrophe troubling Christians. The distorted image of the Jews as contemptible yet dangerous creatures persisted for centuries, and all forms of modern nationalist, racialist, and economic antisemitism—no matter how transformed and secularized—stem from the New Testament, the Church Fathers, and medieval Christian images and perceptions.

ONE

Christian Demonization of the Jews

The origins of the demonization of the Jew are found in the New Testament, in particular the Gospel of John, where Jesus accuses a group of Jews of being "bent on killing me." In 8:44–47, he replies to their assertion that "Abraham is our father":

> Your father is the devil and you choose to carry out your father's desires. He was a murderer from the beginning, and is not rooted in the truth; there is no truth in him. When he tells a lie he speaks according to his nature, for he is a liar and the father of lies. But I speak the truth and therefore you do not believe me. . . . He who has God for his father listens to God's word. You are not God's children; that is why you do not listen.

The writings of the Church Fathers perpetuated the myth that the Jews were a wicked nation of deicides who deserved to suffer. As formulated by Origen (ca. 185–ca. 254), "We may thus assert in utter confidence that the Jews will not return to their earlier situation, for they have committed the most abominable of crimes, in forming the conspiracy against the Saviour of the human race. . . . Hence the city where Jesus suffered was necessarily destroyed, the Jewish nation was driven from its country, and another people was called by God to the blessed election."[1] During the Middle Ages Jews were viewed as Satan's agents, who, armed with his superhuman powers, robbed and murdered Christians in fulfillment of their master's will. Medieval art, poetry, drama, sermons, and theological writings demonized the Jews and ridiculed Judaism: Jews were given horns, tails, and a noxious odor, all signs that they were descendants of the devil. The powers attributed to Jews as magicians or sorcerers and the many diabolic enterprises they supposedly engaged in—including necromancy, the black art of communicating with the dead—also stemmed from their pact with Satan. Passion plays performed during Lent in the Easter season depicted Jews gleefully and sadistically torturing Christ as he struggled under the weight of the cross and then mutilating his crucified body. A corollary of the Jew as Satan's agent was the phantasmagoria of the Antichrist. Variously, he was said to be a Jew, the Wandering Jew, Satan himself, or the offspring of Satan and a Jewish prostitute. The Antichrist, in league with "the Jews," would conquer the world and destroy Christendom. A fourteenth-century theologian predicted that the Antichrist, "with the help of Jewish money, would conquer the world in two and a half years."[2] The belief that the Jews were a conspiratorial people plotting deviously to dominate the world, a key component of modern secular antisemitism, originated centuries earlier in medieval Christendom.

This demonization of the Jew, which bore no relationship to the actual behavior of Jews or to their highly ethical religion, and the "theology of victimization," which held that the Jews were collectively and eternally cursed for denying Christ, became powerful myths, which, over the centuries, poisoned Christians' hearts and minds against Jews, spurring innumerable humiliations, persecutions, expulsions, and massacres. Demonization and the consequent dehumanization of the Jew are the foundation of antisemitism.

St. John Chrysostom

"[The synagogue is] a lodging-place for demons, a fortress of the devil,"
386–387

The Greek Church Father, St. John Chrysostom, 340s–407, was one of the great figures in the history of Christianity, a seminal and abiding influence on its doctrines, liturgy, and piety, and for centuries on its attitude toward the Jews and Judaism. Baptized in 368 and ordained to the clergy in 381, he soon became the most famous preacher in Antioch, renowned for his combative eloquence—what Robert L. Wilken aptly calls "the rhetoric of abuse"[3]—in attacking heretics, pagans, and the Jews (Chrysostom means "the golden-mouthed").

Chrysostom's eight orations against Judaizers and Jews were delivered in Antioch in 386–387. The principal purpose of these discourses was to discourage Christians from Judaizing—from attending Jewish services or continuing to practice some Jewish rituals and observances. His pathological metaphors of Jews and Judaism as disease, drunkenness, and madness; his dehumanization of Jews as dogs, pigs, and goats, even comparing them to wild beasts "fit for killing" or old plough horses "fit for slaughter"; and his demonization of them—"the devil's jaws"— molded the outlook of Christians for centuries and contributed to antisemitism's lethal power. The centerpiece of Chrysostom's theology of Jews and Judaism is "their odious assassination of Christ": "This supreme crime lies at the root of their woe and degradation," for which "no expiation [is] possible, no indulgence, no pardon." The term "Christ-killer," which Chrysostom employs several times, came into the Christian vocabulary in the fourth century and initially referred to the Jews of Jesus's time; in Chrysostom's usage, however, this frightful term was applied to all Jews at all times in all places.

The sermons shaped Christian attitudes toward the Jews and Judaism in medieval Latin Christendom, Byzantium, and Russia (they were translated into Russian in the eleventh century); their most venomous accusations reappear in Luther's diatribes and a whole host of antisemitic polemicists down to Hitler. Chrysostom's rhetoric is purple and exceptional, but his theology of Judaism remained standard until the Second Vatican Council of the 1960s. It is true that his primary motive was to attack the Judaizers rather than the Jews. In that setting the sermons, excerpted below, were not necessarily lethal, but in the radically changed context of subsequent centuries their meaning changed and their impact was devastating.

What is this disease? The festivals [Rosh Hashanah, the New Year, and Yom Kippur, the Day of Atonement] of the pitiful and miserable Jews are soon to march upon us one after the other and in quick succession. . . . There are many in our ranks who say they think as we do. Yet some of these are going to watch the festivals. And others will join the Jews in keeping their feasts and observing their fasts. I wish to drive this perverse custom from the Church right now. . . .

And so it is that I hasten to anticipate this danger and prevent it. . . .

But do not be surprised that I called the Jews pitiable. They really are pitiable and miserable. When so many blessings from heaven came into their hands, they thrust them aside and were at great pains to reject them. . . . From their childhood they read the prophets, but they crucified him whom the prophets had foretold. We did not hear the divine prophecies but we did worship him of whom they prophesied. And so they are pitiful because they rejected the blessings which were sent to them, while others seized hold of these blessings and drew them to themselves. . . .

Many, I know, respect the Jews and think that their present way of life is a venerable one. This is why I hasten to uproot and tear out this deadly opinion. . . . [T]he synagogue is not only a brothel and a theater; it also is a den of robbers and a lodging for wild beasts. . . . [W]hen God forsakes a people, what hope of salvation is left? When God forsakes a place, that place becomes the dwelling of demons.

But at any rate the Jews say that they, too, adore God. God forbid that I say that. No Jew adores God! Who says so? The Son of God says so. For he said: "If you were to know my Father, you would also know me. But you neither know me nor do you know my Father" [John 8:19]. Could I produce a witness more trustworthy than the Son of God?

If then, the Jews fail to know the Father, if they crucified the Son, if they thrust off the help of the Spirit, who should not make bold to declare plainly that the synagogue is a dwelling of demons? God is not worshipped there. Heaven forbid! From now on it remains a place of idolatry. But still some people pay it honor as a holy place. . . .

. . . In our churches we hear countless discourses on eternal punishments, on rivers of fire, on the venomous worm, on bonds that cannot be burst, on exterior darkness. But the Jews neither know nor dream of these things. They live for their bellies, they gape for the things of this world, their condition is no better than that of pigs or goats because of their wanton ways and excessive gluttony. They know but one thing: to fill their bellies and be drunk, to get all cut and bruised, to be hurt and wounded while fighting for their favorite charioteers. . . .

. . . Indeed the synagogue is less deserving of honor than any inn. It is not merely a lodging place for robbers and cheats but also for demons. This is true not only of the synagogues but also of the souls of the Jews, as I shall try to prove at the end of my discourse. . . .

But I must get back again to those [Christians] who are sick. Consider, then, with whom they are sharing their fasts. It is with those who shouted: "Crucify him, Crucify him" [Luke 23:21], with those who said: "His blood be upon us and upon our children" [Matthew 27:25].[4] . . . Is it not foolish . . . to enter into fellowship with those who have committed outrages against God himself? Is it not strange that those who worship the Crucified keep common festival with those who crucified him? Is it not a sign of folly and the worst madness?

Since there are some who think of the synagogue as a holy place, I must say a few words to them. Why do you reverence that place? Must you not despise it, hold it in abomination, run away from it? They answer that the Law and the books of the prophets are kept there. What is this? Will any place where these books are be a holy place? By no means! This is the reason above all others why I hate the synagogue and abhor it. They have the prophets but do not believe them; they read the sacred writings but reject their witness—and this is a mark of men guilty of the greatest outrage.

Tell me this. If you were to see a venerable man, illustrious and renowned, dragged off into a tavern or den of robbers; if you were to see him outraged, beaten, and subjected there to the worst violence, would you have held that tavern or den in high esteem because that great and esteemed man had been inside it while undergoing that violent treatment? I think not. Rather, for this very reason you would have hated and abhorred the place.

Let that be your judgment about the synagogue, too. For they brought the books of Moses and the prophets along with them into the synagogue, not to honor them but to outrage them with dishonor. When they say that Moses and the prophets knew not Christ and said nothing about his coming, what greater outrage could they do to those holy men than to accuse them of failing to recognize their Master, than to say that those saintly prophets are partners of their impiety? And so it is that we must hate both them and their synagogue all the more because of their offensive treatment of those holy men. . . .

Therefore, flee the gatherings and holy places of the Jews. Let no man venerate the synagogue because of the holy books; let him hate and avoid it because the Jews outrage and maltreat the holy ones, because they refuse to believe their words, because they accuse them of the ultimate impiety. . . .

Finally, if the ceremonies of the Jews move you to admiration, what do you have in common with us? If the Jewish ceremonies are venerable and great, ours are lies. But if ours are true, as they *are* true, theirs are filled with deceit. I am not speaking of the [Hebrew] Scriptures. Heaven forbid! It was the Scriptures which took me by the hand and led me to Christ. But I am talking about the ungodliness and present madness of the Jews.

Certainly it is the time for me to show that demons dwell in the synagogue, not only in the place itself but also in the souls of the Jews. . . .

Do you see that demons dwell in their souls and that these demons are more dangerous than the ones of old? And this is very reasonable. In the old days the

Jews acted impiously toward the prophets; now they outrage [Jesus Christ] the Master of the prophets. Tell me this. Do you not shudder to come into the same place with men possessed, who have so many unclean spirits, who have been reared amid slaughter and bloodshed? Must you share a greeting with them and exchange a bare word? Must you not turn away from them since they are the common disgrace and infection of the whole world? Have they not come to every form of wickedness? Have not all the prophets spent themselves making many and long speeches of accusation against them?[5] What tragedy, what manner of lawlessness have they not eclipsed by their blood-guiltiness? . . .

Tell me this. If a man were to have slain your son, would you endure to look upon him, or to accept his greeting? Would you not shun him as a wicked demon, as the devil himself? They slew the Son of your Lord; do you have the boldness to enter with them under the same roof? After he was slain he heaped such honor upon you that he made you his brother and coheir. But you dishonor him so much that you pay honor to those who slew him on the cross, that you observe with them the fellowship of the festivals, that you go to their profane places, enter their unclean doors, and share in the tables of demons. For I am persuaded to call the fasting of the Jews a table of demons because they slew God. If the Jews are acting against God, must they not be serving the demons? . .

What is it that you are rushing to see in the synagogue of the Jews who fight against God? . . . You should stay at home to weep and groan for them, because they are fighting against God's command, and it is the devil who leads them in their revels and dance. . . .

Meanwhile, I ask you to rescue your brothers [the Judaizers], to set them free from their error, and to bring them back to the truth. . . . I want them to . . . free themselves from their wicked association with the Jews. I want them then to show themselves sincere and genuine Christians. I want them to shun the evil gatherings of the Jews and their synagogues, both in the city and in the suburbs, because these are robbers' dens and dwellings of demons. . . .

. . . [Y]ou frequented shrines that are no better than hucksters' shops or dens of thieves. . . .

. . . Now you give it a more worthy name than it deserves if you call it [the synagogue] a brothel, a stronghold of sin, a lodging-place for demons, a fortress of the devil, the destruction of the soul, the precipice and pit of all perdition, or whatever other name you give it.[6]

NOTES

1. Quoted in Léon Poliakov, *The History of Anti-Semitism*, vol. 1, *From the Time of Christ to the Court Jews*, trans. Richard Howard (New York: Vanguard, 1974), 23.

2. Salo W. Baron, *A Social and Religious History of the Jews*, 2nd ed., 18 vols. (New York: Columbia University Press, 1952-1983), 11: 133.

3. Robert L. Wilken, *John Chrysostom and the Jews: Rhetoric and Reality in the Late 4th Century* (Berkeley: University of California Press, 1983), 123.

4. Chrysostom holds the position, which was commonplace for centuries, that all Jews are responsible for Christ's passion and death. The fundamental change came with Vatican II's *Nostra Aetate* of 1965 (see page 219). A prime mover of that decree was Cardinal Bea, who explained Matthew 27:25 as the cry of a Jerusalem crowd that had no right to speak for the whole Jewish people.

5. Chrysostom argues from the guilt of their forebears to the guilt of contemporaneous Jews.

6. From Saint John Chrysostom, *The Fathers of the Church*, vol. 68, *Discourses against Judaizing Christians*, trans. and ed. Paul W. Harkins (Washington, D.C.: Catholic University of America Press, 1979), 3-5, 10-11, 14-15, 18-19, 21, 23-25, 28, 92, 144-145, 150, 174.

TWO

The Libel of Ritual Murder

During the Middle Ages bizarre myths about Jews emerged. They were seen as agents of Satan conspiring to destroy Christendom and as sorcerers employing black magic against Christians. Perhaps the most absurd (and dangerous) charge against the Jewish people was the accusation of ritual murder—that the Jews, requiring Christian blood for making the Passover matzoh, sacrificed a Christian child. These accusations were learnedly maintained and theologically justified by a number of treatises, beginning with the Spanish Dominican Raymond Martini's *Pugio fidei* (Dagger of Faith against Moors and Jews, 1278), which is an enormous volume with all the trappings of scholarship that seemed to buttress its claims. Despite the vehement denials of Jews and the prohibition on consumption of blood or of meat containing blood by biblical prescription and Jewish law, as well as the protests of some enlightened Christian leaders, hundreds of such libelous accusations were made, resulting in the torture, trials, murder, and expulsion of many Jews. Some medieval popes resolutely condemned ritual murder as an utterly false accusation. Thus Innocent IV in 1247 enjoined all Christians not to accuse Jews "of using human blood in their religious rites, since in the Old Testament they are instructed not to use blood of any kind, let alone human blood." In 1272, Pope Gregory X elaborated on Innocent IV's pronouncement:

> And most falsely do these Christians claim that the Jews have secretly and furtively carried away their children and killed them, and that the Jews offer sacrifice from the heart and blood of these children, since their law in this matter precisely and expressly forbids Jews to sacrifice, eat, or drink the blood, or to eat the flesh of animals having claws. This has been demonstrated many times at our court by Jews converted to the Christian faith: nevertheless very many Jews are often seized and detained unjustly because of this.
>
> We decree, therefore, that Christians need not be obeyed against Jews in a case or situation of this type, and we order that Jews seized under such a silly pretext be freed from imprisonment, and that they shall not be arrested henceforth on such a miserable pretext.[1]

But trapped by a mythical image of Jews as demonic creatures lusting after Christian blood, medieval Christians, including zealous clergy, continued with the bizarre allegations and the torture and murder of hapless Jews accused of the crime. It was common from the first instance of the accusation, "St. William the Martyr of Norwich," England, in 1144, to view the child "victim" as a "martyr" and to enshrine the site of the "martyrdom." Until late in the twentieth century these shrines, visited by pilgrims and tourists, including busloads of schoolchildren, perpetuated the blood-libel slander. It was only with Vatican Council II in the 1960s that shrines like that of "St. Simon of Trent" were dismantled and the idea of ritual murder decisively condemned.

The Libel of Ritual Murder in Gloucester

"they had made him a glorious martyr to Christ," 1168

In the following passage, an English chronicle reports the death of one young Harold of Gloucester, purportedly murdered by Jews in 1168; this account from the *Historia Sti. Glocestriae* (History of the Saint of Gloucester) is the only near-contemporaneous report on any of the many boys celebrated as martyrs.

[The eight-year old] boy Harold, who is buried in the Church of St. Peter the Apostle, at Gloucester, near the altar of St. Edmund the Archbishop and of St. Edward King and Confessor, . . . is said to have been carried away secretly by the Jews, in the opinion of many,[2] on February 21, and by them hidden till March 16. On that night, on the sixth of the preceding feast, the Jews of all England coming together as if to circumcise a certain boy, pretend deceitfully that they are about to celebrate the feast [of Passover] appointed by law in such case, and deceiving the citizens of Gloucester with that fraud, they tortured the lad placed before them with immense tortures. It is true no Christian was present, or saw or heard the deed, nor have we found that anything was betrayed by any Jew. But a little while after when the whole convent of monks of Gloucester and almost all the citizens of that city, and innumerable persons coming on the spectacle, saw the wounds of the dead body, scars of fire, the thorns fixed on his head, and liquid wax poured into the eyes and face, and touched it with the diligent examination of their hands, those tortures were believed or guessed to have been inflicted on him in that manner. It was clear that they had made him a glorious martyr to Christ, being slain without sin, and having bound his feet with his own girdle, threw him into the river Severn. [The body is taken to St. Peter's Church, and there performs miracles.][3]

Sebastián de Horozco

"Ritual Murder" at La Guardia, Spain, 1490s

The following account of accusation and punishment for ritual murder and desecration of the Eucharist comes from La Guardia in Spain. It is unusual not because the accusation was utterly groundless, but because the "child of La Guardia," a "Holy Child," never existed—he was simply a figment of the imagination, an example of pious fraud for the sake of profits and royal propaganda later used to justify the expulsion of the Jews from Spain in 1492. Its unreality and baselessness notwithstanding, the whole story was taken up and propagated in the Spanish-speaking world by the great Spanish poet and dramatist, Lope de Vega, in his play *El Niño de la Guardia* (The Child of La Guardia), ca.1606. The narrative below is from Sebastián de Horozco's *La historia del niño innocente de la Guardia* (The History of the Innocent Child of La Guardia), written in 1533.

Certain Jews, some of those who were involved in the crucifixion of this blessed child and others who were not to be present at it, being in the kingdom of France, these Jews, it being believed that they were among those who fled from Castile when the king, Don Ferdinand, and the queen, Doña Isabella, Catholic Monarchs of blessed memory, constituted and ordained the Holy Inquisition [1478], announcing that all the Jews who were in their kingdoms should be baptized and become Christians, or else leave them within a certain period [1492]. Many Jews, damned with evil hearts, gathered in France, looking for a way in which they could revenge themselves on the Christians. . . . It was revealed to them by diabolical revelation, or by the advice of some Jewish sage, or rather sorcerer . . . that, taking the heart of an innocent boy, without sin, and the most Holy Sacrament of the altar [the Eucharist], all burnt and reduced to dust, and thrown into the water which the Christians would drink, as soon as they drank it they would go mad and die. And in this way they would be revenged.

> [To obtain the heart, the Jews supposedly suborned a poor French nobleman, with many children and little with which to support them, promising him great wealth if he would give them the heart of one of his sons. The nobleman's wife persuaded him to counter with a trick.]

The woman, being astute, and also because women, as may be seen by experience, or by their nature, are accustomed to giving very clear and useful advice, replied, almost without need for thought, "Sir, do not worry, I'll tell you how we can fool these Jews, without your killing your son and without their realizing it. . . . We have this sow, which is small. Take it and kill it, and we'll take out its heart, and we'll say it comes from our son, and we'll have to hide our son, so that he won't be found." [After speaking to the Jews], this man went home and, as the woman had advised him, killed his sow, took its heart out and gave it to the Jews. They, when they saw the heart, really believing that it was the child's, took it with great delight, and they paid the nobleman a lot of money, with which he escaped easily from his misery.

Having already got the heart, it remained for them to find a way of getting hold of the most Holy Sacrament, and as they could not find it [for themselves], they agreed to secure their goal as follows. They wanted to have [the Eucharistic host] complete, just as it was in the tabernacle. . . . They thought up this ruse. Near them, there lived an old woman who was very poor, much poorer than the nobleman, and they went to her and said, "Sister, it will be well worth your while to do what we are going to ask you." [They offered her the bribe of a piece of cloth to smuggle the communion host out of the church.] So when the accursed old woman went on another day to receive [Holy] communion, she found a way to bring the most holy sacrament to the Jews, who took it and kept it to do spells with it. . . . And they paid the diabolical old woman what they had promised, and much more, so that she would keep all this secret.

Having now searched for what they wanted to make their spell, the heretics [Jews or *conversos*, see page 29] burnt to dust both the pig's heart, which they thought was a boy's, and the most Holy Sacrament, and went and threw [the residue] into the passing river, to infect or bewitch all the water or waters which the Christian people used for drinking, so that when they drank it they would all die. . . . These Jews, or some of them, or some of their descendants, having returned to Castile, and being now Christians at least in name, sought to return to and finish their evil deed. . . . They looked through Castile for a suitable place, one which in location and appearance resembled Jerusalem, and it seems that they found no place more suited to their purpose than this town of La Guardia. And for this purpose there was, it seems, in Ávila or in the area of Ávila, a Jewish rabbi, a great scholar, or rather a great sorcerer, to whom went these bad Christians and heretics, called the Francos, who were four brothers or relatives and other companions, eleven in all, and with them an accountant of the Order of Saint John of Jerusalem, a citizen of Tembleque, a person of great style and authority, who was to be the Pilate who gave the sentence like a robber. . . .

These Francos were citizens and dwellers in this town of La Guardia, with their wives and children and property, and their businesses: they were carters. And, going to Toledo and back, they succeeded in finding or hearing of a blind woman who had a little son aged about seven or eight, called Christopher [Christovalico: "little Christopher"]. And they found a trick and way to get hold of the child with gifts, giving him some red booties. And the child, in his innocence, went off with them, because he liked what they gave him. And in this way they stole the son from the poor blind woman, his mother. . . . For certain, it is an amazing thing and it moves hearts to tears of compassion to see how far they took the child, giving him blows with the cross on his back, and [this cross] so thick and solid as it must have been, and such a bitter thing when it is known that he received, on account of the accursed Jews, 6200 strokes. . . . And they gave him a thousand strokes more than they gave Christ, as was discovered from the confession of the aforesaid Jews.

The poor blind woman, mother of this holy child martyr . . . had never seen light. And at the moment when her son died, at that very point, she received her sight. . . . The aforesaid Jews, after they had crucified the child and extracted his heart, went to bury him deeply, almost a quarter of a league from the spot, close by a hermitage called Our Lady of Pera, doing all this very secretly at night, so as not to be noticed. . . .

[According to the tale, after the Jews had obtained the heart of an innocent Christian boy, they bribed a Christian with "a Courtrai hood . . . which had cost thirty [silver] *reales*, the same as the thirty pieces for which Christ was sold by Judas."[4] The Jews were discovered and turned over to the court of the Inquisition where priests regularly applied torture to gain confessions.]

. . . And when they confessed they were sentenced to the fire. Four of them, because they did not believe [in Christ], were tortured and burnt alive. The others, who asked for mercy, were suffocated and then burnt.

And, before they were judged, one of them (it was said to be Juan Franco) was taken to show [the inquisitors] the place where they had buried the innocent child, and they dug in the place where he was buried. And until today his body has never been found, nothing of his, not a bone, nor the shoes or hose with which he was buried. Neither was anything found except the empty tomb of the size in which they had made it, and no more. This was a mysterious thing, that nothing of that holy child has ever appeared up to today, not even the heart which the Jew took to Ávila, which went wrapped in some very bloodstained cloths. Only the cloths were found, but without any blood. And thus it may be piously believed that Our Lord mysteriously wished that nothing of [the child] should remain or appear, but that he should go in bone and flesh to enjoy His holy glory in paradise. In addition to the above, it happened that, at this time, many sows which entered those caves or chambers [near La Guardia] died.

When the identity of the holy, innocent child had been discovered, they went to Toledo to look for his mother, and they found her, able to see. And she described how she had lost her son at that time and on that day, and how she was blind from birth, and on that day she had been able to see, and she did not know how it had happened. And [the inquisitors] found it to be true that, at the same day and hour that the holy child had expired, she had recovered her sight. And in this she represented Longinus, who lived with the blood and water from the side of Our Lord [having pierced it with a lance[5]], in the same way this woman with the martyrdom and death of her son.[6]

Menasseh ben Israel

Refutation of "That Strange and Horrid Accusation" That Jews Use
Christian Blood for Ritual Purposes, ca. 1640

Ritual murder was a vicious defamation that Jews vehemently denied as totally contrary to their faith. A particularly compelling refutation of the charge was made by Menasseh ben Israel (1604–1657), a distinguished Dutch rabbi of Portuguese Marrano descent (see page 29). Many of his numerous works were addressed to non-Jews, seeking to explain Jewish life and traditions to them, and he enjoyed the friendship of many Christians. He is remembered chiefly for his visit to England at the head of a delegation in 1656 seeking to negotiate the return of Jews to England, from which they had been expelled in 1290. During Menasseh's visit the Jews and Judaism were attacked by, among others, William Prynne, a bigoted Puritan lawyer and pamphleteer and bitter opponent of Oliver Cromwell, who repeated many familiar anti-Jewish vilifications, most notably the blood accusation. *Vindicae Judaeo-rum* (A Vindication of the Jews) is Menasseh's rejoinder; the longest section, a classic rebuttal of the blood libel, is excerpted below. *Vindicae* is probably addressed to a friend of Menasseh's and of the Jewish cause, John Sadler, "Most Noble, and Learned Sir," who commissioned Menasseh's reply. Against much opposition from clergy and businessmen, Cromwell's government permitted Jews to reside again in England. *Vindicae* was often reprinted and translated at times of Jewish persecution and in the struggle for emancipation. In sharp contrast to the Continent, accusations of ritual murder in Britain were condemned in the *Rex v. Osborne* case of 1732 as defamation of "a whole body of men, as if guilty of crimes scarce practicable and totally incredible."

And in the first place, I cannot but weep bitterly, and with much anguish of soul lament that strange and horrid accusation of some Christians against the dispersed and afflicted Jews that dwell among them, when they say (what I tremble to write) that the Jews are wont to celebrate the [Passover] feast of unleavened bread, fermenting it with the blood of some Christians, whom they have for this purpose killed: when the calumniators themselves have most barbarously and cruelly butchered some of them. Or to speak more mildly, have found one dead and cast the corpse, as if it had been murdered by the Jews, into their houses or yards, as lamentable experience hath proved in sundry places: and then with unbridled rage and tumult, they accuse the innocent Jews as the committers of this most execrable act, which detestable wickedness hath been sometimes perpetrated, that they might thereby take advantage to exercise their cruelty upon them; and sometimes to justify and patronize their massacres already executed. But how far this accusation is from any semblable appearance of truth, your worship may judge by the following arguments.

1. It is utterly forbid the Jews to eat any manner of blood whatsoever, Leviticus Chapter 7: 26 and Deuteronomy 12, where it is expressly said, *And ye shall eat no manner of blood,* and in obedience to this command the Jews eat not the blood of any animal. And more than this, if they find one drop of blood in an egg, they cast it away as prohibited. And if in eating a piece of bread, it happens to touch any blood drawn from the teeth or gums, it must be pared and cleansed from the said blood, as it evidently appears in *Sulchan Aruch* [an authoritative guide to Jewish religious life and law compiled in the sixteenth century by Joseph Caro] and in our ritual book. Since then it is thus, how can it enter into any man's heart to believe that they should eat human blood, which is yet more detestable, there being scarce any nation now remaining upon earth so barbarous, as to commit such wickedness?

2. The precept in the Decalogue *Thou shalt not kill* is of general extent; it is a moral command. So that the Jews are bound not only, not to kill one of those nations where they live, but they are also obliged by the law of gratitude, to love them. They are the very words of R. Moses of Egypt [Maimonides] in *Mishneh Torah*, in his treatise of Kings, the tenth Chapter, in the end, *Concerning the nations, the ancients have commanded us to visit their sick and to bury their dead, as the dead of Israel, and to relieve and maintain the poor, as we do the poor of Israel, be-*

cause of the ways of peace, as it is written, God is good to all, and his tender mercies are over all his works. Psalm 145:9. And in conformity hereto, I witness before God blessed forever, that I have continually seen in Amsterdam where I reside, abundance of good correspondence, many interchanges of brotherly affection, and sundry things of reciprocal love. I have thrice seen when some Flemish Christians have fallen into the river in our ward, called Flemburgh, our nation cast themselves into the river to help them out, and to deliver their lives from death. And certainly he that will thus hazard himself to save another, cannot harbour so much cruel malice as to kill the innocent, whom he ought out of the duty of humanity to defend and protect.

3. It is forbidden, Exodus 21:20, to kill a stranger; *If a man smite his servant, or his maid with a rod, and he die under his hand, he shall surely be punished. . . .* The text speaks of a servant that is one of the Gentile nations. . . . And the Lord commands, that if he die under the hand of his master, his master shall be put to death, for that as it seems, he struck him with a murderous intent. . . . If, therefore, a Jew cannot kill his servant or slave that is one of the nations, according to the law, how much less shall he be empowered to murder him that is not his *enemy,* and with whom he leads a quiet and a peaceable life? and therefore how can any good man believe that against his holy law, a Jew (in a strange country especially) should make himself guilty of so execrable an act? . . .

5. If the Jews did repute and hold this action (which is never to be named without an epithet of horror) necessary, they would not expose themselves to so eminent a danger, to so cruel and more deserved punishment, unless they were moved to it by some divine precept; or at least, some constitution of their wise men. Now we challenge all those men who entertain this dreadful opinion of us, as obliged in point of justice to cite the place of Scripture, or of the Rabbis, where any such precept, or doctrine is delivered. And until they do so, we will assume so much liberty, as to conclude it to be no better than a malicious slander. . . .

7. The Lord, blessed forever, by his prophet Jeremiah Chapter 29:7, gives it in command to the captive Israelites that were dispersed among the heathens, that they should continually pray for and endeavor the peace, welfare and prosperity of the city wherein they dwelt and the inhabitants thereof. This the Jews have always done, and continue to this day in all their synagogues, with a particular blessing of the Prince or Magistrate, under whose protection they live. . . . [I]f we are bound to study, endeavor and solicit the good and flourishing estate of the city where we live, and the inhabitants thereof, how shall we then murder their children, who are the greatest good, and the most flourishing blessing that this life doth indulge to them. . . .

9. [Our Christian accusers say] that this is practiced by [the Jews] in hatred and detestation of Jesus of Nazareth. And that therefore they steal Christian Children, [striking] them in the same manner that he was buffeted; thereby to rub up and revive the memory of the aforesaid death. And likewise they imagine that the Jews secretly steal away crosses, crucifixes, and such like graven images, which Papists privately and carefully retain in their houses, and every day the Jews mainly strike and buffet, shamefully spitting on them, with such like

ceremonies of spite, and all this in hatred of Jesus. . . . For surely we cannot believe, that a people, otherwise of sufficient prudence and judgement, can persuade themselves into an opinion that the Jews should commit such practices, unless they could conceive they did them in honor and obedience to the God whom they worship. And what kind of obedience is this they perform to God blessed forever, when they directly sin against that special command *Thou shalt not kill?* Besides this cannot be committed without the imminent and manifest peril of their lives and fortunes, and the necessary exposing themselves to a just revenge. Moreover, it is an anathema to a Jew to have any graven images in his house, or any thing of an idol, which any of the nations figuratively worship, Deuteronomy 7:26.

10. Matthew Paris . . . writes, how that in the year 1240, the Jews circumcised a Christian child at Norwich, and gave him the name Iuruin, and reserved him to be crucified, for which cause many [Jews] were most cruelly put to death. The truth of this story will evidently appear upon the consideration of its circumstances. He was first circumcised, and this perfectly constitutes him a Jew. Now for a Jew to embrace a Christian in his arms and foster him in his bosom, is a testimony of great love and affection. But if it was intended that shortly after this child should be crucified, to what end was he first circumcised? . . . Surely this supposed prank . . . looks more like a piece of the real scene of the popish Spaniards' piety, who first baptized the poor Indians and afterwards out of cruel pity to their souls, inhumanely butchered them; than of the strict-law-observing Jews, who dare not make a sport of one of the seals of their covenant.

11. Our captivity under the Moslems is far more burdensome and grievous than under the Christians. . . . It would therefore follow, that if this sacrificing of children be the product and result of hatred, that they should execute and disgorge it much more upon the Moslems, who have reduced them to so great calamity and misery. So that if it be necessary to the celebration of the Passover, why do they not as well kill a Moslem? But although the Jews are scattered and dispersed throughout all these vast territories, notwithstanding all their spite against us, they never yet to this day forged such a calumnious accusation. Wherefore it appears plainly, that it is nothing else but a slander. And such a one, that considering how the scene is laid, I cannot easily determine whether it speak more of malice or of folly: certainly [Ottoman] Sultan Selim made himself very merry with it, when the story was related to him by Moses Amon, his chief physician.

12. [As prescribed by Exodus 22] I swear, without any deceit or fraud, by the most high God, the creator of heaven and earth, who promulgated his law to the people of Israel, upon Mount Sinai, that I never yet to this day saw any such custom among the people of Israel, and that they do not hold any such thing by divine precept of the law, or any ordinance or institution of their wise men, and that they never committed or endeavored such wickedness, (that I know, or have credibly heard, or read in any Jewish authors) and if I lie in this matter, then let all the curses mentioned in Leviticus and Deuteronomy come

upon me, let me never see the blessings and consolations of Zion, nor attain to the resurrection of the dead. By this I hope I may have proved what I did intend, and certainly this may suffice all the friends of truth, and all faithful Christians to give credit to what I have here averred. . . .

13. Notwithstanding all this, there are not wanting some histories that relate these and the like calumnies.[7]

NOTES

1. Quoted in Jacob R. Marcus, *The Jew in the Modern World: A Source Book: 315-1791* (1938; reprint, New York: Harper and Row, 1965), 153-154.

2. Even the chronicler puts it doubly doubtfully.

3. From Joseph Jacobs, *The Jews of Angevin England: Documents and Records* (London: Putnam's, 1893), 45-46.

4. The traitor Judas of time-honored Christian theology, Shakespeare's "base Judean," is depicted radically differently in the "Gospel of Judas" that was published in English translation in 2006. The manuscript was discovered in Egypt in the 1970s; written in Coptic, it dates from the third or fourth century but is likely to derive from a Greek version that dates possibly from ca. 140 and was a canonical text of a Christian community opposed to or rival of others that adhered to one or more of what became the four Gospels of the New Testament. Its depiction of Judas as Jesus's most loyal disciple is the diametric opposite of the New Testament's. It is highly critical of the disciples, to which Judas becomes an exception because he recognizes who Jesus is, whence he comes, and what his mission is. Jesus then reveals to him the secrets of salvation and the cosmos: "Knowing that Judas was reflecting upon something that was exalted, Jesus said to him, 'Step away from the others and I shall tell you the mysteries of the kingdom'," and he commands Judas to hand him over to be executed. The discovery of the Gospel of Judas is a very important contribution to our understanding of early Christianity; whether it will ultimately rehabilitate the image of Judas—"the treasonous, treacherous, greedy, demonized Judas [who] is synonymous with 'the Jews'"—and remove a potent source of Christian antisemitism is uncertain; it is clearly consistent with the traditional but often ignored Christian theology of the crucifixion as providential and beneficent. See *The Gospel of Judas: From Codex Tchacos*, ed. Rodolphe Kasser et al. (Washington, D.C.: National Geographic, 2006) and the review by Philippa Townsend, Eduard Iricinschi, and Lance Jenott, "The Gospel of Judas," *New York Review of Books*, June 8, 2006, pp. 32-37; for Judas's centrality to antisemitism, Marvin Perry and Frederick M. Schweitzer, *Antisemitism: Myth and Hate from Antiquity to the Present* (New York: Palgrave Macmillan, 2002, 2005), 37-38.

5. "St. Longinus," from the Greek for lance, *lonkhe*, was said to be the centurion who pierced Jesus's side and then saw that he was "a/the son of God," John 10:34, Matthew 27:54.

6. Excerpted from John Edwards, ed. and trans., *The Jews in Western Europe 1400-1600* (Manchester, England: Manchester University Press, 1994), 110-112, 114, 116.

7. From Lucien Wolf, ed., *Menasseh ben Israel's Mission to Oliver Cromwell: Being a Reprint of the Pamphlets Published by Menasseh ben Israel to Promote the Re-admission of the Jews to England* (London: Macmillan, 1901), 108-115; for clarity, we have modernized some spelling, grammar, and punctuation.

THREE

The Accusation of Host Desecration

Two forms of popular, religious libel of Jews arose in the Middle Ages, ritual murder and host desecration. According to the blood libel, Jews were believed to require innocent Christian blood for a variety of magical, medicinal, and ritual purposes. Similar parallels and a similar logic appear in the libel of desecration of the Eucharist, the holy host of communion, believed to be the body of Jesus Christ. The accusation arose in the later thirteenth century, following the promulgation in 1215 by the Fourth Lateran Council of the doctrine of transubstantiation, that the bread and wine of the Eucharistic sacrament were transformed by priestly action and divine power into the body and blood of Jesus Christ; this dogma meant that the communion wafer possessed miraculous powers. Other enactments by the Lateran and subsequent church councils segregated the dangerous Jews from vulnerable Christians and safeguarded the host from sacrilege by prohibiting Jews from appearing in public during Holy Week or when the holy sacrament was being carried to the sick or dying, or in solemn procession on the feast of Corpus Christi (body of Christ).

As early as the 1240s Jews were accused of stealing hosts for a variety of evil purposes. Before long the archetypal pattern of host profanation emerged: A Jew or "the Jews" bribed a Christian man or woman to break into a church and steal the consecrated hosts or surrender one that had been received in holy communion; at home, in synagogue or in a secret subterranean conclave, the Jews—mockingly exclaiming "How absurd the Christians are to believe such nonsense"—"tortured Jesus again" by stabbing, beating, boiling, or burning the hosts; the host would "bleed," cry out, or a crucifix or an image of the Christ child would appear. Unable to hide or destroy the hosts, the Jews would be caught, "confess," and be burnt alive, their property confiscated and used to erect a church or chapel on the site; those who escaped the fire were either massacred, converted, or expelled. The outcome was interpreted and celebrated in the new cult of the shrine of the Holy Blood Sacrament, which signified that Christian teachings about Jews were true and that persecution of Jews was justifiable. This is what Miri Rubin characterizes as "the recovery into cultic triumph of the, now miraculous, host."[1] New liturgies and rituals developed, featuring annual processions and shrines exhibiting the miraculous host and often the knife purportedly used by Jews to stab it. Unlike ritual murder, which some medieval popes condemned, the host libel flourished with papal sanction, symbolized by the institution in 1264 of the solemn feast of Corpus Christi, which was often a day to harass and molest Jews.

In Bavaria in 1298, on the report of wild rumors about Jewish "abuse" of the holy sacrament, great bands of knights, townsmen, and peasants led by a butcher identified in some accounts as "King" Rintfleisch, "a base, poor, and hot-tempered man," swept over the countryside and through the towns and villages for most of the summer massacring thousands of Jews until Albert, the Habsburg ruler of that politically fragmented and socially restive area, stopped the killing. A generation later, 1336–1338, a similarly lethal storm swept over the same area and into neighboring lands (Alsace, Austria, Swabia, Switzerland), this time led by the equally brutal leader, "King" Armleder. In addition to "revenge" on the Jews for "cruelties against Christ," the marauders were bent on punishing them for their "usuries." The plague of host desecrations spread widely in Europe. Once the Reformation began, almost all Protestant denominations condemned transubstantiation as superstition; hence the host libel disappeared from Protestant countries but continued for five centuries in Catholic areas.

Rabbi Avigdor Kara of Prague

"All the Afflictions," 1389

A notable instance of the charge of host profanation occurred in 1389 in Prague, the capital of Bohemia in the modern Czech Republic. During Holy Week, a Jew was said to have thrown a stone that hit the monstrance—the container of the hosts carried by a priest in procession—and caused the hosts to spill out on the ground, thus insulting Christ and his priest; this angered the people of Prague who, led by the "prophet" Johannes or Gesco Quadratus (John the Square), attacked the Jews, systematically tearing off their arms and legs, killing nearly all of them. They also burned Jewish books and pillaged the wealth and property of the Jews' homes, collecting them together by order of the town council to pay the fine that the Jews' protector, King Wenceslaus IV, would surely impose. For his part, the perpetually impecunious Wenceslaus systematically renounced his legal and financial prerogatives over the Jews, reduced or abolished interest rates and canceled debts payable to them, in return for "indemnities" paid to him by the townsmen and clergy, who were caught up in a struggle with him for political and ecclesiastical autonomy. Content to profit from the spoils, Wenceslaus acquiesced to the 1389 massacre. Contemporary accounts justified despoliation of the Jews' property and the piling up of their bodies to be burnt to ashes as righteous punishment for blaspheming the Eucharist and proper cleansing of the region of the pollution of usury. A spiral of accusation and violence persisted to a culmination in neighboring Austria in 1421, when its Jews were either massacred or expelled from Vienna and all of Austria; here too accusations of host profanation were larded together with resentment against "Jewish usury" and the ducal policy of protecting "his Jews."

A moving response to the Jewish suffering in Prague in 1389 was the poem *Et kol ha-tela'a* (All the Afflictions) by Rabbi Avigdor Kara of Prague (d. 1439). A noted poet and kabbalist (Kabbalah is the Jewish mystical tradition), Kara was an eyewitness to the massacres of 1389 and one of the few survivors. Kara's tombstone is still to be seen in the famous Jewish cemetery in Prague. His poem is biblically based, narrating the Christian onslaught through many biblical citations and allusions; it was incorporated in Jewish liturgy and is still recited in Prague as part of the liturgy on the Day of Atonement. In contrast to the Christian narratives, Kara reports Jews committing suicide to avoid humiliation, torture, and slaughter at the hands of the berserk Christian mobs. He says the community's books and their authors, readers, and interpreters were all destroyed in the fire that burnt their bodies, sparing neither young nor old, neither women nor children. To uproot all vestiges of the Jewish community, the murderous looters vandalized gravestones and other traces of the centuries-long Jewish presence. Following are portions of Rabbi Kara's lamentation.

All the afflictions which have befallen us, no one can tell,
    nor all that has been visited upon us.
      All this has happened and yet we have not forgotten God's name,
      the God of the Hebrews has been etched upon us.

Burning shame and indignity we have suffered, for so many trials and
    tribulations,
      trouble and loss which cannot be counted.
      Each affliction seems to suffice in its time, with nowhere to turn,
      as it replaces the memory of earlier ones.

*   *   *

Blood touched blood in that spring month
    on the last day of Passover, the feast of sweet salvation. . . .

Evil men's counsel was heard on this woeful day,
    rushing, running nameless sons of villainy,
    Each of them with weapon in hand, bows and arrows,
    with axes they came, like wood-cutters.

From every gate, from every opening they entered,
    gathering in groups, hovering in troops,
    their chants tremulous and joyful,
    as they spilt pure blood for swift robbery, to do and to have done with.

*   *   *

Having waited till nightfall they plotted their attack
    as they saw a Jew they seized him with a glance.
    First they try to persuade him,
    and then the killer strikes him dead.

*   *   *

Just like the father of many, the father of few
    turns his intention to heaven and his soul towards the act.

Father spares not his baby, his infant—
all his fruits shall become sacred offerings.

Killing is the task of the most timid,
and mothers spare not their sons, nor save them.
An offering by each who is thus moved,
male and female will be sacrificed.

Left without comfort as the head of the holy congregation, its guardian, falls;
the rabbi, his pious brother and his only son.
Is there such a sage, his book in hand?
He will be lamented, woe to the master, woe to his flowering.

*   *   *

Now my soul is eaten up for these great men, experts in book and in discourse,
for leaders and cantors and community benefactors,
for scholars and men of manners [ethics].
Take them from me, they are my congregation.

Old synagogue was the meeting-place of their families
their house of a prayer.
There the sword of fire will devour them.
They were sacrificed whole to their God.

Proud boys and girls were subjected to
yet another abomination, father of all defilement [forced conversion].
Until when, O God, will your sons and daughters be given
to another people, and your eyes remain closed?

Rushing they entered the new and old synagogues.
I cried in a faint voice
as they mocked, burnt and shredded holy books,
The Torah given by Moses as our inheritance.

Shout, hasten, rush, rob, loot,
grab their silver, steal gold and all that you can find.
They are free for the taking and their property and belongings too.
All those who find them may devour and be deemed guiltless.

Tear away the clothes of the fallen haughtily,
our boys and old men, struck by the sword of war.
Naked they are thrown for shame and calumny,
the human corpse fallen into the soil of the earth.

Unto us the fallen are too numerous to name,
the infant with the elder, youths and maids.
Why, they are in your number, Lord of all souls.
God will know, since he is the knower of all secrets.

Verily, God, call a halt to the many killed and fallen,
we have been nothing but robbed and beaten for so long.
We have become an example and testimony to the nations,
the Zuzims in Ham and the Emims. [See Genesis 14:5.]

Why, they have committed atrocities and acted in malice,
> devised schemes to cover up the killing—
> burning Israel's bodies with gentiles—
> and mix Israel's seed with gentiles.

Your free house they have destroyed, the place where my fathers are buried,
> unearthing bones and breaking their headstones.
> My conscience has sunk and my feelings are low
> and my soul was terrified. How long will you allow this to go on?

All around me moan and groan
> pressed by the trouble of their brothers and the oppression of their enemies.
> Captured and tortured, beaten and afflicted,
> here is the cry of my people from afar.

Call, O God, a day of consolation, and put an end to sin and evil.
> Gather the exiled and draw routes in the desert.
> To those who deserve the consolation of Isaiah uplift quickly.
> Because my salvation is soon to come, my justice to appear.[2]

The Passau Host Desecration of 1478

"A horrible thing which was done at Passau by the Jews"

A particularly notorious example of the accusation of host desecration occurred in Passau, Bavaria, in 1478. Christoff Eysengreisshamer, a Christian and well-known petty thief who specialized in robbing churches, confessed under torture that he had stolen eight holy hosts at the behest of the Jews of Passau. He said they paid him one Rheinish gulden, or thirty pfennig for each host, which was the familiar motif of Judas's sale of Jesus for thirty pieces of silver. Under torture, Passau's Jews confessed to the crime of distributing hosts to Prague and other cities, and of stabbing the hosts in the synagogue causing blood to spurt from them. As in earlier instances of host desecration it was reported that the Jews tried to burn the hosts in a roaring baker's oven, but two doves flew out and a child with two angels protecting it appeared. Along with Eysengreisshamer, ten Jews were executed, some forty were forcibly converted, and the remnant of the community expelled; Jewish homes were pillaged and the synagogue was destroyed to be replaced by a church suitably designed to exhibit the precious relics and draw pilgrims. Not many years later an artist carved woodcuts with pictures and a text depicting these events, and sold copies to the crowds of pilgrims who visited the shrine. Following is a translation of the German text inscribed on the woodcuts.

It happened [when Lord Ulrich, Prince and Bishop of Passau reigned] that a wanton and desperate fellow, usually known as Christoff Eysengreisshamer, unmindful of his soul's salvation and lusting for temporal goods, made an agreement, Judas-like, with the Jews after inquiring whether if he brought them the Sacred Host, the body of our Lord Jesus Christ, they would buy it. . . .

After the deal had been made, the seller and callous sinner, in his wickedness, laid a snare for the Holy Sacrament. . . . [O]n the Friday before St. Michael's day, he broke open the receptacle in which the Host is reserved in St. Mary's church in Freyung-in-the-Abbey [near Passau] and stole eight pieces of the Holy Sacrament, seized hold of them with his sinful hands, and wrapped them in a kerchief. He carried them on his person from that Friday till Sunday morning and then in his faithlessness turned them over to the Jews to whom he sold them for a *Rheinisch Gulden*, each Host thus amounting to thirty *Pfennig*. This was an insult to the holy Christian Church.

The Jews—blasphemers of God—kept the Hosts and skeptically brought them to their synagogue, seized hold of the body of Christ with their sinful hands in order to crucify him with savage eagerness and thus test the Christian faith. A Jew took a sharp knife, and when he had stabbed the Host on the altar in the synagogue, blood flowed out of it, and the face of a child appeared. The Jews, very much frightened, took counsel and sent two sacraments to Prague, two to [Wiener-]Neustadt, and two to Salzburg. And when they threw [the remaining] two wafers into a glowing baker's oven they saw two angels and two doves fly out of it.

Later the evil-doer was seized . . . while breaking into a church at Germannsberg. He was then led prisoner to the episcopal palace at Passau, where he voluntarily confessed this great crime, and told even more about the Jews. Thereupon the above-mentioned devout Right Reverend Bishop of Passau, Ulrich, who, as a Christian prince, was quite properly very much grieved by this crime, decided to exact adequate punishment. He commanded the noble and gracious knight, Lord Sebastian von der Alben—at that time his Grace's marshal—to seize all the Jews of Passau and to question them about the truth. They [ten male Jews] all with one accord confessed, and showed the knife, the stone, the place, and the oven where they had committed and perpetrated such a deed with the Holy Sacrament.

Four of them converted to the Christian faith and were brought to justice on Tuesday after Judica in Lent. . . . The new Christians were executed by the sword; the Jews, by fire; and two of them were torn with pincers [and then burnt alive]. A few weeks after the others, the seller [Christoff] was executed, as the law demands, with glowing pincers—all of which he bore with great patience, remorse, and devoutness, and also confessed publicly all that he had done.[3]

NOTES

1. Miri Rubin, *Gentile Tales: The Narrative Assault on Late Medieval Jews* (New Haven, Conn.: Yale University Press, 1999), 1.

2. From Rubin, *Gentile Tales*, 196-198.

3. From Jacob R. Marcus, *The Jew in the Medieval World: A Source Book: 315-1791* (1938; reprint, New York: Harper and Row, 1965), 156-158.

FOUR

Jews Blamed for the Black Death

The Black Death, which ravaged Europe in 1348–1351, was the greatest natural disaster in history. It took the lives of some twenty-four million people, about one-
quarter of Europe's population. Jews also suffered terribly from the plague, although whether their losses were proportionately less owing to ritual requirements
of cleanliness cannot be established. Teachers and physicians could only say that
this calamity was God's will, but in short order it was attributed to Jews who were
accused—as they had been on several occasions over the preceding century—
of poisoning the wells and streams; these servants of Satan were engaged in a
conspiracy to destroy Christendom. Despite decrees of Pope Clement VI prohibiting violence against Jews and denying that Jews spread the disease, mobs—often
spurred on by competitors, debtors, and fanatical clergy—slaughtered Jews by
sword, club, and fire everywhere except Avignon, the papal residence. Some three
hundred Jewish communities in Germany (including the Low Countries, Bohemia,
and Switzerland), southern France, and northeastern Spain, were wiped out; a
"Memorial Book" of Nuremberg records about 345 towns and villages where Jews
were attacked in those years. Except for a few German cities, casualty statistics are
non-existent and allow only a rough estimate of twelve thousand to twenty thousand victims of marauding Christian mobs. Surviving the Middle Ages, the myth of
an international Jewish conspiracy would incite enormous violence against Jews in
the modern world.

Jacob von Königshofen

*"If they [the Jews] had been poor and if the feudal lords had not been in debt
to them, they would not have been burnt," 1349*

When the town council of Strasbourg resisted pressure to do away with its Jews, it
was deposed and a new council gave in to the mob. The city's Jews were arrested
and burned. After 1387 Jewish peddlers were allowed through the "Jews' gate"
into the "Jews' street" until sundown, but no Jews could reside in Strasbourg until
the eighteenth century. The following description of the carnage is by Jacob von
Königshofen (1346–1420), a Strasbourg archivist who lived close to the scene of

the tragedy and relied on accounts of a predecessor who most likely witnessed the misfortune.

In the year 1349 there occurred the greatest epidemic that ever happened. Death went from one end of the earth to the other, on that side and this side of the sea, and it was greater among the [Muslim] Saracens than among the Christians. In some lands everyone died so that no one was left. Ships were also found on the sea laden with wares; the crew had all died and no one guided the ship. . . . This epidemic also came to Strasbourg in the summer of the above-mentioned year, and it is estimated that about sixteen thousand people died.

In the matter of this plague the Jews throughout the world were reviled and accused in all lands of having caused it through the poison which they are said to have put into the water and the wells—that is what they were accused of—and for this reason the Jews were burnt all the way from the Mediterranean into Germany, but not in Avignon, for the pope protected them there.

Nevertheless they tortured a number of Jews in Berne and Zofingen [Switzerland] who then admitted that they had put poison into many wells, and they also found the poison in the wells. Thereupon they burnt the Jews in many towns and wrote of this affair to Strasbourg, Freiburg, and Basel in order that they too should burn their Jews. But the leaders in these three cities in whose hands the government lay did not believe that anything ought to be done to the Jews. However in Basel the citizens marched to the city hall and compelled the council to take an oath that they would burn the Jews, and that they would allow no Jew to enter the city for the next two hundred years. Thereupon the Jews were arrested in all these places and a conference was arranged to meet at Benfeld [Alsace, February 8, 1349]. The Bishop of Strasbourg [Berthold II], all the feudal lords of Alsace, and representatives of the three above-mentioned cities came there. The deputies of the city of Strasbourg were asked what they were going to do with their Jews. They answered and said that they knew no evil of them. Then they asked the Strasbourgers why they had closed the wells and put away the buckets, and there was a great indignation and clamor against the deputies from Strasbourg. So finally the Bishop and the lords and the Imperial Cities agreed to do away with the Jews. The result was that they were burnt in many cities, and wherever they were expelled they were caught by the peasants and stabbed to death or drowned.

[The town council of Strasbourg, which wanted to save the Jews, was deposed on February 9-10, and the new council gave in to the mob, who then arrested the Jews on Friday the 13th.]

On Saturday—that was St. Valentine's Day—they burnt the Jews on a wooden platform in their cemetery. There were about two thousand people of them. Those who wanted to baptize themselves were spared. [Some say that about a thousand accepted baptism.] Many small children were taken out of the fire and baptized against the will of their fathers and mothers. And everything that was owed to the Jews was cancelled, and the Jews had to surrender all pledges and notes that they had taken for debts. The council, however, took the cash that the Jews possessed and divided it among the workingmen proportionately. The money was indeed the thing that killed the Jews. If they had been poor and if the feudal lords had not been in debt to them, they would not have been burnt. After this wealth was divided among the artisans some gave their share to the Cathedral or to the Church on the advice of their confessors.

Thus were the Jews burnt at Strasbourg, and in the same year in all the cities of the Rhine, whether Free Cities or Imperial Cities or cities belonging to the lords. In some towns they burnt the Jews after a trial, in others, without a trial. In some cities the Jews themselves set fire to their houses and cremated themselves.[1]

NOTE

1. From Jacob R. Marcus, *The Jew in the Medieval World: A Source Book: 315-1791* (1938; reprint, New York: Harper and Row, 1965), 45-47.

FIVE

Expulsion of the Jews from Spain

Spain in the thirteenth century was the environment in Europe most hospitable to Jewish life: Jews continued to be prominent in government, medicine, commerce, and finance; their intellectual life as expressed in scholarship and rabbinical studies flourished as never before; the autonomy of their communities was hardly impaired. But in the fourteenth century the violence that was so rife elsewhere in Europe began to spill over into Spain. Accusations of ritual murder and host desecration became more frequent. In the 1340s massacres stimulated by the Black Plague erupted, if less ferociously than in Germany. The fatal turn came in the Easter season of 1391, when a rabid archdeacon, Ferrand Martínez, confessor to the queen mother and a power at court, preached such ferocious sermons that the most primitive passions of his listeners were unleashed, with the result that Ash Wednesday of 1391 saw the bloody sacking of the Jewish quarter of Seville, despite the efforts of civil authorities and some clergy to quell the berserk mobs. An orgy of bloodletting and destruction spread like wildfire over the whole of Spain, presenting the Jews with the choice of baptism or death. In many towns the whole community was exterminated, their quarter was everywhere left in ashes, and before the wave had spent itself as many as fifty thousand were dead. There was little retribution beyond the execution of twenty-five instigators by King John I of Aragon and Martínez's arrest by King Henry III of Castile.

Uniquely in Spain and probably a measure of their acculturation and allegiance to the host society, the great majority of Spanish Jewry acceded to baptism rather than death. The papacy, following canon law, opposed forced baptism, but no ecclesiastical authority ever denied the indelible efficacy of the sacrament once it had been performed, regardless of the motive of the giver or recipient. Baptism could not be renounced, and such *conversos* (converted Jews) or New Christians, became subject to the Inquisition (see below). The two hundred thousand New Christians of 1391 were augmented in subsequent decades by sword-point conversions, such as followed the fiery preaching of the Franciscan St. Vincent Ferrer in 1411. So it went, down through the fifteenth century.

Many of the New Christians (at least initially, but it is impossible to say what proportion) were so only in form; in everything but name they remained Jews, and so too their children. These crypto-Jews or Marranos—as they were dubbed in Castilian, meaning pig—developed as a separate body but remained in surreptitious contact with their coreligionists, those who had managed to hide and avoid the grim choice of apostasy or death. Such Jews could and did practice their religion openly, technically still enjoying the old freedom and autonomy but increasingly exposed to raging mobs and inflammatory preachers. As for the technically Christian Marranos, all doors had to open to them. They made their way in great numbers into the highest positions in the legal profession, the civil service, the army, universities, and the church. Much of the government's financial administration was in their hands, and they made themselves felt in municipal government. The wealthier families intermarried with the proudest of the nobility, and before two or three generations there was hardly a noble family, not excluding the royal house of Aragon, that did not have its tincture of "Jewish blood." It was this circumstance that gave rise in the course of the fifteenth century to a new form of antisemitism, racial rather than the age-old religious kind, for it was deemed shameful and punishable at law to have Jewish ancestry, no matter how remote.

The potent allegiance of many of the Marranos to Judaism antagonized pious Christians, upon whose urging the Spanish Inquisition was established in 1478. It was headed by the Dominican Tomás de Torquemada, who as Queen Isabella's confessor and himself of New Christian extraction propelled the bloody business. Torquemada devised the harsh rules of procedure of the Inquisition and imparted to it its spirit of calm ruthlessness, glacial persistence, and slaughterhouse efficiency. To Torquemada and the crown it was self-evident that the Inquisition could make no headway against the Marranos retaining Jewish rites and customs so long as there were Jews in Spain who openly and legally professed Judaism. It did not suffice to decimate them by massacre and forced conversion, or to reduce them to poverty and degradation by steady erosion of their rights and autonomy. The inquisitors began to press for expulsion, and here too Torquemada's initiative was decisive.

The year 1492 was an eventful one in Spanish history: it saw the fall to Spanish arms of Granada, the last Moorish kingdom in the peninsula, the expedition of Columbus, and the expulsion of the Jews. All these developments reflect the crusading ardor that was the hallmark of medieval Spain and the Reconquest.[1] The monarchs' motive for expulsion was fundamentally religious: they wanted the conversion of the Jews to Catholicism and, as the decree states, to prevent New Christians from being encouraged and assisted by Jews, their erstwhile coreligionists and kin, to return to Judaism. Ferdinand and Isabella, who were known as *los reyes catolicos* (the Catholic monarchs), in a decree later the same year invited the expellees who returned baptized as Catholics to have their property and other rights restored.

The Royal Edict of 1492

"throw the . . . Jews out of our kingdoms"

It is not known how many Jews fled in 1492 (perhaps one hundred fifty thousand to two hundred thousand), how many remained and converted, or how many accepted the offer to be baptized and return to Spain. By the early sixteenth century, the Jews had been expelled from most of Western and central Europe, and Poland-Lithuania and the Ottoman Empire were emerging as the principal centers of Jewish life. Below is the royal edict issued in the spring of 1492, allowing the Jews about three months to comply.

You [officials and ecclesiastics] well know, or should know, that . . . we were informed that in these our kingdoms there were certain bad Christians who Judaised and apostasised from our holy Catholic faith, for which much of the reason was the communication by the Jews with the Christians. . . . [The Inquisition] discovered many guilty people, as is well known, and as we are informed by the inquisitors and by many religious people, ecclesiastical and secular, a great danger to Christians has clearly emerged, this having followed, and still continuing, from the activity, conversation [and] communication which [these Christians] have maintained with Jews. [These Jews] demonstrate that they always work, by whatever ways and means they can, to subvert and remove faithful Christians from our holy Catholic faith, to separate them from it, and attract and pervert [them] to their wicked belief and opinion, instructing them in the ceremonies and observances of their Law.

They organise meetings at which they read to them and teach them what they have to believe and observe according to their Law, succeeding in circumcising them and their sons, giving them books from which they recite their prayers, and announcing to them the fasts they have to fast and joining with them to read and to teach them the stories of their Law, notifying them of the great festivals before they arrive, informing them of what they have to observe and do in [these festivals]. They give [to the Christians] and bring to their houses unleavened bread and ritually slaughtered meat, instructing them in the things from which they must abstain, both foodstuffs and other things for the observance of their Law, and persuade them, in so far as they can, to keep and guard the Law of Moses, making them to understand that there is no other law or truth except that one. This is evident from many statements and confessions, both by the Jews themselves and by those who were perverted and deceived by them, all of which has resulted in great harm and detriment to, and opprobrium of, our Holy Catholic Church.

Seeing that we were informed of much of this before now, and that we know that the true remedy for all these injuries was to reduce to nothing communication between the said Jews and the Christians, and throw them out of all our kingdoms, we desired to content ourselves with ordering them to leave all the cities, towns and villages of Andalusia, where it seemed that they had done the most damage, believing that would be enough to stop [the Jews] of the other cities and towns of our kingdoms and lordships from doing the above. We are informed that neither that [measure] nor the judicial acts which have been carried out against some of the said Jews, who have been found most culpable of the said crimes and offences against our holy Catholic faith, are enough to be a complete remedy. For this reason and to avoid and put an end to so great a shame and offence to the Christian faith and religion, because every day it is found and becomes apparent that the said Jews increasingly pursue their bad and wicked project wherever they live and have converse [with New Christians], and so that there should be no further occasion for offence to our holy faith, among those whom God has so far chosen to keep safe, as well as those who fell, amended their ways and returned to Holy Mother Church, which [danger], given the weakness of our human nature and the devil's cunning and suggestion, continually and at every opportunity warring against us, could happen, if the principal cause of all this is not removed, [means we have] to throw the said Jews out of our kingdoms. . . .

Therefore we, with the counsel and opinion of certain prelates and grandees and knights of our kingdoms, and of other persons of knowledge and understanding in our Council, after much deliberation about [the matter], agree to order all the Jews and Jewesses of our kingdoms to leave, and never return or come back to them, or any one of them. And in this matter we order this our letter to be given, by which we give order to all Jews and Jewesses of whatever age they may be, who live and dwell in our aforesaid kingdoms and lordships, both those native to them and non-natives, by whatever means and for whatever reason they have come and may reside within them, that by the end of the month of July coming, in this current year, they should leave all our aforesaid kingdoms and lordships, with their sons and daughters, Jewish menservants and maidservants and household members, great or small, of whatever age they may be, and that they should not dare to return to them or reside in them, nor in any part of them, for dwelling or passage or in any other way, on pain that, if they fail to do thus and comply, and are found to have been in our aforesaid kingdoms and lordships and to have come into them by any means, they may incur the penalty of death and confiscation of all their goods for our Chamber and Exchequer, which penalties they may incur in accordance with this same act and law without further process, sentence or declaration.

And we give orders and forbid that any person at all in our aforesaid kingdoms, of whatever estate, condition or dignity they may be, should dare to receive or welcome or defend or guard publicly or secretly, any Jew or Jewess, from the said term of the end of July, henceforth for evermore, whether in their lands, or their houses or in any other part of our kingdoms and lordships, on pain of the loss of all their goods, vassals and fortresses and other properties, and also the loss of any grants that they may hold from us through our Chamber and Exchequer. . . .

We give license and faculty to the said Jews and Jewesses to take their goods and property out of all our said kingdoms and lordships, by sea and by land, provided that they do not take out gold and silver or minted coins, or the other things forbidden [for export] by the laws of our kingdoms.

[A contemporary Christian chronicler, Andrés Bernáldez, who believed the Jews deserved their fate because "they were deniers and enemies of the truth" that the promised messiah had come, recorded how the Jews lost everything: "For Christians took their many estates, very many rich houses and landed properties for a few coins, and [the Jews] went about begging to sell them, but they could not find anyone to buy them. They exchanged a house for an ass, and a vineyard for a small piece of cloth or linen, because they could not take out either gold or silver."][2]

NOTES

1. Reconquest—The series of wars traditionally inaugurated by Charlemagne and partly inspired by Christian crusading fervor in response to the Muslim conquest of almost all the peninsula, 711-715, and culminating in the extinction of Muslim rule in 1492 by Ferdinand and Isabella.

2. From John Edwards, ed. and trans., *The Jews in Western Europe 1400-1600* (Manchester, England: Manchester University Press, 1994), 49-52; the excerpt from Bernáldez, ibid., 53-54.

SIX

The Spanish Inquisition and the Conversos

Organized in 1478, the Spanish Inquisition was a royal institution, in fact the only one common to all Spain. Although it served royal ends, it was run by priests and ecclesiastics motivated by church doctrines about Jews and Judaism. The Inquisition was established for surveillance of the *conversos* or New Christians, the descendants of the Jews who were forcibly converted in 1391 and after, to make sure they ceased to engage in Jewish rites and customs.

The Trial of Elvira del Campo, 1567–1568

The fate of Elvira del Campo—a descendant of converts who considered herself Catholic, married to an Old Christian, and pregnant at the time—typifies the relentless modus operandi of the Inquisition. Servants and neighbors testified that she refused to eat pork and that she put on clean clothes on Saturdays—compelling evidence for them that she was a Marrano or secret Jew. These and other seemingly innocent practices had been enjoined upon Elvira at age eleven by her dying mother. Elvira acknowledged these acts but denied heretical intent; told that she would be tortured to establish intent, she fell to her knees and begged to know what the inquisitors wanted her to say. Her pregnancy only inspired the court to accelerate her trial. The fact that she was a good Christian—as she seems undoubtedly to have been—in the testimony of clergy and others was unavailing.

The following account of her subjection to torture was first presented by the famous historian of the Spanish Inquisition, Henry Charles Lea (1825–1909); it is the record of the proceedings from the Inquisition's archives in Toledo as transcribed by the secretary to the inquisitors. Four days after this torture session when, as the much-practiced inquisitors knew, the limbs stiffened and the pain worsened, Elvira del Campo was again summoned, stripped, tortured, and so broken that she confessed to Judaizing. The sentence was confiscation of her property, three years' imprisonment, and wearing the penitential garb of a convicted heretic, the sanbenito. By then she had been a year in prison, where her infant was born, whose fate is unknown. A few months later, as Lea wrote, "the imprisonment was commuted to spiritual penances, and she was told to go where she chose. Thus, besides the horrors of her trial, she was beggared and ruined for life, and an ineffaceable stain was cast upon her kindred and descendants."

She was carried to the torture-chamber and told to tell the truth, when she said that she had nothing to say. She was ordered to be stripped [to humiliate as well as to remove any protection from cutting ropes] and again admonished, but was silent. When stripped, she said "Señores, I have done all that is said of me and I bear false-witness against myself, for I do not want to see myself in such trouble; please God, I have done nothing." She was told not to bring false testimony against herself but to tell the truth. The tying of the arms was commenced; she said "I have told the truth; what have I to tell?" One cord was applied to the arms and twisted and she was admonished to tell the truth but said she had nothing to tell. Then she screamed and said, "I have done all they say." Told to tell in detail what she had done she replied "I have already told the truth." Then she screamed and said "Tell me what you want for I don't know what to say." She was told to tell what she had done, for she was tortured because she had not done so, and another turn of the cord was ordered. She cried "Loosen me, Señores and tell me what I have to say: I do not know what I have done, O Lord have mercy on me a sinner!" Another turn was given and she said, "Loosen me a little that I may remember what I have to tell; I don't know what I have done; I did not eat pork for it made me sick; I have done everything; loosen me and I will tell the truth." Another turn of the cord was ordered, when she said "Loosen me and I will tell the truth; I don't know what I have to tell—loosen me for the sake of God—tell me what I have to say—I did it, I did it—they hurt me Señor—loosen me, loosen me and I will tell it." She was told to tell it and said, "I don't know what I have to tell—Señor I did it—I have nothing to tell—Oh my arms! release me and I will tell it." She was asked to tell what she did and said, "I don't know, I did not eat because I did not wish to." She was asked why she did not wish to and replied "Ay! Loosen me, loosen me—take me from here and I will tell it when I am taken away—I say that I did not eat it." She was told to speak and said "I did not eat it, I don't know why." Another turn was ordered and she said "Señor I did not eat it because I did not wish to— release me and I will tell it." She was told to tell what she had done contrary to our holy Catholic faith. She said "Take me from here and tell me what I have to say—they hurt me—Oh my arms, my arms!" which she repeated many times and went on "I don't remember—tell me what I have to say—O wretched me!—I will tell all that is wanted, Señores—they are breaking my arms—loosen me a little—I did everything that is said of me." She was told to tell in detail truly what she did. She said "What am I wanted to tell? I did everything—loosen me for I don't remember what I have to tell—don't you see what a weak woman I am?—Oh! Oh! my arms are breaking." More turns were ordered and as they were given she cried "Oh! Oh! Loosen me for I don't know what I have to say—Oh my arms! I don't know what I have to say—if I did I would tell it." The cords were ordered to be tightened when she said "Señores have you no pity on a sinful woman!" She was told, yes, if she would tell the truth. She said, "Señor tell me, tell me it." The cords were tightened again and she said "I have already said that I did it." She was ordered to tell it in detail, to which she said "I don't know how to tell it Señor, I don't know." Then the cords were separated and counted, and there were sixteen turns, and in giving the last turn the cord broke.

She was then ordered to be placed on the *potro* [or *escalera*, a kind of rack equipped with sharp-edged rungs, pulleys, and ropes]. She said, "Señores, why will you not tell me what I have to say? Señor, put me on the ground—have I not said that I did it all?" She was told to tell it. She said "I don't remember—take me away—I did what the witnesses say." She was told to tell in detail what the witnesses said. She said "Señor, as I have told you, I do not know for certain. I have said that I did all that the witnesses say. Señores release me, for I do not remember it." She was told to tell it. She said "I do not know it. Oh! Oh! They are tearing me to pieces—I have said that I did it—let me go." She was told to tell it. She said "Señores, it does not help me to say that I did it and I have admitted that what I have done has brought me to this suffering—Señor, you know the truth—Señores, for God's sake have mercy on me. Oh Señor, take these things from my arms—Señor release me, they are killing me." She was tied on the *potro* with the cords, she was admonished to tell the truth and the *garrotes* were ordered to be tightened [meaning that sticks were twisted causing the ropes to cut deeper into the arms and legs]. She said "Señor do you not see how these people are killing me? Señor, I did it—for God's sake let me go." She was told to tell it. She said "Señor, remind me of what I did not know—Señores have mercy upon me—let me go for God's sake—they have no pity on me—I did it—take me from here and I will remember what I cannot here." She was told to tell the truth, or the cords would be tightened. She said "Remind me of what I have to say for I don't know it—I said that I did not want to eat it—I know only that I did not want to eat it," and this she repeated many times. She was told to tell why she did not want to eat it. She said "For the reason that the witnesses say—I don't know how to tell it—miserable that I am that I don't know how to tell it—I say I did it and my God how can I tell it?" Then she said that, as she did not do it, how could she tell it—"They will not listen to me—these people want to kill me—release me and I will tell the truth." She was again admonished to tell the truth. She said, "I did it, I don't know how I did it—I did it for what the witnesses say—let me go—I have lost my senses and I don't know how to tell it—loosen me and I will tell the truth." Then she said: "Señor I did it, I don't know how I have to tell it, but I tell it as the witnesses say—I wish to tell it—take me from here—Señor as the witnesses say, so I say and confess it." She was told to declare it. She said "I don't know how to say it—I have no memory—Lord, you are witness that if I knew how to say anything else I would say it. I know nothing more to say than that I did it and God knows it." She said many times, "Señores, Señores, nothing helps me. You, Lord, hear that I tell the truth and can say no more—they are tearing out my soul—order them to loosen me." Then she said, "I do not say that I did it—I said no more."

Then she said "Señor, I did it to observe that Law." She was asked what Law. She said, "The Law that the witnesses say—I declare it all Señor, and don't remember what Law it was—O, wretched was the mother that bore me." She was asked what was the Law she meant and what was the Law that she said the witnesses say. This was asked repeatedly but she was silent and at last said that she did not know. She was told to tell the truth or the *garrotes* would be tightened but she did not answer. Another turn was ordered on the *garrotes* and she was admonished to say what Law it was. She said "If I knew what to say I would say it. Oh Señor, I don't know what I have to say—Oh! Oh! they are killing me— if they would tell me what—Oh, Señores! Oh, my heart!" Then she asked why they wished her to tell what she could not tell and cried repeatedly "O, miserable me!" Then she said, "Lord bear witness that they are killing me without my being able to confess." She was told that if she wished to tell the truth before the water was poured she should do so and discharge her conscience. Then the linen *toca* [a strip of cloth to guide the water] was placed [in her throat] and she said "Take it away, I am strangling and am sick in the stomach." A jar of water was then poured down, after which she was told to tell the truth. She clamored for confession, saying that she was dying. She was told that the torture would be continued till she told the truth and was admonished to tell it, but though she was questioned repeatedly she remained silent. Then the inquisitor, seeing her exhausted by the torture, ordered it to be suspended.[1]

NOTE

1. From Henry Charles Lea, *A History of the Inquisition of Spain,* 4 vols. (New York: Macmillan, 1907), 3:24-26.

SEVEN

The Persecution of
Portuguese Jews

Most of the Spanish exiles fled to Portugal in 1492, perhaps as many as a hundred thousand, where they had to pay a head tax that was very lucrative to King Manuel. Manuel desired the hand in marriage of a Spanish princess, but Ferdinand and Isabella would entrust no daughter of theirs to a land still besmirched by the presence of Jews, whereupon Manuel turned fanatic and in 1497 decreed the forced conversion of all children four to fourteen, thinking that their parents would follow them to the baptismal font. Although many Jews smothered their children and killed themselves and others fled the country, most of the children were distributed across the kingdom in Christian homes and their elders, allowed no choice whatsoever, submitted to baptism, what the chronicles call the "General Conversion." On Easter 1506 in Lisbon, these New Christians were attacked by Old Christians, who were instigated by rabid monks to engage in ferocious riots and pillage that lasted several days, causing much death and destruction. Portugal followed Spanish precedent in founding its own Inquisition in 1540 to track the New Christians or Marranos. In a relatively short time, however, these New Christians rose rapidly from the status of the despised and rejected of the ghettos who, as Jews, with few exceptions, had been confined to humble occupations and blocked from normal social activity, and quickly gained entry—once conversion had, on paper, removed the religious-legal barriers—into the professions, commercial enterprises, the universities, and public careers in church and state, where they succeeded all out of proportion to their numbers. However, prejudice and discrimination against them persisted, based increasingly on race—supposedly genetic traits that set Jews apart from other people—as one area of life after another came to require "purity of blood" as a criterion for entry into professions, associations, religious orders, universities, and so forth. In Portugal the legal-racial distinction between New and Old Christians, and a host of discriminations occasionally punctuated by massacres and inquisitorial trials, endured until 1774, when it was ended by the royal minister, Pombal; supposedly, the king had ordered New Christians or anyone with the slightest tincture of Jewish blood to wear yellow hats, but desisted when Pombal provided three such hats, one for himself, one for the inquisitor-general, and one for the king. (In Spain, the racial distinction lasted till 1860.)

Damião de Gois

Expulsion, Forced Conversion, and Massacre, 1507

The two excerpts from the contemporary Christian chronicler of the reign of King Manuel of Portugal, Damião de Gois, tell the harrowing story of the expulsion and forced conversion of Portuguese Jews in 1497 and, nearly a decade later, the massacre of these New Christians by their fellow Catholics, the Old Christians. The ferocious cruelty that drove the killers seemed to stem from envy, fear, and hatred.

Many of the Jews born in the kingdom [of Portugal] and of those who came from Castile received the water of baptism, and those who did not want to convert then began to arrange matters suitably for their embarkation. At this time the king, for reasons that moved him thus, ordered that on a certain day their sons and daughters, aged fourteen and below, should be taken from them and distributed among the towns and villages of the kingdom, where at his own expense [the king] ordered that they should be brought up and indoctrinated in the faith of our saviour Jesus Christ. . . .

Because there was less secrecy among the members of the [royal] council than had been expected, concerning what had been ordered in this matter, on the day on which [this] was to happen, it was necessary for the king to command that the execution of this order should be implemented at once throughout the kingdom, before by means and devices the Jews might have sent their children abroad. This action was the cause, not only of great terror, mixed with many tears, pain and sadness among the Jews, but also of much fright and surprise among the Christians, because no [human] creature ought to suffer or endure having his children forcibly separated from him. . . . [M]any of them killed their children, by suffocating them and drowning them in wells and rivers, as well as other methods, preferring to see them die in this way rather than be separated from them, without hope that they would ever see them again; and, for the same reason, many of [the parents] killed themselves. . . .

Now it appears that we might be regarded as neglectful if we did not state the reason why the king ordered the children of the Jews to be taken from them, but not those of the Moors, because they too left the kingdom because they did not wish to receive the water of baptism and believe what the Catholic Church believes. The reason was that from the seizure of the Jews' children no harm could result for the Christians dispersed throughout the world, in which the Jews, because of their sins, do not have kingdoms or lordships, cities and towns, but rather, everywhere they live they are pilgrims and taxpayers, without having power or authority to carry out their wishes against the injuries and evils which are done to them. But for *our* sins and punishment,

God allows the Moors to occupy the greater part of Asia and Africa and a great part of Europe, where they have empires and kingdoms and great lordships, in which many Christians are under tribute to them, as well as many whom they hold as captives. For all these [reasons], it would be very prejudicial to take the Moors' children way from them, because it is clear that they would not hesitate to avenge those to whom such an injury was done on the Christians living in the lands of other Moors, once they found out about it, and above all on the Portuguese, against whom they would have a particular grievance in this regard. And this was the reason why [the Muslims] were allowed to leave the kingdom with their children and the Jews were not, to all of whom God permitted through his mercy to know the way of truth, so that they might be saved in it.

[De Gois describes the massacre of New Christians by Old Christians in 1506.]

In the monastery of St Dominic in [Lisbon], there is a chapel named after Jesus and in it a crucifix, in which at that time a sign was seen, to which [the monks] gave the colour of a miracle, although those who were to be found in the church judged to the contrary. Among the [skeptics], a New Christian said that a lighted candle appeared to him, which was placed beside the image of Jesus, and that some men from the lower orders who were there hauled him out of the church by his hair and killed him and immediately burned his body in the Ressio [a quarter of Lisbon].

To this disturbance many people came, to whom a friar gave a sermon, calling them together against the New Christians. After this two friars came out of the monastery with a crucifix in their hands, shouting, "Heresy! heresy!" This made such an impression on many foreigners, [who were] ordinary people, sailors from ships which had come at that time from Holland, Zeeland, Hoesteland [probably the Baltic region] and other places, as well as men of the land [Portuguese], of the same [social] condition and low quality, that, more than five hundred having assembled, they began to kill all the New Christians they found in the streets. They threw the dead and dying bodies onto, and burnt them on, a bonfire. . . . In this business they were helped by slaves and serving-lads, who with great diligence carted wood and other materials to light the fire. On this Easter Sunday they killed more than five hundred people.

This crowd of wicked men and friars, who, without fear of God, walked through the streets inciting the people to so great a cruelty, was joined by a thousand peasants, of the same kind as the others, and on [Easter] Monday they continued their wickedness together with greater cruelty. And seeing that by now they could not find any [more] New Christians in the streets, they attacked with battering rams and ladders the houses in which they knew [the converts] were. They hauled them out, and, dragging them through the streets with their sons, wives and daughters, they threw them indiscriminately, dead and alive, onto the bonfires, without any mercy. And so great was the cruelty that they even executed children and babies in the cradle, taking them by the legs, cutting them into pieces and smashing them against walls. In these cruelties, they did not forget to sack the houses and steal all the gold, silver and jewels which they found in them, the matter reaching such a frenzy that they dragged [even] from the churches many men, women, boys and girls, tearing them away from the tabernacles [containing the Eucharistic bread] and from the images of Our Lord and Our Lady and the other saints, which they had embraced for fear of death, killing and burning without distinction, [and] without fear of God, both women and men.

On this day more than a thousand souls perished, without there being anyone in the city who dared resist, because of the small number of people of quality who were in it, those of highest rank being away because of the plague. If the magistrates and other justices showed an intention to attend to so great an evil they met so much resistance that they were forced to retreat where they could be sure that what had happened to the New Christians would not happen to them.

Among the Portuguese who occupied themselves with this business, which was so ugly and inhuman, there were some who, to avenge themselves for the hatred and illwill that they had for certain "pure" Christians, gave the foreigners to understand that the New Christians were their enemies, and, in the streets or in their houses, wherever they came across them, they killed them, without anyone being able to impose order on such a disaster.

Once this day had gone by, which was the second of this persecution, on [Easter] Tuesday these damned men went back to pursue their cruelty, but not as much as on the other days, because by now they could not find anyone to kill, since all the New Christians who escaped this great fury were placed in safety by honourable and merciful people, who did whatever they could; and the time and its disorder permitted them, without being able to avoid the deaths in this tumult of more than nineteen hundred souls, who by all accounts were killed by these wicked and perverse men in the events of much of that day. In the afternoon of that same day, a senior councillor, Aires de Silva, and the governor [of Lisbon], Dom Alvaro de Castro, came to the city with those of their forces whom they could assemble, the fury of [the rioters] being by now almost exhausted and at peace, as they were tired of killing and without hope of being able to carry out any more robberies than they had already done.

This news reached the king [who] . . . was very sad and angry about it, and so . . . he immediately sent [two officials] with powers to punish those who were found guilty, of whom many were imprisoned and hanged for justice, mainly among the [Portuguese] natives, because the foreigners returned to their ships with the stolen goods and spoils that they could carry, and each went back to his own hometown. The friars who [had] paraded through the city with the crucifix were defrocked and, after being sentenced, were burnt. And the king ordered proceedings through his official representative against [the people] in the city [of Lisbon] and its territory, as well as its officials, as a result of which many lost their offices and property, and sentence was given against the city and its territory.[1]

NOTE

1. From John Edwards, ed. and trans., *The Jews in Western Europe 1400-1600* (Manchester, England: Manchester University Press, 1994), 61-67.

EIGHT

Luther and the Jews

Martin Luther (1483–1546) played a decisive part in launching the Protestant Reformation and founding the Lutheran church. Of peasant stock and an Augustinian monk, Luther was swept up in a strenuous personal quest for salvation. Haunted by his consciousness of sin and profound unworthiness, Luther was obsessed with the fear that he was doomed and could not win salvation by following the path decreed by Catholicism. He came to believe that "by faith alone" the individual attains redemption, that God, in his infinite and unfathomable grace, would save those justified by faith. In the course of his quest, Luther ignited a revolution that attacked the fundamental teachings of the Catholic Church with regard to the efficacy of the sacraments and good works, the authority of the priesthood, the papal headship of the church, the validity of canon (church) law, and the relevance of scholastic theology and philosophy.

Luther also took up the issue of the Jews, but here he was traditionalist rather than revolutionary, and in fact his antisemitism is quintessentially medieval. In his tract of 1523, *That Jesus Christ Was Born a Jew,* Luther hoped for and expected the conversion of the Jews. It is a standard interpretation that Luther was disposed to be friendly toward the Jews, but that in old age, frustrated in not winning their conversion, he turned into an extreme antisemite. However, as the Lutheran scholar Andreas Pangritz insists, Luther was consistent in his theology of Judaism throughout his life—he was dismissive and contemptuous.[1] Even in the 1523 treatise he asserts that the blind Jews refuse to see that Jesus is the fulfillment of Hebrew scripture, that the law of Moses is abrogated, that the Romans' destruction of Jerusalem and the Temple was just punishment for deicide, and the like. For the moment it will suffice, Luther says, if the Jews "begin recognizing this man Jesus as the true Messiah," and he concludes with the ominous warning that he will "let the matter rest for the present, until I see what I have accomplished."

Martin Luther

On the Jews and Their Lies, *1543*

In 1543 Luther wrote *On the Jews and Their Lies,* a hate-filled treatise, which looks back to St. John Chrysostom and the patristic theologians, and forward to Hitler and the Nazi regime. Hitler himself hailed the Luther who, "With one blow, heralded a new dawn. . . . He saw the Jew as we are only beginning to see him today."[2] In the aftermath of the 1938 *Kristallnacht* pogrom in Germany, Lutheran bishop Martin Sasse of Thuringia published excerpts from this work and introduced them with a preface celebrating Hitler and Luther: "On 10 November 1938, on Luther's birthday, the synagogues in Germany are aflame. . . . [T]he power of the Jews in economic affairs in the New Germany is finally broken by the German people, and thus is capped the blessed struggle of our Führer for the complete liberation of our people. . . . In this hour the voice must be heard of the man, who, as the German Prophet of the sixteenth century . . . became the greatest antisemite of his time, the warner of his people against the Jews."[3] The notorious Julius Streicher (see page 182) testified at his trial in Nuremberg in 1946 that, "Dr. Martin Luther would very probably sit in the defendants' dock today if his book had been taken into account by the Prosecution. He said in this book *On the Jews and Their Lies* that Jews are a serpent's brood and one should burn down their synagogues and destroy them."[4]

What is distinctive of Luther's antisemitic diatribe is its flaming rhetoric and scatological vocabulary, his incandescent hatred stemming from his frustration in failing to convert the Jews as well as being stigmatized as a Judaizer. In content Luther's treatise is the familiar medieval accusations of a people cursed, pathologically deranged in mind and body, given to lying and deception, the Talmud as an armory of weapons to injure Christians, Jews as capitalist exploiters and usurers, arch-criminals and ritual murderers,[5] agents of Satan and subverters of Christianity who are out to rule the world, a carnal people who have forfeited the covenant; in short, "a plague, pestilence, pure misfortune." What angers Luther most and most often is, as he presupposes, the Jews' lying blindness in misreading their own scripture, since it foretells the coming of the Messiah and that he is Jesus the Risen Christ; but "if God were to give me no other messiah than such as the Jews wish and hope for, I would much, much rather be a sow than a human being." Luther's remedies—first of annihilation by conversion, later by murderous expulsion and pillage—are also familiar, then and since. Luther's arch-antagonist in debate, the Catholic Johannes Eck, wrote a remarkably similar attack and equally venomous, equally medieval antisemitic work. Luther's antisemitism together with his fervent German patriotism and authoritarianism added up to a dire legacy. In 1994 the Evangelical Lutheran Church in the United States explicitly repudiated Luther's writings on the Jews (see page 241). Following are passages from *On the Jews and Their Lies.*

I [do not] propose to convert the Jews, for that is impossible. . . . They have failed to learn any lesson from the terrible distress that has been theirs for over fourteen hundred years in exile. Nor can they obtain an end or definite terminus of this. . . . [God's] wrath is proof that the Jews, surely rejected by God, are no longer his people, and neither is he any longer their God. . . .

All the prophets censured them for . . . an arrogant, carnal presumption devoid of spirit and of faith. They were also slain and persecuted for this reason. . . . Our Lord also calls them a "brood of vipers"; furthermore, in John 8 [:39, 44] he states: "You are of your father the devil." . . .

. . . The entire course of the history of Israel and Judah is pervaded by blasphemy of God's word, by persecution, derision, and murder of the prophets. Judging them by history, these people must be called wanton murderers of the prophets and enemies of God's word. Whoever reads the Bible cannot draw any other conclusion. . . . So it became apparent that they were a defiled bride, yes, an incorrigible whore and an evil slut with whom God ever had to wrangle, scuffle, and fight. . . . [T]he wicked Jews cannot be God's people and . . . their lineage, circumcision, and law of Moses cannot help them. . . .

The devil with all his angels has taken possession of this people. . . . [God] often wanted to exterminate them, but Moses interceded for them. . . . They are like the devil, who knows very well that God's word is the truth and yet with deliberate malice contradicts and blasphemes it. . . .

[D]ear Christian, be on your guard against the Jews, who, as you discover here, are consigned by the wrath of God to the devil, who has not only robbed them of a proper understanding of Scripture, but also of ordinary human reason, shame, and sense, and only works mischief with Holy Scripture through them. Therefore they cannot be trusted and believed in any other matter either, even though a truthful word may drop from their lips occasionally. For anyone who dares to juggle the awesome word of God so frivolously and shamefully as you see it done here . . . cannot have a good spirit dwelling in him. Therefore, wherever you see a genuine Jew, you may with a good conscience cross yourself and bluntly say: "There goes a devil incarnate." . . .

[D]ear Christian, be advised and do not doubt that next to the devil, you have no more bitter, venomous, and vehement foe than a real Jew who earnestly seeks to be a Jew. . . . Therefore the history books often accuse them of contaminating wells, of kidnapping and piercing children, as for example at Trent, Weissensee, etc. They, of course, deny this. Whether it is true or not, I do know that they do not lack the complete, full, and ready will to do such things either secretly or openly where possible. This you can assuredly expect from them, and you must govern yourself accordingly. . . .

. . . They live among us, enjoy our shield and protection, they use our country and our highways, our markets and streets. Meanwhile our princes and rulers . . . permit the Jews to take, steal, and rob from their open moneybags and treasures whatever they want. That is, they let the Jews, by means of their usury,[6] skin and fleece them and their subjects and make them beggars. . . . For the Jews, who are exiles, should really have nothing, and whatever they have must surely be our property. . . .

[T]heir Talmud and their rabbis record that it is no sin for a Jew to kill a Gentile, but it is only a sin for him to kill a brother Israelite. Nor is it a sin for a Jew to break his oath to a Gentile. Likewise, they say that it is rendering God a service to steal or rob from a Goy, as they in fact do through their usury. For since they believe that they are the noble blood and the circumcised saints and we the accursed Goyim, they cannot treat us too harshly or commit sin against us, for they are the lords of the world and we are their servants, yes their cattle. . . .

[T]heir own vile external life. . . . abounds with witchcraft, conjuring signs, figures, and the tetragrammaton of the name, that is, with idolatry, envy, and conceit. Moreover, they are nothing but thieves and robbers who daily eat no morsel and wear no thread of clothing which they have not stolen and pilfered from us by means of their accursed usury. Thus they live from day to day, together with wife and child, by theft and robbery, as arch-thieves and robbers, in the most impenitent security. For a usurer is an arch-thief and a robber who should rightly be hanged on the gallows seven times higher than other thieves. . . .

But for us Christians they stand as a terrifying example of God's wrath. . . . The example of the Jews demonstrates clearly how easily the devil can mislead people, after they once have digressed from the proper understanding of Scripture, into such blindness and darkness that it can be readily grasped and perceived simply by natural reason, yes, even by irrational beasts. And yet they who daily teach and hear God's word do not recognize this darkness but regard it as the true light. . . . It serves them right that, rejecting the truth of God, they have to believe instead such abominable, stupid, inane lies, and that instead of the beautiful face of the divine word, they have to look into the devil's black, dark, lying behind, and worship his stench. . . .

[The Jews wish to] lay their hands on the land, the goods, and the government of the whole world. . . . This gives you a clear picture of their conception of the fifth commandment and their observation of it. They have been bloodthirsty bloodhounds and murderers of all Christendom for more than fourteen hundred years in their intentions, and would undoubtedly prefer to be such with their deeds. Thus they have been accused of poisoning water and wells, of kidnapping children, of piercing them through with an awl, of hacking them in pieces, and in that way secretly cooling their wrath with the blood of Christians, for all of which they have often been condemned to death by fire. . . .

. . . Furthermore, we do not know to the present day which devil brought them into our country. We surely did not bring them from Jerusalem. . . . For they are a heavy burden, a plague, a pestilence, a sheer misfortune for our country. Proof for this is found in the fact that they have often been expelled forcibly from a country. . . . With their accursed usury they hold us and our property captive. . . . Should the devil not laugh and dance if he can enjoy such a fine paradise at the expense of us Christians? . . . From all of this we Christians see—for the Jews cannot see it—what terrible wrath of God these people have incurred and still incur without ceasing. . . .

What shall we Christians do with this rejected and condemned people, the Jews? Since they live among us, we dare not tolerate their conduct, now that we are aware of their lying and reviling and blaspheming. If we do, we become sharers in their lies, cursing, and blasphemy. Thus we cannot extinguish the unquenchable fire of divine wrath, of which the prophets speak, nor can we convert the Jews. With prayer and the fear of God we must practice a sharp mercy to see whether we might save at least a few from the glowing flames. We dare not avenge ourselves. Vengeance a thousand times worse than we could wish them already has them by the throat. I shall give you [the princes and civil powers] my sincere advice:

First, to set fire to their synagogues or schools and to bury and cover with dirt whatever will not burn, so that no man will ever again see a stone or cinder of them. This is to be done in honor of our Lord and of Christendom, so that God might see that we are Christians, and do not condone or knowingly tolerate such public lying, cursing, and blaspheming of his Son and of his Christians. . . .

Second, I advise that their houses also be razed and destroyed. For they pursue in them the same aims as in their synagogues. Instead they might be lodged under a roof or in a barn, like the gypsies. This will bring home to them the fact that they are not masters in our country, as they boast, but that they are living in exile and in captivity, as they incessantly wail and lament about us before God.

Third, I advise that all their prayer books and Talmudic writings, in which such idolatry, lies, cursing, and blasphemy are taught, be taken from them.

Fourth, I advise that their rabbis be forbidden to teach henceforth on pain of loss of life and limb. For they have justly forfeited the right to such an office. . . .

Fifth, I advise that safe-conduct on the highways be abolished completely for the Jews. For they have no business in the countryside, since they are not lords, officials, tradesmen, or the like. Let them stay at home. . . . If you great lords and princes will not forbid such usurers the highway legally, some day a troop may gather [to lynch] them, having learned from this booklet the true nature of the Jews and how one should deal with them and not protect their activities. . . .

Sixth, I advise that usury be prohibited to them, and that all cash and treasure of silver and gold be taken from them and put aside for safekeeping. The reason for such a measure is that, as said above, they have no other means of earning a livelihood than usury, and by it they have stolen and robbed from us all they possess. . . .

Seventh, I recommend putting a flail, an ax, a hoe, a spade, a distaff, or a spindle into the hands of young, strong Jews and Jewesses and letting them earn their bread in the sweat of their brow, as was imposed on the children of Adam (Gen. 3 [:19]). . . .

In brief, dear princes and lords, those of you who have Jews under your rule—if my counsel does not please you, find better advice, so that you and we all can be rid of the unbearable, devilish burden of the Jews, lest we become guilty sharers before God in the lies, the blasphemy, the defamation, and the curses which the mad Jews indulge in so freely and wantonly against the person of our Lord Jesus Christ, his dear mother, all Christians, all authority, and ourselves. . . .

And you, my dear gentlemen and friends who are pastors and preachers, I wish to remind [you] very faithfully of your official duty, so that you too may warn your parishioners concerning their eternal harm, as you know how to do—namely, that they be on their guard against the Jews and avoid them so far as possible. . . .

Accordingly, it must and dare not be considered a trifling matter but a most serious one . . . to save our souls from the Jews, that is, from the devil and from eternal death. . . .

. . . [Rulers and clergy] must act like a good physician who, when gangrene has set in, proceeds without mercy to cut, saw, and burn flesh, veins, bone, and marrow. Such a procedure must also be followed in this instance. . . . I have done my duty. Now let everyone see to his. I am exonerated.[7]

NOTES

1. Andreas Pangritz, "Once More: Martin Luther and the Jews," in *Remembering for the Future: The Holocaust in an Age of Genocide*, 3 vols., ed. John K. Roth and Elisabeth Maxwell (New York: Palgrave, 2001), 2: 604-611, 615.

2. Quoted in Neil Baldwin, *Henry Ford and the Jews: The Mass Production of Hate* (New York: Public Affairs, 2001), 290.

3. Quoted in Mark U. Edwards, mimeograph of a lecture he gave at a 1983 conference in New York City on Christian attitudes toward Jews.

4. International Military Tribunal, *Nuremberg War Crimes Trials*, CD-ROM (Seattle: Aristarchus Knowledge Industries, 1995), 12: 982.

5. By contrast, the German humanist, scientist, and Lutheran theologian Andreas Osiander (1498-1552) advanced twenty reasons condemning ritual murder as spurious.

6. Luther's treatise *Trade and Usury* (1520; rev., 1524) excoriates trade and commerce as "this great, filthy, widespread business" but astonishingly makes only fleeting, neutral references to Jews and does not equate them with usury. *Trade and Usury*, trans. Charles M. Jacobs, in vol. 45 of *Luther's Works*, ed. Helmut T. Lehmann (Philadelphia: Fortress Press, 1962), 260.

7. From *On the Jews and Their Lies*, ed. Franklin Sherman, trans. Martin H. Bertram, in vol. 47 of *Luther's Works* (Philadelphia: Fortress Press, 1971), 137-139, 141, 160, 166, 174, 185, 200, 213-214, 217-218, 226-227, 242, 253, 256, 264-270, 272-274, 285, 292.

NINE

The Misuse of Learning:
The Professor as Antisemite

In the twelfth and thirteenth centuries, when Christian scholars first became keen students of Hebrew and discovered the Talmud,[1] the result was a new chapter in persecution. Churchmen concluded that the Talmud was "of earth," not divine inspiration, that therefore Judaism was not a biblical religion but a heresy that denied Jews the right to be tolerated within Christendom. Supported by popes who stated repeatedly that the Talmud was filled with "blasphemies against God and his Christ," this view justified a campaign by Dominican and Franciscan friars to forcibly convert Jews. Churchmen used the Talmud to defame Jews, accusing the rabbis of demanding that their fellow Jews heed the Talmud's putative precepts to kill, injure, cheat, and deceive Christians at every opportunity. Thus, "a new stereotype was born," comments Gavin Langmuir, "that of the mysterious Talmudic Jew."[2]

Johann Andreas Eisenmenger

Judaism Exposed, *1710*

Johann Andreas Eisenmenger (1654–1704) was a professor of oriental languages at Heidelberg. He spent twenty years writing this two-volume work that runs to more than two thousand pages. Learned in Hebrew, Aramaic, and Arabic, he consulted as many as two hundred works on Judaism, indicating that he was familiar with almost all the sources expected of a scholar of Judaism in his time. Eisenmenger quotes extensively and at length, and scholars have ascertained that his citations are essentially accurate as are his literal translations into German. Nevertheless, as a devout Christian and because his controlling assumptions about Judaism are the age-old religious antipathies, he became a learned denigrator of the Jews and Judaism. The subtitle of his book reveals its tenor: It is, he says, a "thorough and truthful report concerning the manner in which the stiff-necked Jews blaspheme against and abominably dishonor the Holy Trinity, the Father, Son, and Holy Ghost, shame the Holy Mother of Christ, ridicule the New Testament, the Gospels, and Apostles and curse and scorn all of Christianity in the extreme." Chapter themes are just as explicit: he examines how Jews "ridicule . . . the sacraments and Christian clergy," "how they render the food of Christians loathsome and unclean," "their doctrine that all Christians be damned," "schemes and plots to deceive the authorities," "what to believe concerning the oath of a Jew," and so forth.

Eisenmenger is thus an example of the misuse of learning. Steeped in traditional antisemitism and anti-Judaism, he uses his knowledge to justify age-old phobias. His quotations—from the Talmud and rabbinic literature—are distorted to "prove" the ancient accusations against Jews. For example, the Bible specifies that the Amalekites' memory shall be "blotted out from under heaven," and the Talmud says such things as "a gentile who observes the Sabbath deserves death," as does the Gentile "who studies the Torah." These and numerous similar statements stem from historical periods very different from the one in which Eisenmenger was writing; they reflect the pagan age in which they were written, when Jewish religious texts condemned idolaters, in language that is characteristically poetic and hyperbolic. Had he read Maimonides (1135–1204), the greatest Jewish scholar of the Middle Ages, he might have understood that both Christianity and Islam were regarded as historical extensions of Judaism, as providing Gentiles the way to the one God of Israel; had he read Menahem Ha-Me'iri, writing in the early fourteenth century, he would have found a mature theory of religious tolerance rather than the exclusiveness that he assumed characterized Judaism in his own time as it undoubtedly had in Talmudic times. Ha-Me'iri recognized the obsolescence of many of the Talmud's strictures and condemnations of non-Jews, stating that "In our days nobody heeds these things." He explained that "all these [negative] things were said at the time when those Gentiles were cleaving to their idolatry, but now idolatry has disappeared from most places." Referring clearly to Christianity and Islam, Ha-Me'iri insisted that "in so far as we have to deal with nations which . . . believe in the Godhead, there is no doubt that [friendly relations and open dealings are possible]"; for example, Ha-Me'iri quotes the demand, "One should not let a house to a Gentile" and explains how it is to be disregarded: "This prohibition applies fundamentally only to those idolaters who kept their idols in their house, and sacrificed to them there."[3] Eisenmenger, unhistorically, takes all such statements in the Talmud at their original face value, but ignores parallel statements like its castigations of Jews, such as, a Jew who "violates the words of the sages deserves death," which if ever meant literally had long been interpreted figuratively. As a consequence of his literal and selective interpretation of texts and obliviousness to the dynamic process of re-interpretation and reformulation exemplified by Ha-Me'iri and others after him, Eisenmenger recapitulates the entire corpus of medieval Judaeophobia and reproduces as established truth all the myths about Jews: ritual murder—with which he is obsessed—host desecration, "criminal" scheming, conspiring to dominate the world and destroy Christianity, greedy exploitation of the poor, poisoning of food and water as Jewish physicians poison their Christian patients, and so forth—all by command of their religion in general and the Bible and Talmud in particular.

Such "Jewish misanthropy" calls for retaliation, according to Eisenmenger. Here too his aims and purposes recall the Middle Ages. First, he wanted Jews to live in degradation—poverty, discrimination, contempt, shackled by economic restrictions, their synagogues and law courts closed down, their writings censored, and so on. Second, and also true to the Christian tradition of tolerating the reprobate Jews in their midst, Eisenmenger sought their conversion. His motive throughout was to convince Jews of the errors of their satanic ways and, having "proven" that Jewish evil stemmed from Jewish religion, he was convinced they would acknowledge the truth of Christianity and all would be well. Thus, unlike the later national-racial antisemites, Eisenmenger, like Christian teaching since the Middle Ages, held out the prospect that the evil Jews were not doomed to remain such.

Entdektes Judentum (Judaism Exposed) was published posthumously, because the German emperor, on the petition of Jewish court agents in his service, proscribed it as "prejudicial to the public and to the Christian religion, and especially to the unlearned." However, the king of Prussia permitted its publication in his kingdom. Thus the treatise—at once scholarly, unhistorical, bigoted and tendentious, polemical, and medieval—began its career. Obsolete and antiquated though it was when it first appeared at the dawn of rationalism and the Enlightenment, *Judaism Exposed* became a foundation text for antisemites like August Rohling (see page 105) and the Nazis; in it they found justification to defame and persecute Jews.

The following excerpt from *Judaism Exposed* on ritual murder is typical of Eisenmenger's aim—making the Jews look wicked—and method—regarding as fact inherited medieval myths. Eisenmenger begins chapter 9 by questioning whether it is permitted to Jews to rescue a Christian whose life is in danger: "it is not only disallowed, but on the contrary, sharply forbidden"; he gives ten reasons why this is so, citing many Talmudic writings as proof.

In addition to these [ten reasons], experience also shows that Jews do not scruple to kill a Christian. As history shows, this pertains not only to mature adults but also to young, innocent children. I shall communicate only a few such cases. . . .

In the year AD1321 the Jews of France caused lepers to poison the wells so that many men died therefrom. And all who were guilty of it were burned by command of King Philipp. . . . The Jews acted thusly also in Switzerland and Alsace. According to Ziegler, this crime has been confessed by the Jews. Concluding that the dissension between the pope and the emperor would lead to the destruction of Christianity, [the Jews] wanted to advance this eventuality through poison. But they received their well-deserved reward when many of them were burned at Basel, Strasbourg, and Mainz. In other places Jews were put in these same poison sacks, which they had placed in the wells, and thrown into the water, whereupon they drowned. Others were stabbed or thrown from houses and otherwise executed by various lethal means, without regard to age or sex.

In the year 1349 the Jews of Meiningen wanted to fall upon the Christians and kill them as they prayed in their churches. A maid overheard the plot and exposed it. Thereupon the Christians left their churches, seized their weapons, and slew all the Jews. . . .

In the year 1665 on May 11 in the Jewish quarter at Vienna, a woman was cruelly murdered by the Jews. She was found in the watering trough used by horses in a sack weighted down by a fifty-pound stone. The corpse had many stab wounds. The head and shoulders and the thighs up to the knees had been slit open. Because the said murder had been accompanied by numerous robberies and other ruthless depravities, his imperial majesty, moved by praiseworthy Christian zeal, decreed the expulsion of the evil-doing Jews. In the year 1670 he had proclaimed with trumpet blasts in the public squares of Vienna that all Jews be eternally banned and that none be any more seen, upon pain of life and limb. Thereafter over 1400 Jewish persons withdrew, part going to Turkey, part to Venice.

Concerning the horrifying murders of tender, innocent little children by Jews there is much to write. . . .

In the year 1250 the Jews of Aragon also stole a child of seven years, crucified him on their Easter [Passover], stabbed him in the chest with a lance, and thus killed him. . . . [I]n London in the year 1257, a Christian child was killed in their annual sacrifice. In the year 1282 it transpired in Munich that an accused witch sold a little boy to the Jews, who punctured the body and murdered him cruelly. And when the suspected witch again stole a child and wanted to bring him to the Jews, she was this time caught by the father and accused. Thereupon, and after suffering torture, she made known the deed and the place where the murdered child had been buried. She was then judged. When now the people of Munich had seen the punctured and killed child, they were so embittered against the Jews that they killed all of them in the area.

In the year 1475 on Maundy Thursday, a Jew named Tobias brought the Jews of Trent, assembled in the house where they had their synagogue, a Christian child named Simon, not yet three years old. Thereupon an old Jew named Moses took the child on his lap, undressed him, and stuffed a cloth in his mouth so that he could not cry out. The others held his hands and feet. The said Moses made a wound with a knife in the right cheek and cut out a small piece of flesh. Those standing around caught up the blood, and each cut out a small piece of flesh until the wound had become the size of an egg. This they also did on other parts of the body. Then they stretched out the hands and arms like a crucifix and stuck needles into the half-dead body, while speaking a few words of this nature: "Let us kill him, just as we did the God of the Christians, Jesus, who is nothing. Thus must all our enemies perish." Finally, the child, having endured this martyrdom, which lasted a full hour, gave up the ghost. [The Jews] hid the body under some wine barrels and then, fearing a search of the house, threw it into the water flowing by the synagogue. This murderous deed, to the greatest derision of the Jews, is depicted under the bridge tower here in Frankfurt with the inscription: "Anno 1475. On Maundy Thursday the child Simon, two and one-half years old, was murdered by the Jews." . . .

. . . In the present day we no longer hear of such cruel deeds in Germany, aside from what, if I remember correctly, I read in a newspaper a few years ago, concerning a murdered child found in Franconia; the Jews fell under suspicion in the case. Because in former days Jews were dealt with very sharply when such crimes were committed, it is not to be doubted that they now refrain from shedding blood solely because of the fear of punishment. Certainly, their hatred of Christians remains as great as it ever was. It is clear from what has been said above, however, that the Jews do not scruple to kill a Christian and that it must be permitted to them, if only it can be done conveniently, secretly, and without danger. . . .

It is also mentioned that in former times, during their Easter feast, Jews made use of [Christian blood] in their sweet cakes, which they call matzos, and mixed in their wine. We read that King Alphonso of Spain conversed with the scholar, Thomas, undoubtedly a Jewish convert, about this. He said to him that a bishop had come to Madrid who preached publicly that the Jews could not hold their Easter feast without Christian blood. He asked whether it were true that such things happened. Thomas answered the king: "Lo, we have seen that a Jew may eat no blood of any living thing. Indeed, they are also forbidden to drink the blood of fish, even though the Talmudists say that it is not called blood. It is scorned and loathsome to them because a Jew is unaccustomed to it, even though he sees that other peoples eat blood. How much more so will he abhor the blood of men, since he has seen no other men who eat it. . . ." From this we can see that Thomas . . . declared the Jews innocent in this matter. [Eisenmenger presents several denials by Jewish writers concerning the use of Christian blood but dismisses them, and delivers his last word on the subject.]

Because, however, many sound writers have written that the Jews do use Christian blood, and demonstrate this with examples, and because most of the children are murdered around Easter, we can suppose that not everything is untrue. I leave it at this as to whether or not the matter is true. Undoubtedly, the Jews murder Christian children mostly at Easter because our Savior Jesus Christ was crucified then. They do it as a mockery of Him. Let that be enough on this matter.

As to the question, whether a Christian, when he is ill, should entrust himself to a Jewish physician and use the remedies prescribed by him, I answer the following. No one should act thus. I shall prove this.

First, because Jews are the . . . bitter enemies of the Christian, as has been adequately shown in [this book], one can expect no good from an enemy. Second, . . . it is allowed [to] them to deprive a Christian of his life. Who would want to trust such men to care for them when, instead of restoring him to health with suitable remedies, he is concerned with killing him with unsuitable ones?[4]

NOTES

1. In two versions, the Babylonian and Palestinian, the Talmud is the compilation of Jewish law and commentary by the Rabbis, ca. 200-500 CE; it is based on the

Mishnah, the code of Jewish law that was edited by Rabbi Judah the Prince, ca. 200 CE, which preserved the oral legal tradition of earlier centuries.

2. Gavin I. Langmuir, *History, Religion, and Antisemitism* (Berkeley: University of California Press, 1990), 297.

3. Quoted in Jacob Katz, *Exclusiveness and Tolerance* (Oxford: Oxford University Press, 1961), 116-117.

4. From *Antisemitism in the Modern World: An Anthology of Texts*, ed. Richard S. Levy (Lexington, Mass.: D. C. Heath, 1991), 33-36.

PART TWO

Modern

In the Middle Ages Jews had faced brutal persecution, but they were not threatened with extinction as a people. Christian culture had nurtured a cosmic hatred for Jews, but Christian morality imposed ethical barriers to systematic genocide as distinct from sporadic massacres stemming from outbursts of popular fury. Ironically, the weakening of Christianity, the Jews' tormentor for almost two millennia, made possible the emergence of an antisemitic (and anti-Christian) pagan ideology that had no qualms about total extermination.

In the nineteenth century, under the aegis of the liberal ideals of the Enlightenment and the French Revolution, Jews gained legal equality in most European lands. They could leave the ghettos and participate in many activities that had been closed to them. Newly emancipated Jews generally aspired to integrate into the majority while still retaining their Jewish identity. Many Gentiles, on the other hand, hoped that emancipation would lead Jews to abandon their faith and become Christians. Seeking to take advantage of this new freedom and opportunity—and drawn by the anonymity and greater tolerance found in large urban centers—large numbers of newly emancipated Jews migrated to the leading cities of Europe, particularly Vienna and Berlin, where many distinguished themselves in business, the arts, the professions, and science. Jews fondly embraced German culture and many converted to Christianity. By the early twentieth century no area of German or Austrian life was unquickened by Jewish energy and creativity.

The success of the Jews—even though the majority, particularly in Eastern and central Europe, remained poor, many desperately so—provided ammunition for extreme nationalists, who were the principal antagonists of Jews. Although fueled by such economic factors and a traditional Christian bias, modern antisemitism rested chiefly on national-racial considerations. A xenophobic nationalism, which viewed the Jews as an alien and conspiratorial race with limitless powers for evil that threatened the nation's existence, had emerged in full force in several European lands in the decades before World War I. The extreme racial nationalism of this period was the seedbed of Hitler's ideology.

Antisemitism generally appealed to the European Right, exponents of tradition and hierarchy who feared the ideals associated with the Enlightenment and French Revolution and the social and economic consequences of the Industrial Revolution. These conservatives attributed all the unsettling forces of the modern age to Jews whom they castigated as Asiatic aliens engaged in a conspiracy to destroy the nation's historic values and institutions and Christianity's sacred beliefs.

Voltaire: The Philosophe as Antisemite

The Enlightenment of the eighteenth century culminated the movement toward modernity that started in the Renaissance. The thinkers of the Enlightenment, the philosophes, attacked medieval otherworldliness and based their understanding of nature and society on reason, unaided by revelation or priestly authority. "The party of humanity," as the philosophes have been called, wanted to establish a more rational and humane society. Their watchwords were criticism, science, secularism, progress, tolerance, education, and freedom in its many guises: intellectual, legal, religious, individual, and commercial. And they attacked slavery, religious intolerance, torture, despotism, and other violations of human dignity and freedom. The philosophes often denounced Christianity, which they equated with superstition, fanaticism, persecution, and suppression of thought. That cluster of attitudes prejudiced several philosophes against Judaism—responsible as the root and source of Christianity and itself marked by "superstition" and "barbarousness"—and seduced some of them, notably Voltaire, into antisemitism.

Other Enlightenment thinkers were favorably disposed toward Jews. Thus John Locke, whose thought is a cornerstone of the Enlightenment, urged in *A Letter Concerning Toleration* that, "[to] speak openly the truth and as becomes one man to another, neither pagan nor Mahometan [Muslim] nor Jew ought to be excluded from the civil rights of the commonwealth because of his religion. . . . If we allow the Jews to have private houses and dwellings among us, why should we not allow them to have synagogues?"[1] In his *Esprit des Lois* (Spirit of the Laws), Montesquieu amplified Locke's call for toleration. He attacked the Portuguese Inquisition for continuing to burn Jews at the stake, and while he shared the philosophes' antipathy for revealed religion, he did not mock Judaism and expressed much sympathy for the persecuted Jews; Montesquieu is most notable for his pioneering explanation of Jewish prominence in business and finance: it was owing to Christian condemnation of these activities as iniquitous callings, Europe's economic backwardness, and the necessity that some economic functions be performed, which were thus open to Jews as despised outsiders. The German philosophe Gotthold Lessing argued, as did many philosophes, that whatever defects Jews exhibited were attributable to their poverty, ghettoization, and cultural backwardness; Lessing was philosemitic and the lifelong friend of Moses Mendelssohn, who was a keen student of modern thought and a faithful Jew. Jean-Jacques Rousseau, perhaps because of his Calvinist background, was well disposed toward Jews, although he too belittled their religion; he admired them for their endurance and believed they "will last as long as the world despite hatred and persecution."[2] In their secular approach to the "Jewish question," the philosophes converted the Jew in Europe, says Peter Gay, from "victim" into "problem," and to many of them the solution was "total assimilation" rather than acceptance.[3]

Voltaire

The Jews: "Still we ought not to burn them"

François-Marie Arouet (1694–1778), known to the world as Voltaire, was the recognized leader of the French Enlightenment. A prolific author whose collected works, correspondence, and notebooks constitute a library in themselves, he was not a systematic or original thinker but a propagandist and polemicist with a rapier-like wit. Voltaire's angriest words were directed against established Christianity, to which he attributed many of the ills of modern society. He rejected revelation and the church hierarchy—"crush that infamous thing" he said of the Roman Catholic Church—and was repulsed by Christian intolerance.

Inconsistent with his principles of humanity and tolerance, Voltaire despised the Jews and Judaism and seems to have had a lifelong obsession with them. Many admirers of the Enlightenment deny that it had an antisemitic dimension parallel to its anti-Christian bias and seek to exonerate Voltaire of Judaeophobia. Editors of Voltaire's works, whether in French or English translation, have often excluded his principal anti-Jewish writings, and biographers discount his animosity as no more than the overflow of his hatred for Christianity. Some scholars suggest that Voltaire turned ferociously against the Catholic Church but retained elements of the fierce antisemitism he had imbibed from his Jesuit teachers. Voltaire spoke admiringly of Jesus but managed to encapsulate many of the crucifixion-inspired accusations—including the blood libel—that have poisoned Christian attitudes toward Jews: Jesus suffered a cruel death owing to a Jewish conspiracy, which Pontius Pilate tried but could not avert, and the Jews brought a cruel condemnation or curse upon their descendants. Other scholars attribute Voltaire's phobia to the unfortunate dealings that he—himself a finagling businessman, one of the wealthiest men in France, a speculator on a grand scale, and moneylender to aristocrats—had with two Jewish bankers; yet his anti-Jewish assertions considerably predate those transactions.

Voltaire's contemporaries were well aware of his Judaeophobia. The liberal Abbé Antoine Guénée asked, "What kind of philosophy is this which, dominated by hatred and dedicated to the blindest prejudice, permits itself these outrageous attacks on a people, the descendants of whom already have more than enough about which to complain? Is this the philosophy of Montesquieu and Locke?"[4] Antisemites since Voltaire's time have drawn ammunition from him. In particular, he became a fountainhead of antisemitism for the Left, including Marx. Some find in Voltaire's

reference to the Jews "as an inferior species of man" or "calculating animals" antici-
pations of the racial ideology of the nineteenth century.[5] In 1942 a French history
teacher served Vichy's antisemitic cause and the German occupation's by compiling a 250-page book culled from Voltaire's antisemitic writings, *Voltaire Antijuif* (The
Anti-Jewish Voltaire). Much of it is drawn from Voltaire's *Dictionnaire Philosophique*
(Philosophical Dictionary), in which 30 or so of its 118 articles attack the Jews as
"our masters and our enemies, whom we believe and detest," as "the most abominable people in the world," and the like, except for the admirable Job who turns
out, however, to be not a Jew but an Arab.

On the other hand, many of his Jewish contemporaries—and their counter-
parts since—admired Voltaire in gratitude for his courageous championing of toleration and freedom from censorship, his combating fanaticism and priestly pre-
tension, and his expressions of empathy with Jewish persecution.

In the works excerpted below Voltaire aimed to demean and demote the Jews
from their honored place with the Greeks and Romans in world history and their
centrality in Christian history. He set about demolishing the Hebrew Bible (although
he knew no Hebrew and little Greek) as history: its chronology is impossible to
square with known history; its statistics do not make sense; its miracles are incredible and irrational. Judaism is derivative, since the primitive Hebrews borrowed
customs, language, beliefs, and practices from the Egyptians and others; they were
ignorant of the soul and immortality, making Judaism materialistic and unspiritual.
Voltaire's mocking belittlement turns biblical history into nothing but atrocities
and massacres, hatred of the stranger, rapes, cattle rustling and thievery, double-
dealing, "usury," and other infamies, making the Bible an immoral work about an
immoral people engaged in divinely ordained criminal activity. Voltaire rarely admitted mistakes, although he made many and often vitiated the sources he used,
and in reissues of his works confined himself essentially to correcting factual errors. To a Jewish admirer Voltaire acknowledged some very biased passages in his
work, admitting "I was wrong to attribute to a whole nation the vices of a few individuals" and pledging to rectify the passages and abandon his prejudices; no re-
visions or recantations ever occurred.[6] In his monumental world history *Essai sur
les Moeurs* Voltaire narrates in a more neutral and occasionally positive way the vicissitudes of Jewish life in the Middle Ages and to his own time, although he continues to harp on their inveterate proclivity for "usury"; even in his last years Jews
remained "the greatest scoundrels who have ever sullied the face of the globe."[7]
Eisenmenger (page 49) pilloried the Jews in trying to prod them into conversion
to Christianity, which, if it happened, would change the Jews from evil to good,
and all would be well; Voltaire, like so many secular antisemites that followed in his
wake, holds out no possibility that Jews can change, and so they would remain a
"problem."

The Philosophy of History, *1765*

I shall not examine what right Joshua had to come and destroy villages [in Ca-
naan], where his name had never been heard of before. The Jews claimed that

they were descended from Abraham [who] traveled in that country about 400 years before. Therefore, said Joshua, your country belongs to us, and we ought to cut the throats of your mothers, wives, and children. . . . It is not at all astonishing that the neighboring people should unite against the Jews, who in their eyes could only appear as a band of execrable robbers and depredators; and not as the sacred instruments of divine vengeance and the future salvation of the human race. . . .

. . . [The Jews] boast of having issued from Egypt like a band of robbers, carrying away everything they had borrowed from the Egyptians. They glory in having spared neither age, sex, nor infancy, in the villages and towns they subdued. They have the effrontery to display an irreconcilable hatred against other nations—they revolt against all their masters—ever superstitious—ever envious of others' good—ever barbarous—and ever servile in misfortune, and insolent in prosperity.

The Philosophical Dictionary, *1756*

1. The Spirit of the Jews and Their History

It is certain that the Jewish nation is the most singular that the world has ever seen; and although, in a political view, the most contemptible of all, yet in the eyes of a philosopher it is, on various accounts, worthy consideration. . . .

. . . The Jews are distinguished among the nations by this—that their oracles are the only true ones, of which we are not permitted to doubt. These oracles, which they understand only in the literal sense, have a hundred times foretold to them that they should be masters of the world; yet they have never possessed anything more than a small corner of land, and that only for a small number of years, and they have not now so much as a village of their own. They must, then, believe, and they do believe that their predictions will one day be fulfilled and that they shall have the empire of the earth. . . .

. . . They were led into slavery [by a succession of conquerors beginning with the Assyrians, followed by Nebuchadnezzer and the Babylonian captivity, the Persians, Alexander the Great and his successors the Ptolemies of Egypt and Selucids of Syria, and the Romans.] [T]hey turned brokers, money-changers, and old-clothes men; by which they made themselves necessary, as they still do, and grew rich. Their gains enabled them to obtain, under Cyrus [the Persian king], the liberty of rebuilding Jerusalem, but when they were to return to their own country, . . . [o]nly the meanest part of the nation returned. . . .

The Jews, ever unfortunate, ever enslaved, and ever revolting, again brought upon them the Roman arms. . . . The seditious spirit of the people impelled them to fresh excesses. Their character at all times was to be cruel; and their fate, to be punished. . . . This memorable siege [of Jerusalem], which ended in the destruction of the city, was carried out by Vespasian and Titus [69-74. Those who survived as prisoners] were exposed in the public markets; and each

Jew was sold [into slavery] at about the same price as the unclean animal of which they dare not eat. In this last dispersion they again hoped for a deliverer; and under [Emperor] Hadrian, whom they curse in their prayers, there arose one Bar Kochba [132-135], who called himself a second Moses—a Shiloh—a Christ. . . . [H]e perished with all his followers. It was the last struggle of this nation, which has never lifted its head again. Its constant opinion, that barrenness is a reproach, has preserved it; the Jews have ever considered as their two first duties, to get money and beget children.

From this short summary it results that the Hebrews have ever been vagrants, or robbers, or slaves, or seditious. They are still vagabonds upon the earth, and abhorred by men, yet affirming that heaven and earth and all mankind were created for them alone. . . .

[W]hat was the philosophy of the Hebrews? The answer will be a very short one—they had none. Their legislator [Moses] himself does not anywhere speak expressly of the immortality of the soul, nor of the rewards of another life. . . . The Jews, in the latter times of their sojourn at Jerusalem, were scrupulously attached to nothing but the ceremonials of their law. The man who had eaten pudding or rabbit would have been stoned; while he who denied the immortality of the soul might be high-priest.

It is commonly said that the abhorrence in which the Jews held other nations proceeded from their horror of idolatry; but it is much more likely that the manner in which they at the first exterminated some of the tribes of Canaan, and the hatred which the neighboring nations conceived for them, were the cause of this invincible aversion. As they knew no nations but their neighbors, they thought that in abhorring them they detested the whole earth, and thus accustomed themselves to be the enemies of all men. One proof that this hatred was not caused by the idolatry of the nations is that we find in the history of the Jews that they were very often idolaters. . . .

[The question is asked] whether the ancient philosophers and lawgivers borrowed from the Jews, or the Jews from them. . . . A great people cannot have received their laws and their knowledge from [the Jews] a little people, obscure and enslaved. . . . This people, after their captivity at Babylon, had no other alphabet than the Chaldean; they were not formed for any art, any manufacture whatsoever. . . . To say that the Egyptians, the Persians, the Greeks, were instructed by the Jews, were to say that the Romans learned the arts from the [barbarian] people of Brittany. The Jews never were scientists, nor geometricians, nor astronomers. So far were they from having public schools for the instruction of youth, that they had not even a term in their language to express such an institution. The people of Peru and Mexico measured their year much better than the Jews. Their stay in Babylon and in Alexandria . . . formed the people to no art save that of usury. They never knew how to mint money. . . . Hence, it is that Jewish coins are so rare, and nearly all false. In short, we find in them only an ignorant and barbarous people, who have long united the most sordid avarice with the most detestable superstition and the most invincible hatred for every people by whom they are tolerated and enriched. Still we ought not to burn them.

2. The Jewish Law

Their law must appear to every polished people, as singular as their conduct; if it were not divine, it would seem to be the law of savages beginning to assemble themselves into a nation; and being divine, one cannot understand how it is that it has not existed from all ages, for them, and not for all men. . . . In this law it is forbidden to eat eels, because they have no scales; and hares, because they chew the cud and have cloven feet. . . . Whoever touches a mouse or a mole is unclean. . . .

We shall not here enter into the details of all these [human] sacrifices, which were nothing more than the operations of ceremonial butchers. . . . It is then but too true that the Jews, according to their law, sacrificed human victims. This act of religion is in accordance with their manners; their own [biblical] books represent them as slaughtering without mercy all that came in their way, reserving only the virgins for their use. It would be very difficult—and should be very unimportant—to know at what time these laws were assimilated into the form in which we now have them. That they are of very high antiquity is enough to inform us how gross and ferocious the manners of that antiquity were. . . .

3. The Dispersion of the Jews

It has been pretended that the dispersion of this people had been foretold, as a punishment for their refusing to acknowledge Jesus Christ as the Messiah: the asserters affecting to forget that they had been dispersed throughout the known world long before Jesus Christ. . . .

Indeed, if while Jerusalem and its temple existed, the Jews were sometimes driven from their country by the vicissitudes of empires, they have still more frequently been expelled through a blind zeal from every country in which they have dwelt since the progress of Christianity and Islam. . . . The Christians pretend to have fulfilled the [biblical] prophecies by tyrannizing over the Jews, by whom they were transmitted. . . .

4. In Answer to Some Objections. . . .

. . . We have been accustomed for ages to hang you up between two dogs; we have repeatedly driven you away through avarice; we have recalled you through avarice and stupidity; we still, in more towns than one, make you pay for liberty to breathe the air: we have, in more kingdoms than one, sacrificed you to God; we have burned you as holocausts—for I will not follow your example, and dissemble that we have offered up sacrifices of human blood. . . . You were monsters of cruelty and fanaticism in Palestine; we have been so in Europe: my friends, let all this be forgotten.

Would you live in peace? Imitate [others who] are dispersed like you; [who], like you, are without a country; who . . . are slaves like you, after being for a long time masters. They say not a word. Follow their example. You are cal-culating animals—try to be thinking ones.

Essai sur les Moeurs et l'Esprit des Nations *(World History)*, *1756*

Spain

All their trade, both foreign and domestic, was carried on by Jews, who had become absolutely necessary in a nation that knew only the use of arms. When toward the end of the fifteenth century, they [Ferdinand and Isabella] began in Spain to inquire into the causes of the wretchedness of the country, it was found that the Jews had accumulated to themselves either by trade or usury all the money in the nation; and upon a computation there appeared 150,000 of this foreign nation amongst them, who were at once so odious and so necessary to the Spaniards. . . . It was therefore debated in the king and queen's council, by what means the nation might be delivered from this underhanded tyranny of the Jews. . . . At length they came to a resolution, in the year 1492, to drive all the Jews out of the kingdom, and share their spoils. . . .

England, France, and Germany

After having seen how the Jews were treated in Spain, let us now examine what was their situation in the other nations of Europe. You know that they everywhere exercised the business of brokers and itinerant traders; as they did in ancient times in Babylon, Rome, and Alexandria. . . .

Their chief vocation from time immemorial [was] the lending of money on pledges. . . .

They were at different times driven out of almost all the towns in Christen-dom, and almost as constantly recalled. [Papal] Rome alone has constantly kept them within her bosom. They were totally driven out of France in 1394. . . . In a word, they were everywhere usurers, in virtue of the privilege and benedic-tion of their own law, and everywhere held in detestation on that account.

Their famous rabbis, Maimonides, Abarbanel, Aben-Ezra, and others, in vain repeated to the Christians in all their writings: "We are your fathers, our Scripture is yours, our books are read in your churches, and our hymns are sung there." They were answered only by being plundered, exiled, and hung between two dogs. In Spain and Portugal it became the fashion to burn these unhappy people. Later times have been more favorable to them, especially in Holland and England; where they were suffered to enjoy their riches and all the rights of society, of which no one is deprived in those countries. . . .

It is no slight proof of the capriciousness of the human mind to see the descendants of Jacob carried in procession to be burned at Lisbon, and at the same time candidates for the most distinguished privileges of a British sub-ject. In Turkey they are neither burned nor admitted to honors; but they have made themselves sole masters of the commerce of that country, and neither the French, the Venetians, the English, nor the Dutch, can buy or sell there but through the intervention of the Jews. . . . They retained all their customs, which were diametrically opposite to those of society in general; and accordingly they were deservedly treated as a people who set themselves up against all others.[8]

NOTES

1. Quoted in Peter Gay, *The Party of Humanity* (New York: Norton, 1971), 98.

2. Quoted in Léon Poliakov, *The History of Anti-Semitism*, vol. 3, *From Voltaire to Wagner*, trans. Miriam Kochan (New York: Vanguard, 1975), 103.

3. Gay, *Party of Humanity*, 97; Peter Gay, *The Enlightenment: A Comprehensive Anthology* (New York: Simon and Schuster, 1973), 747.

4. Quoted in Arthur Hertzberg, *The French Enlightenment and the Jews* (New York: Columbia University Press, 1968), 290.

5. Quoted in Poliakov, *History of Anti-Semitism*, 3:89.

6. Quoted in Gay, *Party of Humanity*, 103.

7. Quoted in Hertzberg, *The French Enlightenment*, 285.

8. From *The Philosophy of History* in *The Best Known Works of Voltaire*, ed. G. W. B. (New York: Blue Ribbon Books, 1927), 402-404, 425-426, 429-430; *The Works of Voltaire* (22 vols.), vol. 5, pt. 2, *Philosophical Dictionary*, trans. William F. Fleming (New York: St. Hubert Guild, 1901), 266, 268, 273-274, 276, 278-281, 283-288, 302-306, 308-309, 313-314; *Works*, vol. 14, pt. 1, *Essai sur les Moeurs et l'Esprit des Nations* (World History), 179-181, 183; *Works*, vol. 16, pt. 1, 45-50. For accuracy and clarity a few changes were made in the translation, punctuation, and paragraphing; for standard French versions see "Juifs," *Dictionnaire Philosophique* in *Oeuvres Complètes de Voltaire*, ed. Louis Moland (Paris: Garnier Frères, 1879), 19: 511-541, and *La Philosophie de l'histoire*, ed. J. H. Brumfit, 2nd ed. (Toronto: Toronto University Press, 1969), vol. 59 of *The Complete Works of Voltaire*, ed. Theodore Besterman et al.

ELEVEN

Continuing Catholic Anti-Judaism and Antisemitism

Into the twentieth century, from the pulpit and in religion-oriented publications, many Catholic clergy and laymen reviled Jews and Judaism, often in venomous language. They perpetuated medieval myths that Jews were eternally condemned as deicides, engaged in ritual murder, and conspired to dominate Christian lands. There is a profound difference between traditional Catholic anti-Judaism and Nazi racial antisemitism. Ordinarily Catholics and other Christians saw Jews as religious inferiors, stricken with an infirmity that conversion to the true faith could alleviate. For the Nazis, however, Jews were condemned by their genes.[1] Whereas Christians sought their conversion, Nazis sought their extermination; even converted Jews and the descendants of converts were not spared the sentence of annihilation. Nevertheless, centuries of Christian anti-Judaism, which taught that Jews were a criminal people deserving of God's perpetual punishment, conditioned many Europeans to agree with the Nazi ideology that Jews were an inherently wicked race that menaced the world.

A Jesuit Journal Propagates Antisemitism:
La Civiltà Cattolica, 1850–1939

The journal *La Civiltà Cattolica* (Catholic Civilization, CC) was established in 1850 to fight the "enemies of Christian civilization" by Jesuits who had fled Rome with Pope Pius IX (1846–1878) to Naples from the revolution of 1848. CC's declared purpose was "to bring the idea and movement of civilization back to that Catholic concept from which it seems to have been divorced for three centuries." CC's initial list of declared enemies included Luther and the Reformation, Voltaire and the Enlightenment, Freemasonry and the French Revolution, liberalism, "the frightening Hydra of socialism," and Protestant Britain. Specific "errors" CC targeted were legal and civil equality, freedom of religion, universal suffrage, public education, freedom of the press, laissez-faire economics, nationalism, Catholic modernism[2] and the *Risorgimento*—the movement to create a unified, liberal, and secular Italy. And CC supported maintenance of the ghetto to which Roman Jews were confined and continuation of the Index[3] and of the Inquisition, which still endured.

In the 1850s CC's few references to Jews were couched in the conventional forms of religious antisemitism utilized by the Church until it was abandoned by the Second Vatican Council in 1965. The Jews were a sinful people with a disposition for moneymaking and greed; they were indelibly stamped with the curse of Cain, the stigma of deicide, and the criminality of ritual murder; the Talmud is the work of the devil. The founding of the Sisters of Zion by two converts devoted to conversion of the Jews elicited this response from *CC:* "It seems that the Lord wishes to use these sisters in breaking the hard-heartedness of this accursed people." Jews were evil, but not universally evil, for there were some good Jews, according to *CC.*

For decades Masonry was portrayed as *CC's* archenemy, but in time its attacks on the Jews mounted. They were maliciously denounced as hateful liberals pressing for a new Italy in which all residents would be citizens enjoying equal rights and as the conspiratorial forces behind the Masons. Increasingly *CC* combined traditional Catholic antisemitism—the Jews as deicides—with the secular and nationalist expressions of Jew-hatred—the Jews as alien Asiatics bent on dominating and exploiting Christian Europe. *CC's* antisemitism evoked little response in Italy, whose fifty thousand to sixty thousand Jews were being increasingly assimilated, many of them achieving prominence in the liberal professions, industry, finance, and politics. And its larger purpose to turn back the tide of modernity also came to nothing. The ratcheting up of *CC's* antisemitism occurred at key points in the war that the Catholic Right was losing to the forces of modernity.

Over time *CC* came to be regarded as the popes' voice, although the official papal publication from its founding in 1864 has been *L'Osservatore Romano.* Pius IX appointed *CC's* editors, underwrote its expenses, and probably reviewed the galleys before publication. Under his successor Pope Leo XIII (1878–1903), *CC's* antisemitism was at its most extreme. It slandered Jews with the charge of ritual murder and endorsed the belief that Jews are required by their religion to exploit and injure Christians. In the opening decades of the twentieth century *CC's* fulminations were directed against Islam and the Muslim Turkish persecutions of the Christian Armenians and against the supposed prominence of Jews among the revolutionaries and leaders of Soviet Russia. After World War I *CC* strongly supported Italian fascism's nationalist and imperialist platform, and applauded the enactment of antisemitic laws by Mussolini's government in 1938. *CC's* antisemitic vituperations persisted throughout World War II and until the new dawn that came with Pope John XXIII (1958–1963). The Church's attitude toward the Jews and Judaism since the Second Vatican Council summoned by John XXIII, 1962–1965, and in such documents as *Nostra Aetate, Notes,* and *We Remember* (see page 219), marks an extraordinary break with Catholic tradition and the views and sentiments expressed by *Civiltà Cattolica.*

1851: The Gospels, Acts, and Epistles, all agree, are of one voice, that the most terrible and implacable enemies of Jesus, author of Christianity, and of his disciples and early followers were *the Jews.* They crucified Jesus, killed Stephen and James, imprisoned Peter and John, did not pardon Paul. . . . [The Church Fathers] Eusebius, Origen, Epiphanius, Tertullian, and Jerome did not hesitate to declare that "In the synagogues the Jews persist in their ancient madness and contempt to curse the Christian people . . . whom they burn alive to hurt and kill in order to amuse themselves . . . [E]ven in the private works of rabbis and in their Pandicts, the Talmud and Gemorrah, it is required that 'Every Jew three times a day curse the Christian people and beg God to destroy them.'" . . . It is therefore clear that the Jews exert themselves in every way to extinguish and hasten the end of Christianity. (*CC*, Series I, vol. 6, p. 659, a Lenten sermon of a non-Jesuit priest.)

1857: Judaism is an Asiatic disease which, like the bubonic plague, cannot be destroyed, its spread contained, or its malignity diminished once it enters European soil. . . . Talmudic Mosesism [ensures that Jews remain a people] who live in the midst of another [incapable of assimilation, prompted by] hatred and revenge against Christians, [whose lack of their own territory], which is God's punishment for their superstitious persistence in a dead belief as well as for deicide, [has made them] a people of overwhelming greed and turbulent spirit. (*CC*, Series III, vol. 7, p. 136, and vol. 8, pp. 352ff., quoting a book under review.)

1858: [Continuing from the book:] It is morally impossible to convert into true European citizens these Israelites, who are so firm in the spirit of their religion which is also their national spirit. It becomes clear, therefore, that little allowance should be given to the invectives of liberals regarding the alleged wrongs of Catholicism in not having permitted entry into their national territory, a people essentially foreign and incapable of being led to civic communal unity and social spirit; even more so, if one reflects that all too soon, through the overwhelming greed and turbulent spirit continuously demonstrated by this miserable people, wherever they have lodged, from the murder in Jerusalem up to the age of Reform [i.e., the contemporary age of liberalism], they would have absorbed everything. Their inability to establish their own territory, which on the part of God could be just punishment for superstitious obstinacy in a dead belief . . . and the obstinate refusal of the Israelites to fully conform. . . . [Given all this], they are condemned by their situation to rely on money as their sole support in life: from this comes the push perpetually to look to increase their wealth. Moreover, by Mosaic law, usury injurious to the gentiles, whatever the motive, . . . came to be conceded to or tolerated of them. . . . [and so,] immersed in the sordid art of moneymaking, this people would pile up simultaneously both boundless wealth and public hate and execration. (*CC*, Series III, No. 10, pp. 273-277, in a lengthy and anonymous article, *Del Credito*, by a *CC* regular.)

1858: [On] the little neophyte Edgardo Mortara: Well, we have to talk about this, even if it is of the slightest importance in itself, because it has been so talked about . . . and given occasion to prejudiced comment. . . . [Seven-year old Edgardo, child of a Jewish family of Bologna in the Papal States, was baptized without his parents' knowledge and taken from them by

papal authorities. Pope Pius IX said he could not return him, because]
It would be inhumanly cruel to [return him to parents who would make
him an apostate, who have seven other children, and don't want him
so much as they don't want him to be a Christian.] They and their co-
religionists—if they want to remain in papal territory—have no right
to claim that canon law be modified to suit the Jewish people. (*CC*, Series III, No. 12, pp. 385, 416; also see *CC*, Series III, No. 12, pp. 373-
374.)

1870: We urge students of social affairs to read and ponder this very stimu-
lating work [Gougenot des Mousseaux's *Le Juif, le judaïsme et la judaï-
sation des peuples chrétiens* (The Jew, Judaism, and the Judaization of the
Christian Peoples), 1869] which should be translated into the language
of our Peninsula, now under the Jews and dominated by them more than
is apparent. . . . It has a special importance because it reveals what is the
chief instrument the Satanic spirit adopts to de-Christianize the world.
This instrument is Judaism. With a rich body of learning, the author
traces the history of Jewish moral corruptions and the atrocious and implacable war, which that deicide nation has continuously waged against
the religion of Jesus Christ. He examines and explains the immoral doctrines of the Talmud and describes how they are practiced, tracing with
vivid strokes of the pen the Jewish influences in the world today. The
gold they have taken from Christians . . . the journalism they control . . .
the role they have in the secret and Masonic brotherhoods which disturb
all social life. . . . [I]n sum, what is called *revolution*, and is distinguished
from all past social ills in its hatred of the Christian, is animated primarily by the Jews, who have become the secret masters of a great part of
Europe. . . . [T]he primary engines of the modern spirit live at the roots
of Judaism. . . . [The attack on the book by a Paris Jewish newspaper]
proves that whoever supports the *revolution* only pushes the Christian
people further into the coils of Judaism which sucks their blood, cor-
rupts them, defiles them, and subjects them . . . to its tyranny. (*CC*, Series VII, No. 11, p. 72.)

1881- [Breaking with some of their medieval predecessors, several nineteenth-
1882: century popes expressed their conviction that ritual murder was historical fact. In numerous articles that amounted to a campaign, the European Catholic press propagated the calumny, often in the crudest
terms. In the 1890s English Catholics petitioned Pope Leo XIII to condemn the accusation of ritual murder, reminding him of the medieval
precedents; the Vatican's formal rejection explained that "ritual murder
is a historical certainty" and to deny it would cause "scandal."]
  The practice of killing [Christian] children for the Paschal Feast
[Passover] is now very rare in the more cultivated parts of Europe, more
frequent in Eastern Europe, and common, all too common in the Middle
East. . . . [In the West, Jews] now have other things to think of than
making their unleavened bread with Christian blood, occupied as they
are in ruling almost like kings in finance and journalism.

It remains . . . generally proven . . . that this bloody rite . . . is a general law binding on the consciences of all Hebrews to make use of the blood of a Christian child, primarily for the sanctification of their souls and . . . to bring shame and disgrace upon Christ and Christianity.

Every year the Hebrews crucify a child. . . . In order that the blood be effective, the child must die in torment.

Opinions of the Hebrew pedants of the Middle Ages differed, as they do now, not about the substance but about the accidents of the bloody Paschal rites. . . . Some held that the blood of a child is essential, others . . . think that the blood of an adult suffices.

In the century which invented printing, discovered America, revived literature and science, half of Europe was full of . . . Masters in Israel [rabbis?] who bought and sold and made use of Christian blood for their piety and devotion. But now the light has been thrown on these deeds, which we now know even more about than our ancestors did.

In Hebrew Jubilee years [every 50 years], the fresh blood of a child is essential, in ordinary years dried blood will do.

Every practicing Hebrew worthy of that name is obliged even now, in conscience, to use in food, in drink, in circumcision, and in various other rites of his religious and civil life the fresh or dried blood of a Christian child, under pain of infringing his laws and passing among his acquaintances for a bad Hebrew. How all this is still true and faithfully observed in the present century, we shall see, God willing, with all the evidence, in the next installment. (*CC*, Series XI, vol. 8, p. 225, in a series of nine articles on the 1475 "ritual homicide" of Simon of Trent; see also Malcolm Hay, *The Foot of Pride* [Boston: Beacon Press, 1950], 311-314.)

1890: [Italy has become] the paradise of the Jews and the Hell of the Christians. (*CC*, Series XII, vol. 7, p. 15.)

Masonry, vivified by the Judaic spirit, has no other *raison d' etre* but hate and rapacity. . . . A single hate burns in the soul of Judaism: hatred for Jesus of Nazareth. . . . A single desire gnaws at their innards: desire for the wealth of this world which, according to their dogma, must belong to them. Thus, its great work through the Masonic sect, which they dominate and which serves them as their instrument, consists in de-Christianizing people under the guise of civilizing them and robbing them under the fiction of national patriotism. (*CC*, Series XII, vol. 7, p. 130.)

1890- The Jew persists in remaining a Jew because his Messianic dream prom-
1891: ises him universal dominion . . . [due to] the Talmud where, in addition to rules for an abominable morality, hate for all mankind is prescribed. . . . This explains why Jews are the sworn enemies of the wellbeing of the nations among whom they reside. (Ibid., pp. 145ff.)

The Jewish nation does not work but trades in the substance and labor of others; it produces nothing but lives and grows fat on the products of the arts and industry of nations that give them refuge. It is the octopus which, with its huge tentacles, embraces and sucks into itself everything:

it has its stomach in the banks . . . its tentacles everywhere: in government contracts and monopolies, credit institutions and banks, mail and telegraph, shipping and railroad companies, in small town and national finance. It represents the reign of capital, financial feudalism, the aristocracy of gold which today replaces that of talent and birth. (*Della Questione Ebraica in Italia*, 1892, 99, 145ff.; the collected articles first appeared in *CC* under that same title in 1890-1891.)

To overthrow the Christian, and especially the Catholic, religion, the Jews have had to work secretly, hiding behind others whom they send ahead, not letting the Jewish trickery be uncovered, getting the fortress to crumble in the name of liberty. . . . And this . . . work . . . has been accomplished through control of Masonry. . . . From this began the emancipation of the Jews in France. This emancipation was the goal secretly intended by the [French] revolution, which invented the famous *rights of man*, to give Jews rights equal to those of Christians. (Ibid., p. 53.)

1891: [What is the remedy?] Let us not say, "Death to the Jew!" Rather, let us say, "Out with the Jew." Live, survive, but far from us. (*CC*, Series XIV, vol. 8, p. 647.)

1898: [Re the Dreyfus case]: Every nation should chase the Jews out. (*CC*, Series XVII, vol. 1, p. 285.)

1901: [The pardon of a Jew in Vienna convicted of ritual murder of two girls caused] great jubilation from the omnipotent house of Israel [but *CC* asserts the reality of ritual murder.] (*CC*, Series XVIII, vol. 3, p. 499f.)

1914: [Re the Mendel Beilis ritual murder case in Russia, *CC* cites ritual murder as proven to be] a sacred dogma among the followers of the Talmud. (*CC*, vol. 2, p. 196f.)

1934: On the Jewish question and Nazi antisemitism! We regret their exaggerations and the fact that their antisemitism does not spring from a religious basis or a Christian and moral conscience. (*CC*, Fasc. 2024f., pp. 126ff., as quoted in Renzo De Felice, *Storia degli Ebrei Italiani sotto il Fascismo* [Turin: Einaudi, 1961], p. 152.)

1938: [Roberto Farinacci, a lieutenant of Mussolini and the leading fascist antisemite, criticized Pius XI's rejection of racial antisemitism and the papal plea that "Spiritually we are all Semites" (see page 219) and praised *CC*, stating that] if, as Catholics we became antisemites, we owe it to the teachings of the Church during the past twenty centuries. . . . We [Catholics] cannot in the space of a few weeks renounce that antisemitic conscience which the Church formed in us over millennia. (Quoted in De Felice, *Storia degli Ebrei Italiani*, p. 384.)[4]

[Utilizing articles from *CC*, British historian Bernard Wasserstein shows that *CC* did not flinch in its antisemitic loathings until Pope John XXIII and the era of Vatican Council II. During World War II it never took notice of German persecution of the Jews; condemned the Jews, as in March 1942, for their "injustice, impiety, infidelity, sacrilege," and the like; while ignoring the concentration camps as they were liberated by the Allied armies, expressed deep sympathy with the German refugees fleeing from the East and lamented the "pious" deaths of the Nazi war criminals hanged after the Nuremberg trials in 1946; reiterated in 1951 that Satan had rendered Jewish consciousness full of "national egoism, racial pride, greed, desire for vengeance, hypocrisy, hardness toward their neighbors"; and the following year bemoaned the fact that Germany was held responsible for war crimes and would make restitution (*Wiedergutmachung*) for some of the lost Jewish property.][5]

A Children's Story Perpetuates the Myth of Ritual Murder, Andreas of Rin, 1462, 1911

The tale of Andreas of Rin (Andrew of Rinn) is one of many medieval ritual murder episodes. A cult honoring the boy, supposedly murdered by Jews, flourished for centuries; in the 1960s, in the spirit of the Second Vatican Council, the church acknowledged that the event was a crime against Jews and the cult was dismantled. The version that appears below is taken from the German *Katholischer Kindergarten oder Legende für Kinder* (The Catholic Kindergarten or Legends for Children), a popular nineteenth-century anthology of kindergarten stories that reached its seventh edition in 1911, and was also translated into several European languages. The anthology, which was sponsored by a bishop, contains several blood-curdling tales of Jewish evil and danger to innocent children. Its foreword assured parents and parish priests: "These are selected excerpts which can enhance the weak understanding of children and warm their hearts. . . . This book carefully omits anything which might harm the tender conscience and the innocent heart." Apparently, grotesque tales about Jewish blood lust were intended for the moral refinement of Catholic youngsters. As W. Z. Bacharach emphasizes in his path-breaking study of parish sermons in nineteenth-century Germany, such preaching, Sunday school lessons, and stories (the tale of Andreas was read and discussed on July 12, commemorating his "saint's day") imbued Germans with a starkly negative image of the Jews, who were seen as evil, dangerous, cruel, and bloodthirsty. Such Christian antisemitic stereotypes were given considerable authority by Bishop Konrad Martin's *Blicke in's Talmudischen Judenthum* (Glimpses into Talmudic Judaism, 1876), exposing Jewish criminality and concluding after extended inquiry that accusations of Jewish ritual murder of Christian children at Eastertide were, in fact, true and conditioned people to accept the vile lies about Jews circulated by Nazi propagandists.

Between the towns of Hall and Innsbruck in the Tyrol, stretches a wide and beautiful mountain range. Many pleasant villages and lonely farms are scattered amidst the green mountain scenery. One of the villages is Rin; about fifteen minutes away stands the house where Andreas was born, on November 26, 1459. His father was Simon Oxner and his mother's name was Maria. They were poor but honest peasants. The boy's godfather was Hans Maier, of the Weisel farm in Rin. The parents were his tenants. About a year and a half after Andreas was born, his father died, and his mother brought him up alone.

At that time, many traders used to pass along the road near the farm, en route to the great fairs which were held four times a year in the town of Bozen in the southern Tyrol. Among them were many Jews. In 1462, ten Jews traveled this road on their way to the fair, which was named after Jesus. As they were passing by the farm, little Andreas, aged two, was sitting and playing outside the door. He was a charming child. When the Jews saw him, they agreed among themselves to kidnap him secretly and kill him out of hatred of Jesus. Had it not been for the mother, who was nearby, they would have taken him on the spot. They went to the nearby tavern, where little Andreas' godfather, Hans Maier, a drunkard, was sitting. The Jews now tried to obtain the child through him.

They conversed with him about different things and asked him about Andreas. Hans told them all he knew, and said that he was the child's guardian and godfather. The Jews praised the child, saying that he deserved a better education than his poor mother could give him; and asked Hans to intercede with the mother to give them the little boy; they would take him with them, be as parents to him, and give him a prosperous and comfortable life. And they promised Hans a hat full of gold coins if he gave them the child.

Miserly Hans, dazzled by the gold, agreed to give them little Andreas when they returned four weeks later from the fair in Bozen.

And thus it came about. The ten Jews, with their teachers or rabbis, returned four weeks later to Rin. It was on July 9th, a Friday, that they returned to the tavern. They asked to spend their Sabbath there. Hans Maier joined them at the bar; he drank a great deal at their expense. They remained there on Sunday as well.

Hans, the godfather, had learned meanwhile that Andreas' mother was leaving early on Monday morning for Ambras to pick vegetables. At this time, he intended to hand over the child to the Jews. Early in the morning, before the mother set out on her journey, she handed the child trustingly and confidently to his godfather and guardian and asked him, with maternal concern, to guard her beloved only child until she returned. The godfather made a false promise.

So the mother went out to the fields to pick vegetables. It was six in the morning. When she had left, and not a soul was nearby, Hans led the Jews through the entrance into the room. There they counted out the promised money into his hat, and he gave them the child. But outside, a great storm began to rage. Lightning flashed, and the thunder was so loud that the entire house shook and the windows rattled. The workers in the fields scattered in all directions, hastening home.

The Jews were very frightened; they feared that the mother would return, so they left the farm and returned to the tavern. There they waited till the storm died down. Then once again they sneaked into the house, where Hans Maier and Andreas had remained. By various promises they persuaded the little boy to go out of the house and with them. They fled into the forest, where the trees and bushes grew thickly. After some time they reached, in the heart of the forest, a large stone protruding from the ground. Its surface was flat but inclined like a crooked table. There they halted. Now the rabbi seized the child and cast him on the stone. They tied his hands behind his back and bound his feet, and they gagged him with a piece of cloth lest his cries reveal their hiding place.

Now they began to stab and dismember the unhappy child, cursing and vilifying him. They opened his veins and caught his blood; finally they untied his bonds and laid him down, arranging his limbs in the position of a crucifix; then the bloodthirsty rabbi cut his throat. The blood of the sweet and innocent child poured out of his many wounds. These inhuman people did not content themselves with these cruel acts of torture and murder. By the stone stood a birch tree. They took the body and hung it on the tree. And the stone, on which they perpetrated the crime, has been called since then "The Jew-stone," and can be seen to this day. Then they fled for their lives.

While all this was happening at the Jew-stone in Rin, the mother was in the field. Before the storm began, she felt ill, and suddenly fainted. When the storm died down, she awakened and returned to her work. Suddenly she felt a drop of blood dripping on her right hand; it was still fresh and hot. Maria was startled and showed it to the others; she wiped away the drop with a fearful heart. But immediately afterwards, a second and third drop of fresh blood fell on her hand; the mother wondered at it and was afraid; she felt that it augured ill. Her concern for her child gave her no peace. She rose up, and hastened from Ambras to the farm. She ran to the room first of all to see the cradle where her child lay. But he was not there. In great distress, she sought him throughout the house and then throughout the neighbourhood. Finally she found the godfather, and asked him where he had taken Andreas and where the child was. First, Hans pretended to know nothing. But, because of her cries and sobs, he tried to comfort her and told her to be calm since Andreas was well. He led her to the room and showed her the hat filled with gold. He told her that the masters had promised him that the boy would be given a good education and that they would guarantee his prosperity; he even offered her some of the money. But as he put his hand into the hat, the money turned into dry leaves. Now fate had betrayed the betrayer himself. The mother urged him to reveal where the Jews had gone with her child. Hans, now shocked at the divine punishment, admitted everything and admitted that the Jews had taken the child to the forest.

The mother hastened to the forest. She cried out, weeping and calling Andreas' name. She reached the stone, saw the cloth and the bloodstains, and soon discovered the corpse of the little boy hanging on the birch tree. Her heartbreaking cries soon brought people to the spot. They cut down the body and placed it in the arms of the fainting mother. After overcoming her first grief, she arose and went straight to the priest, told him what had happened and discussed the funeral arrangements with him.

Now they carried the sacred corpse to the church in Rin; there he was buried in the courtyard not far from the pulpit.[6]

NOTES

1. The Marranos of medieval and early modern Portugal and Spain afford an instance of racial antisemitism under Catholic auspices.

2. Catholic modernism was a movement of Catholic intellectuals who sought to liberalize the Church to make it more accepting of modern liberal political ideals and modern science and to re-examine the Gospels and Catholic teaching in the light of modern biblical scholarship. Realization of most of its aims came only with Vatican Council II.

3. A list of prohibited and of expurgated books that endangered faith or morals, instituted in 1559 by Pope Paul IV during the Counter-Reformation and not abolished until Vatican Council II in the 1960s; it was often revised and reissued. In those four hundred years the works of many prominent European thinkers were added to the list.

4. All translations from *CC* made for this volume are by Professor Emerita Eleanor Ostrau of Manhattan College.

5. Quotes from *CC* in Bernard Wasserstein, *Vanishing Diaspora: The Jews in Europe since 1945* (Cambridge, Mass.: Harvard University Press, 1996), 131-132.

6. From Walter Zwi Bacharach, *Anti-Jewish Prejudices in German-Catholic Sermons*, trans. Chaya Galai (Lewiston, N.Y.: Edwin Mellen, 1993), 144-147.

TWELVE

The Jew as Evil Capitalist: Marx and Sombart

Beginning in the Middle Ages, Jews became important actors in European economic life. Over the centuries Jewish economic activity gave rise to myriad myths and fantasies: the Jew as Shylock or capitalist exploiter, on one hand, and the Jew as Marxist predator or socialist agitator, on the other, the twain meeting as international Jewish bankers conspiring with international Jewish Bolsheviks to destroy, enslave, and dominate. The peculiar role of Jews in the European economy and the historic myths that evolved regarding this role ultimately sprang from the theological anti-Judaism promulgated by Christian thinkers. Since the earliest Christian commentators, the image of Jesus's "cleansing of the Temple" and the expulsion of the money changers (Mark 11:15–19) have been used to condemn Jewish business activity, contrasting the crass materialist mentality of Judaism to the spirituality of Jesus and Christianity. Judas was cited as the quintessential Jewish bloodsucker, he who sells his soul for "blood money," and all such were damned as "children of the devil." Without this theological condemnation, the Jew would have been a merchant, banker, or property owner, normal and respectable, rather than wicked money-grubber, usurer, and leech, as Christians came to perceive them. Condemnation of the Jews as economic exploiters followed from their theological condemnation as a criminal people.

Jewish prominence or dominance in certain economic callings, at certain times and places, has its origin in the Christian Middle Ages, when Jews survived as peddler-merchants and moneylenders. The merchant's function, considered economically unimportant and morally suspect, was frowned on by Christians and thus left open to Jews among other outsiders. Coming from the economically advanced Islamic world where commerce labored under no religious prohibition or taboo, enjoying far-flung contacts and access to credit, and largely barred from land ownership, Jews were able to fill the vacuum left by Christian aversion and European backwardness.

By 1100 commerce had grown more important and respectable; it became an enterprise coveted by Christians, who displaced Jews, often, as during the Crusades, by sack and massacre. Jews also were eliminated by monopolistic Christian merchant guilds that enjoyed many advantages over Jewish rivals, such as the patronage and protection of monarchs, princes, town governments, and ecclesiastics.

In many parts of Europe, Jews, forced out of trade, turned to an area still open to them by the Church's war on usury (taking of interest) as well as by European backwardness in banking and finance. Although there is ample record of ecclesiastical efforts to enforce the prohibition of usury law on Jews, including cutting off whole communities from contact with Christians and interdicting their food supply, in general the Church granted *de facto* toleration to Jewish moneylending.

In the course of the thirteenth century, the same pattern we have seen in commerce repeated itself in finance: From being an indispensable pioneer, the Jewish moneylender was transformed into an expendable competitor who was expelled by force and by his inability to match Christian financial organizations, like those of the Lombards, "the Pope's usurers."[1] In this matter, however, kings loomed as large as the popes and canonists. For a Jew to function as a banker, he needed royal permission in the form of a charter, which was costly to purchase and annually to renew. There was little chance for him to collect debts without the king's aid, for which the royal fee was about 10 percent, although often it was much more; debts outstanding were subject to a hefty tax on the creditor, which was a chief source of royal revenue. If a Jew died without heirs, all his property and the debts payable to him went to the king; surviving heirs had to pay any sum the king demanded, usually about a third. Kings ordinarily did not borrow from the Jews but periodically simply bilked these "serfs of the royal chamber" of any amount according to the needs of the treasury or the whims of the monarch. When it suited their purposes, kings reduced or canceled the interest and/or principal of anyone's debts owed to Jews; sometimes they made such debts payable to the crown. The pound of flesh extracted by the king from the Jewish moneylender, he had, perforce, to extract from his clients. Indeed the king, in reality the Jew's silent partner, was the chief maker of the Shylock image. The cycle ended when the Jewish community was, as a result of royal exactions, bankrupted and then, of no further utility, expelled, as from England in 1290.

In the early modern period, 1500–1789, there emerged a far-flung economic network of Jewish communities that centered in the Netherlands. This international nexus linked the Jews expelled from Spain in 1492 and Spanish and Portuguese Marranos (see page 29), many of whom settled in the Ottoman Empire; the *arendars* (agents of Polish kings and nobles) and merchants of the vast area of Poland-Lithuania-Ukraine; and the court Jews, astute businessmen and administrators who served the rulers of central Europe as finance ministers and war contractors. Thus Jews participated actively in this period of dynamic growth. They were also major participants in the economic life of Europe in the nineteenth and early twentieth centuries. In France, for example, the Péreire brothers and the Rothschilds were prominent railroad builders and financial organizers; in Germany and Austria-Hungary, Jews demonstrated extraordinary entrepreneurial dynamism and creativity. And in those countries also Jewish economic success was debased by antisemitic myths and chimeras, often updated versions of medieval stereotypes. The Jews were castigated as greedy and materialistic predators eager to exploit and rob Gentiles, behavior that was purportedly sanctioned by the Old Testament and the Talmud. In a Darwinian age in which racial explanations were widely employed, several theorists claimed that such traits were racially determined. Taking many a page from the *Protocols of the Elders of Zion* (see page 139), antisemitic publicists claimed that Jewish capitalists formed an international cabal to control the world's finances. Among numerous writers, some of them prominent, who helped shape these myths and impart "scientific" authority to them, two Germans, Karl Marx and Werner Sombart, and an American, Henry Ford (see page 144), stand out. Antisemites, both from the elite and the mob, used their conclusions to buttress their own bigotry.

The American automobile magnate Henry Ford exemplifies this bizarre combination of economic antisemitism with the Jewish conspiratorial menace set forth in the *Protocols.* He said in 1920, "International financiers are behind all war. They are what is called the international Jew: German Jews, French Jews, English Jews, American Jews. I believe that in all those countries except our own the Jewish financier is supreme . . . here the Jew is a threat." He was convinced that "international Jewish Bankers" triggered World War I, "pushed" the United States into the war in 1917, and, as he said in 1940, that Hitler and Mussolini were "puppets upon whom someone is playing a dirty trick," namely the conspiratorial Jews.[2] "The Jew is a mere huckster," Ford said, "a trader who doesn't want to produce, but to make something [profit] out of what somebody else produces. Our money and banking system is the invention of the Jews, for their own purposes of control, and it's bad."[3] Likewise, Jews invented capitalism, the stock market, and economics.

In broad historical view, the Jews represented what the French historian Fernand Braudel called "civilizations of the diaspora type."[4] The Christian Armenians (sometimes styled "Jewish Christians" for their entrepreneurial pluck) played much the same role in the Ottoman Empire (and were the victims of genocidal persecutions from 1895 to the 1920s); from the early modern period Armenians became international merchants, brokers, and bankers from Amsterdam to the Philippines. The Chinese who are scattered about Southeast Asia and elsewhere fall into the same socioeconomic category and are sometimes called "the Jews of the East"; they, too, are often calumniated as being "aggressive" and "materialistic" as if they were all "rich middlemen" or "film magnates" of "unlimited acquisitiveness" who displace the natives in a conspiratorial "silent invasion." The massacre of ethnic Chinese and pillaging of their places of business in 1998 in Indonesia are reminders of the age-old hatred and envy of a minority that is perceived as foreign and unduly privileged and prosperous. Other examples of dynamic minorities include the Parsees of India, who fled from their native Persia when the Islamic Arabs conquered it and were renowned for a thousand years in the East for their commercial sagacity and spirit of enterprise; the Indians—until they were expelled in 1972 by Idi Amin—from Uganda; and the Nestorian Christians in Egypt and Asia.

Each of these communities had several things in common: literacy, better education than the host society, and links with the outside world. What appears to be the key to the whole issue is education, or simply literacy, that fitted them to perform economic functions that the host society could not, initially, perform for itself. Until modern times most people, including some medieval kings, were illiterate. Since the first century BCE, when a system of mandatory elementary education was instituted in Judaea, Jews, in fulfillment of a religious obligation, normally were educated. Such education—he who "prays through study"—made Jews profound students of the Torah and Talmud but also sharpened their faculties and equipped them to carry on economic operations. This tradition of respect for education was put to great advantage in the nineteenth century by Jews newly emancipated from the ghetto; in response, antisemites conjured up an enormous catalogue of accusations that filled the skies with chimerical myths but failed to touch the ground of fact and actuality.

Karl Marx

"The Jewish Question," 1843

Karl Marx (1818–1883) was born into a family that could boast a long line of distinguished rabbis. But his father, an attorney, in order not to lose his livelihood and middle-class status, was baptized a Lutheran as was his son at age six or seven. Marx grew up in a household where the family's Jewish extraction remained an unmentionable secret; this silence probably contributed to the acrimony that characterized Marx's attitude toward Jews and Judaism, which was likely to have been reinforced by his Christian education at the Gymnasium (a former Jesuit academy where most of his fellow students were Catholics) in his native Trier, Germany. He was judged to be qualified for university admission by the state examining board because, among other criteria, he was "competent in Christian doctrine" and had submitted his essay on "The Union of the Faithful with Christ" in his application. Many of Marx's formal works, especially the essay written in 1843 on the "Jewish Question," and his letters and conversations brim over with contempt for *Judentum,* which can mean the Jews, Judaism, or Jewishness, or all three at once. Marx was thoroughly ignorant of any and all of *Judentum's* manifestations. Nevertheless, his interpretation of Judaism and his pronouncements on Jews, together with his equation of *Judentum* with capitalism, profoundly influenced socialist movements and the parties on the Left and, when they came into power, shaped their attitudes and policies toward the Jews, at times tragically. Marxist scholars gloss over the antisemitism of this essay, arguing that his animus was directed at the dehumanizing alienation of commerce and bourgeois society rather than *Judentum,* and that by the "emancipation of society from Judaism" Marx meant the emancipation of society from all religion, including Christianity; yet Marx enunciated none of this in so many words, and given the essay's ranting vehemence, the argument remains unconvincing. To be sure, Marx supported granting Jews citizenship with equal rights, yet to qualify Jews would have to cease being Jews. The early editors of Marx's correspondence, journalism, and books went to great lengths to soften or eliminate his antisemitic bigotry, but in the Stalinist era editors went to great lengths to restore it.

Marx's harsh condemnation of Jewry and all its works chimed in too readily with voices of the century demanding that "the Jew in the Jew must be done to death" or with proposals to cure "the Jewish disease"—trade and finance—by destroying the Jewish commercial classes. In his later years Marx never retracted the brutally contemptuous condemnation of Jews and Judaism as capitalism personified. From the 1840s to his death in 1883 his conversation, letters, and journalism are full of invective and anti-Jewish epithets, like his complaint of a town that is crawling with "Jews and fleas," that Jews are "dirty" and multiply "like lice"; they are Europe's "loan-mongers" and have been so since "Christ drove the money-changers from the temple 1855 years ago"; and much else of the same tenor. In Edmund Silberner's considered judgment, "If the pronouncements of Marx are not chosen at random, but are examined as a whole, . . . [he] *must* be regarded as an outspoken anti-Semite."[5]

Almost all nineteenth-century socialists followed Marx in characterizing Jews as capitalists, as aggressively dominant in trade and finance, and as having an irredeemable predisposition for exploitation. At the same time German and Austrian Social Democratic parties and the French Socialist Party often denounced antisemitism as the way the ruling classes distracted attention away from the real sources of the workers' exploitation and onto the Jews. Marx provided fuel for right-wing antisemites who, because of Marx's Jewish ancestry, defined Marxism/communism/socialism as "Jewish," as he had defined capitalism and with some of the same kinds of calamitous consequences for Jews. His essay was put to antisemitic use by Hitler and Nazi antisemites, Soviet antisemites and their Eastern European imitators, and Arab-Islamic antisemites. To Julius Carlebach, "Marx is a logical and indispensable link between Luther and Hitler."[6]

Following are excerpts from Marx's 1843 essay, "The Jewish Question," a stockpile of antisemitic motifs.

The German Jews seek emancipation. What kind of emancipation? Civil and political emancipation. . . .

For us the question of Jewish capacity for emancipation becomes the question of which element in society must be overcome in order to abolish *Judentum* [Judaism, Jewry, Jewishness]. For the Jews' capacity for emancipation depends on the Jews' relation to the emancipation of our whole enslaved world.

Let us look at the actual, secular Jew of our time . . . the Jew of everyday life.

What is the Jew's foundation in our world? Material necessity, private advantage.

What is the object of the Jew's worship in this world? Usury/huckstering. What is his worldly god? Money.

Very well then; emancipation from usury/huckstering and money, that is, from practical, real Judaism, would constitute the emancipation of our time.

The organization of society so as to abolish the preconditions of usury/huckstering, and hence its possibility, would render [the existence of] the Jew impossible. His religious conviction would dissolve like a stale miasma under the pressure of the real life of the community. . . . [S]hould the Jew recognize his materialistic nature as valueless and work for its abolition, he would be working for simple human emancipation and the shedding of his historical development to the present. . . .

Thus we recognize in Judaism generally an anti-social element which has reached its present strength through a historical development in which the Jews eagerly collaborated. Jewish emancipation [from money and huckstering] means, in the final analysis, the emancipation of humanity from Judaism.

The Jew has already emancipated himself [but] in the Jewish way: "The Jew, who is, for example, merely tolerated in Vienna [Marx is quoting the Hegelian philosopher and biblical scholar Bruno Bauer in this reference to the banker Salomon Rothschild], determines by his money-power the fate of the entire German Empire. The Jew, who is without rights in the smallest German state, decides the fate of Europe. . . . While corporations and guilds are closed to the Jew or are not yet favorable to him, the daring of [Jewish] private industry mocks the obstinacy of medieval institutions."

This is no isolated fact. The Jew has emancipated himself in the Jewish fashion not only by acquiring money-power but through money's having become (with him or without him) the world-power and the Jewish spirit's having become the practical spirit of the Christian peoples. The Jews have emancipated themselves to the extent that Christians have become Jews.

For example, "The pious and politically free inhabitant of New England," reports Colonel Thomas Hamilton [in *Men and Manners in America*, 2 vols., 1833], "is a kind of Laocoön [a classical statue of a man] who makes not the slightest effort to free himself from the snakes which are strangling him. Mammon is the God of these people: they worship him not only with their lips but with all the powers of their bodies and soul. The earth in their eyes is nothing but one great stock exchange and they are convinced that they have no other mission here below than to become richer than their neighbors. Usury has taken hold of all their thoughts, excitement derives from some change in its object. When they travel, they carry their office or store, so to speak, with them on their backs and speak of nothing but interest and profits and if they turn their eyes for an instant from their own business it is only to turn them to the business of others."

Indeed, the materialistic rule of the Jew over the Christian world has in the United States reached . . . everyday acceptability. . . .

. . . [T]he Jew is deprived of political rights in theory while in practice he wields enormous power and exercises wholesale a political influence whose retail use is [by law] denied him.

The contradiction between this actual political power and Jews' political rights is [explained by] the universal . . . power of money. . . .

Judaism has maintained itself alongside Christianity . . . because the materialistic spirit of Judaism has kept itself alive in Christian society and achieved there its highest expression. . . .

Bourgeois society continuously brings forth the Jew from its own entrails.

What was the essential foundation of the Jewish religion? Practical needs, egotism.

The monotheism of the Jew is therefore actually a polytheism of many [material] needs. . . .

Money is the zealous one god of Israel, beside which no other god may stand. Money degrades all the gods of mankind and turns them into commodities. Money is the universal and self-constituted value set upon all things. It has therefore robbed the whole world, of both nature and man, of its original value. Money is the essence of man's life and work, which have become alienated from him. This alien monster rules him and he worships it.

The god of the Jews has [thus] become secularized and is now a worldly god. The bill of exchange is the Jew's real god. His god is the illusory bill of exchange.

The view of nature gained under the dominion of money and private property is a genuine contempt, a materialistic degradation of nature, such as exists in Jewish religion, if only in fancy.

It is in this sense that Thomas Müntzer[7] complains that "all creatures have become property, the fish in the water, the birds in the air, the plants on the ground—the creatures, too, must become free."

What is stated abstractly in Jewish religion, namely, contempt for theory, art, history and man as an end in himself, is the actual and conscious point of view, held to be virtuous by the man of money. Even the relations between the sexes, between man and woman, become an object of commerce. The woman is auctioned off.

The chimerical nationality of the Jew is the true nationality of the merchant, particularly of the man of money.

The law of the Jew, lacking all solid foundation, is only the religious caricature of morality and of law in general. . . .

Jewish Jesuitism—that practical Jesuitism which [is found] in the Talmud [by which Jews rationalize their evasion of laws and thus undermine public good in pursuit of private aims and egotistical ends].

[Judaism as a religion is incapable of further development.] Jewry/Judaism cannot create a new world; it can only [parasitically] draw the world's newly made creations and relationships into the sphere of its activities, because practical need, whose motivation is private interest, acts passively and never initiates growth, but only feeds on the growth of society. . . .

Christianity sprang from Judaism; it has now dissolved itself back into Judaism.

The Christian was from the start the theorizing Jew; the Jew therefore the practical Christian, and the practical Christian has once more become a Jew.

Christianity overcame real Judaism in appearance only. . . .

Christianity is the sublime thought of Judaism. Judaism is the everyday practical application of Christianity. . . .

As soon as society can abolish the empirical nature of the Jew, that is, usury/huckstering and its preconditions, being a Jew will become impossible because his [religious] conviction will no longer have any object, since the subjective basis of Judaism (practical need) will have become humanized and the conflict between man as a sensual individual and as a species will have been abolished.

The social emancipation of Jewry is the emancipation of society from Jewry/Judaism.[8]

Werner Sombart

The Jews and Modern Capitalism, *1911*

Werner Sombart (1863–1941) was a German economic historian and academic who wrote on the bourgeoisie, the proletariat, the rise of modern capitalism, and German economic history. In *The Jews and Modern Capitalism* (1911), Sombart sought to provide the evidence to support Marx's essay "The Jewish Question." Sombart thus began his research with a thesis and "proved" it by selected evidence utilizing archetypes and stereotypes—"the Jewish essence" and Jewish characteristics that remained "unchanged over the ages"—and employing tainted antisemitic sources; the data that contradicted his assertions he cast aside. He never learned Hebrew and knew nothing of Jewish religious thought and philosophy—of the Jewish ethic—before he undertook his book, an accidental detour from his main pursuit, the rise of modern capitalism. In his early career, capitalism was the enemy, and so he blamed it on the Jews in *The Jews and Modern Capitalism.* In later life, when he became an enthusiastic Nazi, capitalism underwent rehabilitation and socialism-communism became the enemy, which he characteristically blamed on the Jews. Throughout his life as a scholar, Sombart was given to oversimplification and exaggeration and was driven by shifting ideological premises in his pursuit of *Homo Judaeus* as *Homo capitalisticus* and then *Homo communisticus.* Volkish nationalism (see page 104) appears to have been the one constant ideological element of his outlook. Although intrinsically defective and incomplete, like Marx's 1843 essay, *The Jews and Modern Capitalism* has had an unwarranted influence and been readily exploited by antisemites to underwrite their distortions.

Sombart's interpretation of Jewish capacity in business and finance is fundamentally racist: the race shaped and determined the religion. Together race and religion imparted to Jews a set of characteristics—adaptable, impersonal, worldly, rational, abstract, "extremely intellectual," anti-mystical, materialistic, mobile, restless, nomadic, sexually puritanical, and ascetic—that fitted them, in Sombart's view, to found capitalism and be its most successful and ruthless practitioners: "I think that the Jewish religion has the same leading ideas as Capitalism. I see the same spirit in the one as in the other."

In seeking to attribute capitalism to the villainous Jews, Sombart greatly exaggerated and oversimplified their importance. He held that Jews invented virtually all the tools and devices and institutions of capitalism, including capitalism itself, that product of "the spirit of Judaism." In fact, however, most of these instruments and the new forms in business and public finance were well established by the time the Jews came on the scene; once they were actively engaged in their use, the Jews and others such as the Puritans contributed—no doubt disproportionately to their numbers—to capitalism's further development.

Sombart reiterates the hoary, hackneyed accusation of a double moral standard, that Jews behave in one way toward fellow Jews and in another, less ethical or unscrupulous way, toward Gentiles. This too rested on a religious foundation, namely Deuteronomy 23:20: "You may charge interest to a foreigner but not on a loan to a fellow-countryman." But Sombart and those who argue this way generalize excessively on the basis of one of the 613 Commandments. He seemed to think that it alone governed economic relations with the out-group and that it did so uniformly and unchangingly over the centuries since the Babylonian Captivity. But over the centuries the rabbis interpreted this and other biblical and talmudic precepts in a multitude of ways. Sombart and many another economic historian were decidedly at fault for failing to read the rabbis—had they pondered Rashi, Maimonides, Nachmanides, and many others, they would have found that the sages vehemently forbade taking advantage of Gentiles, that some commentators permitted charging interest to Jews and Gentiles but forbade taking it from the Jewish or Gentile poor, that far from being fixed and static there was an evolutionary development of rabbinical teaching on economic behavior. If Sombart had troubled to acquire a firsthand acquaintance with five hundred years of rabbinical commentary and legal interpretation, he certainly would have found that dealing with strangers was not a matter of ethical indifference to Jews and that *strangers* had long ceased to be synonymous with *enemies.*

In placing excessive emphasis on biblical inspiration and talmudic direction, Sombart ignores a far more important factor in explaining Jewish economic performance, that as a small minority of strangers subject to prejudice and persecution, Jews were driven to sharpen their economic skills in order to survive. Nowhere in Sombart's work is there any indication that other peoples—the Armenians, Parsees in India, Chinese in Southeast Asia—functioned in similar ways. He eschewed any kind of comparative method, which would have shattered his whole interpretative scheme. Rather, he persisted in an a priori racial-religious explanation of Jewish economic behavior as well as in his Marxian formula that capitalism is nothing more than the workings of the "spirit of Judaism." Nor did Sombart consider the sociological fact that for centuries Jews were barred from artisan guilds and deprived of land, and therefore might be expected to concentrate their efforts in commercial and financial enterprises. With the pioneering sociologist of religion Max Weber (1864–1920), it may be said that "one fact could not be seriously questioned, namely that Judaism played a conspicuous role in the evolution of the modern capitalistic system."[9] But one is not dependent on Sombart's misreading of this phenomenon to come to that realization, and it remains puzzling why serious scholars have taken The Jews and Modern Capitalism, excerpted below, so seriously for so long.

The time has really arrived when the myth that the Jews were forced to have recourse to moneylending in medieval Europe, chiefly after the Crusades, because they were debarred from any other means of livelihood, should be finally disposed of. The history of Jewish moneylending in the two thousand years before the Crusades ought surely to set this fable at rest once and for all. The official version that Jews could not devote themselves to anything but moneylending, even if they would, is incorrect. The door was by no means always shut in their faces; the fact is they preferred to engage in moneylending. This has been proved. . . . The Jews had a natural tendency towards this particular business, and both in the Middle Ages and after rulers were at pains to induce Jews to enter into other callings, but in vain. Edward I made the attempt in England; it was also tried in the eighteenth century in the [Prussian] Province of Posen, where the authorities sought to direct the Jews to change their means of livelihood by offering them bounties if they would. Despite this, and despite the possibility of being able to become handicraftsmen and peasants like all others, [Jews ignored the opportunity: here Sombart overlooks the fierce resistance by craftsmen and peasants to any prospect of Jewish competition]. . . .

We find that the Jew rises before us unmistakably as more of a businessman than his neighbour; he follows business for its own sake; he recognizes, in the true capitalistic spirit, the supremacy of gain over all other aims. . . .

I know of no better illustration than the *Memoirs of Glückel von Hameln*, a mine of information, by the way, about Jewish life and thought in the early capitalistic age. Glückel, the wife of a merchant in Hamburg, lived between 1645 and 1724, the period when the Jewish communities of Hamburg and Altona shot up to a position of prosperity, and in almost every respect we may regard this remarkable woman as a type of the Jew of that day. Her narrative grips the reader because of its natural simplicity and freshness. . . . [A] complete personality is revealed to us in a life rich in experience. . . . If I cite just this splendid book in order to show the predominating interest of money among Jews in those days, it is because I believe that this characteristic must have been general, seeing that even in so gifted a woman as Glückel it also stands out. In very truth, money is the be-all and end-all with her, as with all the other people of whom she has anything to say. Accounts of business enterprise occupy but a small space in the book, but on no less than 609 occasions (in 313 pages) does the authoress speak of money, riches, gain, and so forth. The characters and their doings are mentioned only in some connexion or other with money. Above all, we are told of good matches—good from the financial point of view. To marry her children is in fact the chief object of Glückel's business activities. "He also saw my son, and they were almost on the point of coming to terms, but they could not close because of a thousand marks." Incidents of this kind abound in the book. Of her second marriage she says, "in the afternoon my husband wedded me with a valuable gold ring an ounce in weight." I cannot help regarding the peculiar conception of marriage-making, which used to be current among Jews, as symptomatic of the way they looked upon money, and especially the tendency among them of appraising even the most precious things in life from a purely business point of view. Children, for example, have their value. That was a matter of course among Jews in those days. "They are all my darling children, and may they all be forgiven, as well those on whom I had to spend a lot of money as those on whom I spent nothing," writes Glückel. It was as marriageable persons that they had a price, which varied with the state of the market. Scholars, or the children of scholars, were much in demand. In one case we are told that a father speculated in his children. Similar incidents are abundant enough to warrant the conclusion that they must have been typical. [Sombart makes no reference to Glückel's and her husband's mystical, uncapitalistic maintenance for three years in the 1660s of barrels of food and clothing on a ship ready to sail to the land of Israel at a moment's notice when the call should come from the messiah, false as he turned out, Shabbetai Zevi.] . . .

One or two contemporary opinions must be quoted: "These people [the Jews] have no other God but the unrighteous Mammon, and no other aim than to get possession of Christian property. . . ."

Let me avow it right away: I think that the Jewish religion has the same leading ideas as Capitalism. I see the same spirit in the one as in the other. . . .

. . . Rationalism is the characteristic trait of Judaism as of Capitalism; Rationalism or Intellectualism—both deadly foes alike to irresponsible mysticism and to that creative power which draws its artistic inspiration from the passion world of the senses.

The Jewish religion knows no mysteries, and is perhaps the only religion on the face of the globe that does not know them. It knows not the ecstatic condition wherein the worshipper feels himself at one with the Godhead, the condition which all other religions extol as the highest and holiest. [Sombart would seem never to have heard of the Kabbalah, the vast and influential corpus of Jewish mysticism.] . . .

The kinship between Judaism and Capitalism is further illustrated by the legally regulated relationship—I had almost said the businesslike connexion, except that the term has a disagreeable connotation—between God and Israel. The whole religious system is in reality nothing but a contract between Jehovah and His chosen people. . . .

The contract usually sets forth that man is rewarded for duties performed and punished for duties neglected; the rewards and punishments being received partly in this and partly in the next world. Two consequences must of necessity follow: first, a constant weighing up of the loss and gain which any action needs must bring, and secondly, a complicated system of bookkeeping, as it were, for each individual person. . . .

I put the question [why the good prosper and the evil fail] to myself in this way. Let us imagine old Amschel Rothschild [1745-1812] on a Friday evening, after having "earned" a million on the Stock Exchange, turning to his Bible for edification. What will he find there touching his earnings and their effect on the refinement of his soul, an effect which the pious old Jew most certainly desired on the eve of the Sabbath? Will the million burn his conscience? Or will he not be able to say, and rightly say, "God's blessing rested upon me this week.

I thank Thee, Lord, for having graciously granted the light of Thy countenance to Thy servant. In order to find favour in Thy sight I shall give much to charity, and keep Thy commandments even more strictly than hitherto"? Such would be his words if he knew his Bible, and he did know it.

For his eye would rest complacently on many a passage in the Holy Writ. In his beloved Torah he would be able to read again and again of the blessing of God. "And He will love thee and bless thee and multiply thee, He will also bless the fruit of thy body and the fruit of thy ground, thy corn and thy wine and thine oil . . . thou shalt be blessed above all peoples" (Deut. 7:13-14). And how moved he would be when he reached the words, "For the Lord, thy God, will bless thee, as He promised thee; and thou shalt lend unto many nations, but thou shalt not borrow" (Deut. 15:6). Then suppose he turns to the Psalms, [where he would also find many verses to sanctify his acquisitiveness]. . . .

. . . The Prophets also promised Israel earthly rewards if he kept to God's way and walked therein. If Amschel turned to the 60th chapter of Isaiah he would find the prophecy that one day the Gentiles should bring their gold and silver to Israel.

But perhaps Amschel's favourite book would be Proverbs. . . . Here he would be warned that riches alone do not bring happiness. . . . [But possibly such warnings] may not after all trouble him much when he remembers the numerous passages in this very book which commend riches. So numerous indeed that it may be said they give the tone to the whole of Proverbs. . . .

. . . [O]ld Amschel must have conned with delight [the passage in Ecclesiastes that "money answereth all things" (10:19)]. If any Rabbi had told him that [the wisdom books of the Bible regard] the wealthy man almost as a sinner and wealth as the source of evil, . . . Amschel would have replied, " My dear Rabbi, you are mistaken. Those passages are warning against the dangers of wealth. But a rich man who avoids the dangers is thereby the more righteous. . . . And why, my dear Rabbi" (so Amschel might continue), "do you not mention the passages which speak [approvingly] of the man who has amassed millions? . . ."

"Should I be ashamed of my millions, my dear Rabbi" (Amschel would conclude the imaginary conversation), "should I not rather look upon them as God's blessing? Recall what the wise Jesus ben Sirach said of great King Solomon (47:18): "By the name of the Lord God, which is called the Lord God of Israel, thou didst gather 'gold as tin, and didst multiply silver as lead.' I also will go, Rabbi, and in the name of the Lord God will gather gold as tin and silver as lead."

In the Talmud the passages that express the same point of view are frequent enough. . . .

[Sombart describes Judaism's rationalization of life as a fundamental feature of capitalism.]

To begin with, a number of good qualities or virtues which are indispensable to any economic order owe their existence to rationalization—e.g., industry, neatness, thrift. But the whole of life, if lived in accordance with the ordinances of the "Wise," ministers to the needs of wealth-getting. Sobriety, moderation and piety are surely qualities which stand the businessman in good stead. In short, the whole ideal of conduct preached in Holy Writ and in Rabbinic literature has something of the morality of the small shopkeeper about it—to be content with one wife, to pay your debts punctually, to go to church or synagogue on Sunday or Saturday (as the case may be) and to look down with immeasurable scorn on the sinful world around. . . .

We see then that a good deal of capitalistic capacity which the Jews possessed was due in large measure to the sexual restraint put upon them by their religious teachers. . . . I refer to the influence of the very wise regulations of sexual intercourse, of eating and drinking and so on. (Incidentally it is worthy of note that Jewish law has long restricted the marriage of the unfit.)

One other point in conclusion. . . . What in reality is the idea of making profit, what is economic rationalism, but the application to economic activities of the rules by which the Jewish religion shaped Jewish life? Before capitalism could develop the natural man had to be changed out of all recognition, and a rationalistically minded mechanism introduced in his stead. There had to be a transvaluation of all economic values. And what was the result? The *homo capitalisticus,* who is closely related to the *homo Judaeus,* both belonging to the same species, *homines rationalistici artificiales.*

And so the rationalization of Jewish life by the Jewish religion, if it did not actually produce the Jewish capacity for capitalism, certainly increased and heightened it. . . .

[In the following paragraphs Sombart expounds the presumed double standard employed by Jews in dealing with Gentiles.]

What was the effect on economic life of this [ghetto] seclusion and separation of the Jewish social organism? Directly the Jews stepped outside the Ghetto gates their intercourse was with strangers. . . . [T]his attitude was a direct consequence of the teaching of Judaism, that in treating the people among whom they lived as "others," the Jews were but obeying a divine behest. Here, too, their conduct was hallowed, and it received a sanction from the peculiar system of laws relating to "strangers."

The most important and most frequently discussed legal ordinance in this system was that affecting the taking of interest. In the old Jewish theocracy, as in every society in early civilization, loans without interest were the regular means of rendering assistance by a man to his neighbour. But it may be observed that even in the earliest collection of laws interest was allowed to be taken from "strangers."

The Jewish code was no exception: The best example of this may be found in Deuteronomy 23:20. . . . "You may charge interest to a foreigner but not on a loan to a fellow-countryman." [Sombart quotes several additional biblical and talmudic passages referring to interest.] . . .

What was the importance in economic life of the laws concerning strangers? It was twofold. First, intercourse with strangers was bereft of all considerations, and commercial morality (if I may put it so) became elastic. I admit that there was no absolute necessity for this to come about, but all the conditions were given for it to do so, and it must have been an everyday occurrence in certain circles. "If a non-Jew makes an error in a statement of account, the Jew may use it to his own advantage; it is not incumbent upon him to point it out." . . . Is it not obvious that the good Jew must needs draw the conclusion that he was not bound to be so particular in his intercourse with non-Jews? With Jews he will scrupulously see to it that he has just weights and a just measure; but as for his dealings with non-Jews, his conscience will be at ease even though he may obtain an unfair advantage. It is not to be denied that in some cases honesty towards non-Jews was inculcated. But to think that this should have been necessary! . . .

It is a . . . task to determine to what extent this or that [religious] doctrine still finds acceptance. Does, for example, the talmudic adage, "Kill even the best of the Gentiles," still hold good? Do the other terrible aphorisms ferreted out in Jewish religious literature by Pfefferkorn, Eisenmenger [see page 49], Rohling, Dr. Justus and the rest of that [antisemitic] fraternity, still find credence, or are they, as the Rabbis of to-day indignantly protest, entirely obsolete?

[The Jews as a Pure Race]

. . . [F]rom the days of Ezra to these the Jews have kept strictly apart. For more than two thousand years they have been untouched by other peoples; they have remained ethnically pure. That drops of alien blood came into the Jewish body corporate through the long centuries of their dispersion no one will deny. But so small have these outside elements been that they have not influenced to any appreciable degree the ethnical purity of the Jewish people.

It seems pretty clear now that in the past the number of proselytes admitted into Judaism was considerably over-estimated [which also assured "ethnical purity"].

We come back then to the fact that for some twenty centuries the Jews have kept themselves ethnically pure. One proof of this is found in the similarity of the anthropological [i.e., racial] characteristics of the Jews all over the globe, and, moreover, in that the similarity has been remarkably constant through the centuries. . . .

The anthropological homogeneity of the Jewish stock at the present time has been established by numerous anatomical experiments and measurements. . . .

. . . Jewish characteristics are rooted in the blood of the race, and are not in any wise due to educative processes [or environment].

If any one wished in a sentence to account for the importance of the Jews in the world's civilization, and more particularly in economic life, he could do so by saying that it was due to the transplanting of an Oriental people, among Northern races, and the culture union of the two. [These remarks are typical of Sombart's chapter on "The Race Problem," which, in the original German edition, is longer and more tendentious than the English version.][10]

NOTES

1. Salo Wittmayer Baron, *A Social and Religious History of the Jews*, 2nd ed., 18 vols. (New York: Columbia University Press, 1952-1983), 12: 135.

2. Quotations in Howard M. Sachar, *A History of the Jews in America* (New York: Knopf, 1992), 319; Albert Lee, *Henry Ford and the Jews* (New York: Stein and Day, 1980), 122.

3. Quoted in Morton Rosenstock, *Louis Marshall, Defender of Jewish Rights* (Detroit: Wayne State University Press, 1965), 138.

4. Fernand Braudel, *The Mediterranean and the Mediterranean World in the Age of Philip II*, trans. Sian Reynolds (New York: Harper and Row, 1973), 2: 804.

5. Edmund Silberner, "Was Marx an Anti-Semite?" *Historia Judaica*, 11 (April 1949): 50; for the quotations in this par. 31-40; Silberner calls the 1843 essay Marx's "frontal attack."

6. Julius Carlebach, *Karl Marx and the Radical Critique of Judaism* (London: Routledge and Kegan Paul, 1978), 352.

7. Thomas Müntzer, ca. 1489-1525, radical Protestant and bitter antagonist of Luther; preacher of a war of extermination by the "League of the Elect" against the unrighteous ("usurers," corrupt clergy, and princely exploiters of the poor) to inaugurate Jesus's return and the reign of heaven; a leader of the peasant's revolt in Germany, which was bloodily suppressed by the princes who captured, tortured, and executed Müntzer; Müntzer was apotheosized in Marxist tradition as a revolutionary seeking to establish economic equality and a classless society.

8. From *Karl Marx: A World without Jews*, ed. with an introduction by Dagobert D. Runes (New York: Philosophical Library, 1959), 1, 36-45. For clarity minor editorial changes were made.

9. Max Weber, *The Sociology of Religion*, trans. Ephraim Fischoff (Boston: Beacon Press, 1963), 248.

10. From Werner Sombart, *The Jews and Modern Capitalism*, trans. M. Epstein, intro. Bert F. Hoselitz (Glencoe, Ill.: Free Press, 1951), 287-288, 137-139, 200, 202, 209-212, 224, 226-227, 232, 197, 266, 269, 298-299.

THIRTEEN

French Antisemitism and the Dreyfus Affair

During the Revolution, in 1790 and 1791, France was the first country in Europe to emancipate its Jews. The stipulation was that in return for equal rights as citizens Jews would renounce all special rights as members of a separate community: everything to the Jews as individuals, nothing to the Jews as a group. Many Jews followed that path of assimilation, and in celebrating the centennial of the Revolution in 1889 exulted that France had generously adopted them, that "there are no longer any but Frenchmen in France." Nevertheless, antisemitism exploded in the late nineteenth century. Jews were denounced as powerful and greedy capitalists; as modernists and secularists who undermined traditional French culture and the Catholic faith; and as alien intruders who were displacing true Frenchmen from the professions, civil service, and the army officer corps (there were about three hundred Jewish officers, ten of them generals). The monarchist and ultranationalist Charles Maurras (1868–1952) explained that Jews had gained "control of Money. But Money had delivered everything else into their hands."[1] The collapse in 1882 of the Union Générale (a Catholic bank created to break the presumed banking monopoly of Jews and Protestants) was represented as proof of Jewish conspiracy and Rothschild treachery, although it was really incompetence and mismanagement that brought it down. As in other countries, these accusations against French Jews (at most seventy-five thousand in a total population of thirty-eight million) reflected the antisemites' paranoia and irrationality. In late 1894 Alfred Dreyfus, a Jewish captain serving on the army general staff, was arrested on the false accusation of giving military secrets to the Germans; the ensuing Dreyfus Affair entailed turmoil and near civil war for a dozen years (see page 96).

Several antisemitic demagogues emerged in this period, including the Marquis de Morès (1858–1896). Educated by the Jesuits and as a military officer at St. Cyr (where he was a classmate of the future Marshal Philippe Pétain), Morès was a swashbuckling adventurer who failed at every business venture he put his hand to in France and overseas. He read the demagogic journalist Édouard Drumont (see below) and learned that it was the Jews who foiled all his ventures. Morès plunged into antisemitic agitation. Marching about Paris, Morès and his gang, dressed in black cowboy hats and purple shirts, terrorized Jewish meetings and celebrations.

His pamphlets attacked finance capitalism, industrial corporations, parliamentary government, Britain, and, with whom all these were supposedly linked, the Jews. He called himself a "socialist" and worked to create a great political party uniting conservatives and nationalists with workers and socialists, who remained unconvinced, and Morès and his allies suffered one humiliating election defeat after another. Morès had the idea of a national party uniting the socialist masses and the nationalist classes cemented by antisemitism, but was not the leader to effect it, whereas Hitler succeeded.

One of the by-products of the Dreyfus Affair was the party and journal *Action Française* founded by Maurras, the eminent writer and poet, one of the forty "Immortals" as a member of the Académie Française. Maurras's formula of "integral nationalism" meant no Jews, Masons, Protestants, or foreigners, and the "re-Christianization of France"; how integral antisemitism was to Maurras's nationalism emerges from this assertion: "Everything seems impossible or frightfully difficult without the providence of anti-Semitism. Thanks to it, everything works out, everything is smoothed over and becomes simpler. If we were not anti-Semitic out of patriotic determination, we would become so simply out of a sense of opportunity."[2] He was the fiercest enemy of the republic—"the Jewish state"—and desired "Europe to be Catholic again." He was an agnostic Catholic for whom the Gospels were the work of "four shabby Jews," Christianity a religion for the "rabble," and mass just for the masses; his Catholicism was cultural and social, seeing in Catholic doctrines a source of social cohesion and national identity. Like Drumont, Maurras was obsessed with "Jewish domination" and saw it realized in 1936 with the premiership of Léon Blum, a Jew and a socialist. Maurras malevolently called for murdering Jewish officials and politicians: "There is a man to be shot . . . in the back," he said of Blum, "He must not be missed."[3] His "spiritual" brand of antisemitism, combining the nationalist-racist form with traditional Catholic Judaeophobia, was the version that prevailed in France under the Vichy regime of 1940–1944. When found guilty and sentenced to life imprisonment in 1945 for collaboration with the Nazis, Maurras shouted at his judges, "It is Dreyfus's revenge."

In the 1930s the fascist movement in France grew by leaps and bounds. There were in 1936 over a million French fascists, twice as many as Hitler's followers in 1932. Yet, in response to the Great Depression, the French electorate voted for democrats and socialists rather than fascists and extreme nationalists, and it elevated Léon Blum to be premier. It was only military defeat by the Germans in 1940 and the abrogation of normal politics that enabled the antisemitic Vichy regime to come to power. There is abundant continuity between the antisemitism of the Dreyfus era and that of Vichy. Several key Vichy figures, including Marshall Philippe Pétain, its head, retained an unmodified antisemitism that had been conditioned by the Dreyfus Affair. It was then that Maurras's and Drumont's disciples came into their own. Vichy's anti-Jewish legislation and its roundups and deportation of Jews to Nazi death camps, all without German pressure, had a measure of popular support. It would seem that the call of the crowds when Captain Dreyfus was degraded of rank in 1894, "Death to the Jews," was implemented a half century later by Pétain's government.

Édouard-Adolphe Drumont

Jewish France, *1886*

The journalist Éduoard-Adolphe Drumont (1844–1917), the fashioner of a vast corpus of antisemitica, became the center of a cult maintained over several generations and even into the present by emulating admirers. "I wish to describe the Jewish conquest [of France]," Drumont begins *La France Juive: Essai d'histoire contemporaine* (Jewish France: An Essay in Contemporary History, 1886), asserting that the real rulers of France and ruiners of Europe are the Jews. Its thousand pages went through many hundreds of reprintings and editions, no less than 114 in a single year. In 1892 Drumont launched his daily paper, *La Libre Parole* (Free Speech) for a quotidian dose of poison for the public. Throughout his career Drumont attacked the Jews and prominent persons who had or were said to have any affiliation or merely sympathy for Jews from antiquity down to his own time. He denounced the French Revolution for emancipating the Jews and turning France into a "Jewish Republic." Drumont was careful that his diatribe was theologically correct and acceptable, and indeed Catholic clergy were among his most enthusiastic readers; he had acquired religion by the 1880s, when he began to attend mass daily and married his mistress in a Catholic ceremony so as to be hailed "a faithful son of the Church." Drumont gave journalistic purple-passage expression to every myth and prejudice about Jews, sounding every demagogic note from Left to Right: Jewish "usury" and capitalist exploitation for the workers and socialists; Jews are "foreign," "alien," "oriental," and can never be French for nationalists and racists; "the image of Christ humiliated, insulted, lacerated by thorns, crucified . . . [by] Jews, as obstinate in their deicide [today] as in the time of [the High Priest in Jesus's time] Caiaphas" for Catholics.[4] A lengthy chapter spells out the massive guilt of Jews for ritual murder. Running like a red thread through the whole is Drumont's phobia of the Jews as frightful conspirators. His remedy for this "Jewish peril": restore the ghetto, compel the wearing of the yellow badge, confiscate their "excessive" wealth, expel them from France; he did not exclude massacre, for he approved the murderous pogroms in Russia. Throughout the Dreyfus Affair, he demagogically attacked Dreyfus as a traitor and Judas and avowed that an acquittal "will give immediate signal for the massacre of the Jews; their execution in France is very easy" and, he averred in the much-used refrain attributed to him, "St. Bartholomew [a notorious massacre of Huguenots in 1572] was a half measure. We'll start it all over again against the Jews and this time we'll exterminate them all."[5]

Drumont and his chief collaborator Morès fused nationalism, socialism, antisemitism, and Catholicism into a mass-appealing political movement; this synthesis —deftly straddling Left and Right—was pursued by his disciples and successors, several of whom were journalists and editors of his newspaper. This persuades some scholars that France was the birthplace of fascist ideology. One of Drumont's last surviving lieutenants, Jean Drault, exulted in 1935, "What Drumont proclaimed, Hitler has achieved."[6] In France, however, antisemitism on the Left has often been the twin of the Right's and just as fierce. A tradition of socialist, economic anti-semitism stems from Pierre-Joseph Proudhon, François Fourier, Alphonse Toussenel, and other nineteenth-century denigrators of the Jews' putative role in the creation of capitalism and exploitation of the poor. Drumont's anti-capitalism dovetailed neatly with the Left's invective against "Moses & Co."

A critical part in transmitting Drumont's legacy and ending the "overwhelming silence" that followed his death and eclipse in 1917 was played by the great Catholic novelist Georges Bernanos, whose La Grande Peur des Bien-pensants: Édouard Drumont (The Great Fear of the Right-Thinking, 1931) was a long celebration of Drumont's life, social and religious ideas, and incandescent hatred of the Jews. For the novelist, Drumont was "a visionary historian" and La France Juive "a magic book." The Drumont-inspired antisemites were enthusiastic supporters of the Vichy regime and the Nazi occupation. There was a galaxy of anti-Jewish writers—antisémites de plume (of the pen)—that included Maurice Barrès, Bernanos, Léon Bloy, Maurice Blanchot, Robert Brasillach, Louis-Ferdinand Céline, Léon Daudet, Pierre Drieu La Rochelle, Jean Giraudoux (the playwright, for a time minister of information), Charles Maurras, and many others as prominent as they. In their numerous writings and journalistic efforts they continued to nurture themselves on Drumont's toxin and publicly celebrated various anniversaries of his life; his widow was so impressed she proclaimed "Drumont would have been proud of you."[7] Their pathology is illustrated by the literary critic and novelist Robert Brasillach (1909–1945, the only major writer to be executed for treason) and the novelist L.-F. Céline (1894–1961). A wounded, decorated veteran of World War I who luxuriated in sloughs of hate, rage, and psychosis, Céline prophesied a Continent-wide extermination of Europeans perpetrated by the "vengeful" Jews. He preferred "twelve Hitlers" to "one Blum" and wanted to avert the war that the Jews were bent on igniting, "A war for the joy of the Jews."[8] "I became an antisemite and not just a little bit to laugh about, but ferociously, to my very depths, enough to blow up all the kikes."[9] Céline's writings stand among the most vicious anti-Jewish denunciations in the entire corpus of antisemitism: "Racism first of all! Racism above all. Disinfection! Cleansing! Only one race in France: Aryan." He and Brasillach continue to be treasured as cult figures in France by the radical cultural and political Right.[10]

For decades after World War II antisemitism was never more than temporarily discredited in France and occasionally flared up unexpectedly, as in 1967 when the war hero and president, Charles de Gaulle, singled out the Jews as "an elite people, sure of themselves and domineering," who, wherever they reside, "provoked ill-feeling." The Jewish intellectual Raymond Aron commented, "We all know this style and these adjectives. They belong to Drumont."[11] In recent years high French officials and clergy have tried to make amends, and under the Gayssot law written or published Holocaust denial is a punishable offense.[12]

The passage below is from *La France Juive,* in which Drumont contrasts Jews with Aryans in exactly the way Hitler was to do in *Mein Kampf.*

Let us examine now the essential traits which differentiate Jews from other people, beginning with ethnographic, physiological, and psychological comparisons of the Semite with the Aryan. These are two distinct races irremediably hostile to each other, whose antagonism has troubled the past and will cause still more trouble in the future.

The generic name Aryan derives from a Sanskrit word signifying "noble," "illustrious," "generous," standing for the superior family of the Indo-European family. . . . All the nations of Europe are descended by a straight line from the Aryan race, from which all great civilizations have sprung. . . . The Aryan or Indo-European race alone possesses the notion of justice, the sentiment of freedom, and the concept of the beautiful. . . .

From the earliest moment of history we find the Aryan at war with the Semite. The dream of the Semite, indeed its obsession, has always been to reduce the Aryan into servants, to throw them into subjection. . . . Today Semitism feels sure of victory. It has replaced violence by wily tricks. The noisy invasion has been replaced by silent, progressive, slow penetration. Armed hordes no longer announce their arrival by shouts, but separate individuals, gathering in small groups, opportunistically infiltrate the state, taking possession of all important positions, all the functions in the country from the lowest to the highest. Spreading out from the area of Vilna [now Lithuania, then in Russia] they have occupied Germany, leaped over the Vosges mountains, and conquered France.

There was nothing brutal in this advance; it was a soft takeover accomplished in an insinuating manner of chasing the indigenous people from their homes, their source of income, in a velvety way depriving them of their goods, their tradition, their morals, and eventually their religion. . . . By their qualities as well as their faults, the two races [Jews and Aryans] are condemned to hurt each other.

The Semite is mercantile, greedy, scheming, subtle, crafty. The Aryan is enthusiastic, heroic, chivalrous, disinterested, straightforward, trusting to the point of naiveté. The Semite is earthbound, seeing nothing beyond the present life. The Aryan is the child of heaven, relentlessly preoccupied with superior aspirations. One lives among realities, the other among ideals.

The Semite operates by instinct; he has the vocation of a trader, a genius for exchange, for every occasion to take advantage of his fellow man. The Aryan is devoted to life on the land, a poet, a monk and above all a soldier. War is his true element; he exposes himself joyfully to danger; he braves death. The Semite lacks any creative faculty. By contrast the Aryan is an inventor. The Jew has not made the least invention. He rather exploits, organizes, and utilizes the inventions of creative Aryans, guarding them as though they were his own. . . . The Aryan organizes voyages of adventure and discovers America. The Semite . . . attends to all that has been explored and developed in order to enrich himself at the expense of others.[13]

Jews in the French Army, 1892

In the following selection, "Jews in the Army" in *La Libre Parole* (May 23, 1892), Drumont complains about Jews serving in the French army two and a half years before the Dreyfus Affair erupted.

Longer than the rest of contemporary society, the army has avoided Jewish influence. This immunity is due to the army's traditional esprit and to the very nature of its mission.

What would the kikes do in its ranks? . . . Why wear oneself out, why rough it, why always have empty pockets, when it is so easy, on the stock market or through shady business dealings, to make a fortune without hardship and without deprivation?

If Jews cared little about entering the army, the army cared even less about having them. Beyond all religious consideration, there exists among the vast majority of military men a feeling of instinctive repulsion against the sons of Israel. One sees in them the usurer who completes the ruination of the indebted officer, the tradesman who speculates on the soldier's hunger, the spy who traffics without shame in the secrets of national defense. Everywhere and always, in peace as in war, the army has seen the Jew stand against it—against its duties, against its well-being; against its honor.

Since 1870 and the adoption of compulsory military service, the situation has altered. Israelites are no longer allowed to exempt themselves, for an average of two thousand francs, from all duty toward the fatherland. . . .

They had barely placed a foot in the army when they searched, by every means, to gain influence. They understand the opportunity there for the spread of power; already lords of finance and administration, already dictating judgments to the courts, they will definitely be masters of France on the day they command the army. Rothschild will deliver the mobilization plans—and one can imagine toward what end!

Happily, we are not there yet. The Semitic invasion is like the breeding of microbes: When the environment is not favorable, the growth process suffers. Though there have been some hints of weakness, the army has joined the combat with a remarkable strength of resistance. In undertaking this series of articles, we want to encourage the army in this holy struggle. At the same time, we want to uncover the criminal deeds that would have the immediate effect of endangering the country's interests. . . .

The tendency to avoid the army, which was widespread before 1870, has abated since then in a very notable way. But there remains a considerable proportion of Jews who, unable to find careers with the state, turn to positions offered by private industry, commerce, or banking.

Those Jews who have entered the army have found a way of setting themselves up in the most agreeable posts . . . in the choicest situations. With each opening that attracts twenty qualified candidates, it is the Jew who climbs over his nineteen Christian competitors. . . .

Are these statistics not striking testimony to the favoritism enjoyed by the sons of Israel?[14]

The Dreyfus Affair: "Death to the Jews!"

In the last days of 1894 Captain Alfred Dreyfus (1859–1935), the first Jew to be posted to the general staff, was secretly court-martialed on the basis of forged evidence and sentenced to prison for life on Devil's Island for selling military secrets to the Germans. Colonel Georges Picquart, antisemite though he was, reopened the case by reporting that the handwriting on a critical document was that of Major Marie-Charles-Ferdinand Walsin-Esterhazy, an unscrupulous adventurer and gambler always desperate for money, who was tried but acquitted and later, in 1898, fled to England where he spent the rest of his life; Picquart was assailed by his superior, General Charles-Arthur Gonse, with the question, "What business is it of yours if this Jew is on Devil's Island?" and dismissed from the army.[15] Esterhazy's acquittal inspired Émile Zola's famous "*J'Accuse*" open letter attacking the decision as corrupt, for which the novelist was tried and convicted but fled abroad to avoid conviction and imprisonment in a second trial. Another forged document—one of many launched during the affair—was shown to be by Major Hubert-Joseph Henry, who committed suicide. By then Dreyfus's brother Mathieu had come forward with new evidence; but in 1899, at the second court-martial, public this time, Dreyfus was again convicted of treason, "guilty, with extenuating circumstances," and sentenced to "ten years' detention." "Since when have there been 'extenuating circumstances' for treason?" Dreyfus asked.[16] A few days later the president of the republic pardoned him. Despite an amnesty act that ended all suits and prosecutions arising out of the affair, Dreyfus persisted until a new inquiry and trial unanimously nullified the 1899 verdict and vindicated Dreyfus in 1906, when he and Picquart were restored to the army and promoted.

Throughout those twelve years France was torn apart in a virtual civil war that threatened its republican institutions and unleashed torrents of antisemitic invective in the press, particularly among the Right—nationalists, the army, the Church, royalists, conservatives, and other anti-republicans; the Left was more divided, as some socialists and Marxists looked with indifference on Dreyfus's plight, seeing in the antisemitic upheaval only a "bourgeois" matter. The Right viewed the conflict as the struggle of "les deux France," the two Frances—in Drumont's formulation, the old "Catholic France" versus the new "Jewish France" and "Jew Republic." The Right's motto, minted by Drumont, was "France for the French" and "Death to the Jews." A medley of antisemitic groups utilized rallies, posters, inflammatory journalism of mass circulation, and rhetorical violence, which often translated itself into physical violence. The decade was punctuated by riots and agitation like the fifty-five to seventy-five violent eruptions that broke out in the several weeks following Zola's *J'Accuse.* Because public authority and the police worked to protect the Jews (unlike in Russia), there were few if any deaths, although lots of bruises and broken limbs and much destruction of Jewish homes, shops, and synagogues. The agitation was on a large scale, organized rather than spontaneous, often through the efforts of local clergy who distributed leaflets from the church door and provided lists of names and addresses of Jews, the better to terrorize them. The hysteria spread strongly to the rural areas, so that no corner of France was untouched. According to a police report during this "inexhaustible rage of antisemitism" in 1898, the priest of Saint-Martin said that "Someday they [the Jews] will have to be exterminated."[17] Morès's ravings were not untypical: "[T]he occult chiefs of Judaism have decided that next year Israel would eat unleavened bread saturated with the blood . . . of Christian babies. . . . We must destroy the Jews, chase every last one of them from our midst, or perish at their hands."[18]

The affair was generated and sustained in large measure by the Parisian press and the yellow journalism of Drumont. The Catholic press relentlessly and cruelly defamed Jews as traitors and vermin and urged boycotting their businesses, excluding them from the civil service, and ridding the nation of them. (In 1998, the centennial of Zola's J'Accuse, the paper of the Catholic order of the Fathers of the Assumption, La Croix, apologized for its antisemitic vituperation during the affair.) The world press riveted its attention on the affair, repulsing French claims that it was an internal matter, and was often indignant, editorializing, for example, that the 1900 World Exhibition in Paris should be boycotted as penalty. With the exception of antisemitic and Catholic newspapers, the European-American press condemned the persecution of Dreyfus, markedly so once Esterhazy confessed his guilt to a reporter of the London Observer. Many, perhaps most, newspapers were skeptical of Dreyfus's conviction in 1894 and astounded and outraged by the second conviction in 1899. Several editors also asserted that France was guilty of betraying the Revolution of 1789 and the Enlightenment. European Catholic papers generally maintained Dreyfus's guilt. L'Unità Cattolica, the Catholic daily of Florence, Italy, parroted Drumont in asserting that the Dreyfus Affair was a "colossal international conspiracy for combating the Church and the social order."[19] La Civiltà Cattolica (see page 65) appropriated material wholesale from La Libre Parole and fittingly commended Drumont for his "most tenacious war against the Jews."[20]

The following selections reveal the vicious antisemitism surging through France at the turn of the century. The first group is from Drumont's paper, La Libre Parole, which leaked the news of Dreyfus's arrest and greatly increased its circulation (to 106,000 in 1899), which had been faltering since its founding in 1892—in fact, by 1894 Drumont was virtually bankrupt and on the verge of selling La Libre Parole.

La Libre Parole, 1894

"The Jewish Judas"

A) The affair of Captain Dreyfus, which has aroused attention even in foreign countries, is only an episode in Jewish history. Judas has sold the compassion and love of God.

B) What a terrible lesson, this disgraceful treason of the Jew Dreyfus! A well-to-do man, the son-in-law of a wealthy merchant, officer in our Army, who holds the most sought-after posts, sells our mobilization plans and the names of his comrades entrusted with foreign missions. Never have we had a similar outrage in our fatherland.

Concerning the Jewish Judas, Frenchmen, for eight years I have been warning you each day.

C) "The Soul of Dreyfus"

[The fact is] that man, if one takes into consideration his origins and his type, has done in the Army exactly what he would have done in a bank or in a stable of a race course: he has sold information to a competitor. He has committed an abuse of confidence, but he has not committed a crime against his country. In order for a man to betray his country, it is necessary first of all that he has a country, and that country cannot be acquired by an act of naturalization. That country is the land of one's forefathers. . . .

What is needed is a law making it a prerequisite for nationality at least three generations of French descent. In resisting this idea the Jews are preparing for their own destruction.

All the maneuvers of Jewdom are directed against the inevitable resistance of the national element, against the soul of France. In insisting impudently on imposing on us their own conception of equality, the Jews have prepared with their own hands the most frightful catastrophe of their tragic history. . . .

[My book] *Jewish France* dates from 1886! That was eight years ago, and that is precious little time for the march of an idea.

Lord, I am not going to boast of that effort! I have always been the most feeble of men, the most sentimental, the most easy to discourage. The courage I have shown in awakening my country you have given to me. Protect me, oh Lord!

All this I say to those who have extended congratulations to me and words of encouragement, to those who have hindered me in the past but now recognize that I was right, and especially to those young people of the anti-Semitic committees which have been organized in Paris, in Lyons, in Dijon, in Montpellier.

My books have rendered an immense service to our dear France, in revealing to her the Jewish peril, in preventing her from being delivered bound hand and foot to the enemy, from being ambushed in a moment of war by the Dreyfuses and Reinachs [a family of Jewish bankers]. I am happy to have written those books, but I do not merit praise on the subject, for I could not write them alone. I have merely obeyed the voice of a superior will: "Speak!" I have spoken.[21]

An Antisemitic Poster

"The Jews have ruined us," 1898

This selection, a poster of 1898, was of a kind widely distributed by antisemitic organizations.

FOR MORE THAN TEN YEARS, PATRIOTS LIKE DRUMONT AND
MORÈS HAVE BEEN DENOUNCING *THE JEWISH PERIL*.
THEY UNMASKED THE MONOPOLIES, THE STOCK MARKET
TAMPERING OF A VILE HANDFUL OF HEBREWS SPILLING INTO
FRANCE FROM ALL THE GHETTOS OF GERMANY.
NO ONE WANTED TO HEAR DRUMONT AND MORÈS. ANTISEMITES
WERE TREATED LIKE PROPHETS OF DOOM.
NOW WE HAVE THE ACT OF TREASON. JUDAS DREYFUS SOLD OUT
FRANCE FOR A LITTLE MORE THAN THIRTY PIECES OF SILVER.
YOU'D HAVE TO BE BLIND NOT TO SEE THE JEWISH PERIL.
FRENCHMEN! THE NATION IS IN DANGER!
THE JEWS, HAVING RUINED US, DIVIDED US, AND DISHONORED US,
ARE IN THE PROCESS OF TURNING FRANCE ON ITS HEAD
FOR THE GREATEST PROFIT OF UNIVERSAL YIDDISCHRY.
SO LET US UNITE TO TURNP JEWISH OMNIPOTENCE ON ITS HEAD.
AND WHILE WE WAIT TO DRIVE THOSE DANGEROUS PARASITES, THE JEWS,
OUT OF FRANCE, LET US DESTROY THEIR INFLUENCE BY EVERY MEANS.
IT IS BEGINNING TO BE TIME TO RETURN
FRANCE TO THE FRENCH!
DOWN WITH THE SYNDICATE! DOWN WITH THE JEWS AND THE TRAITORS!
LONG LIVE THE ARMY![22]

The Reflections of a Small Businessman in Caen

"Evil is the Jew," 1898

The following excerpt from "The Reflections of a Small Businessman of Caen" was distributed in that town of Normandy at the end of 1898.

All of you workers, employees, shopkeepers, retirees, citizens of Caen of every condition, do you know where evil comes from? Yes, you know! Evil is the money-grubber! Evil is the Jew! . . . French women, you who are most often responsible for the shopping: the weapon to fight the money-grubber, the Jew, is in your hands! You are making the Jew rich, wives and daughters of shopkeepers, housewives, bourgeois women, patronesses, nuns, the Jew is driving your fathers and husbands to ruin, and thanks to his people's solidarity, he is invading everything—positions, offices, jobs—and throwing your sons out on the sidewalk. The Jew you are supporting, daughters of France, with the money he has stolen from you, has believed it right to form a syndicate to exempt from deserved punishment the traitor Dreyfus, who sold the blood of your brothers! You will oppose the Judaic invasion. For your purchases, go exclusively to shopkeepers of Caen, to Frenchmen![23]

The Henry Monument

"Jews . . . are the vampires of France," 1898–1899

When it appeared that the case against Dreyfus might unravel, Lieutenant Colonel Hubert-Joseph Henry (he had been promoted) forged a letter to strengthen the case against him and it was used as well in the proceedings against Zola. When the forgery (the "faux Henry") was discovered, Henry committed suicide and Esterhazy fled to England. Hailing Henry as hero and martyr who gave his life "for the honor of the army and the good of the country," Drumont's paper *La Libre Parole* launched a highly successful drive for a memorial fund for Henry's widow, who was viewed as the symbol of a betrayed nation. Many of the contributors took the opportunity to vent their hatred of Jews, as appears in the following examples drawn from the book recording the donations, a revelation of the fervor of popular antisemitism in France.

A lieutenant of the colonial infantry. For the shame of the Jews and the triumph of honest men. 3 francs.

L. M., ex-second lieutenant of the 159th infantry. Long live France! Down with the kikes and freemasons who insult the army! 5 fr.

An administrative officer, in retirement. For the expulsion of the Yids. 5 fr.

A superior officer who would be delighted to see France in the hands of the French. 5 fr.

A section of officers from a frontier fortress who await with impatience the order to try new cannon and new explosives on the 100,000 Jews [there were at most 75,000 French Jews, half of them in Paris] who poison the country. 25 fr.

A veteran of 1870, who considers the Jews the ten plagues of Egypt reunited. 2 fr.

Galey (Abbot), for the defense of the eternal law against the Puritan quackery and Judeo-Huguenot swindling. 5 fr.

A rural priest, who offers up the most ardent prayers for the extermination of the two enemies of France: the Jew and the Freemason. 5 fr.

A teacher, sworn enemy of stateless people. 1.50 fr.

A teacher from the Jura, who does not fail to tell his students that Jews and their friends are the vampires of France. 1 fr.

A future medical student, already sharpening his scalpels to dissect the Maccabee Dreyfus, bored through by a dozen bullets of a firing squad. 0.25 fr.

A group of policemen who would be very happy to thump hard and fast on Dreyfusards and filthy Yids, while, *by command and under pain of dismissal*, they are compelled to protect these rogues. 12.50 fr.

A royalist widow who misses the old bygone days when Jews were kept in their place. 2 fr.

A widow, who raises her son for God and France and in hatred of Freemasons and Jews. 0.15 fr.

A woman with great admiration for Drumont, who would like to see him govern France with the power of a king or emperor. 0.15 fr.

Sabatier (Madame Achille). Saint Joan of Arc, patron of our sweet France, deliver us from the Jews! 20 fr.

H. L., brother of an infantry lieutenant, for [French President] Felix Faure when he kills as many kikes as rabbits. 0.50 fr.

XXXX. Finding not enough Jews to massacre, I propose cutting them in two, in order to get twice as many. 0.50 fr.

When will the alarm bell sound to rid France of the evil Yids? 1 fr.[24]

La Croix

"It is a question for them of universal domination. . . . " 1899

La Croix (The Cross) was the newspaper of the Catholic Fathers of the Assumption. Founded in 1882, it was the favorite reading of the parish clergy and was virulently antisemitic; it rivaled Drumont's *La Libre Parole,* to which it was often only an echo chamber but exceeded its circulation (190,000 in 1899). It was given to conspiracism, such as the editorial reproduced here from August 18, 1899, and an indication of how rife such theories were in France, indeed in Europe, at that time; a few years later the journal *Revue internationale des Sociétés Secrètes* was founded in Paris.

The editorial below is written in very poor, ungrammatical French, deliberately so, perhaps, as the work of "Le Paysan" ("the peasant," who in fact was the editor of *La Croix,* Father Vincent de Paul Bailly, a shrewd creator of a mass circulation daily but no intellectual). The plot here—that Dreyfus's attorneys Fernand Labori and Charles Demange and other Dreyfusards in league with the Masons and employing great amounts of gold at the behest of a "king of the Jews" were conspiring to free Dreyfus—is a variant on the "Dreyfus Syndicate" rumor that was spread repeatedly by the antisemitic press, *La Libre Parole* and *La Croix* in the lead, since 1896 or 1897 in response to the growing demand at home and abroad for a retrial. It posited an international conspiracy to spring Dreyfus free from Devil's Island by Jews, Protestants, Masons, and international bankers, especially the Rothschilds and the Germans, who, supposedly, supplied thirty-five million francs and threw "hands full of gold" to bribe French officials. Any reversal in the fortunes of the anti-Dreyfusards was explained as the machinations of this "Treason Syndicate." Pope Leo XIII was alarmed by the excesses and vituperation of French Catholics and, fearing eventual reprisals by the French government, called for restraint by Catholic journalists but to no avail. In 1900 the government dissolved the Assumptionist order (it had never bothered to register under the law and so was technically illegal) and a more moderate editorial leadership was forced on *La Croix*. From 1901 to 1905 a series of laws enacted the separation of church and state in France.

The attempted crime perpetrated against Monsieur Labori [who was shot on his way to the court in an attempt to assassinate him] has given rise to all sorts of suspicions and explications. It seems fair to us that, until today, the most reasonable has not been proposed to the judge.

When one wishes to find the unknown author of a crime, you need to ask who the crime will benefit. *Is fecit cui prodet* [That person committed (the crime) whom it advances], say the jurisconsults. But if the attempt at a crime marvelously serves the interests of Dreyfus' defense, it serves less well those of the advocate whose life has been endangered and whose blood has been spilled.

It doesn't help the general staff and the army at all! The story of the decisive proof found in Monsieur Labori's napkin is ridiculous.

In setting this hypothesis aside, although it is quite possible, is it only the foolishness or the excitement of the assassin working for himself that remains suspect?

The Labori, the Demange, the Dreyfusard journalists, are becoming by the month only the vulgar agents of the supreme occult control, very powerful, that plays in this moment the largest part that the Jewish people have ever played.

It is a question for [the Jews] of universal domination affirmed by the all-powerfulness of gold.

Can one believe that the king of the Jews or those who hold that place—because if there was one, it seems that he is hidden in Russia—can one believe that the king of the Jews or his ministers will hesitate for a similar interest to employ or not any kind of effective tactic?

It is for this kind of Jews that Dreyfus works, more perhaps than for himself.

To deliver France to the enemy seems to have been commanded . . . if that enters into some plan of high politics . . . as a consequence of some alliance that has been concluded. . . .

In this case, it seems useless to search out the monetary interest here, it might exist only as an accessory.

In revenge, the motive of the extraordinary defense that wasted millions and placed into movement enormous forces becomes apparent: the honor of the Jewish government was engaged. . . . In three years, said Dreyfus who knows its power, the relief ought to arrive! . . .

Le Paysan [The Peasant].[25]

NOTES

1. Quoted in Paula Hyman, "The French Jewish Community from Emancipation to the Dreyfus Affair," in *The Dreyfus Affair: Art, Truth, and Justice*, ed. Norman L. Kleebatt (Berkeley: University of California Press, 1987), 30.

2. Quoted in Zeev Sternhell, "Roots of Popular Anti-Semitism in the Third Re-

public," in *The Jews in Modern France*, ed. Frances Malino and Bernard Wasserstein (Hanover, N.H.: University Press of New England, 1985), 115.

3. Quoted in Pierre Birnbaum, *Anti-Semitism in France: A Political History from Léon Blum to the Present*, trans. Miriam Kochan (Oxford: Blackwell, 1992), 237.

4. The last passage of *La France Juive*.

5. Quoted in James E. Brennan, *The Reflection of the Dreyfus Affair in the European Press, 1897-1899* (New York: Peter Lang, 1998), 105, 20.

6. Quoted in Malcolm Hay, *The Foot of Pride* (Boston: Beacon Press, 1950), 192.

7. Quoted in Frederick Busi, *The Pope of Antisemitism: The Career and Legacy of Edouard-Adolphe Drumont* (New York: University Press of America, 1986), 167.

8. Quoted in Omer Bartov, *Murder in Our Midst: The Holocaust, Industrial Killing, and Representation* (Oxford: Oxford University Press, 1996), 199, nn. 52, 54.

9. Quoted in Busi, *The Pope of Antisemitism*, 163.

10. Alice Kaplan, *The Collaborator: The Trial & Execution of Robert Brasillach* (Chicago: University of Chicago Press, 2000), 219-220, 231-233.

11. Quoted in Pierre Birnbaum, *Jewish Destinies*, trans. Arthur Goldhammer (New York: Hill and Wang, 2000), 217; see generally Pierre-André Taguieff, *Rising from the Muck: The New Anti-Semitism in Europe*, trans. Patrick Camiller (Chicago: Ivan R. Dee, 2004).

12. Jean Daniel, *The Jewish Prison: A Rebellious Meditation on the State of Judaism*, trans. Charlotte Mandell (Hoboken, N.J.: Melville House, 2005), passim.

13. From Marvin Perry et al., eds., *Sources of the Western Tradition*, 6th ed. (Boston: Houghton Mifflin, 2006), 2:232.

14. From Michael Burns, ed., *France and the Dreyfus Affair: A Documentary History* (New York: Bedford/St. Martin's Press, 1999), 10-11.

15. Quoted in Louis L. Snyder, ed., *The Dreyfus Case: A Documentary History* (New Brunswick, N.J.: Rutgers University Press, 1973), 155.

16. Quoted in Snyder, *The Dreyfus Case*, 336.

17. Quoted in Birnbaum, *Jewish Destinies*, 144.

18. Quoted in Michael Burns, *Dreyfus, a Family Affair 1789-1945* (New York: HarperCollins, 1991), 144.

19. Quoted in Brennan, *The Reflection of the Dreyfus Affair*, 474.

20. Quoted in Brennan, *The Reflection of the Dreyfus Affair*, 411, dated Jan. 24, 1898.

21. A) is from the daily edition of *La Libre Parole* for Nov. 3, 1894; B) is from the weekly edition for the same date; C) appeared Dec. 26, 1894; all excerpted from Snyder, *The Dreyfus Case*, 93, 95-96.

22. From Pierre Birnbaum, *The Anti-Semitic Moment: A Tour of France in 1898*, trans. Jane Marie Todd (New York: Hill and Wang, 2003), 45-46.

23. From Birnbaum, *The Anti-Semitic Moment*, 288.

24. From Burns, *France and the Dreyfus Affair*, 130-131.

25. Lead editorial of *La Croix* by Le Paysan, "Le Profit," Aug. 18, 1899, p. 1; translated for this volume by Professor Jeff Horn, Manhattan College.

FOURTEEN

German Volkish Antisemitism

In the nineteenth century, with the spread of the liberal ideals of the Enlightenment and the French Revolution, most European states granted Jews citizenship and legal equality. Motivated by the fierce desire of outsiders to prove their worth and spurred by deeply embedded traditions that valued education and family life, many Jews achieved striking successes as entrepreneurs, financiers, lawyers, journalists, physicians, scientists, and scholars as well as in theater, music, and literature. Nowhere was this success more impressive than in German-speaking lands. For example, in the first decade of the twentieth century Jews, who constituted about 10 percent of Vienna's population, accounted for 59 percent of its physicians, 65 percent of its lawyers, 63 percent of its industrialists, and 71 percent of its financiers—all but one of the major banking houses were Jewish. Vienna's cultural life before World War I was to a large extent shaped by Jewish writers, performers, composers, critics, and patrons. By the early 1930s German Jews, amounting to less than 1 percent of the population, accounted for 10.9 percent of the physicians, 10.7 percent of the dentists, 5.1 percent of the editors and authors, and 16.3 percent of the attorneys. By the early 1930s, 30 percent of the Nobel laureates in Germany were Jews. A degree of their social acceptance is seen in the *Kaiserjuden* (the kaiser's Jews), famous Jews who were accepted at court, members of the Bleichröder, Rothschild, Warburg, Rathenau, and Ballin families. Many Germans, however, reacted negatively to the astounding ascent of German (and Austrian) Jews, seeing in it the eclipse of traditional German ways and values. Especially after the worldwide depression of 1873, which struck particularly hard in central Europe, did the collective need for scapegoats focus attention on the Jews and bring forth old and new stereotypes.

German antisemitism was closely linked to Volkish thought, an ominous expression of that romantic German nationalism that exalted everything German—the medieval past, German language and landscape, fatherland and Teutonic tribes and Teutonic gods, the simple peasant life and pre-industrial village community—and denounced everything non-German, particularly the liberal-humanist Enlightenment tradition that was identified with France, the West, and most particularly the "alien" Jews. An especial target of Volkists was modernity as exemplified by urbanization, industrialization, and an impersonal, highly rationalized capitalism that Volkish nationalists claimed undermined the traditional organic community.

Volkish thinkers were much attracted to racist doctrines, which held that race was the key to history; for them it was fundamentally important to safeguard the pure German race and the unique German "racial soul." They maintained that not only physical features but also moral, esthetic, and intellectual qualities distinguished one race from another. In their view a race demonstrated its vigor and achieved greatness when it preserved its purity and conquered and subjected "inferior" races; intermarriage between races—"miscegenation"—was contamination that would result in genetic, cultural, and military decline. Like their Nazi successors, Volkists claimed that the German race was purer, and thus superior to, all other races. Its superiority was revealed in such physical characteristics as blond hair, blue eyes, and fair skin: all marks of inner qualities lacking in other races. German racists claimed that the Germans were the purest descendants of the ancient Aryans. According to their version of the myth of the Aryan race, the Germans had inherited the superior racial qualities of the Aryan creators of European civilization.

The endless stream of antisemitic publications and the innumerable discussions of the "Jewish problem" in the press, decade after decade down to 1914, attest to the Germans' strange obsession with people amounting to barely 1 percent of the population. Several prominent journalists, academics, and clergy helped make antisemitism more respectable among the elite. Journalist Wilhelm Marr (1819–1904), "the patriarch of antisemitism," minted the neologism "antisemitism" as a "scientific" term intended to establish race instead of religion as the decisive factor in relations with the Jews. In *The Victory of Jews/Judaism over Germandom* (1879), which went through numerous printings and editions, Marr warned his fellow Germans of the Jewish peril. Heinrich von Treitschke (1834–1896), a respected historian and professor at the University of Berlin and member of the Reichstag from 1871 to 1884, coined the phrase, much used as a motto by the Nazis and other rabid antisemites, "The Jews are our misfortune." A more distinctly racist approach was taken by the economist Eugen Dühring in his book of 1880, *The Jewish Question;* according to this professor at the University of Berlin, the Jews were so irrevocably evil, they must not be tolerated. As early as 1865 he demanded their "killing and extirpating." Canon August Rohling's reduction of Judaism to the Talmud, and the Talmud to a criminal code requiring ritual murder and a long list of wicked and illegal actions, caused a profound stir because, in contrast to numerous cranks, he was supposedly a learned professor; even after his *Talmud Jew* (1871) was discredited and he was disgraced as a fraud, Rohling was not repudiated by the Catholic Church. Others, like Paul de Lagarde, a prominent university professor, designated Judaism a skeleton or fossil and called for Christianity to be de-Judaized, for a "de-Semiticized Christianity."

As the highest level of society stood Adolf Stöcker, court preacher and chaplain to the kaiser, who launched the Christian Social Workers' Party in 1878. Stöcker argued that Jewish capitalists and journalists were solely responsible for the turmoil and deprivation suffered by the workers and the people at large. Owing to their corrupting influence on the young, Jewish teachers were especially culpable. "What we demand of modern Jewry," he explained, was legislation to "eradicate" Jewish journalistic attacks on Christianity, curb Jewish capital, remove Jewish teachers from the elementary schools, and thus extinguish the "social abuse" caused by the Jews—in short, dis-emancipation.

In 1892, following the precedent of Conservatives in the Prussian parliament who had voted 95 to 1 to espouse antisemitism, the Conservative Party, the most prestigious party in Germany, nailed antisemitism to its masthead, its platform spelling out that "We will do battle against the many-sided, aggressive, decomposing, and arrogant Jewish influence on the life of our people" and specifying a battery of prohibitions and restrictions that would apply to Jews.[1] A motion to "repudiate the excesses of antisemitism" was defeated. All this ferment in high and low places—professional organizations, churches, clubs and fraternal bodies, schools and universities, parties and pressure groups—made antisemitism acceptable, indeed, as Fritz Stern remarks, "virtuous."

In the view of many Volkish antisemites, the Jews stood in the way of the fulfillment of the German Volk's (people, race) destiny. Writers like Houston Stewart Chamberlain described the inescapable conflict of "the races," Germans and Jews, who would struggle "to the death." He equated the Jews with every conceivable danger and threat: liberalism, parliamentarism, socialism, and materialism. Germans, he said in 1888, "are menaced by a complete moral, intellectual, and material ruin if a strong reaction does not set in in time against the supremacy of the Jews, who feed upon them and suck out—at every grade of society—their very life blood."[2] Chamberlain was a favorite of Kaiser Wilhelm II, Wagner (his father-in-law), and Hitler.

Many writers, following what they thought to be the line of Darwinian biology and anthropology, postulated that Jews represented an arrested development in evolution and were thus not fully human; for example, Theodor Fritsch (see page 114) placed Jews in an intermediate zone between Nordic man and the apes, while others designated Jews as vermin, insects, and parasites, categories which the Nazis would later use. American historian George Mosse noted, "The dehumanization of the Jew is perhaps one of the most significant developments in the evolution of the Volkish ideology."[3] This was an ominous sign, for by the end of the century the racist antisemitic ideology penetrated the youth movement and educational system at all levels, providing a breeding ground for future Nazis.

The antisemitic political parties declined sharply as of 1903 and no significant anti-Jewish legislation was passed by the outbreak of World War I. But much damage had been done. For many Germans, including members of the elite, Jew-hatred had become pervasive, legitimate, and even virtuous.

In Vienna the Christian Social Party, the strongest antisemitic organization in Europe, gained political power. Led by Karl Lueger, mayor from 1897 to 1910, it ruled the city of Vienna from 1897 to 1914. But it failed to inflict much harm on the Jews of Vienna (beyond purging them from teaching and municipal jobs and instigating boycotts of Jewish businesses) or Austria because of the constitution, the Emperor Franz Joseph, and the imperial legislature where the antisemites fell short of a majority and did not come into power until Hitler in 1938.

All these themes—populist agrarian, Volkish, nationalist, and racist forms of antisemitism—are exemplified by the following documents, as are the various solutions of isolation, expulsion, and annihilation.

Richard Wagner

"Judaism in Music," 1850, 1869

In many ways the immensely popular German composer Richard Wagner (1813–1883) exemplified the Volkish synthesis of nationalism, antisemitism, racism, and demagoguery, most notably in his essay, "Das Judentum in der Musik," which can be translated as "Judaism" or "The Jews" or "Jewishness in Music." In this essay, first published under a pseudonym in 1850 and republished with some additions under his own name in 1869, Wagner, who resented the fame of the Jewish composers Felix Mendelssohn (who had converted to Lutheranism) and Giacomo Meyerbeer, asserted that Jews debased German music. They could not possess nor express the feelings that animated the German soul; they had their own, distinct folk soul, which had been formed by a degenerate culture. Devoid of creative imagination and concerned only with self-centered materialist pursuits, Wagner contended, Jews were incapable of making a creative contribution to German or European culture. Because Jews were the opposite of German artists, who set aside personal gain to pursue pure ideals, Wagner maintained that Jews must inescapably have a detrimental influence on German cultural life. He expressed the view many of the German elite shared regarding recently emancipated Jews who could now leave the ghettos to which they had been confined for centuries and participate in public and professional life as citizens: Germans, he said, shun contact with Jews because of "our deep-seated, involuntary feeling of repugnance for the Jewish nature." And in the essay's concluding passage, which is freighted with the most blatant kind of age-old Judaeophobia, Wagner stipulated that the only solution was "Untergang!" (destruction or annihilation). Whether he meant annihilation literally or the disappearance of the Jews as a people and of Judaism as a religion, many of his admirers and followers—most assuredly Hitler and the Nazis—took Wagner strictly by the letter.

In later essays published in the Wagnerian journal, the *Bayreuther Blätter,* and in private conversation and correspondence, Wagner's antisemitism grew ever more vitriolic and racist. "I hold the Jewish race to be the born enemy of pure humanity and everything noble in it. It is certain that it is running us Germans to the ground."[4] Wagner and his immediate circle, including his wife Cosima, reviled Judaism as a curse, considered Jews inferior and degenerate, and maintained that they were taking over Germany. They frequently referred to Jews as vermin, bacilli, and lice, the very language that Nazi mass murderers would employ. Holding that artistic creativity was a function of ethnicity, Wagner saw Jews as the deadly opponent of the German spirit, the contaminators of the arts in Germany, and he rejected their participation in the regeneration of the national culture that he hoped to inspire. He also felt that Jesus was not Jewish but "Aryan" and called for severing Christianity from its Jewish roots, believing that the connection ruined it. German antisemites regarded themselves as Wagner's apostles: They sent him their anti-semitic writings for approval and viewed the master's home as a shrine. The young Hitler was obsessed with Wagner's music-dramas, which he felt embodied the Germanic soul, and they may have inspired him to believe that he was the man of destiny summoned to regenerate Germany and save it from the Jews. When he was agitating for power in the 1920s, Hitler attended the Bayreuth festivals that performed Wagner's operas, an indication that he had adopted Wagner's nationalist and antisemitic ideas. And Wagner's family—among them his son-in-law Houston Stewart Chamberlain, the apostle of Teutonic superiority and Jewish degenerateness who saluted Hitler as "the true awakener"—and followers hailed Hitler as the savior of the German soul. Once in power the Nazis utilized for propaganda purposes the words and music of Wagner, of whom they made a cult. As Hitler put it on various occasions, "Whoever wants to understand National Socialist Germany must know Wagner."

The following excerpt is from Wagner's "Judaism in Music."

[Our] desire to give the Jews their rights sprang much more from principle than from real sympathy, and all the talking and writing about Jewish emancipation failed to mask our unwillingness to have any actual dealings with them.

So here we reach the starting-point of our enquiry: we shall attempt to understand the involuntary repulsion aroused in us by the personality and customs of the Jews, in order to justify this instinctive feeling which is obviously stronger and more overpowering than our desire to be free of it. We are deliberately distorting our own nature if we feel ashamed to proclaim the natural revulsion aroused in us by Jewishness. . . . As the world is constituted today, the Jew is more than emancipated, he is the ruler. And he will continue to rule as long as money remains the power to which all our activities are subjugated. . . .

We have no need to prove that modern art has been taken over by the Jews; this is a fact that leaps to the eye unbidden. . . . But if emancipation from Judaism seems to us a prime necessity, we must test our strength for this war of liberation. We shall not gain this strength merely by an abstract definition of the situation, but by an intimate knowledge of the nature of our deep-seated, involuntary feeling of repugnance for the Jewish nature. By this unconquerable feeling, what we hate in the Jewish character must be revealed to us, and when we know it we can take measures against the Jewish character. By revealing him clearly, we may hope to wipe the demon from the field, where he has been able to thrive only under the protective cover of darkness, a darkness that we good-natured Humanists ourselves have offered him to make his appearance less disgusting.

In ordinary life the Jew, who as we know possesses a God of his own, strikes us first by his outward appearance which, what ever European nationality we belong to, has something unpleasantly foreign to that nationality. We instinctively feel we have nothing in common with a man who looks like that. This must, in past times, have been upsetting to the Jew: nowadays, however, not only does he not mind this, his successes lead him to consider his difference from us as an advantage. Ignoring the moral aspect of this unpleasant freak of nature, and considering only the aesthetic, we will merely point out that to us this exterior could never be acceptable as a subject for a painting; if a portrait painter has to portray a Jew, he usually takes his model from his imagination, and wisely transforms or else completely omits everything that in real life characterises the Jew's appearance. One never sees a Jew on the stage: the exceptions are so rare that they serve to confirm this rule. We can conceive of no character, historical or modern, hero or lover, being played by a Jew, without instinctively feeling the absurdity of such an idea. . . . This is very important: a race whose general appearance we cannot consider suitable for aesthetic purposes is by the same token incapable of any artistic presentation of its nature.

Considerably more important is the effect upon us of Jewish speech, and this is the point at which we should consider Jewish influence on music. The Jew speaks the language of the country in which he has lived from generation to generation, but he always speaks it as a foreigner. . . . To begin with, the fact that the Jew speaks modern European languages only as learnt and not as a native, makes it impossible for him ever to speak colloquially, authoritatively or from the depths of his being. A language, its expression and its evolution are not separate elements but part of an historical community, and only he who has unconsciously matured in this community can take any part in what it creates. But the Jew has stood quite apart from this community. . . . To create poetry in a foreign language has always been impossible, even for the greatest geniuses. Yet our entire European civilisation and art have remained foreign to the Jew; for he has taken no part in the evolution of either. At best he has been a cold, even a hostile onlooker. In this language, this art, the Jew can only imitate, he can create neither poem nor work of art.

We are repelled in particular by the purely aural aspect of Jewish speech. Contact with our culture has not, even after two thousand years, weaned the Jew away from the peculiarities of Semitic pronunciation. The shrill, sibilant buzzing of his voice falls strangely and unpleasantly on our ears. His misuse of words whose exact shade of meaning escapes him, and his mistakenly placed phrases combine to turn his utterance into an unbearably muddled nonsense. Consequently, when we listen to Jewish speech we are involuntarily struck by its offensive manner and so diverted from understanding of its matter. This is of exceptional importance in explaining the effect of modern Jewish music on us. When we listen to a Jew talking we are unconsciously upset by the complete lack of purely human expression in his speech. The cold indifference of its peculiar "blabber" can never rise to the excitement of real passion. And if we, in conversation with a Jew, should find our own words becoming heated, he will always be evasive, because he is incapable of really deep feeling. He will never be excited by a mutual exchange of feelings with us, but only by matters of particular egotistic interest to his vanity or to his sense of profit. This, together with his manner of speaking, makes him to our ears more ridiculous than sympathetic. . . . If these defects in his manner of speaking render the

Jew almost incapable of artistic enunciation of his feelings, how much less capable he will be of expressing those feelings in song. Song is, after all, speech heightened by passion: music is the language of passion. If the Jew's already ridiculously vehement manner of speech is to be heightened, we shall be further alienated from him. If we were repelled by his appearance and his speech, his song will engage our attention only to the extent that we exclaim at so absurd a phenomenon. It is understandably in song, as the most indisputably vivid expression of personal feeling, that the offensive peculiarity of the Jewish nature reaches its peak. But it is for every aspect of art, not only those connected with song, that on a natural hypothesis we must consider the Jew unsuited.

The Jews' ideas on visual observation have rendered it impossible for any visual artist to emerge from them: their eyes have always busied themselves far more with practical affairs than with beauty or the spiritual substance of the material world. As far as I can discover, no Jewish architect or sculptor has appeared in our time. Whether recent painters of Jewish descent can really be considered creative artists, I must leave to the judgment of connoisseurs; presumably, however, the attitude of these artists to their art does not essentially differ from that of modern Jewish composers towards music, a subject we shall now consider in detail.

The Jew, completely incapable of communicating artistically with us either by his appearance or his speech, and least of all by his singing, has nevertheless succeeded in completely taking over public taste in that most popular of modern arts, music. . . .

[Resolution of the Jewish question, Wagner, addressing the Jews directly, concludes,] cannot be achieved easily or in comfortable complacency, but only by sweat, want, anguish and the depths of sorrow and suffering. Without a backward glance, take part in this work of redemption through self-destroying struggle, for then we are one and indivisible. But remember only one thing can bring redemption from the curse laid on you, and that is the redemption of Ahasuerus [the Wandering Jew, i.e., the Jewish people]—Destruction! [Untergang].[5]

Hermann Ahlwardt

"The Jews versus the Germans," 1895

In the following selection, Hermann Ahlwardt (1846–1914), an antisemitic member of the Reichstag (parliament) and author of *The Desperate Struggle between Aryan and Jew,* addresses the national legislature on March 6, 1895, with a plea to close Germany's borders to Jewish immigrants, especially those fleeing Russian pogroms. This speech and his pamphlets, which were very popular, share much with Luther before and Hitler after him. All three paint a very negative picture of Jews and use many of the same words and phrases: The Jews are "a poison in the land," economic predators, demonic conspirators pursuing power and domination; they are aliens possessing vile racial traits that set them apart from Germans. Ahlwardt conjured up every imaginable accusation and stereotype. Even though he was a convicted embezzler and self-confessed liar, his example of antisemitic demagoguery and political appeal helped persuade the Conservative Party to add to its platform in 1892 the principle to "do battle against the many-sided aggressive, decomposing, and arrogant Jewish influence." The aim to extinguish Jewish emancipation and civil rights was the common property of the German elites and the Pan-German movement, and it remained the Conservative party's plan into the Nazi era. In his demagogic polemic and simplemindedness, Ahlwardt most closely resembles Julius Streicher (see page 182).

It is certainly true that there are Jews in our country of whom nothing adverse can be said. Nevertheless, the Jews as a whole must be considered harmful, for the racial traits of this people are of a kind that in the long run do not agree with the racial traits of the Teutons. Every Jew who at this very moment has not yet transgressed is likely to do so at some future time under given circumstances because his racial characteristics drive him on in that direction. . . .

Experience in all fields of nature shows that innate racial characteristics which have been acquired by the race in the course of many thousands of years are the strongest and most enduring factors that exist, and that therefore we can rid ourselves of the characteristics of our race no more than can the Jews. One need not fight the Jew individually, and we are not doing that, by the way. But, when countless specimens prove the existence of certain racial characteristics and when these characteristics are such as to make impossible a common life, well, then I believe that we who are natives here, who have tilled the soil and defended it against all enemies—that we have a duty to take a stand against the Jews who are of a quite different nature.

We Teutons are rooted in the cultural soil of labor; each of us seeks to work for others and demands in return that others work for him. It is on this soil of culture that we have worked our way up from barbarity to our present state of civilization. It is different with the Jews. The Jews do not believe in the culture of labor, they do not want to create values themselves, but want to appropriate, without working, the values which others have created; that is the cardinal difference that guides us in all our considerations.

The Jews want to grab what others have produced by their work; we ourselves would be content, if we could only get what we have labored for. . . . Herr Deputy Rickert here has just expounded how few Jews we have altogether and that their number is steadily declining. Well, gentlemen, why don't you go to the main business centers and see for yourselves whether the percentages indicated by Herr Rickert prevail there too. Why don't you walk along the [main business streets] Leipzigerstrasse [in Berlin] or the Zeil in Frankfurt and have a look at the shops? Wherever there are opportunities to make money, the Jews have established themselves, but not in order to work—no, they let others work for them and take what others have produced by their labor. . . .

Gentlemen, the Jews are indeed beasts of prey, they work like beasts of prey. You cannot alter this fact. . . .

The Jews have an attitude toward us which differs totally from that of other peoples. It is one thing when a Pole, a Russian, a Frenchman, a Dane immigrates to our country, and quite another thing when a Jew settles here. . . . Once our [Polish, etc.] guests have lived here for ten, twenty years, they have come to resemble us. For they have stood with us on the same cultural soil of labor. . . . After thirty, forty years, they have become Germans and their grandchildren would be indistinguishable from us except for the strange-sounding names they still bear. The Jews have lived for 700 or 800 years, but have they become Germans? Have they placed themselves on the cultural soil of labor? They never even dreamed of such a thing; as soon as they arrived, they started to cheat and they have been doing that ever since they have been in Germany.

The Jews should not be admitted, whether or not there is overpopulation, for they do not belong to a productive race, they are exploiters, parasites. . . .

[Answering Rickert's argument that it would be a shame if fifty million Germans were afraid of a few Jews, Ahlwardt continued,] Herr Rickert, who is just as tall as I am, is afraid of one single cholera bacillus—well, gentlemen, the Jews are just that, cholera bacilli!

Gentlemen, the crux of the matter is Jewry's capacity for contagion and exploitation. . . . How many Germans have perished as a result of this Jewish exploitation, how many may have hanged themselves, shot themselves, drowned themselves, how many may have ended by the wayside as tramps in America or drawn their last breath in the gutter, all of them people who had worked industriously on the soil their fathers had acquired, perhaps in hundreds of years of hard work. . . . Ah, why were they foolish enough to let themselves be cheated? But the Germans are by no means so foolish, they are far more intelligent than the Jews. All inventions, all great ideas come from the Germans and not from the Jews. No, I shall tell you the national difference: The German is fundamentally trusting, his heart is full of loyalty and confidence. The Jew gains this confidence, only to betray it at the proper moment, ruining and pauperizing the German. This abuse of confidence on the part of the Jews is their main weapon. And these Jewish scoundrels are to be defended here! Is there no one to think of all those hundreds of thousands, nor of those millions of workers whose wages grow smaller and smaller because Jewish competition brings the prices down? One always hears you must be humane to the Jews. The humanitarianism of our century, this humaneness of beasts of prey is our curse. Why aren't you for once humane toward the oppressed? You'd better exterminate those beasts of prey and you'd better start by not letting any more of them into the country. . . .

If you come to a city [near the German-Russian border where the "real Jews" live] like Flatow, Meseritz, Bomst, etc., you will hardly find any German shops at all. Business is completely in Jewish hands and the Jew exploits every-body at will! And you speak of a cultural mission! How does he carry out this cultural mission with respect to the peasants? Why don't you ask them what they are getting for their grain? They work from 3AM until 9 PM until they drop, and you ask who derives the profit from the crop! Most of the people are so poor that they cannot wait until the harvest is in. They must ask for advance payment, and the Jew gets the poor people's grain for next to nothing. Without the Jew no one can sell cattle or grain, no one can buy a pair of shoes. The Jew carries out his cultural mission by maintaining these regions in a state of bar-barism. The people there are all poor. Wherever the Jews put in their appear-ance, the Germans become poor. Once they are completely impoverished, the Jews leave. . . .

[Taking issue with the liberals' argument of Jewish achievement in the arts, Ahlwardt asserted,] Art in my opinion is the capacity for expressing one's innermost feelings in such a way as to arouse the same feelings in the other person. Now the Jewish world of emotions and the Teutonic world of emotions are two quite different things. German art can express only German feelings; Jewish art only Jewish feelings. Because Jewry has been thrusting itself for-ward everywhere, it has also thrust itself forward in the field of art and there-fore the art that is now in the foreground is Jewish art. Nowadays the head of a family must be very careful when he decides to take his family to the the-ater lest his Teutonic feelings be outraged by the infamous Jewish art that has spread everywhere.

The Jew is no German. If you say, the Jew was born in Germany, he was nursed by a German wet-nurse, he abides by German laws, he has to serve as a soldier—and what kind of a soldier at that! let's not talk about it—he fulfills all his obligations, he pays his taxes—then I say that all this is not the crucial fac-tor with regard to his nationality; the crucial factor is the race from which he stems. Permit me to make a rather trite comparison which I have already used elsewhere in my speeches: a horse that is born in a cowshed is far from being a cow.

A Jew who was born in Germany does not thereby become a German; he is still a Jew. Therefore it is imperative that we realize that Jewish racial char-acteristics differ so greatly from ours that a common life of Jews and Germans under the same laws is quite impossible because the Germans will perish.

Gentlemen. . . . I beg you from the bottom of my heart not to take this matter lightly but as a very serious thing. It is a question of life and death for our people. . . .

We wouldn't think of going as far as the Austrian anti-Semites in the Fed-eral Council and to move that a bounty be paid for every Jew shot or to de-cree that he who kills a Jew shall inherit his property. [A reference to Ernst Schneider, a lieutenant of Karl Lueger in the Austrian Christian Social Party, who punctuated his speeches with this kind of humor.] We have no such in-tention. We shall not go as far as that. What we want is a clear and reasonable separation of the Jews from the Germans. An immediate prerequisite is that we slam the door and see to it that no more of them get in. [The motion to prohibit Jewish immigration was defeated 167 to 51.][6]

Theodor Fritsch

Handbook of the Jewish Question, 1887

Theodor Fritsch (1852–1933) was a German engineer, of lower middle class origin and outlook, and a ferocious antisemite throughout his long life. His antisemitic phobias are expressed in his *Antisemiten-Katechismus* (Antisemitic Catechism), which was first published in 1887 by his Hammer Press; the work was constantly expanded in new editions under the title *Handbuch der Judenfrage* (Handbook of the Jewish Question), reaching its twenty-sixth by 1907 and fortieth by 1936. One of its features is an enormous number of antisemitic quotations—seeming proof texts—from the Roman historian Tacitus to Richard Wagner. In this and other writings he attacked Freud's "poison" and Einstein's "delusion" and warned against the "Jewish peril" and the "Jewification" of German art and culture—so as to put all on notice he named innumerable Jewish conductors, musicians, singers, actors, and impresarios. Jewish doctors were especially dangerous for the national health, and the numerous Jewish pediatricians put German children at colossal risk.

Fritsch lived on to become a Nazi Party member and sit in the Reichstag. At the time of his death in September 1933, he was extolled by the Nazis as *der Altmeister* (the great old teacher) and had been honored by Hitler as a precursor; the *Handbuch* is one of the few books that Hitler is definitely known to have read. The *Handbuch,* excerpted below, was standard reading in German schools under the Nazis and it served as intellectual teething material for the Hitler Youth.

A. Antisemitic catechism: What are the Jews really guilty of?

1. Jews engage in usurious dealings with peasants, artisans, officials and officers.
2. Their sharp business practices lead to the decline of honest trade and make it their prey.
3. They ruin handicraft and cause formerly independent artisans to submit to wage slavery.
4. They force wages and prices down to a level where honest labor can hardly exist any longer and the threat of a bloody revolution constantly grows.
5. They have a monopoly of the press and use it to deceive the people as to the true causes of their misery and to divert discontent toward wrong targets (government, church, *Junkers*, police, officials).
6. They demoralize the people by feeding them sensational and obscene news, degrading our entire culture.
7. They committed fraud on a gigantic scale at the time of the financial crash [of 1873].
8. They influence legislation through Jewish parliamentarians (Lasker, Bamberger,

etc.) and through paid non-Jewish underlings, with the aim of furthering their own designs (fraudulent insolvency, gambling at the stock exchange, freedom of movement).

9. They commercialize all values: offices, titles, prestige, honor, love; causing moral devastation especially among the nation's young womanhood. ("The Jews' low sensuous disposition and their lack of decency make them the most unscrupulous seducers.") They run the white slave trade.

10. They have lured into their nets and bribed many prominent persons; the few men of character who resist are mercilessly slandered in the Jewish press.

11. They dominate even governments through shrewd financial operations, have pull with all cabinets through international contacts so that "no individual state can dare to take steps against the Jews without being set upon by neighboring states."

B. Ten German Commandments of Lawful Self-Defense: The Racists' Decalogue

I. Be proud of being a German and strive earnestly and steadily to practice the inherited virtues of our people, courage, faithfulness and veracity, and to inspire and develop these virtues in thy children.

II. Thou shalt know that thou, together with all thy fellow Germans, regardless of faith or creed, hast a common implacable foe. His name is Jew.

III. Thou shalt keep thy blood pure. Consider it a crime to soil the noble Aryan breed of thy people by mingling it with the Jewish breed. For thou must know that Jewish blood is everlasting, putting the Jewish stamp on body and soul unto the farthest generations.

IV. Thou shalt be helpful to thy fellow German and further him in all matters not counter to the German conscience, the more so if he be pressed by the Jew. Thou shalt at once take into court any offense or crime committed by the Jew in deed, word or letter, that comes to thy knowledge, lest the Jew abuse the laws of our country with impunity.

V. Thou shalt have no social intercourse with the Jew. Avoid all contact and community with the Jew and keep him away from thyself and thy family, especially thy daughters, lest they suffer injury of body and soul.

VI. Thou shalt have no business relations with the Jew. Never choose a Jew as a business partner, nor borrow nor buy from him, and keep your wife, too, from doing so. Thou shalt sell nothing to him, nor use him as an agent in thy transactions, that thou mayest remain free and not become slave unto a Jew nor help to increase his money, which is the power by which he enslaves our people.

VII. Thou shalt drive the Jew from thy own breast and take no example from Jewish tricks and Jewish wiles, for thou shalt never match the Jew in trickery but forfeit thy honor and earn the contempt of thy fellow Germans and the punishment of the courts.

VIII. Thou shalt not entrust thy rights to a Jewish lawyer, nor thy body to a Jewish physician, nor thy children to a Jewish teacher lest thy honor, body and soul suffer harm.

IX. Thou shalt not lend ear nor give credence to the Jew. Keep away all Jewish writings from thy German home and hearth lest their lingering poison may unnerve and corrupt thyself and thy family.

X. Thou shalt use no violence against the Jews because it is unworthy of thee and against the law. But if a Jew attack thee, ward off his Semitic insolence with German wrath.[7]

Konstantin von Gebsattel

The Jewish Threat, 1913

In the elections for the Reichstag in January 1912, the socialist SPD (Social Democratic Party) won a third of the votes and a quarter of the seats. Among many schemes to preserve the Hohenzollern autocracy and arrest the march of democracy and socialism was a plan for a new constitution drafted by Konstantin von Gebsattel, a retired general in the Bavarian army. In October 1913 he sent it to the Crown Prince, who endorsed it enthusiastically and relayed it to the chancellor, who in turn enlisted the father, Kaiser Wilhelm II, to write his son and reject the general's constitution. This thoroughly reactionary document included proposals for drastically changing the status of the Jews in Germany. Like a great many anti-semites, von Gebsattel claims he is not one, that he knows and admires some Jews. This does not inhibit him from making proposals that anticipate the Nazi racial laws, "Aryanization," and the yearning for a führer.

I am not an anti-Semite. I know some Jews, particularly business people, whom I respect and admire. On the other hand one would have to be blinder than Hödur [the Nordic god of darkness] if one refused to see that our entire life is dominated and endangered by the Jewish spirit: internal affairs by the press in Jewish hands, financial affairs by the great banks directed by Jews, legal affairs by the huge number of Jewish lawyers in the big cities, cultural affairs by the many Jewish university professors and the almost exclusively Jewish theatre directors and critics. The Jewish and Germanic spirits contradict each other like fire and water: the latter is deep, positive and idealistic, the former superficial, negative, destructively critical and materialistic. The danger threatening Germandom and thus also the German Reich is grave and immediate; the more dangerous because it is cleverly disguised and because the Jewish press has succeeded in persuading a large section of the nation that anyone who fights against the excesses of Judaism is backward and inferior. I, on the other hand, maintain that anyone who fails to take up this struggle even for one day is avoiding his urgent duty in a cowardly way. . . .

The Jews should be placed under the law pertaining to aliens and should remain the guests of the German people. Naturally they will be exempt from military service and will pay instead an army tax, which will perhaps be up to twice as high as the taxes paid by Germans. Obviously they will not be allowed to enter public service, to be judges, officials, university professors, lawyers, officers; they will, however, be allowed to become businessmen, directors of private banks, doctors. The acquisitions of sizeable landed estates will also be forbidden to them, and here the borderline will have to be drawn very low. For quarrels among themselves one could perhaps give them their own courts, but for quarrels with Teutons, they will come before the normal courts, as in the case of criminal proceedings.

There is a danger that such laws might cause the Jews to emigrate to states where they hope to receive equal treatment with Christians, or rather, where they hoped to seize the entire executive power for themselves. I am utterly convinced that Sombart [see page 82] is wrong when he declares that the expulsion of the Jews was the reason for the economic collapse of states in the Middle Ages, and I would point there rather to the Germanic [*sic*] prophet Count Gobineau. That German commerce does not need Jews is proven by the Fuggers, the Welsers and the Hanseatic League, none of which succumbed to Jewish influence. I also know of not one case where a Jew has achieved great things in industry. I do admit, however, that a total emigration of Jews would be undesirable, and that we should try to use their good qualities to our advantage. I also do not know whether the German Reich could withstand the great capital loss involved, which I estimate in milliards. It would, in any case, be a travesty of justice if we were to permit our guests to take with them the great riches which they have only gained by being more commercially-minded and unscrupulous than their hosts, so doing great damage to the nation's prosperity. Any Jew wishing to emigrate must therefore leave the major share of his property to the state. It will therefore be necessary when the state of siege is proclaimed, to close the borders and the banks until the Jewish fortune has been assessed.

A mixing of Jewish and Germanic races is not desirable, but cannot be prevented. Baptism must not, however, change the status of the Jew and the Jewess, nor of their children. . . . Not until there is not more than one-quarter Jewish blood in the grandchildren should they be able to acquire the rights of the Teutons. . . .

As the Jews are only guests and not citizens, they should not be allowed to participate in the discussions about the constitution, the rights of the citizen, etc. They must therefore be prohibited from editing and writing for newspapers, on pain of severe punishment. They will only be allowed to publish a fixed number of Jewish newspapers, specifically marked as such, solely about Jewish matters and devoid of all opinion and comment on affairs of state. . . .

May the man come soon who will lead us along this path.[8]

The Pan-German League

Imposing Restrictions on Jews

Organized in 1894, the ultranationalist Pan-German League called for German expansion in Europe and overseas. It also expressed strongly antisemitic views, as illustrated by the following passage written in 1912 by Heinrich Class (1868–1953), then president of the league (see page 156).

A return to health in our national life, in all its branches—cultural, moral, political, and economic—and the maintenance of that recovered health is only possible if Jewish influence is either completely expunged or screwed back to a bearable, innocuous level. Let us be clear in the discussion of these necessities that the innocent must suffer along with the guilty. . . .

Today, the borders must be totally and unconditionally barred to any further Jewish immigration. This is absolutely necessary, but no longer sufficient. Just as self-evident, foreign Jews who have not yet acquired citizenship rights must be speedily and unconditionally expelled, to the last man. But this is also not enough. . . . We must demand that resident Jews be placed under an Aliens' Law. . . .

A Jew, according to the above Aliens' Law, is anyone who belonged to a Jewish religious corporation as of 18 January 1871, as well as all the descendants of such persons who were Jews at that date, even when only one parent was or is [a Jew by the above definition]. All public offices remain closed to Jews whether of a paid or honorary nature, whether national, state, or municipal. They will not be allowed to serve in the army or navy. They will hold neither the active nor the passive right to vote. The professions of lawyer and teacher are denied them, also that of theater director.

Newspapers which have Jewish collaborators must make this fact known. The others, which we generally call "German" newspapers, may neither be owned by Jews nor have Jewish editors or reporters. Banks that are not purely personal enterprises may not have Jewish directors. In future, rural property may not be owned by Jews or be mortgaged to Jews. As compensation for the protection Jews enjoy as foreigners, they shall pay double the taxes of Germans.[9]

NOTES

1. Quoted in John Weiss, *Ideology of Death: Why the Holocaust Happened in Germany* (Chicago: Ivan R. Dee, 1996), 115-116.

2. Quoted in Geoffrey G. Field, *Evangelist of Race: The Germanic Vision of Houston Stewart Chamberlain* (New York: Columbia University Press, 1981), 90.

3. George L. Mosse, *The Crisis of German Ideology: The Intellectual Origins of the Third Reich* (New York: Grosset and Dunlap, 1964), 140.

4. Quoted in Jacob Katz, *The Darker Side of Genius: Richard Wagner's Antisemitism* (Hanover, N.H.: University Press of New England, 1986), 115.

5. From Richard Wagner, "Das Judentum in der Musik" (Judaism/Jews/Jewishness in Music), *Richard Wagner: Stories and Essays*, ed. Charles Osborne (New York: Library Press, 1973), 24-39.

6. From Paul W. Massing, *Rehearsal for Destruction: A Study of Political Anti-Semitism in Imperial Germany* (New York: HarperCollins, 1949), 300-305.

7. From Massing, *Rehearsal for Destruction*, 306-307, 77-78.

8. From J. C. G. Röhl, ed., *From Bismarck to Hitler: The Problem of Continuity in German History* (New York: Barnes and Noble, 1970), 49-51.

9. Downloaded from http://h-net.org/german/g/text/kaiserreich/class.html, trans. Richard S. Levy.

FIFTEEN

Zionism as a <u>Defense</u> against Jew-Hatred

Virulent antisemitism and the success of the Italians, Germans, Serbs, and others in achieving unification or independence stirred nationalist feelings among Jews. <u>Jewish nationalism took the form of Zionism</u>—a movement advocating the return of Jews to the land of Israel, their ancient homeland. The longing of Jews for a return to the land of their biblical roots is deeply <u>embedded in Jewish tradition</u>. What made Zionist dreams increasingly compelling, however, was the growing persecution of Jews in Eastern Europe, particularly the outbreak of pogroms in Russia starting in 1881. The attackers looted, burned, raped, and murdered, generally with impunity for several days until the security forces got organized or as long as the local police stood by indifferently.

Several writers in the 1880s, mostly Russian or Polish, formulated the ideology of a Jewish national resurgence. They argued that Jewish existence outside the ancient homeland was <u>sterile,</u> that the Jewish spirit was cramped and stultified in the Diaspora, that there was <u>no cure for antisemitism,</u> that there had to be a normalization of the Jewish occupational pattern with a return to crafts and working the land. As Dr. Leon Pinsker (1821–1891), a physician, assimilationist, and Russian patriot said,

> We do not count as a nation among other nations and we have no voice in the council of the peoples even in matters that concern ourselves. Alien countries are our fatherlands, dispersion is our unity, the world's hostility to us constitutes our solidarity. Our weapon is adaptability, our future is tomorrow. What a contemptible role for the people that once had its Maccabees![1]

Zionism is an age-old part of Judaism and <u>finds expression in the prophet Isaiah</u> and other biblical books. It is the yearning to return to the ancient homeland from which Jews were enslaved and exiled by the Romans following the cataclysmic Jewish revolt of 66–73 CE. Yet prior to the Holocaust, Zionism had only limited appeal in Western Europe and the United States. There Jews were the beneficiaries of emancipation, enjoying legal equality and civil rights as citizens. For most of them the road of Jewish destiny was <u>continued acculturation and social integration</u>. In the much-used formula, they were Englishmen, Frenchmen, Belgians, Dutchmen, Italians, or Germans "<u>of Jewish persuasion.</u>" They denied that world Jewry constituted a nationality: ["America is our fatherland, the local synagogue is our temple."] They were

def [marginal note]

profoundly moved by the suffering of the millions of Jews in Eastern Europe, but their program—in addition to generous charity and facilitating eastern Jews' immigration to Western Europe, the British Empire, and the United States—was to campaign for constitutionally protected civil and political rights for the Jewish minority (as well as other minorities) in both the old and newly created states of Eastern Europe. For much of modern Jewish history a debate went on between two conceptions of the status of Jews in the modern world. These are the nationalist-Zionist versus the acculturationist-assimilationist, an argument that the Holocaust and Israel reborn raised anew in the most searing terms but still without resolving it.

By 1914 Jewish nationalism had quickened. Zionism was reinforced by the murderous pogroms in Russia, violence in Romania, a growingly vicious antisemitic movement in Austria-Hungary, where the capital of Vienna was governed by the antisemitic Christian Social Party led by the demagogue Karl Lueger, the Dreyfus Affair, when mobs in the land of the Enlightenment and French Revolution were shouting "Death to the Jews," and the Aliens Act of 1905, which, after a strident public campaign and several royal commissions, restricted immigration to Britain. The principal force in the creation of the Zionist movement was Theodor Herzl.

Theodor Herzl

The Jewish State, *1896*

The odyssey of Theodor Herzl (1860–1904), exactly paralleling the earlier one of the physician Leo Pinsker, indicates the dilemma facing prosperous European Jews, beneficiaries of emancipation and content with the prospect of assimilation to the point of the disappearance of the Jews as a distinct people. Herzl was the son of a wealthy financier in Budapest, went to the University of Vienna where he joined a German fraternity, admired the new Germany of Bismarck and its Prussian ways, shared a German hostility to Slavs, and was indifferent to Judaism, so indifferent that he urged that the Jews convert to Christianity or be baptized at birth in order to expunge the defects inherited from the ghetto and efface all possible differences that separated them from Gentiles. Herzl initially believed antisemitism was a remnant of the Middle Ages that was rapidly ebbing away, but began having second thoughts in 1883, when mass rites to mourn the death of Richard Wagner turned raucously antisemitic, and, not long after, his beloved fraternity formally forced all Jews out. In the 1890s Herzl was a reporter in France covering the trial of the antisemitic firebrand Édouard Drumont and then the Panama Canal scandal, and was astounded on both occasions, and again in the Dreyfus proceedings a few years later, to hear the crowds shouting "Death to the Jews!" At the same time he was a witness to the riotous clamor in Vienna of Karl Lueger's antisemitic campaign to become mayor: "Lueger will become mayor, the Jew will be destroyed" was a popular chant. Herzl came to believe that antisemitism was an incurable disease; Jews would never be safe in Europe and had to have their own homeland.

Stung by recrudescent antisemitism, especially the Dreyfus Affair, which he reported on from Paris for the leading Vienna newspaper, Herzl concluded that if Jews were not safe in France, the pioneer in their emancipation, they would not be safe anywhere. Herzl's analysis of the Jewish predicament was anticipated in the Zionist classic *Rome and Jerusalem* (1862) by Moses Hess (1812–1875) and the works of Leon Pinsker, but, unaware of their writings, Herzl formulated his ideas independently. His importance is that he summoned the first Zionist Congress, at Basle, Switzerland, in 1897, and was inspired to launch the World Zionist Organization. He engaged in diplomatic negotiations in order to gain a charter for "a publicly guaranteed homeland for the Jewish people in Israel," but these efforts never came to anything beyond vague hopes. At the end of the 1897 conference, he confided to his *Diary,* "At Basle I created the Jewish state. If I were to say this out loud everybody would laugh at me. In five years, perhaps, but certainly in fifty, everybody will agree"—so it turned out in 1948.

In 1896 Herzl published his program in a book, *Der Judenstaat* (The Jewish State), in which he envisaged a glorious future for an independent Jewish state harmoniously cooperating with the local population. In the following year he presided over the first Congress of Zionist Organizations, attended mostly by Jews from central and Eastern Europe. In its program the congress, adopting Herzl's words, called for "a publicly guaranteed homeland for the Jewish people in the land of Israel." Subsequently, Herzl negotiated with the German emperor, the British government, and the sultan of the Ottoman Empire (of which Palestine was a part) for diplomatic support. In 1901 the Jewish National Fund was created to help settlers purchase land in Palestine. At his death, Herzl firmly expected a Jewish state to arise sometime in the future.

The excerpts that follow from Herzl's *Der Judenstaat,* written "in a white heat," demonstrate how fundamental contemporary and historic antisemitism was for Herzl's motivation. Given the nationalist ferment brewing everywhere, and the malignant antisemitism that was often its accompaniment, Herzl argued that security for Jews could be attained only by a separate national state of their own, preferably but not necessarily in the ancient homeland of Palestine.

We are a people—one people.

We have honestly endeavored everywhere to merge ourselves in the social life of surrounding communities and to preserve the faith of our fathers. We are not permitted to do so. In vain are we loyal patriots, our loyalty in some places running to extremes; in vain do we make the same sacrifices of life and property as our fellow-citizens; in vain do we strive to increase the fame of our native land in science and art, or her wealth by trade and commerce. In countries where we have lived for centuries we are still cried down as strangers, and often by those whose ancestors were not yet domiciled in the land where Jews had already had experience of suffering. . . . I think we shall not be left in peace.

Oppression and persecution cannot exterminate us. No nation on earth has survived such struggles and sufferings as we have gone through. Jew-baiting has merely stripped off our weaklings; the strong among us were invariably true to their race when persecution broke out against them. . . .

. . . [O]ld prejudices against us still lie deep in the hearts of the people. He who would have proofs of this need only listen to the people where they speak with frankness and simplicity: proverb and fairy-tale are both Anti-Semitic. . . .

No one can deny the gravity of the situation of the Jews. Wherever they live in perceptible numbers, they are more or less persecuted. Their equality before the law, granted by statute, has become practically a dead letter. They are debarred from filling even moderately high positions, either in the army, or in any public or private capacity. And attempts are made to thrust them out of business also: "Don't buy from Jews!"

Attacks in Parliaments, in assemblies, in the press, in the pulpit, in the street, on journeys—for example, their exclusion from certain hotels—even in places of recreation, become daily more numerous. The forms of perse-cutions vary according to the countries and social circles in which they oc-cur. In Russia, imposts are levied on Jewish villages; in Rumania, a few per-sons are put to death; in Germany, they get a good beating occasionally; in Austria, Anti-Semites exercise terrorism over all public life; in Algeria, there are travelling agitators; in Paris, the Jews are shut out of the so-called best so-cial circles and excluded from clubs. [Shades of anti-Jewish feeling are innu-merable] But this is not to be an attempt to make out a doleful category of Jew-ish hardships.

I do not intend to arouse sympathetic emotions on our behalf. That would be a foolish, futile, and undignified proceeding. I shall content myself with putting the following questions to the Jews: Is it not true that, in countries where we live in perceptible numbers, the position of Jewish lawyers, doctors, technicians, teachers, and employees of all descriptions becomes daily more intolerable? Is it not true, that the Jewish middle classes are seriously threat-ened? Is it not true, that the passions of the mob are incited against our wealthy people? Is it not true, that our poor endure greater sufferings than any other proletariat? I think that this external pressure makes itself felt everywhere [In our economically upper classes it causes discomfort, in our middle classes con-tinual and grave anxieties, in our lower classes absolute despair.]

Everything tends, in fact, to one and the same conclusion, which is clearly enunciated in that classic Berlin phrase: "*Juden Raus!*" [Jews out!]

I shall now put the Question in the briefest possible form: Are we to "get out" now and where to?

Or, may we yet remain? And, how long?

Let us first settle the point of staying where we are. Can we hope for better days, can we possess our souls in patience, can we wait in pious resignation till the princes and peoples of this earth are more mercifully disposed towards us? I say that we cannot hope for a change in the current of feeling. . . . The nations in whose midst Jews live are all either covertly or openly Anti-Semitic. . . .

. . . We might perhaps be able to merge ourselves entirely into surround-ing races, if these were to leave us in peace for a period of two generations. But they will not leave us in peace. For a little period they manage to tolerate us, and then their hostility breaks out again and again. . . .

Thus, whether we like it or not, we are now, and shall henceforth remain, a historic group with unmistakable characteristics common to us all.

We are one people—our enemies have made us one without our consent, as repeatedly happens in history. Distress binds us together, and, thus united, we suddenly discover our strength. Yes, we are strong enough to form a State, and, indeed, a model State. We possess all human and material resources necessary for the purpose. . . .

Let the sovereignty be granted us over a portion of the globe large enough to satisfy the rightful requirements of a nation; the rest we shall manage for ourselves.

The creation of a new State is neither ridiculous nor impossible. We have in our day witnessed the process in connection with nations which were not largely members of the middle class, but poorer, less educated, and consequently weaker than ourselves. . . .

Palestine is our ever-memorable historic home. The very name of Palestine would attract our people with a force of marvelous potency. If His Majesty the Sultan were to give us Palestine, we could in return undertake to regulate the whole finances of Turkey. We should there form a portion of a rampart of Europe against Asia, an outpost of civilization as opposed to barbarism. We should as a neutral State remain in contact with all Europe, which would have to guarantee our existence. The sanctuaries of Christendom would be safeguarded by assigning to them an extra-territorial status such as is well-known to the law of nations. We should form a guard of honor about these sanctuaries, answering for the fulfillment of this duty with our existence. This guard of honor would be the great symbol of the solution of the Jewish Question after eighteen centuries of Jewish suffering.[2]

Max Nordau

On the Lessons of History and Zionism, 1899

Max Nordau (1849–1923) was a Hungarian physician who saw the task of Zionism as the creation of a "muscular Judaism" and the "normalization" of Jewish society so that Jews were distributed proportionally in all economic fields and occupations. Nordau was a principal lieutenant of Theodor Herzl and a dynamic force in the Zionist movement until World War I. It was customary for Nordau at the annual meetings of the World Zionist Organization to give a keynote address on the condition and prospects of the Jewish communities worldwide. He emphasized the material misery of nine-tenths of world Jewry but thought the "moral misery" of the emancipated, assimilated Jews even worse, because these "new Marranos" renounced their Jewish heritage without gaining acceptance and admission to the host society. While Nordau assumed antisemitism and persecution would continue in the future, he believed that mass murder was impossible because, as he said in an early speech, "There is now a European conscience, a world conscience which—

even if not yet broad enough—prescribes certain outward forms and does not easily tolerate mass crimes"; shortly before World War I, however, he concluded that the situation in tsarist Russia had deteriorated so extremely that its Jews were in grave danger and every government stood by indifferently, "although this is an incomparably greater crime than any war, for no war has ever yet destroyed six million human lives." The following is from Nordau's speech of April 17, 1899, arguing characteristically that history has determined that the only sure path for the Jews is a return to Zion.

Heed the lessons of history, which speak a threatening warning to you! . . .

The Jews know that the only sources of their misery and suffering are fanaticism, superstition, brutality, and despotism. So as soon as they believed that one of these four repugnant powers in the world was becoming weaker, there arose in them the hope that their misery will have an end. Yet until now this hope has always been futile.

Since the Reformation promised to emancipate the Christian world from spiritual coercion, the Jews welcomed the movement for it also promised justice to them. Nicholas of Lyre taught Martin Luther Hebrew. The rabbis initiated the reformers in all the secret lore of the Jewish tradition and placed in their hands the weapons of biblical exegesis. In Christendom the Old Testament came back to a place of honor. Yet once the Reformation had triumphed, the reformers used their new understanding of scripture to prove that the Jews are cursed by God, and they treated them worse than under Catholicism previously.

The authors of the French *Encyclopaedia* launched their assault against dogmatism. The Enlightenment began the struggle against supernatural belief and the church. Immediately the Jews were the philosophes' most inspired apostles. Since fanaticism was the mortal enemy, the Enlightenment had to be holy. The Enlightenment was victorious, and dogmatic fanaticism was overcome and thereafter could generate only rearguard actions. Nevertheless, the Jews won nothing with these developments. Now they were pursued, no longer indeed on account of their beliefs, but, on the contrary, in the name of a scientific anthropological principle   one which the enlightened sons of the nineteenth century found utterly respectable—they are persecuted because of their race.

The French revolution overthrew despotism, proclaimed the rights of man, and brought freedom to the world. Here indeed was salvation at last! The Jews again believed it with fervor and found it holy. They carried on the movement in distant, backward countries, and everywhere they participated with passion in the national struggles for freedom. Thus the Revolution of 1848 was considered to be virtually a Jewish movement. Yet today, the liberals tolerate their Jewish comrades-in-arms in their ranks only with embarrassment and in irritation, or, without ceremony, they reject them because they fear they will be considered Jew-protectors and are afraid to alienate the people. . . .

[W]e have the right to say to the Jewish socialist leaders [who are anti-Zionist and claim that antisemitism will disappear when socialism and a secular society triumph]: the Reformation broke many chains, those of the Jews it rendered stronger; the Enlightenment freed the spirit, but hatred against the Jews—pardon, against the Semites—they intensified rather than softened; the principles of the French revolution have conquered the world, although the liberals of today indicate to the Jews, whether in a civilized or coarse way, that no one wants their collaboration in the work for political freedom. Socialism will bring the same disappointment as the Reformation, the Enlightenment, and the political reform movement [for democracy and national self-determination in the nineteenth century]. Should we live to see socialist theory become practice, you will be surprised to find once more in the new order your old acquaintance: antisemitism. And it will not help you that Marx and [Ferdinand] Lassalle [founder of the Social Democratic Party of Germany] were Jews. If I may compare something small to something large, very large: the founder of the Christian religion was also a Jew; but it is unbeknownst to me that Christendom on that score feels any gratitude toward the Jews. I do not doubt that the theorists of socialism will remain faithful to their teachings, that they will never turn into racists. Yet as practical leaders they will have to reckon with reality, and in the foreseeable future the feelings of the masses will force an antisemitic—or let us say, a no-Jews [*asemitische*]—policy upon them, just as the leaders of the liberal-minded middle class parties were compelled to accept. Then they will say: socialist solidarity extends only over the higher races, not over the lower ones, and one will simply find the Jewish people in humanity's second class, stuck among the Negroes and the yellow coolies.

May the Jewish proletariat, may the socialist ideologists among the educated Jews, hear and heed our voice. Zionism works for them. . . . Certainly, Zionism affords you the possibility to live up to all your ideals, to enjoy contentment, to vindicate your outlook and philosophy of life, and to uplift your proletarianized, rightless people by normalization.[3]

NOTES

1. Excerpted in "Memorandum Submitted to the Anglo-American Committee of Inquiry," prepared by the Jewish Agency for Palestine (Jerusalem, March 1946), 19-20.

2. From Theodor Herzl, *The Jewish State: An Attempt at a Modern Solution of the Jewish Question* (New York: American Zionist Emergency Council, 1946), 76-77, 85-86, 91-93, 96.

3. From Max Nordau, *Zionistische Schriften* (Berlin: Jüdischer Verlag, 1923), 268-271, trans. Frederick M. Schweitzer for this volume.

SIXTEEN

Persecution and Pogroms in Tsarist Russia

Until Hitler and Nazi Germany, Russia was the classic land of antisemitism and Jewish persecution. Down to 1917 some 650 laws, decrees, ukases, and the like mangled Jewish life in a web of regulations, requirements, and prohibitions. Legal and political emancipation for Jews, which was being enacted throughout Europe during the nineteenth century, appeared an impossibility for the well over five million Jews of autocratic Russia, three-quarters of the world's Jewish population.

A particularly onerous demand was imposed by Nicholas I (1825–1855), who instituted the conscription of Jews for military service—until then they were exempt on payment of a fee. The *kahals* (local governing councils of Jewish communities) were made responsible for drawing up the lists of recruits and sending out the posses to seize boys as young as seven or eight. They were sent to a canton to be prepared for army training by rough-cut drill sergeants who conducted the cantons as forcing houses of Christianization and Russification. Many of the boys died of ill treatment, committed suicide, drowned themselves when being baptized in the river, or like the Marranos of old practiced Christianity by day and Judaism by night. Parents maimed their sons to disqualify them for military service, and the communities were riven by hate and fear because the oligarchic *kahals* favored the well-to-do, well-connected, and influential. Nicholas's policy was Russification of Jews by pitiless coercion.

Alexander II, 1855–1881, the so-called liberal tsar, ended conscription of children and allowed some Jewish students and professionals to reside outside the Pale of Settlement, the region of Russia to which Jews were confined. Reflecting the growth of the *Haskalah* (the Jewish Enlightenment and modernist movement), Jews flocked into Russian-speaking, government-provided schools that ranged from the grades to university. Such schooling was the onset of a marked Russification of some Jews and enabled them to enter the professions and pursue new commercial opportunities. Although excluded from the civil service and the army and navy officer corps, as of the 1860s Jews notably became lawyers, physicians, bankers, pharmacists, engineers, international merchants, journalists, and publishers, and did so far beyond their proportion in the population at large, paralleling developments in central and Western Europe and the United States. Nevertheless, most Jews remained un-Russified and abysmally poor in that land of the *luftmensch* (literally man of air, pauper living by his wits) and *schnorrer* (beggar, often a cringing manner). Jews were little engaged as entrepreneurs in industry owing to the paucity of capital in the Pale and the handicaps posed by bureaucratic regulation, although they had a significant role as sub-contractors and suppliers for railway construction, oil, and chemicals. Industrialization afforded Jews some openings as factory workers, and there was a fairly steady rise to 1914 in the number of craftsmen and artisans.

Such gains as Jews made fed into the phobias about Jewish "scheming" to dominate "the basic population," as the Christian population was referred to in bureaucratese. A principal bearer of antisemitism was "the nascent middle class," which, according to Arcadius Kahan, either feared or lacked the know-how to compete with Jews: "As competitors, the Jewish middle class was formidable, relying upon inherited and acquired experience, knowledge, and adaptability," and above all on "their heightened perception of new opportunities."[1]

The assassination of Alexander II in 1881 triggered pogroms in about 160 Jewish communities, although Jews had very little to do with the murder. Hesia Halfman, a woman, provided a hiding place for the assassins and was the lone Jew involved in the conspiracy, but the government alleged that Jews were the leaders and executors of the plot, thus providing the regime justification for a new batch of anti-Jewish laws. The violence occurred mostly in Russian Poland and Ukraine where local gangs of townsmen and peasants pillaged Jewish homes and shops, punctuating their maraudings with rape and murder for, as many explained to government reporters, the Jews' "murder of the Tsar and economic oppression."[2] The public authorities, both local and central, often stood by, whether out of incompetence or complicity.

There were three great waves of pogroms in Russia, 1881–1884, 1903–1906, and 1917–1921, interspersed with individual explosions or smaller clusters. The standard perception, at the time and since, is that pogroms were planned and perpetrated by the tsarist government as part of its "pogrom system" to distract attention from government failures, economic distress, and military defeats to forestall revolutionaries and striking workers by deflecting discontent onto the hated Jews. This view that the government deliberately instigated pogroms or allowed them to continue out of indifference or antisemitic hatred has been called into question. Certainly almost everyone involved from Tsar Alexander III down was vilely antisemitic. The tsar reportedly rejoiced in his soul whenever he heard that Jews were beaten up. But a law-and-order mentality prevailed in Russia as in Europe in the nineteenth century, and it would have been unlikely, if not unthinkable, to stir up mob anger or mobilize the masses, because they might turn on the authorities. It is also true that police were not much trained in crowd control, the army even less so; sometimes small units of police or soldiers were overwhelmed and retreated, and sometimes they joined the rioters or looters.

As the reaction to the assassination of Alexander II unfolded and a concerted effort was undertaken under Alexander III to bolster the autocracy, the liberal policy of his predecessor of integrating the Jews into Russian society was largely abandoned. Under the "Temporary Rules" of 1882 (they lasted until the revolution of 1917), Jews were progressively blocked by quotas and prohibitions from education and the professions; these developments were paralleled, if not overshadowed, by deepening impoverishment, legal and administrative chicanery, and massive migration out of the country.

After 1884 pogroms tapered off. The government, however, imposed new restrictions on Jews and local officials felt empowered to extort bribes from Jews by threats and blackmail. Russian public opinion, partly under the influence of German and Austrian antisemitic currents, turned increasingly Judaeophobic. Russian Slavophiles, who treasured native ways and traditions, adapted the antisemitic vocabulary slandering Jews as "aliens" and "parasites" who conspired to inflict "the corrupt spirit of the West" and its noxious capitalism on Holy Mother Russia. Revolutionaries like the *Narodniks,* followers of the pathologically antisemitic anarchist Michael Bakunin, adopted much the same view and worked to rouse the peasantry against the *"Zhids."* They saw in the pogroms harbingers of massacre and the revolution to come. With almost no exceptions, Russia's great writers like Tolstoy and Turgenev were notable for their silence (the bitterly and blindly antisemitic Dostoyevsky died in 1881), as was the press for its indifference. While antisemitism in Russia was normally of the religious kind and the Shylock kind, with the Slavophiles and Russifiers it became increasingly nationalistic and in Hans Rogger's words, "as close to racism as it is possible to be without an explicit [pseudo-scientific] theory," such as prevailed in France and Germany.[3]

In the reign of the last tsar, Nicholas II (1894–1917), the government pursued its official policy of antisemitism and the police state emerged more and more clearly. A simple-minded believer in his divine right to rule and a virulent Jew hater, Nicholas financed antisemitic publications and sanctioned accusations of ritual murder. As the revolutionary movement advanced and was paralleled by liberal demands for a constitution and an end to antisemitic policies, the government responded with allegations of an international, Jewish-led plot. These were the circumstances in which the infamous *Protocols of the Learned Elders of Zion* (see page 139) was forged by the tsar's secret police. The violent propaganda scapegoating Jews for every ill and danger incited a series of pogroms that outraged enlightened opinion at home and abroad; of these Kishinev in 1903 (see below) was among the worst.

The regime persisted in disseminating antisemitic propaganda blaming the Jews for the loss of the war with Japan (1904–1905) and igniting revolution, and Nicholas patronized organizations like the Black Hundreds (in many ways a prototype of the Nazi SS) and the Union of the Russian People that incited riots and terror in which the police, Cossack horsemen, and army units participated as well as local authorities, peasants, and artisans. For a time the revolution of 1905 held out the promise that subjection to a police state would be replaced by a constitutional monarchy, and for the first time Jewish emancipation became a subject of public debate. The revolution did lead to the formation of an elected Duma (parliament) and the proclamation of basic rights. The press attacked the Duma as "Jewish," elected by "Jewish money," and wire-pulled by "international Jewry." Not for the first time the intensely antisemitic Russian Orthodox Church took an energetic part in preaching Jew-hatred in the name of tsar, church, and motherland. By 1907 the revolutionary impulse had petered out and the autocracy was restored, although the emasculated Duma continued to meet, and there were few pogroms until World War I, the revolution of 1917, and civil war lasting to 1921.

The Kishinev Pogrom, Easter 1903

None of the many pogroms in the period before World War I had a greater impact on world public opinion than that of Kishinev, the capital of Bessarabia, a province in southwestern Russia. Formerly under Turkish rule, Kishinev's fifty-thousand Jews accounted for over a third of its population. Jews, who had the advantage of education in a population that was overwhelmingly illiterate, were the backbone of the city's economy, being prominent in trade and light industry.

The instigator of the brutal pogrom was Pavolski Khrushevan, a journalist of the Drumont stripe. His newspaper, *The Bessarabian,* which had a virtual monopoly in the province and never had difficulty with the government censor, inflamed the population with a ferocious antisemitic campaign: His headlines screamed out for a "Crusade against the Hated Race," demanded "Death to the Jews," and urged "Down with the Disseminators of Socialism." When a boy was murdered and a girl committed suicide, Khrushevan turned the reports into "proofs" of ritual murder.

Kishinev followed the familiar pattern of pogroms: It began on Easter Sunday and was triggered by rumors and accusations of ritual murder and justified as protest against Jewish domination of the municipal government and the economy. Rioting got out of hand and continued because the incompetent governor delayed until Monday, which was also part of Passover week, to authorize the garrison commander to fully deploy the troops. Berserk mobs in a vengeful fury maimed and killed 44, badly wounded 83, injured, especially as victims of rape, some 500, demolished and pillaged 700 homes and 600 shops, and left 2,000 families ruined. Some police and soldiers stood by indifferently or joined in the pillage. While the interior minister condemned the dithering governor for allowing the disaster to go on for nearly two days and took steps to prevent it from happening again (a pogrom in Gomel later that year was quickly halted), journalists and others explained the assaults as proper punishment for the abuses of the conniving Jews. Rather than the doings of ignorant and exploited peasants (a much-used explanation), it was city workers and craftsmen, competitors of Jewish shops, who wielded the knives and clubs or drove nails through people's eyes. The leaders were students studying to be priests at seminaries, of which there were several in the area. According to the Irish nationalist leader and agricultural reformer Michael Davitt, a non-Jew who traveled extensively in the region, the attackers' motive was fundamentally religious and the method was premeditated. Like many Jews, conscious also of the contemporary Dreyfus Affair in France, Davitt, in *Within the Pale: The True Story of Anti-Semitic Persecutions in Russia* (1903), drew a Zionist lesson from the massacre. Kishinev, he wrote, made him a "convinced believer in the remedy of Zionism." He noted also "the amazing silence" of churchmen, none of whom condemned ritual murder as a false accusation or intervened to halt the cruelty in that Easter season; some even seemed to have given their blessing to the rioters, according to Davitt.

The course of the storm in Kishinev presented in the following account appeared in a report entitled *"Die Judenpogrome in Russland"* (The Jewish Pogroms in Russia) and was prepared by a Zionist organization in London and published in Germany in 1910.

Sunday morning the weather cleared. The Jews were celebrating the last two days of Passover. Not anticipating trouble, they put on their holiday clothes and went to the synagogue. . . .

. . . Suddenly at about 3 PM a crowd of men appeared on the square Novyi Bazar, all dressed in red shirts. The men howled like madmen, incessantly shouting: "Death to the Jews. Beat the Jews." In front of the Moscow Tavern the crowd of some hundred split into several groups of 10-15 men each. There and then the systematic destruction, pillaging, and robbing of Jewish houses and shops began. At first they threw stones in great quantity and force, breaking windows and shutters. Then they tore open doors and windows, breaking into the Jewish houses and living quarters, smashing whatever furniture and equipment they found. The Jews had to hand over to the robbers their jewelry, money, and whatever other valuables they possessed. If they offered the slightest resistance, they were beaten over the head with pieces of their broken furniture. The storerooms were ransacked with special fury. The goods were either carried away or thrown on the street and destroyed. A large crowd of Christians followed the rioters, members of the intelligentsia, officials, students in the theological school, and others. . . .

At 5 PM the first Jew was murdered. The robbers stormed a trolley with a Jewish passenger on board, shouting "Throw out the Jew." The Jew was pushed out and from all sides beaten on his head until his skull cracked and his brains spilled out. At first the sight of a dead Jew seemed to momentarily scare the bandits, but when they saw that the police did not care, they dispersed in all directions, shouting "Kill the Jews!"

On those streets where the pillaging took place Jews had to give up all attempts at self-defense. . . . But on the square Novyi Bazar the Jewish butchers gathered to defend themselves and their families. They bravely fought back and chased away the attackers, who were as cowardly as they were wild. Then the police came and arrested the Jews.

That was the final signal for the organizers of the mob. Until 10 PM the unleashed passions were vented in plunder, robbery, and destruction. Seven other murders took place. . . .

The Jews spent the night from Sunday to Monday in indescribable fear, yet hoping that the terror might be over.

During that night the leaders of the pogrom prepared further attacks, as in war. First the gangs which during the previous evening had arrived from the countryside were equipped with weapons. All weapons were of the same kind: axes, iron bars, and clubs, all strong enough to break doors and shutters, and even metal cabinets and safes. All men wore the same outfit: the red work shirts were worn by all members of the rabble, by peasants, workers, petty bourgeois, even seminary students and police. The second systematic action was the marking of all Jewish houses by the committee organizing the pogrom. During the night all Jewish houses and shops were painted with white chalk. Next came the organization of a permanent information and communication network among the various gangs. Several bicyclists were engaged, who subsequently played an important role. The bicyclists were high school students, theological students, and officials. The organization covered more than the city of Kishinev. Messengers were sent out to the nearest villages inviting the peasants: "Come to the city and help plunder the Jews. Bring big bags." Around 3 AM the preparations were finished. The signal for the attack was given.

The terror that now followed can hardly be described—orgies of loathsome savagery, blood-thirsty brutishness, and devilish lechery claimed their victims. Forty-nine [sic] Jews were murdered in Kishinev. When one hears about the excess of horror, one recognizes that only a few victims were lucky enough to die a simple death. Most of them had to suffer a variety of unbelievable abuse and repulsive torture unusual even among barbarians.

From 3 AM to 8 PM on Monday the gangs raged through the ruins and rubble which they themselves had piled up. They plundered, robbed, destroyed Jewish property, stole it, burned it, devastated it. They chased, slew, raped, and martyred the Jews. Representatives of all layers of the population took part in this witches' Sabbath: soldiers, policemen, officials, and priests; children and women; peasants, workers, and vagabonds.

Major streets resounded with the terrifying roar of murdering gangs and the heartrending cries of the unfortunate victims. . . . The storerooms and shops were robbed, as on the previous day, down to the last item. . . . In the Jewish houses, the gangs burst into the living quarters with murderous howls, demanding all money and valuables. . . . If, however, the Jews could offer nothing or did not respond quickly enough, or if the gangsters were in a murderous mood, the men were knocked down, badly wounded, or killed. The women were raped one after the other in front of their men and children. They tore the arms and legs off the children, or broke them; some children were carried to the top floor and thrown out of the window. . . .

Early Monday morning a Jewish deputation hurried to the Governor of the province to plead for protection. He answered that he could do nothing, since he had no orders from St. Petersburg [the capital]. At the same time he refused to accept private telegrams from St. Petersburg.

The vain appeal of the Jews to the governor was followed by a catastrophic worsening of their fate. The gangs henceforth could count on the patronage of the highest authority. . . .

In ever-rising fury the robbery, murder, and desecration continued. Jews had their heads hacked off. Towels were soaked in their blood and then waved like red flags. The murderers wrote with Jewish blood on white flags in large letters: "Death to the Jews!" They slit open the bodies of men and women, ripped out their guts and filled the hollows with feathers [a frequent motif of pogroms]. They jumped on the corpses and danced, roaring, and drunk with vodka—men and women of "the best society." Officials and policemen laughed at the spectacle and joined in the fun. They beat pregnant women on their stomachs until they bled to death. . . .

They cut off the breasts of women after raping them. . . . Nails were driven into Chaja Sarah Phonarji's nostrils until they penetrated her skull. They hacked off the upper jaw of David Chariton, with all his teeth and his upper lip. Another man, Jechiel Selzer, had his ears pulled off before being beaten on the head until he became insane. . . .

These are some of the inhumanities committed during the pogrom. They are certified as true by eyewitnesses and the testimony of Christian physicians and Russian newspapers, which had passed through the most anti-Semitic and despotic censorship.

The synagogues were stormed and plundered with special spite. In one synagogue the *gabbai* [sexton] braved death in front of the Holy Ark holding the Torah. Dressed in the *tallis* [prayer shawl] and with the *tephalin* [phylacteries] on his forehead, he prepared for the onslaught of the murderers in order to protect the sacred scrolls. He was cut down in the foulest manner. Then they tore, here and elsewhere, the Torah from the holy ark and cut the parchment into small scraps (Christian children later sold them on the streets for a few kopeks as mementos of Kishinev). After that the mobsters demolished, here as elsewhere, the synagogue's interior.

The barbarism of these scenes was so shattering that no less than 13 Jews went out of their minds. . . .

It would be unjust and ungrateful not to mention those Christians who in those days of mad brutality proved themselves true human beings and illustrious exceptions. They deserve to be remembered with special esteem because they were so few.[4]

A Ritual Murder Trial in the Twentieth Century: The Beilis Case—International Protests, 1912

A conference of Russian nobles in 1911 had demanded that the empire must get rid of its Jews, and it listened approvingly to the claims of "experts" that Jews, as ordained by the Talmud, required Christian blood to perform their religious observances and rituals. This was an invitation to accuse. That same year the ultranationalist Union of the Russian People fabricated just such a libel against Mendel Beilis (1874–1934), the superintendent of a brick factory in Kiev and the only Jew living in the vicinity of the site where the body of a thirteen-year-old Christian boy was found. This family man with five children was incarcerated, tortured, and interrogated for nearly two years, as the police and the ministry of justice cooked up "testimonies" and assembled "experts" and "witnesses." In actuality a criminal gang had committed the deed fearing that the youth would inform on them to the police. The tsarist government knew this but hoped a trial and conviction would win support for the regime. The following leaflet was distributed at the youngster's funeral:

Orthodox Christians

The Yids [a derogatory term for Jews] have tortured Andryusha Yu-schinsky to death. Every year, before their Passover, they torture to death several dozens of Christian children in order to get their blood to mix with their *matzos.* They do this in commemoration of our Saviour, whom they tortured to death on the cross. The official doctors found that before the Yids tortured Yuschinsky they stripped him naked and tied him up stabbing him in the principal veins so as to get as much blood as possible. Russians! If your children are dear to you beat up the Yids. Beat them until there is not a single Yid left in Russia. Have pity on your children! Avenge the unhappy martyr! It is time! It is time![5]

By the time the trial began in December 1913, public opinion abroad and in Russia (although decidedly not in Russian Poland) turned against the government, seeing in the trial another episode in the contest that had begun with the revolution of 1905 between the forces of reaction and autocracy and those of modernity and constitutionalism. Famous lawyers (almost none of them Jews because they were virtually barred from legal education and the profession) exposed the prosecution's witnesses and experts as frauds and ignoramuses. The whole story of the sham staging of the trial by the ministry of justice came out in the press at home and abroad, and there were formal interventions and popular protests. Declarations were made by eminent private individuals in Britain, France, Germany, and Russia itself. The signatories asserted unequivocally that the accusation of ritual murder was an inherited medieval superstition that often precipitated mob violence against Jews.

Despite being stacked with prejudiced and near-illiterate peasants, the jury acquitted Beilis on grounds of lack of evidence. It made no pronouncement, however, on the utter falseness of the blood libel, leaving it available for antisemites to continue to peddle. World War I saw the evaporation in Russia of all the goodwill manifest during the trial the year before. Much of the fighting on the eastern front engulfed the Pale of Settlement, and Jews were accused of spying, war profiteering, abetting the German/Austrian cause, and were expelled, tried, and executed for "treason." In later years Beilis sought to live in Palestine but eventually the family moved to the United States, where he wrote his memoirs, *The Story of My Life* (1925).

The British Protest

[The following statement was signed by the Anglican archbishops of Canterbury, York, Armagh, the Catholic archbishop of Westminster, and the heads of other Christian denominations, statesmen, justices, scholars, and editors.]

We desire to associate ourselves with the protests signed in Russia, France, and Germany by leading Christian Theologians, Men of Letters, Scientists, Politicians and others against the attempt made in the City of Kieff [Kiev] to revive the hideous charge of Ritual Murder—known as the "Blood Accusation"—against Judaism and the Jewish people.

Animated by the sincerest friendship for Russia, we can have no idea of meddling with the domestic concerns of that country. Much less do we wish to prejudice in the slightest degree the course of the criminal trial with which this accusation has become identified. In the terms of the published protest of our Russian colleagues and friends and in their intimation that they welcome support from other countries, we have the best assurances that our motives will not be misinterpreted.

The question is one of humanity, civilisation and truth. The "Blood Accusation" is a relic of the days of Witchcraft and Black Magic, a cruel and utterly baseless libel on Judaism, an insult to Western culture and a dishonour to the Churches in whose name it has been falsely formulated by ignorant fanatics. Religious minorities other than the Jews, such as the Early Christians, the Quakers, and Christian Missionaries in China, have been victimised by it. It has been denounced by the best men of all ages and creeds. The Popes, the Founders of the Reformation, the Khalif of Islam, Statesmen of every country, together with all the great seats of learning in Europe, have publicly repudiated it.

It is the more necessary that these testimonies should be renewed because, among the ignorant and inflammable populace of Eastern Europe, the "Blood Accusation" has often given rise to terrible outbreaks of mob violence against the Jews, and there is grave reason to fear that its present resuscitation may endanger many innocent lives in the crowded Jewries of the Russian Empire.

The French Protest

[The following statement was signed by the famed novelist Anatole France and many other "leaders of French opinion."]

The undersigned, friends of Russia and strangers to Judaism, denounce to public opinion the absurd accusation of Ritual Murder brought against the Jew Beilis, of Kieff.

They affirm as follows:

1. That, so far from requiring blood for its rites, the religion of Israel prohibits its use both for ceremonial purposes and for food, and that this absolute prohibition is rigorously respected by all the Jewish sects.

2. That in all ages and in all countries religious minorities have been victims of this same calumny—the early Christians under the Roman Emperors, as well as quite recently the missionaries in China.

They express the hope that such accusations may no longer find credence in any civilised country.

The German Protest

[The following statement was signed by the mayor of Berlin, members of the Reichstag (parliament), and many "other leaders of public opinion."]

Mob agitators have eagerly seized on the crime, and have boldly asserted that the boy Yuschinsky was slaughtered by Jews in order to drain his blood and use it for ritual purposes in obedience to an alleged Jewish religious law. This unscrupulous fiction, spread among the people, has from the Middle Ages until recent times led to terrible consequences. It has incited the ignorant masses to outrage and massacre, and has driven misguided crowds to pollute themselves with the innocent blood of their Jewish fellow-men. And yet not a shadow of proof has ever been adduced to justify this crazy belief. The most esteemed Christian authorities on Jewish literature have proved incontrovertibly that the Jews have never been exhorted by their religion to murder their fellow-men.

We deem it the duty of every one to whose heart the moral progress of mankind is dear to raise his voice against such deplorable absurdities. We thus join in the Protest of the most esteemed Russian scholars, authors, and artists, believing that such a protest should not be limited by frontiers, but should concern the heart of the whole civilised world.

The Russian Protest

[The following statement was signed by members of the Council of State and of the Duma (parliament), professors, politicians, scientists, writers, artists, "and nine illustrious women leaders."]

To the Russian Public, on the blood libel upon the Jews.

In the name of justice, reason and humanity, we raise our voices against this new outbreak of fanaticism and black mendacity. . . .

In connection with the still uninvestigated murder of the boy Yuschinsky at Kieff, the false story of the use of Christian blood by Jews has been sown broadcast once more among the people. This is a familiar device of ancient fanaticism. In the early ages AD, the pagan priests used to accuse the Christians of partaking of the Communion with the blood and flesh of a pagan infant killed for the purpose of the Eucharist. Thus it was that this dark and malicious legend arose. The first blood shed on its account, by the prejudiced sentences of Roman judges and amid the shouts of the ignorant pagan crowd, was the blood of Christians. And the first to disprove it were the Fathers and the teachers of the Christian Church. . . .

But the greatest sufferers from this fiction are the Jews who are scattered among other nations. The *pogroms* caused by it have drawn a trail of blood through the dark history of the Middle Ages. At all time murders happen, the motives and authorship of which are a source of perplexity. Where there is a Jewish population it is a simple matter to explain such crimes by the alleged ritual use of blood. Such a thing excites ignorant superstition, and thus influences the evidence of witnesses, deprives the judges of calmness and impartiality, and leads to judicial errors and *pogroms*.

Frequently the truth has eventually come to light, though too late. Sensible and just men would then be seized by shame and indignation. Many Popes and spiritual and secular rulers have branded the malicious superstition and forbidden the authorities to lend to its investigation a religious meaning. Among us such a ukase [an imperial proclamation] was issued on March 18th, 1817, by the Emperor Alexander I, and was confirmed on January 30th, 1835, in the reign of the Emperor Nicholas I. In 1870 the Greek Patriarch Gregory also condemned the blood legend applied to the Jews, and declared it to be a "disgusting prejudice of men infirm in their faith."

But ukases are mouldering in State archives while superstitions skulk abroad, and now the old lie, fraught with violence and *pogroms*, is being circulated again, even from the tribune of the State Duma.

In this lie there is the ring of the same malice which once incited the blind pagan crowd against the early followers of the Christian doctrine.... Dark and criminal passions always follow in its train, while it always tends to blind the populace and pervert justice.

But sentiments of love and truth must always combat it.[6]

NOTES

1. Arcadius Kahan, *Essays in Jewish Social and Economic History*, Roger Weiss, ed. (Chicago: University of Chicago Press, 1986), 37, 87.

2. Quoted in Hans Rogger, "Conclusion and Overview," in *Pogroms: Anti-Jewish Violence in Modern Russian History*, ed. John D. Klier and Shlomo Lambroza (Cambridge: Cambridge University Press, 1992), 337.

3. Hans Rogger, *Jewish Policies and Right-Wing Politics in Imperial Russia* (Berkeley: University of California Press, 1986), 36.

4. From Marvin Perry et al., eds., *Sources of the Western Tradition* (Boston: Houghton Mifflin, 1999), 2:218-219.

5. From Maurice Samuel, *Blood Accusation: The Strange History of the Beilis Case* (New York: Knopf, 1966), 17.

6. From Cecil Roth, *The Ritual Murder Libel: The Report by Cardinal Lorenzo Ganganelli* (London: Woburn Press, 1935), 101-105.

SEVENTEEN

The Myth of an
International Jewish Conspiracy

"[A]ntisemitism is the father of all conspiracy theory," says Paul Johnson.[1] The earliest Christian texts—the New Testament and Church Fathers—reduce Jews and Judaism to the quintessence of evil, the enemies of all spiritual values. Medieval Christians believed that Jews sought to draw people away from Christ's spiritual message by pandering to their vile materialistic desires. In this way they could realize their aim of destroying Christianity. In the mid-fourteenth century at the time of the Black Plague, it was believed that an international conspiracy of Jews—a "cabal" centering this time in Toledo, Spain—contrived to distribute poison all over Europe in order to pollute the water supply and kill massive numbers of Christians. Jews were attacked, "punished," with a lethal ferocity that recalls the massacres during the Crusades 250 years earlier. In times of crisis conspiracy myths flourish and more recruits flock to them as true believers. During the Reformation, Martin Luther was one of the great transmitters of medieval Jewish conspiracy ideas: The Jews, he believed, were in league with his German enemies and rivals, with the Muslim Turks, and with the popes to destroy his new teaching and Europe with it; Jews, Turks, and popes were the "triple arm of the Antichrist."

For the paranoid believer in conspiracy theory, says Richard Hofstadter, "History *is* a conspiracy, set in motion by demonic forces of almost transcendent power, and what is felt to be needed to defeat it is not the usual methods of political give-and-take, but an all-out crusade."[2] The conspirators are seen as powerful, sinister, and evil agents who engage in secret plots in order to realize their macabre designs. Variously, over the centuries, the conspirators were/are Masons, Catholics and Jesuits, Mormons, the "Slave Power" and anti-abolitionists of the antebellum South, and many more, but above all and most of all the Jew, in Hofstadter's phrase "a perfect model of malice, a kind of amoral superman."[3]

The Jews became indispensable in explaining catastrophes and downfalls in the nineteenth century. They were regarded as the force behind the French Revolution—according to the pioneer conspiracist, the Abbé Barruel, "the most dreadful of crimes"[4]—the revolution of 1848, the depression of 1873, and the assassination of Tsar Alexander II in 1881. It was widely asserted by nationalists on all sides that war was triggered in 1914 by those perennial warmongers, the Jews, particularly the international Jewish bankers. German nationalists attributed their nation's ills to Jewish conspirators: the military defeat and loss of the war, the overthrow of the monarchy, the establishment of the "Jewish" Weimar Republic, the Versailles "diktat" and reparations, the inflation of 1923, the Great Depression of 1929, and everything else that threatened or frustrated the Germans, including the Bolshevik Revolution.

The Protocols of the Learned Elders of Zion, 1890s–1905

A fundamental belief of antisemites is that Jews have formed a secret government that is, at this very moment, conspiring to dominate the world. To support this bizarre assertion, antisemites cite the *Protocols of the Learned Elders of Zion,* "the canonical text in the history of conspiracy theory," which was forged by the tsar's secret police in Paris, possibly as early as the 1890s, certainly by 1903–1905.[5] The forger concocted a tale of an alleged meeting of Jewish elders in the ancient Jewish cemetery of Prague, where, in those eerie surroundings, they plot to take over the world.

First published in 1905, it had Tsar Nicholas II's enthusiastic approval—"What depth of thought!" "How prophetic!" "How perfectly they [the Elders] have fulfilled their plan!" he annotated his copy.[6] At the time Russia was engaged in a catastrophic war with Japan and quaking with revolution and a constitutional crisis that for a period put the monarchy in jeopardy. Nicholas was particularly incensed with Britain, which had been in alliance with Japan since 1902. He blamed the calamitous cycle of events on the Jews.

After World War I, says Richard S. Levy, the work was taken very seriously, even by public figures, as it had been in 1905 by the tsar and the kaiser, for it

> satisfied a deep emotional need in the postwar world, providing a simple, all-embracing explanation for a bewildering series of events. The fall of dynasties, the decline of the aristocracy, bloody wars, national humiliation, the emergence of international communism, worthless currencies, the weakening hold of traditional religion, pornography, the "new woman," jazz, and a host of other unsettling trends were, each and every one, to be accounted for as parts of a well-thought-out Jewish plan.[7]

The *Protocols* remains a staple of antisemites throughout the world—millions of copies in many languages have circulated—even though it was definitively proven by Philip Graves to be a forgery as early as 1921. Since the attacks on the World Trade Center and the Pentagon on September 11, 2001, radical Arab-Islamist clerics have blamed the attacks on the Jews, invoking the *Protocols* as proof. In Muslim countries, the *Protocols* (first translated into Arabic in 1925) stands second only to the Qur'an in the frequency and authority with which it is quoted.

In various versions of the *Protocols,* excerpted below, the anonymous narrator is reportedly the Chief Rabbi, Satan, or Theodor Herzl.

From Protocol No. 1

2. What I am about to set forth, then, is our system. . . .

8. Whether a State exhausts itself in its own convulsions, whether its in-

ternal discord brings it under the power of external foes—in any case it can be accounted as irretrievably lost: it is in our power. The despotism of Capital, which is entirely in our hands, reaches out to it a straw that the State, willy-nilly, must take hold of: if not, it goes to the bottom. . . .

11. The political has nothing in common with the moral. The ruler who is governed by the moral is not a skilled politician, and is therefore unstable on his throne. He who wishes to rule must have recourse both to cunning and to make-believe. Great national qualities, like frankness and honesty, are vices in politics, for they bring down rulers from their thrones more effectively and more certainly than the most powerful enemy. Such qualities must be the attributes of the kingdoms of the *goyim* [Hebrew for Gentiles], but we must in no wise be guided by them. . . .

15. Our power in the present tottering condition of all forms of power will be more invincible than any other, because it will remain invisible until the moment when it has gained such strength that no cunning can any longer undermine it. . . .

22. Behold the alcoholised animals, bemused with drink, the right to an immoderate use of which comes along with freedom. It is not for us and ours to walk that road. The peoples of the *goyim* are bemused with alcoholic liquors; their youth has grown stupid . . . from early immorality, into which it has been inducted by our special agents—by tutors, lackeys, governesses in the houses of the wealthy, by clerks and others, by our women in the places of dissipation frequented by the *goyim*.

23. Our countersign is—Force and Make-believe . . . we must not stop at bribery, deceit and treachery when they should serve towards the attainment of our end. In politics one must know how to seize the property of others without hesitation, if by it we secure submission and sovereignty.

24. . . . [F]or the sake of victory, we must keep to the programme of violence and deception. The doctrine of vengeance is precisely. . . . the means [by which] we shall triumph and bring all governments into subjection to our super-government. It is enough for them to know that we are merciless, for all disobedience will then cease.

25. Far back in ancient times we were the first to cry among the masses of the people the words "Liberty, Equality, Fraternity," words many times repeated since those days by stupid poll-parrots who from all sides round flew down upon these baits and with them carried away the well-being of the world, true freedom of the individual, formerly so well guarded against the pressure of the mob. The would-be wise men of the *goyim*, the intellectuals, could not make anything out of the uttered words in their abstractness; did not note the contradiction of their meaning and inter-relation: did not see that in nature there is no equality, cannot be freedom: that Nature herself has established inequality of minds, of characters, and capacities. . . . [A]nd this aided the success of our cause.

26. In all corners of the earth the words "Liberty, Equality, Fraternity," brought to our ranks, thanks to our blind agents, whole legions who bore our

banners with enthusiasm. And all the time these words were canker-worms at work boring into the well-being of the *goyim*, putting an end everywhere to peace, quiet, solidarity, and destroying all the foundations of the *goya* [Gentile] States. As you will see later, this helped us to our triumph: it gave us the possibility, among other things, of getting into our hands the master card—the destruction of the privileges, or in other words of the very existence of the aristocracy of the *goyim*, that class which was the only defense peoples and countries had against us. On the ruins of the eternal and hereditary aristocracy of the *goyim*, we have set up the aristocracy of our own educated class headed by the aristocracy of money. The qualifications for this aristocracy we have established in wealth, which is dependent upon us, and in the ideas, which our learned elders disseminate.

From Protocol No. 2

2. The administrators, whom we shall choose from among the public, with strict regard to their capacities for servile obedience, will not be persons trained in the arts of government, and will therefore easily become pawns in our game in the hands of men of learning and genius who will be their advisers, specialists bred and reared from early childhood to rule the affairs of the whole world. . . .

3. Do not suppose for a moment that these statements are empty words: think carefully of the successes we attained with Darwinism, Marxism, Nietzsche-ism. To us Jews, at any rate, it should be plain to see what a disintegrating importance these efforts have had upon the minds of the *goyim*. . . .

5. In the hands of the States of to-day there is a great force that creates the movement of thought in the people, and that is the Press. . . . But the *goyim* States have not known how to make use of this force; and it has fallen into our hands. Through the Press we have gained the power to influence while remaining ourselves in the shade; thanks to the Press we have got the gold in our hands. . . .

From Protocol No. 3

1. To-day I may tell you that our goal is now only a few steps off. There remains a small space to cross and the whole long path we have trodden is ready now to close its cycle of the Symbolic Snake, by which we symbolise our people. When this ring closes, all the States of Europe will be locked in its coil as in a powerful vise. . . .

7. We appear on the scene as alleged saviours of the worker from this oppression [poverty] when we propose to him to enter the ranks of our fighting forces—Socialists, Anarchists, Communists—to whom we always give support in accordance with an alleged brotherly rule (of the solidarity of all humanity) of our social masonry. The aristocracy, which enjoyed by law the labour of the workers, was interested in seeing that the workers were well fed,

healthy and strong. We are interested in just the opposite—in the diminution, the killing out of the *GOYIM*. Our power is in the chronic shortness of food and physical weakness of the worker because by all that this implies he is made the slave of our will, and he will not find in his own authorities either strength or energy to set against our will. Hunger creates the right of capital to rule the workers. . . .

8. By want and the envy and hatred which it engenders we shall move the mobs and with their hands we shall wipe out all those who hinder us on our way. . . .

11. *This hatred will be still further magnified by the effects of an economic crisis, which will stop dealing on the exchanges and bring industry to a standstill.* We shall create by all the secret subterranean methods open to us and with the aid of gold, which is all in our hands, *a universal economic crisis whereby we shall throw upon the streets whole mobs of workers simultaneously in all the countries of Europe.* These mobs will rush delightedly to shed the blood of those whom, in the simplicity of their ignorance, they have envied from their cradles, and whose property they will then be able to loot.

12. *"Ours" they will not touch, because the moment of attack will be known to us and we shall take measures to protect our own.* . . .

14. . . . Remember the French Revolution, to which it was we who gave the name of "Great": the secrets of its preparations are well known to us for it was wholly the work of our hands. . . .

16. At the present day we are, as an international force, invincible. . . .

From Protocol No. 5

5. *For a time perhaps we might be successfully dealt with by a coalition of the GOYIM of all the world:* but from this danger we are secured by the discord existing among them whose roots are so deeply seated that they can never now be plucked up. We have set one against another the personal and national reckonings of the *goyim*, religious and race hatreds, which we have fostered into a huge growth in the course of the past twenty centuries. . . . We are too strong—there is no evading our power. *The nations cannot come to even an inconsiderable private agreement without our secretly having a hand in it.*

6. . . . And it was said by the prophets that we were chosen by God Himself to rule the whole earth. God has endowed us with genius that we may be equal to our task. . . . All the machinery of all States go by the force of the engine, which is in our hands, and that engine of the machinery of States is—gold. The science of political economy [was] invented by our learned elders. . . .

From Protocol No. 9

2. . . . Nowadays, if any States raise a protest against us it is only *pro forma* at our discretion and by our direction, *for their anti-Semitism is indispensable to us for the management of our lesser brethren.* . . .

3. For us there are no checks to limit the range of our activity. Our Super-Government subsists in extra-legal conditions, which are described rightly by the energetic and forcible word—Dictatorship. I am in a position to tell you with a clear conscience that at the proper time we, the law-givers, shall execute judgment and sentence, we shall slay and we shall spare, we, as head of all our troops, are mounted on the steed of the leader. We rule by force of will, because in our hands are the fragments of a once powerful party [the Liberals], now vanquished by us. *And the weapons in our hands are limitless ambitions, burning greediness, merciless vengeance, hatreds and malice.*

4. *It is from us that the all-engulfing terror proceeds. We have in our service persons of all opinions, of all doctrines, . . . monarchists, demagogues, socialists, communists, and utopian dreamers of every kind. We have harnessed them all to the task: each one of them on his own account is boring away at the last remnants of authority, is striving to overthrow all established forms of order. . . .*

10. *We have fooled, bemused and corrupted the youth of the goyim by rearing them in principles and theories, which are known to us to be false although it is by us that they have been inculcated.*

From Protocol No. 10

9. When we introduced into the State organism the poison of Liberalism, its whole political complexion underwent a change. States have been seized with a mortal illness—blood poisoning. All that remains is to await the end of their death agony.

From Protocol No. 11

4. The *goyim* are a flock of sheep, and we are their wolves. And you know what happens when the wolves get hold of the flock? . . .

8. God has granted to us, His Chosen People, the gift of the dispersion, and in this which appears in all eyes to be our weakness, has come forth all our strength, which has now brought us to the threshold of sovereignty over all the world.

9. There now remains not much more for us to build up on the foundation we have laid.

From Protocol No. 12

8. Literature and journalism are two of the most important educative forces, and therefore our government will become proprietor of the majority of the journals. This will . . . put us in possession of a tremendous influence upon the public mind. . . . thereby creating confidence in us and bringing over to us quite unsuspicious opponents, who will thus fall into our trap and be rendered harmless. . . .

12. All our newspapers will be of all possible complexions—aristocratic,

republican, revolutionary, socialist, even anarchical. . . . Like the Indian god Vishnu they will have a hundred hands, and every one of them will have a finger on any one of the public opinions as required. When a pulse quickens these hands will lead opinion in the direction of our aims. . . . Those fools who will think they are repeating the opinion of a newspaper of their own camp will be repeating our opinion or any opinion that seems desirable for us. In the vain belief that they are following the organ of their party they will in fact follow the flag which we hang out for them.

From Protocol No. 14

1. When we come into our kingdom it will be undesirable for us that there should exist any other religion than ours of the One God, with whom our destiny is bound up by our position as the Chosen People and through whom our same destiny is united with the destinies of the world. We must therefore destroy all other religions. . . .

5. *In countries known as progressive and enlightened we have created a senseless, filthy, abominable literature.* For some time after our entrance to power we shall continue to encourage this pornography in order to provide a telling relief by contrast to the speeches, party programme, which will be distributed from exalted quarters of ours. . . . Our wise men, already trained to become leaders of the *goyim*, will compose speeches, projects, memoirs, articles, which will be used by us to influence the minds of the *goyim*, directing them towards such understanding and forms of knowledge as determined by us.

From Protocol No. 15

7. If we have been able to bring them [non-Jews] to such a pitch of stupid blindness, is it not a proof and an amazingly clear proof, of the degree to which the mind of the *goyim* is undeveloped in comparison with our mind? This it is, mainly, which guarantees our success.[8]

Henry Ford

The International Jew, *1920*

In 1920 the *Dearborn Independent,* a newspaper owned by Henry Ford, printed a series of antisemitic articles endorsing the thesis of the *Protocols of the Learned Elders of Zion* that Jews were secretly conspiring to conquer the world. The articles were quickly published in book form as *The International Jew* (1920), which became an instant bestseller—a half-million copies were soon in circulation. Although the articles were not actually written by Ford but by others assigned the task and each volume appeared anonymously, it was always known to be his initiative and responsibility. Faced with a libel suit and sure defeat, in 1927 Ford publicly recanted his views and apologized to the Jewish people for any hurt he might have caused them. But the damage had been done: Antisemitism had been backed by a famous and popular American. During the hard times of the Great Depression of 1929 when antisemitism in the United States grew significantly more menacing, several demagogues made use of Ford's work. In Germany Hitler pronounced himself a disciple of Ford and in German translation *The International Jew* sold "by the ton" as a Nazi Party publication. In Brezhnev's Soviet Union and the contemporary Arab-Islamic Middle East, *The International Jew* was updated as "World Zionism." Translated into Arabic, Ford's work, Hitler's *Mein Kampf,* the *Protocols,* and the nineteenth-century allegation of ritual murder, August Rohling's *The Talmud Jew,* circulate widely as the four most authoritative sources on the "Jewish-Zionist question." Despite occasional protestations that he was no antisemite and did not wish to harm Jews, Ford, steadfast in the tradition of the *Protocols,* blamed the Jews for World War II. (The Ford family has since made amends to Jews and done much to combat antisemitism.)

The following excerpts from *The International Jew* repeat the myth of Jewish economic domination and demonstrate how heavily the work relied on the *Protocols.*

The Jew is the world's enigma. Poor in his masses; he yet controls the world's finances. Scattered abroad without country or government, he yet presents a unity of race continuity which no other people has achieved. Living under legal disabilities in almost every land, he has become the power behind many a throne. There are ancient prophecies to the effect that the Jew will return to his own land and from that center rule the world, though not until he has undergone an assault by the united nations of mankind.

The single description which will include a larger percentage of Jews than members of any other race is this: he is in business. It may be only gathering rags and selling them, but he is in business. From the sale of old clothes to the control of international trade and finance, the Jew is supremely gifted for business. More than any other race he exhibits a decided aversion to industrial employment, which he balances by an equally decided adaptability to trade. . . .

. . . In America alone most of the big business, the trusts and the banks, the natural resources and the chief agricultural products, especially tobacco, cotton and sugar, are in the control of Jewish financiers or their agents. Jewish journalists are a large and powerful group here. "Large numbers of department stores are held by Jewish firms," says the *Jewish Encyclopedia,* and many if not most of them are run under Gentile names. Jews are the largest and most numerous landlords of residence property in the country. They are supreme in the theatrical world. They absolutely control the circulation of publications throughout the country. . . .

The strength of Jewish money is in its internationalism. It stretches a chain of banks and centers of financial control across the world, and plays them on the side of the game that favors Judah. This center was, and for the moment is, in Germany, at Frankfurt-on-the-Main, but feverish anxiety now accompanies the fear that it may have to be moved. Destiny is overtaking the Jewish World Power. The gold which is their god—"the God of the living" is what they call their god—is being brought overseas on every available ship and locked up in the vaults of Jewish bankers in North and South America, not to enrich this hemisphere but to mobilize Jewish financial power for any desperate stroke. Financial Jewry is afraid. It has a right to be afraid. Its conscience, still bloody from the war whose gains have not yet stopped, is in a troubled state. . . .

It is not . . . the success of the individual Jewish banking house that concerns us. Flabby-minded non-Jews who have been blinded by pro-Jewish propaganda find difficulty in seeing that point. They say that the individual Jewish businessman has as much right to his business success as has anyone else. Which is a perfect Jewish platitude! Certainly he has. Whoever stated that he had not? But when you are dealing with a world chain of financial consulates, all of them linking up in a world system, none of them to be regarded as American banks, or British banks, or French banks, or Italian banks, or German banks, but all of them members of the Jewish World Banking System, you are obviously not dealing with individuals who are trying to make a living. You are then dealing with a mighty force for good or ill, and thus far, sad truth to know, the ill is mountainous in comparison. . . .

The reader of the *Protocols* is much impressed by the financial notes that are sounded throughout their proposals. The Jewish defense against the *Protocols*, that they were written by a criminal or madman, is intended only for those who have not read the *Protocols*, or who have overlooked the financial plans they offer. Madmen and criminals do not coolly dissect one money system and invent another, as do the Protocolists.

It will be worthwhile, in view of the sidelights that these articles have thrown on the money question, to recall some of the forecasts and plans made in these most remarkable documents which have been attributed to the Wise Men of Zion, the world leaders of the inner council. . . .

Protocol VI is interesting in this connection:

> "We shall soon begin to establish huge monopolies, colossal reservoirs of wealth, upon which even the big Gentile properties will be dependent to such an extent that they will all fall, together with the government credit, on the day following the political catastrophe."

Although these words were written with Europe in view (the United States not yet having been Judaized) their import is clear. At the present moment the number of business concerns in the hands of Jewish creditors, through "loans," is very large. The Jewish idea in business is to "borrow," instead of making the business stand on its own feet. The trail of that idea is seen all over our land today. . . .

. . . The Jewish program profited by the split which Jewish ideas had been able to make between the upper and lower classes of "Gentile" society. "Divide and Rule" is the Jewish motto, as quoted in the *Protocols*. "Divide the working class from the directing class. Divide the Catholic and Protestant churches."

In brief divide Christendom on economic, creedal, social and racial lines, while the Jew remains a solid body, able because of his solidarity to handle a divided world. And this plan has succeeded. Out of the disorder of the World War look how high the government of Judah has been placed in Russia, Austria, Germany, France, Italy, England and in the United States.

All the Jewish bankers are still in Russia. It was only the non-Jewish bankers who were shot and their property confiscated. Bolshevism has not abolished Capital; it has only stolen the Capital of the "Gentiles." And that is all that Jewish socialism or anarchism or Bolshevism is designed to do. Every banker who is caricatured with dollar marks on his clothes is a "Gentile" banker. Every capitalist publicly denounced in Red parades is a "Gentile" capitalist. Every big strike—railroad, steel, coal—is against "Gentile" industry. That is the purpose of the Red movement. It is alien, Jewish and anti-Christian. . . .

. . . The Jewish expectation of World Rule is, of course, absurd, although the mass of Jews sincerely hold it. Their condemnation is that they regard every degeneracy in society as bringing them a step nearer their goal, which explains the great assistance they give to all degenerative processes.

> "When we ascend the thrones of the world, such financial expediencies, not being in accord with our interest, will be definitely eliminated." . . .

The international Jewish banker who has no country but plays them all against one another, and the international Jewish proletariat that roams from land to land in search of a peculiar type of economic opportunity, are not figments of the imagination except to the non-Jew who prefers a lazy laxity of mind.

Of these classes of Jews, one or both are at the heart of the problems that disturb the world today. The immigration problem is Jewish. The money question is Jewish. The tie-up of world politics is Jewish. The terms of the [Versailles] Peace Treaty are Jewish. The diplomacy of the world is Jewish. The moral question in movies and theaters is Jewish. The mystery of the illicit liquor business is Jewish.[9]

Nesta Webster

Drawing-Room Antisemitism, 1920s

The indefatigable English researcher and "queen of conspiracy theorists," Nesta Helen Webster (1876–1960) was born into an immensely wealthy family of Christian fundamentalists. She was essentially self-educated, an autodidact of a kind familiar in the annals of antisemitism. In 1910 she suffered a religious crisis that induced her to believe that she was the reincarnation of a French countess whose family had suffered at the hands of the French revolutionaries. Between 1916 and 1938 Webster wrote five books—at least one of them a bestseller—on the French Revolution, which featured the conspiratorial influence of Illuminism and Freemasonry. Webster reduced European history to the story of the "World Revolution," "a deep-laid conspiracy" that was propelled by an "occult force [that is] terrible, unchanging, relentless, and wholly destructive, [and] constitutes the greatest menace that has ever confronted the human race"; it is "the plot against [Christian] civilization." The primum mobile of the "World Revolution," according to Webster, was the Illuminati, a society founded in Bavaria about 1776 by Adam Weishaupt and dedicated to rationalism; organized on the model of the Jesuits and Freemasonry, it conspired, she says, to abolish monarchy and aristocracy, church and religion, private property and inheritance, and to replace marriage and family by free love and institutional rearing of children, and patriotism by internationalism. The society was dissolved in 1785 by order of the Bavarian ruler and presumably came to an end. Instead, she says, Illuminism furtively preserved itself by "illuminizing" the Masons, meaning that Illuminati doctrines, teachings, and methods were grafted on to Freemasonry's organization, which itself had emerged secretly from the surreptitiously reconstituted Knights Templar of the Middle Ages.[10]

Illuminism-Freemasonry's vehicles were the French Enlightenment and the Revolution of 1789. A plethora of revolutionaries and secret societies, Webster maintained, engulfed Europe after the revolution. These secret societies, "under orders from a profusion of invisible chiefs" and making use equally of "dupes" and "adepts," directed the "World Revolution." Among the gravest threats was "the disintegrating doctrines of international socialism" that culminated in Lenin and the Bolshevik Revolution of 1917. Stretching over "the civilized world," this vast conspiratorial network had "penetrate[d] every sphere of human endeavour—art, literature, education, women's movements, religious movements—and gain[ed] control of the means of publicity—the press, the theatre, the cinema, and also broadcasting"; unless countermeasures were taken, all civilization would be "submerged."[11]

By 1850 the part played by the Jews in the great "World Revolution" began to be "as clear as day" to Webster. They had been gaining "power" since the 1780s, when by a "mole-like" process they began to filter into the Masonic lodges and other secret societies, gradually ascending the ranks to positions of leadership and control. The French Revolution delivered the people from the nobility and church only to hand them over to the Jews, whose emancipation was a conspiratorial proceeding inspired by Illuminism-infected leaders. In the 1790s Jews were "working below ground," but emerged as "the driving force behind the Masonic insurrection of 1848" in Germany. Their essential function was "the building up of capitalism."[12] Webster quotes extensively from the economic historian and later Nazi adherent Werner Sombart (see page 82), that it was largely the Jews who invented capitalism, what she calls "Super-Capitalism," as a conspiratorial instrument of exploitation and control, introduced "cut-throat competition," and monopolized money-lending. Jews and "the Judaized plutocracy"—all "leeches"—exploited the workers and peasants by "usury." The Rothschilds began as kings of the "loan-floaters," then became monarchs of the railroads, and finally, "There is only one power in Europe, and that is Rothschild." Accordingly, "the Jews are not genuine revolution-

aries, but only throw themselves into revolutions for their own ends. While profess-
ing to believe in Liberty and Equality they secretly deride such ideas, but make use
of them to destroy existing governments in order to establish their own domination in religion, property, and power."[13]

In 1921 Webster described Soviet Bolshevism as "a wholly Jewish movement."
As for the *Protocols,* she accepted Philip Graves's proof of its being a forgery, but
felt that the *Protocols* did "represent the programme of world revolution," as was
visible in its "prophetic nature" and "extraordinary resemblance to the protocols
of certain secret societies in the past." In *Secret Societies and Subversive Movements,*
she declared that "the immense problem of the Jewish power [is] perhaps the most
important problem with which the modern world is confronted"; the Jew would
use this power "to achieve world-domination and to obliterate the Christian faith."
Although the Jews were scattered and divided among themselves over the world,
they nevertheless unite "like quicksilver," for "there is immense solidarity" among
them, which "constitutes the real Jewish Peril."[14] Once Hitler came to power in
1933, Webster turned from Germanophobe to Germanophile and remained as
antisemitic as ever. She wrote in an April 1933 magazine article "That Hitler is doing the best thing for Germany seems at present undeniable" and scoffed at Nazi
persecution of Jews as exaggerated or false.[15] But in the aftermath of *Kristallnacht*
(night of glass), the pogrom of November 9–10, 1938, and the most violent antisemitic explosion in Germany since the Crusades, she felt Hitler had gone too far,
but she managed to find extenuating circumstances and retracted nothing.

Many of Webster's conspiratorial works remain in print and provide a scholarly
facade for antisemites, Holocaust deniers, opponents of the Second Vatican Council's reforms, particularly its declaration on Catholic-Jewish relations *Nostra Aetate*
(see page 219), and conspiracists of all stripes, many of whom, ironically, she
would have opposed. A recent bestselling book that shows Webster's influence is
The New World Order (1991) by Rev. Pat Robertson, the American founder of the
Christian Coalition. His work relies on several well-known antisemitic texts, particularly Webster's writings, frequently reproducing whole paragraphs from them
but without benefit of quote marks or citations. While his book makes only scattered references to Jews, it warns against a dire conspiracy to create a "global, socialist, dictatorial-oriented society" created by international bankers and specula-
tors, terms which are often code words for Jews.[16] Robertson hints at a Jewish link
between "Illuminated Freemasonry" and "World Communism," and reiterates the
libel that "a Wall Street banker such as Jacob Schiff of Kuhn, Loeb and Company
could personally transport $20 million in gold to help salvage the near-bankrupt
government of the new Soviet Russia."[17] He also makes the strange accusation that
the Rothschilds conspired to control the central bank of the United States until it
was abolished in 1836, but that in 1913 international bankers did succeed in creating the Federal Reserve System, "an instrument of immense power." Its architect
was another German-Jewish banker, Paul Warburg, a Rothschild agent and partner
of Schiff in Kuhn, Loeb & Co. Robertson claimed that his book does not invoke any
conspiracy theory of history, and he denied any antisemitic intent, reiterated his "al-

liance" with Jews, his support for Israel, and his assistance to Holocaust survivors, and regretted the offense he gave. That these stale conspiratorial theories propagated by Webster and others were employed by someone who considers himself a friend of the Jewish people shows the enduring power and appeal of these fantasies.

The following attack on Jews as international conspirators is excerpted from the chapter "The Real Jewish Peril" in Webster's *Secret Societies and Subversive Movements*.

"The Real Jewish Peril," 1924

In considering the immense problem of the Jewish Power, perhaps the most important problem with which the modern world is confronted, it is necessary to divest oneself of prejudices and to enquire in a spirit of scientific detachment whether any definite proof exists that a concerted attempt is being made by Jewry to achieve world-domination and obliterate the Christian faith.

That such a purpose has existed amongst the Jews in the past has been shown throughout the earlier chapters of this book. The conception of the Jews as the Chosen People who must eventually rule the world forms indeed the basis of Rabbinical Judaism. . . .

. . . [T]he Jewish religion now takes its stand on the Talmud rather than on the Bible. . . . The Talmud itself accords to the Bible only a secondary place. . . .

Now, the Talmud is not a law of righteousness for all mankind, but a meticulous code applying to the Jew alone. No man being outside the Jewish race could possibly go to the Talmud for help or comfort. In the Talmud [Webster quotes an "authority" in the vein of Eisenmenger (see page 49)], "the precepts of justice, of equity, of charity towards one's neighbour, are not only not applicable with regard to the Christian, but constitute a crime in anyone who would act differently. . . . The Talmud expressly forbids one to save a non-Jew from death, . . . to restore lost goods, etc., to him, to have pity on him. . . ."

But it is in the Cabala [Kabbalah, the vast corpus of Jewish mysticism], still more than in the Talmud, that the Judaic dream of world-domination recurs with the greatest persistence. The *Zohar* [the principal book of the Kabbalah] indeed refers to this as a *fait accompli*, explaining that "the Feast of Tabernacles is the period when Israel triumphs over the other people of the world; that is during this feast we [claim] that we have conquered all the other peoples known as 'populace' and that we dominate them." . . .

The hope of world-domination is therefore not an idea attributed to the Jews by "anti-Semites," but a very real and essential part of their traditions. What then of their attitude to Christianity in the past? . . . [H]atred of the person and teaching of Christ did not end at Golgotha but was kept alive by the Rabbis and perpetuated in the Talmud and the *Toledot Yeshu* [a polemical attack on Christianity in the form of a scurrilous, mocking biography of Jesus; it was not written by the rabbis and has no formal status in Judaism]. The Cabala also contains passages referring both to Christ and to Mohammed so unspeakably foul that it would be impossible to quote here. . . .

It is thus not in the law of Moses thundered from Sinai, not in the dry ritual of the Talmud, but in the stupendous imaginings of the Cabala, that the real dreams and aspiration of Jewry have been transmitted through the ages. . . .

Thus even the Word of God itself is powerless to mitigate the immense megalomania of the Jewish race. . . .

It is here that we must surely see the cause of much of the suffering the Jews have endured in the past. No one of course would justify the cruelty with which they have frequently been treated; nevertheless to maintain there was no provocation on the part of the Jews would be absurd. . . . Moreover, to represent the Jews as a gentle long-suffering people, always the victims but never the perpetrators of violence, is absolutely contrary to historic fact. In the dark ages of the past the Jews showed themselves perfectly capable of cruelties not only towards other races but towards each other.

It is futile then to maintain as do the Jews and their friends . . . that all the faults of the modern Jew are to be attributed to bitterness engendered by persecution. Judaism has always contained an element of cruelty which finds expression in the Talmud. . . .

To attribute the persecution of the Jews to Christianity is . . . ludicrous. . . .

. . . Is there, then, any evidence that there exists amongst Jewry to-day an organized conspiracy, having for its objects world-domination and the destruction of Christianity such as the famous *Protocols of the Elders of Zion* suggest?

The theory of a Jewish world-conspiracy does not, of course, rest on the evidence of the *Protocols*. To judge by the paean of joy that rang through the press after the publication of *The Times* articles [by Philip Graves proving the *Protocols* a forgery], one would imagine that with the so-called "refutation" of this one document the whole case against the Jews had collapsed and that the "anti-Semites" must be forever silenced. But the arguments of the Jews and their friends go further than this; not only do they claim there is no Jewish conspiracy, but no world-plot of any kind. . . .

. . . What is this but a clear recognition of the Hidden Hand? Setting all such evidence as the *Protocols* completely aside, let us examine the reasons for believing in the existence of the Jewish world-conspiracy. Now, we know for certain that the five powers before referred to—Grand Orient Masonry, Theosophy, Pan-Germanism, International Finance, and Social Revolution—have a very real existence and exercise a very definite influence on the affairs of the world. Here we are dealing not with hypothesis but with facts based on documentary evidence. We know in each case the names of many of the leaders, their methods of organization, their centres of action, and the aims they are pursuing. . . .

Whether then the Jewish power is unified or not, Jews are to be found cooperating with, if not directing, all the five powers of which the existence is known. . . .

The role of Jews in social revolution and particularly in Bolshevism hardly needs comment. . . . [T]he founder and patron saint of Bolshevism was the Jew Karl Marx. . . .

In view of [official reports], how is it possible for the Jewish press to pretend that a connexion between Jews and Bolshevism is a malicious invention of the "anti-Semites"? That all Jews are not Bolsheviks and that all Bolsheviks are not Jews is of course obvious; but that Jews are playing a preponderating part in Bolshevism it is absurd to deny. . . .

The influence of the Jews in all the five great powers at work in the world— Grand Orient Masonry, Theosophy, Pan-Germanism, International Finance, and Social Revolution—is not a matter of surmise but of fact. Let us now examine what part they are playing in the minor subversive movements. . . .

Freud, the inventor of the most dangerous form of Psychoanalysis, is a Jew.

[Webster says that psychoanalysis has been controlled by Jews from its inception. She then takes up "degenerate art" and "the deification of ugliness" with which Jews are closely associated, characterizing their work as "inverted and distorted," "hideous," and "sordid." Such art, she thinks, is linked to a Jewish "tendency to perversion." She then links Jews to other "subversive movements."]

The same influence will be noticed in the cinema world, where . . . history is systematically falsified in the interests of class hatred, and everything that can tend, whilst keeping within the present law, to undermine patriotism or morality is pressed upon the public. And the cinema trade is almost entirely in the hands of the Jews.

In the drug traffic Jews are playing a prominent part both here and in America. . . .

Enough, then, has been said to show that, whether as agents or as principals, Jews are playing a part in all subversive movements. . . . At present they are the greatest danger that Christian civilization has to face. . . .

. . . [O]f course [not] all Jews are destructive. Undoubtedly there are good and loyal Jews. . . . But these isolated individuals carry little weight compared to the massed forces of subversive Jewry. . . .

The fact is that the whole educational as well as the whole political and social world is permeated with Jewish influence. Every man in public life, every modern politician, to whatever party he belongs, seems to find it *de rigueur* to have his confidential Jewish adviser at his elbow. . . . This appears to be owing not only to the utility of the Jew in financing projects, but to the almost universal belief in the superior intelligence of the Jewish race which the Jew has succeeded in implanting in the Gentile mind.

But the time has come to ask: Is the Jew really the superman we have been taught to consider him? On examination, we shall find that in the present as in the past his talents are displayed principally along two lines—financial and occult. Usurers in the Middle Ages, financiers to-day, the Jews have always excelled in the making and manipulating of wealth. And just as at the former period they were the great masters of magic, so at the present time they are the masters of the almost magical art of gaining control over the mind both of the individual and of the public. . . .

The Jews, then, provide a high average of cleverness, but have they ever during the last two thousand years produced one mighty genius? Moreover, against this high average of intelligence must be set an equally high average of mental derangement. . . .

. . . At any rate, it is curious to notice that the two symptoms recognized in the first stages of "general paralysis of the insane," the mania that one is the object of persecution and "exalted ideas" . . . are the two obsessions that the Talmud and the Cabala with their dreams of world-domination under an avenging Messiah have inculcated in the mind of the Jew.

But whatever are the causes of this neurosis, it is surely undesirable that a race which exhibits it should be allowed to control the destinies of the British Empire or indeed of any country. . . .

. . . [Emancipation, equality, and privileges are] to a section of Jewry merely a stage on the road to world-domination. For if, as we have seen by documentary evidence, this plan has always existed in the past, is it likely that it has been abandoned at the very moment which seems most propitious for its realization? . . .

To sum up, then, I do not think that the Jews can be proved to provide the sole cause of world-unrest. . . .

But this is not to underrate the importance of the Jewish peril. Although the existence of an inner circle of Masonic "Elders" remains problematical, Jewry in itself constitutes the most effectual Freemasonry in the world. What need of initiations, or oaths, or signs, or passwords amongst people who perfectly understand each other and are everywhere working for the same end? Far more potent than the sign of distress that summons Freemasons to each other's aid at moments of peril is the call of the blood that rallies the most divergent elements in Jewry to the defense of the Jewish cause.

The old complaint . . . would thus appear to be justified, that "the Jews are particles of quicksilver, which at the least slant run together into a block." One must therefore not be deceived by the fact that they often appear disunited. There may be, and indeed is, very little unity amongst Jews, but there is immense solidarity. . . .

It is this solidarity that constitutes the real Jewish Peril and at the same time provides the real cause of "anti-Semitism." If in a world where all patriotism, all national traditions, and all Christian virtues are being systematically destroyed by the doctrines of International Socialism one race alone, a race that since time immemorial has cherished the dream of world-power, is not only allowed but encouraged to consolidate itself, to maintain all its national traditions, and to fulfill all its national aspirations at the expense of other races, it is evident that Christian civilization must be eventually obliterated. . . . Those of us who, sacrificing popularity and monetary gain, dare to speak out on this question have no hatred in our hearts, but only love for our country. We believe that not only our national security but our great national traditions are at stake, and that unless England awakens in time she will pass under alien domination and her influence as the stronghold of Christian civilization will be lost to the world.

[In her conclusion Webster prescribes that] a "Department for the Investigation of Subversive Movements" should have a place in every ordered government.[18]

NOTES

1. Paul Johnson, "Marxism and the Jews," in *Antisemitism in the Contemporary World*, ed. Michael Curtis (London: Westview Press, 1986), 39.

2. Richard Hofstadter, *The Paranoid Style in American Politics and Other Essays* (New York: Knopf, 1966), 14, 29.

3. Hofstadter, *The Paranoid Style*, 31.

4. Quoted in Hofstadter, *The Paranoid Style*, 12.

5. Stephen Eric Bronner, *A Rumor about the Jews* (New York: St. Martin's, 2000), 130; according to the Russian historian Michael Lepechin, who had access to the Moscow archives, the forger was the secret agent Mathieu Golowinski.

6. Quoted in Bronner, *A Rumor about the Jews*, 91.

7. Richard S. Levy, *Antisemitism in the Modern World: An Anthology of Texts* (Lexington, Mass.: D. C. Heath: 1991), 148.

8. From *The Protocols of the Learned Elders of Zion*, trans. Victor E. Marsden (Los Angeles: Christian Nationalist Crusade [an organization of the extremist Protestant antisemite Gerald L. K. Smith], n.d.); for clarity a few verbal changes have been made.

9. From *The International Jew: The World's Foremost Problem, Being a Reprint of a Series of Articles Appearing in* The Dearborn Independent *from May 22 to October 2, 1920*, 4 vols. (N.p.: n.p., 1920), 1: 10–11; 4: 193–199, 203; 3: 243.

10. Nesta H. Webster, *Secret Societies and Subversive Movements* (New York: Dutton, n.d. [1924]), chap. 2.

11. Nesta H. Webster, *The Socialist Network* (London: n.p., 1926), 132.

12. Webster, *Secret Societies*, 165.

13. Webster, *Secret Societies*, 161.

14. Webster, *Secret Societies*, 369, 382, 400–401, 404.

15. Quoted in Richard Gilman, *World Revolution: The Strange Career of Nesta H. Webster* (Ann Arbor, Mich.: Insight Books, 1982), 1: 49.

16. For some of the problematical passages, see Pat Robertson, *The New World Order* (Dallas: World Publishing, 1991), 65, 69, 71, 73, 121, 123, 178, 181, 183; see also Michael Lind, "Rev. Robertson's Grand International Conspiracy Theory," *New York Review of Books*, 42 (Feb. 2, 1995): 21–25; Michael Lind and Jacob Heilbrun, "On Pat Robertson," *New York Review of Books*, 42 (April 20, 1995), 67–71; Ephraim Radner, "New World Order, Old World Anti-Semitism," *Christian Century*, 112, 26 (Sept. 13–20, 1995): 844–849.

17. Rather than Robertson's fantasy, Schiff had loaned a million rubles to the Provisional Government of Alexander Kerensky but had to write it off when that moderate government was overthrown in November 1917 by Lenin and the communists. Actually, Schiff made smaller amounts available to parties opposed to the communist regime,

but in the 1920s and 1930s a standard antisemitic canard claimed that Schiff under-wrote the regime with a $12 million loan, which metamorphosed in Robertson's regur-gitation into $20 million in gold delivered in person. See Naomi W. Cohen, *Jacob H. Schiff: A Study in American Jewish Leadership* (Hanover, N.H.: University Press of New England, 1999), 244-245.

18. From Webster, *Secret Societies*, 370-371, 374-380, 382-385, 387, 392-399, 401-402.

EIGHTEEN

The Intensification of German Antisemitism after World War I

By 1914 what Paul Lawrence Rose calls "revolutionary antisemitism" was adopted by large segments of the German ruling elites and lower middle classes; it saturated the military, judiciary, civil service, and university faculties, indeed, the teaching profession at all levels.[1] Although no antisemitic laws were enacted and antisemitic political parties declined, antisemitism had gained intellectual credence and academic respectability. In 1892 the powerful German Conservative Party grafted antisemitism onto its platform, declaring war on the Jews' "decomposing influence." In the 1912 elections the Social Democrats became the largest single party in the Reichstag, a result that panicked the Conservatives, who responded with even more venomous antisemitism: They proclaimed that the elections were bought with "Jewish gold," demanded that Jews be barred from political life, called for a military despotism to punish the Jews and socialists—they should be "strung up," mouthed Kaiser Wilhelm—and applauded the Pan-German leader Heinrich Class's (see page 118) assertions that one day soon all German Jews would have to be expelled, that indeed they "might have to be wholly eliminated. . . . It is a matter of saving the German soul."[2]

With all its destruction and dislocation, World War I stimulated a new wave of antisemitism in Germany as it did almost everywhere in the Western world. Despite the patriotism of German Jews (twelve thousand were war fatalities), anti-Jewish feeling mounted sharply well before the war's end. Defeat brought the circulation of the stab-in-the-back myth that Jews and socialists had sabotaged the war effort and fostered defeatism. Such hatred and accusation were magnified by the revolution of 1918 that overthrew the kaiser and created a republic, by the Versailles treaty and reparations settlement that were considered to be unjust and humiliating, and by the runaway inflation of the early 1920s that ruined the middle classes. Under the weight of such pressures, antisemitism became cruder and more violent. The philologist and diarist Victor Klemperer (1881–1960) recorded a conversation in September 1919 that gave him an "insight into the horrible [anti-]Jewish agitation that is shamelessly and threateningly being conducted throughout Germany. It is frightening. No one here takes me [a convert] for a Jew. Good people, educated people and so susceptible to this crazy agitation. It is frightening. The Jew is guilty of everything: the war, the revolution, Bolshevism, capitalism, everything. Enlighten them and they see it, but certainly tomorrow they are roused again."[3]

One response to Germany's defeat in the war was the tremendous proliferation of right-wing extremist organizations, each antisemitic in one form or another, ranging from those that were antisemitic entities pure and simple to those that used it as a propaganda weapon. These radical groups—well over four hundred of them had sprung up—overlapped in membership, underwent much fusion and fission, disappeared or changed their name but not essence: They remained dedicated to the violent overthrow of the "Jewish Republic" and the solution of the "Jewish question." The principal ingredients of their ideological brew were Volkish nationalism, "Nordic" racialism, anti-"Jewish capitalism," anti-"Jewish communism," anti-"Jewish predominance in government and public life," and traditional Christian antisemitism. The *Protocols* was the only new element in postwar German antisemitism, once it had been carried to Germany from Russia by Whites— great agricultural estate owners, military officers, and government officials, among others—fleeing the revolution and civil war.

In invective, often marked by conspiratorial delusions, antisemites denounced the Weimar Republic as "Jewish" because the principal author of its constitution was a Jewish professor of political science, Hugo Preuss, and supposedly the government was run by, for, and of Jews. But none of its presidents or chancellors and only five cabinet members (including Preuss) over the whole length of the Weimar Republic were Jews. The best known was Walther Rathenau, whose appointment as foreign minister in 1922 was resented—editorialized a German newspaper—as "an absolutely unheard-of provocation of the people, an even more unheard-of provocation of the Volkish-thinking part of the people."[4] His assassination by *Protocols*-infected fanatics was, by one estimate, one of 376 political assassinations during 1918–1922, victimizing mostly Jews and committed overwhelmingly by the radical Right. Political turmoil and violence dogged the republic throughout most of its short life.

The segments of German society exceptionally susceptible to the radical Right's appeal—including the newly created Nazi Party—were the thousands of war veterans like Hans Knodn (see below), who were organized into violent paramilitary units. Exemplifying the Right's addiction to paranoia and fabrication was Arthur Dinter's phenomenally best-selling novel, *The Sin against the Blood* (1921), which exploited the popular myth that a single sexual contact with a Jew was enough to pollute a German maiden forever so that thereafter all her offspring and descendants would be tainted with "Jewish blood." This was the fantasy world of the *Protocols,* where everyone feared and hated the Jew, whether as capitalist or communist, race defiler or deicide.

With military defeat and the dismemberment of the Habsburg Empire, Austria, too, became, in the view of the new nation's radical Right, a *Judenrepublik* (Jewish republic). At the end of 1918 the Christian Social Party—the party of Karl Lueger, who was mayor of Vienna before the war and had adopted an official antisemitic agenda—stated in its party manifesto, "The corruption and power mania of Jewish circles, evident in the new state [of the Austrian Republic], forces the Christian Social Party to call on the German Austrian people for the most severe defensive struggle against the Jewish peril."[5] The party formed an authoritarian government in 1934 and quickly set about restricting Jewish rights, but lost popularity to the even more extreme Austrian Nazis, who carried out extensive terrorist operations against Jews.

In Austrian society the same elements as in Germany were drawn to the radical Right, except that the Catholic clergy were more to the fore. For example, shortly before Hitler became chancellor in Germany, the bishop of Linz issued a pastoral letter condemning "degenerate Judaism" and Freemasonry for "mammonistic capitalism" and communism: It was, therefore, "the duty of every devout Christian to fight against this harmful influence of Judaism, and it is much to be desired that these dangers and damages arising out of the Jewish spirit should be . . . even more strongly combated by the Aryan and Christian side."[6]

The Nazi Party was simply one of the very numerous radical Right groups in Germany and Austria, not unusual or more extreme and of no special significance until 1929 and the Great Depression. What was distinctive about Hitler and the NSDAP and its Austrian counterpart was their fanatical conviction and their addiction to murderous violence.

Hans Knodn

"The Solution of the Jewish Question," 1920

Hans Knodn was an obscure Volkish crank, veteran of World War I, Freikorps member (free-booting war veterans opposed to the Weimar Republic), and local Nazi Party founder and organizer in the circle of Dietrich Eckardt, a close friend and formative influence on the youthful Hitler. Siding with Hitler's opponents in an intra-party dispute, Knodn was forced out of the NSDAP. He volunteered in 1928 to be a spy for the Soviet Union, and the record of that attempt thwarted all his later efforts to rejoin the NSDAP.

In 1920, Knodn submitted his proposal, "The Solution of the Jewish Question," to the prime minister of Bavaria, Gustav von Kahr (who was murdered by the Nazis in the 1934 purge for opposing Hitler in the 1923 Beer Hall putsch). Knodn's scheme was prepared during a chaotic period in German history: the still lingering shock of defeat; resentment against the Versailles treaty; attempts by both the communist Left and the radical Right to seize power by force; fractious veterans organized in private armies to combat communism; the emergence of hundreds of radical nationalist and antisemitic groups, particularly the National Socialists headed by Hitler; and calls in the name of eugenics for the extinction of "life unworthy of life." The Kahr government filed Knodn's letter away with the notation "No action necessary. These are fantasies."

Knodn's plan for the internment and deportation of Jews—and their murder if the Allies interfered—shows that the idea of interning Jews and holding them as hostages did not originate with Hitler; indeed, it was commonplace among Volkish writers since the late nineteenth century.

Whoever wants to solve the Jewish question in a satisfactory manner must . . . act decisively and oppose without hesitation all countervailing threats. In my view, the following steps should be considered.

1. Within 24 or 48 hours at most, most Jews should be concentrated, that is they should concentrate at certain collecting points. From these places the transportation to the concentration camps should take place. Permission for taking only the most necessary articles of clothing should be given.

2. Jews who try to avoid arrest by flight or bribe will lose their lives; their property will go to the state and should be taken over in practice.

3. The same fate should be accorded Germans who help the Jews in their flight, or permit themselves to be persuaded to that effect or bribed.

4. The Allies will be faced with a *fait accompli* by such a speedy solution of the Jewish question, thus losing their freedom of action, and we must not be silenced any longer by any kind of threat. Should the Allies start military action against us, we must immediately respond with repression against the Jews. Should a blockade be instituted, the Jews will be put to death by starvation. Should the enemy advance, the Jews will be cut down until the advance stops. If not enough foodstuffs are available, the Jews will be given prison rations. The expenses will be covered by Jewry, and the prices charged should be those of countries outside Germany.

5. The internment should be kept up for as long as we are threatened by internal and external enemies. Through this measure we also have an effective tool to keep Bolshevism off because we can respond to an advance of the Bolshevik armies by actions against the Jews. One can expect with certainty that the effect would be stunning and we could prevent that danger from threatening us.

6. We can, in this way, foil all the tricks of international Jewry, which find their expression in the Versailles peace treaty and the Bolshevization of the world. Only in this way can we bring about a revision of the peace treaty.

7. As soon as the internal and external dangers are removed, we must begin with the total deportation of all Jews to Palestine, after taking away all the dishonestly acquired property. Germanic Law will determine whether property was acquired honestly or not.

8. Stepping on German soil should be forbidden to them for all eternity, and should be punishable by the death penalty. This will be the penalty for the unforgivable transgressions which they committed against humanity by starting the world war and the Bolshevik world revolution.

9. International protection should be accorded the Jews in establishing their state, but their state will be under international control. . . . [A] desirable world revolution will ensue, namely the liberation of humanity from the rule of Jewry, the international Jewish and wandering monopoly capital, without incurring serious sacrifice.[7]

NOTES

1. Paul Lawrence Rose, *German Question/Jewish Question: Revolutionary Anti-semitism from Kant to Wagner* (Princeton: Princeton University Press, 1990).

2. Quoted in John Weiss, *Ideology of Death: Why the Holocaust Happened in Germany* (Chicago: Ivan R. Dee, 1996), 36.

3. Quoted in Steven E. Aschheim, *Scholem, Arendt, Klemperer: Intimate Chronicles in Turbulent Times* (Bloomington: Indiana University Press, 2001), 84.

4. Quoted in Peter G. J. Pulzer, *The Rise of Political Anti-Semitism in Germany and Austria* (New York: Wiley, 1964), 307.

5. Quoted in Pulzer, *The Rise of Political Anti-Semitism,* 318.

6. Quoted in Pulzer, *The Rise of Political Anti-Semitism,* 321.

7. Appendix to Herbert A. Strauss, "Hostages of 'World Jewry': On the Origin of the Idea of Genocide in German History," *Holocaust and Genocide Studies: An International Journal,* 3 (1988): 136.

NINETEEN

The Worldview of Adolf Hitler

Adolf Hitler (1889–1945) was born in Austria, the fourth child of a minor civil servant who ill-treated his son. In 1907, the Vienna Academy of Arts rejected his application for admission. After the death of his mother that year (his father had died in 1903), Hitler drifted about Vienna, viewing himself as an art student. Contrary to his later description of these years, Hitler did not suffer great poverty, for he received an orphan's allowance from the state and an inheritance from his mother and an aunt. Hitler was a loner, given to brooding and self-pity. He found some solace by regularly attending Wagnerian operas (much admired by German nationalists for their glorification of German folk traditions), by fantasizing about great architectural projects that he would someday initiate, and by reading. He read a lot, especially in art, history, and military affairs. He also read the racial-nationalist, antisemitic, and Pan-German literature that abounded in multinational Vienna. This literature introduced Hitler to a bizarre racial mythology: a heroic race of blond, blue-eyed Aryans battling for survival against inferior races. The racist treatises preached the danger posed by mixing races, called for the liquidation of racial inferiors, and marked the Jew as the embodiment of evil and the source of all misfortune. As a soldier in World War I he twice won the Iron Cross for bravery, but his frustrations increased with Germany's defeat. After the war he was an army informer against communists and the Left, and he joined and took over the minuscule National Socialist German Workers Party (Nazi/NSDAP), one of the innumerable extremist right-wing groups that had emerged in response to Germany's defeat and loss of territory. Demonstrating extraordinary ability as a demagogic orator, Hitler denounced the Versailles treaty, Marxism, the Weimar Republic, and, above all, the Jews to whom he attributed all of Germany's misfortunes. His attempt to overthrow the Bavarian government failed in the 1923 putsch, after which he was imprisoned a short time and dictated *Mein Kampf*. After the failure of 1923 Hitler sought power by turning his party into a mass movement that would become a political force. A degree of prosperity and normality in Germany deprived him of much appeal until the 1929 depression gave him the opportunity to come to power as chancellor by legal means. In 1933 Hitler was ushered into power by the German elites. He capitalized on support from sympathetic industrialists and secret funds from the army that enabled him and the party to finance a newspaper, a paramilitary force, and election campaigns.

Hitler's thought comprised a patchwork of nineteenth-century antisemitic, Volkish, Social Darwinist, antidemocratic, and anti-Marxist ideas. From them he constructed a worldview rooted in myth and delusion. A racial-nationalist ideology was the driving force impelling his actions and policies, whether as party agitator, ruler of Germany, conqueror of Europe, or destroyer of the Jews. Once Hitler gained power in 1933, his ideology was diffused throughout Germany by the government and party apparatus. Many elements of Nazi ideology had been circulating since the 1870s and were widely familiar and accepted; a great many Germans, as George Mosse said, fell into the grip of the Nazi regime and its ideology "like ripe fruit from a tree."[1] The ideology glorified ruthlessness, war, and conquest. It espoused an intense nationalism and extreme racism that equated the Germans with the superior "Aryan" race and bestowed on them the right to conquer and rule.

For Hitler, race was the key to understanding world history. He believed that Western civilization was at a critical juncture. Liberalism was dying, and Marxism, that "Jewish invention" as he called it, would inherit the future unless it was opposed by an even more powerful worldview. "With the conception of race National Socialism will carry its revolution and recast the world," said Hitler.[2] As the German barbarians had overwhelmed a disintegrating Roman Empire, a reawakened, racially united Germany, led by men of iron will, would undo the humiliation of the Versailles treaty, carve out a vast European empire, and deal a decadent liberal civilization its deathblow. It would conquer Russia, eradicate communism, and reduce to serfdom the subhuman Slavs, "a mass of born slaves who feel the need of a master."[3]

In the tradition of crude Volkish nationalists and Social Darwinists, Hitler divided the world into superior and inferior races and pitted them against each other in a struggle for survival. For him this fight for life, that is, for territory and resources, was a law of nature and history. The Germans, descendants of ancient Aryans, possessed superior racial characteristics; a nation degenerates and perishes if it allows its blood to be contaminated by intermingling with lower races. Conflict between races was desirable, for it strengthened and hardened racial superiors. It made them ruthless—a necessary quality in this Darwinian world. As a higher race, the Germans were entitled to conquer and subjugate other races. Germany must acquire *Lebensraum* (living space) by expanding eastward at the expense of the racially inferior Slavs.

An obsessive and virulent hatred of Jews dominated Hitler's mental outlook. In waging war against the Jews, Hitler believed that he was defending Germany from its worst enemy, a sinister force that stood in total opposition to the new world he envisioned. In Hitler's mythical interpretation of the world, the Aryan was the originator and carrier of culture. As descendants of the Aryans, the German race embodied creativity, bravery, and loyalty. As a counterpart, Jews, who belonged to a separate biological race, personified the vilest qualities. "Two worlds face one another," said Hitler in a statement that reveals the mythical character of his thought, "the men of God and the men of Satan! The Jew is the anti-man, the creature of another god. He must have come from another root of the human race. I set the Aryan and the Jew over and against each other."[4] Everything Hitler despised—liberalism, intellectualism, pacifism, parliamentarianism, internationalism, communism, modern art, and individualism—he attributed to the Jews.

For Hitler, the Jew was the mortal enemy of racial nationalism. The moral outlook of the ancient Hebrew prophets, which affirmed individual worth and made individuals morally responsible for their actions, was totally alien to Hitler's morality, which subordinated the individual to the racial-national community. Hitler once called conscience a Jewish invention. The prophetic vision of the unity of humanity under God and the belief in equality, justice, and peace were also contrary to Hitler's creed that all history is a pitiless struggle between races and that only the strongest and most ruthless deserve to survive.

Hitler's antisemitism served a functional purpose as well. By concentrating all evil in one enemy, "the conspiratorial and demonic" Jew, Hitler provided true believers with a simple, all-embracing, and emotionally satisfying explanation for their misery. By defining themselves as the racial and spiritual opposites of Jews, true believers of all classes felt joined together in a Volkish union. By seeing themselves as engaged in a heroic battle for self-preservation and racial survival against a demonic enemy that embodied evil, they strengthened their will. Even failures and misfits gained self-respect. Antisemitism provided insecure and hostile people with powerless but recognizable targets on whom to focus their antisocial feelings.

The surrender to myth served to disorient the intellect and unify the nation. When the mind accepts an image such as Hitler's image of Jews as vermin, germs, and satanic conspirators, it has lost all sense of balance and objectivity. Such a disoriented mind is ready to believe and to obey, to be manipulated and to be led, to brutalize and to tolerate brutality; it is ready to be absorbed into the collective will of the community. That many people, including intellectuals and members of the elite, accepted these racial ideas shows the enduring power of mythical thinking and the vulnerability of reason. In 1933, the year Hitler took power, Felix Goldmann, a German-Jewish writer, commented astutely on the irrational character of Nazi antisemitism: "The present-day politicized racial antisemitism is the embodiment of myth, . . . nothing is discussed . . . only felt, . . . nothing is pondered critically, logically or reasonably, . . . only inwardly perceived, surmised. . . . We are apparently the last [heirs] of the Enlightenment."[5]

If he had been no more than an ideological crank, Hitler would not have cut such a lethal swath in history. He had such a cataclysmic impact because he combined a fanatical belief in his own ideological system with a tactical genius and political demagoguery that enabled him to attract devoted followers and to wield power long enough to carry out his frightful program.

Adolf Hitler

"Why Are We Antisemites?" 1920
"Finally [the Jew] reaches for his last means: the destruction of the entire culture."

Hitler's speech "Why Are We Antisemites?" of August 13, 1920, dates from three years before the writing of *Mein Kampf*. It is clearly consistent with it, however, and with all his statements about Jews or any ideological theme of any date from 1919 to his last pronouncement in the Berlin bunker in 1945. As he boasted, Hitler's ideas remained fixed, "granite-like," for his mind was incapable of development or revision except in emphasis and proportion to suit a tactical situation. The translation presented below is based on a typescript of thirty-three pages, originally in the main archives of the NSDAP, and now in the Federal Archives of Germany in Koblenz. The text was evidently transcribed from a stenographic account taken down simultaneously at the meeting. The manuscript contains many handwritten corrections, presumably by Hitler himself. While Hitler spoke a number of times in that period on "the Jewish question" or "why we are antisemites," these speeches survive only in fragments or the briefest newspaper reports. This is the only example of a complete text of a Hitler speech from the first year of his membership in the party, a period in which its main activity was propaganda.

The setting for the speech was the banquet hall of the Hofbräuhaus, the most famous large beer hall building in Munich. The evening lasted from 7:30 till 10:30 PM. Hitler spoke for a little over two hours; the remaining time was devoted to questions and comments from the audience and Hitler's responses. The audience was estimated to consist of over two thousand listeners, which indicates that the hall was completely filled. The actual discussion of the Jews takes up about three-fifths of the speech, which evidently produced a great effect on the audience. It was interrupted fifty-eight times by various expressions of agreement: "laughter" or "loud laughter" is noted eighteen times, the shout "very true" ten times, "bravo" twelve times, and "applause" eighteen times. Hitler's speech, which reproduces many of the myths presented in this volume, is an elaborate and systematic justification for the complete exclusion—political, social, economic, biological, cultural—of the Jews from German national life, a denial of their right to exist, and a foretaste of the Nazis' genocidal policies.

The text below contains the sections of "Why Are We Antisemites?" most pertinent to the topic of antisemitism; for greater clarity subtitles have been added.

Unable to Form Their Own State, the Jews Live as Parasites in Other States

If a people lacks these three qualities [a positive attitude toward work, "spiritual inner life," and cultural creativity], it cannot form a state. . . . [T]hrough the long centuries the Jew was always a nomad, even if in the grandest style. He never had that which we designate a state. . . . Even at that time the Jew lived primarily as a parasite on the bodies of other nations, and it was necessarily so; for a nation that does not want to subject itself to work—the sometimes thankless labor of establishing and maintaining a state—doing work in the mines, in the factories, on construction, etc., all of those kinds of work so unpleasant for a Hebrew—such a people will never found a state itself, but always prefer to live as a drone in another state in which these labors are performed by others and in which he is only the intermediary between businesses, the dealer in a favorable situation, or in the vernacular of today: the robber, the nomad who undertakes the same plundering expeditions that he had undertaken in the past. [Loud cries of "bravo" and clapping of hands.]

Thus we can also comprehend immediately why the whole idea of a Zionist state and the founding of such a state is nothing more than a comedy. . . . People try to explain that so and so many Jews have been found who want to go as farmers, as workers, even as soldiers. [Laughter.] And if they really had this impulse in them, Germany today would have great need of these ideal persons to cut peat, to go into the coal mines; they could take part in the enlargement of our factories, our hydroelectric plants, our lakes, etc. But that doesn't occur to them. The whole Zionist state will become nothing but the last completed university of their international tricks and intrigues, and everything will be directed from there, and in addition every Jew will, to a certain extent, receive immunity [from punishment for crimes committed elsewhere] as a citizen of the Palestinian state. [Laughter!] . . .

One can say first of all that the Jew can't do anything about this, that everything is determined by his race, that he can't get beyond this, and therefore it is all the same whether the individual is good or bad, he has to act precisely according to the law of his race. . . . Thus the Jew is everywhere the Jew, who—consciously or unconsciously—furthers decisively the interests of his race.

We see that here already in regard to race there are two great differences; Aryanism means the moral concept of work and, based on this, what we find so often on our lips today: socialism, public spiritedness, the common good before the good of the individual; Judaism means a selfish concept of work and, based on this, Mammonism and materialism, the antithetical opposite of socialism. [Very true.] And in this characteristic, which he cannot get beyond, which is present in his blood, as he himself acknowledges, in this characteristic alone lies the necessity for the Jew to step forth as the absolute destroyer of the state. He can't do anything else, whether he wants to or not. Because of this he is no longer capable of forming his own state, for this always presupposes more or less an abundance of social feeling. Because of this he is only able to live as a parasite in other states, and here we see very clearly that race in itself does not necessarily produce the formation of a state if it does not possess certain definite characteristics that have to be present in the race, that must be inborn on the basis of their blood; and conversely, a race that does not possess these must produce a destructive effect on other nations living on this earth . . . regardless of whether the individual is good or bad.

. . . [B]y means of trickery and deceit, [the Jew] has permeated and infected race after race, always been cast out, but without being insulted, and then sought out another race.

How he pimped and haggled when it was a question of his ideals, willing even to sacrifice his own family. . . . just so that he could do business. . . . The Jew has carried out this pushing and squeezing into other races for millennia, and we know very well that whenever he has dwelt some place for a considerable length of time, the traces of collapse become evident, and that there was finally nothing left for these nations to do but to free themselves from their un-desired guest—or else perish themselves. . . .

The Jew figured out how to sneak into one particular state, Rome at the time of its ascent. We can follow his tracks in southern Italy. Two-and-a-half centuries before Christ, he has already settled everywhere there and people are beginning to shun him. He is already swaggering, he is the dealer, and count-less Roman writings describe for us how there already he was dealing in *every-thing*, just as today, from shoe laces to girls [Very true!], and we know that fi-nally the danger became greater and greater and that the tumult after the murder of Julius Caesar was primarily *incited* by Jews. Already at that time the Jew had figured out how to put himself in a very good position with those in power. . . . We know that none other than the Jew used Christianity, not out of love for Christianity, but in part from the recognition that this new religion rejected earthly power and the authority of the state before all, that it recog-nized only a higher supernatural Lord, that this religion could put the axe to the roots of the Roman state, which was built on the authority of its govern-ment administrators, and the Jew became the bearer of this new religion, its greatest disseminator, and he used it, not to become Christian himself—for that was impossible for him—for he always remained the Jew, just as today our socialist of Jewish race never comes down to join the ordinary worker, but al-ways remains the master and pretends to be the socialist. [Bravos and clapping.] He behaved in exactly the same way 2000 years ago. . . . We know that finally throughout the whole Middle Ages the Jew pushed his way in; we find him in all European states, and everywhere we see him only as a parasite, working with his new principle and his new modes of action, which were still unfamiliar to the various nations at that time and which brought him success; and gradually he turned from a nomad into the avaricious and bloodthirsty robber of modern times, and he went on like this for so long and so far till nation after nation re-belled and tried to shake off this pestilence.

We know very well that it is not true when someone claims today that the Jew was forced to engage in this activity because he was not allowed to ac-quire any landed property. The Jew had been allowed to acquire landed prop-erty everywhere, but he uses the right not to till the soil, but rather for the same purpose that he uses it today—as an object to be traded, as a commodity. Our ancestors were more healthy-minded: they possessed the awareness that the land, the soil, is sacred, that it is a hallowed site for the people, not a prop-erty for haggling, and they excluded the Jew. [Lively agreement and applause.] And even if at some point the Jew had the intention of cultivating the soil and of establishing his own state, in the period when gradually the veils were be-ing lifted from numerous new parts of the world and regions, when whole new continents were being made accessible, the Jew would have had the opportu-nity to go there, take possession of an area, cultivate it, and establish for himself a homeland, [Very true!] if, for this purpose, he had only employed a fraction of his energy, cunning, craftiness, brutality, and ruthlessness, and made use of the financial means at his disposal. For if this energy had sufficed to subjugate whole nations, then it would have sufficed much more easily to establish his own state, if only the basic prerequisite for this had been present at all, i.e., the will to work, not only in the sense of pocketing money, of usurious commerce, but also in the sense of millions who all must be active in order to make a state at all possible and to enable a people to live in a state. In place of this, even at this time, we see him come on the scene as destroyer; right up to our own time, we see here too the great transformation, as the Jew was once only the Court Jew[6] and slyly realized that it is enough to show himself accommodating to his master and to make his master accommodating to him in order to be able to rule all the various nations, that only one thing was necessary to stimulate the desires of these lofty gentlemen—to show them unattainable things and then lend them the money, and by this means to gradually draw them under the spell cast on debtors, and thus to gain power again over the nations. And the same Jews played this game with similar cruelty, who a few years later became the tolerant, humanitarian Jews, the philanthropic Jews, and they, of course, with their sense of humanity and sacrifice in regard to *our* people, have arranged it in such a way that their own fortunes weren't completely spent. [Much laughter.] I said they transformed themselves from Court Jews into Jewish citizens, and why? Because the Jew gradually felt the ground being pulled out from under his feet. Gradually he too had to engage in a struggle for existence against the nations, as they awakened more and more and became ever more indignant. That soon brought him to the necessity of ruling, for all practical purposes, the nations in which he wanted to live. And this again places before him the necessity of first destroying the internal structure of these states. . . .

"International" Jewish Capital Threatens Germany

In order to invest this money one must proceed to destroy whole states, to eradicate whole cultures, to break up national industries, not in order to socialize, but to cast all of it into the jaws of this international capital; for this capital is international; as the only thing on this earth that is international, it is international because its representatives, the Jews, are international due to their diffusion throughout the whole world. [Agreement.] And right here everyone would have to scratch his head and say to himself: If this capital is international because its representatives, the Jews, are spread internationally throughout the whole world, then it would be crazy to think that one could fight this capital internationally with the same members of this race, [Very true.] that one puts out a fire not with fire, but with water, and that one will only be able to break international capital—which belongs to international Jews—by means of national power. [Bravos and clapping.] . . .

The Jew Lowers the Racial Quality of the Nation

The second thing against which the Jew as parasite turns and must turn is national purity as the source of the strength of a people. The Jew, who is national like no other people, who through millennia has not mixed with any other race, who only uses interbreeding to cause others in the most favorable situation to degenerate, this same Jew preaches day after day from thousands of tongues, from 19,000 newspapers in Germany alone, that all peoples on this earth are equal, that an international solidarity should unite these people, that no people may claim a special position, etc., and above all, that no people has a reason to be proud of anything that is called or is national, or that implies a nation, he who himself never thinks of descending to those to whom he preaches internationalism, and he here also knows why.

First, says the Jew, a race must be de-nationalized. First it must forget that its strength lies in its blood, and when it has come to this and possesses no more pride, then the result appears, a second race that is lower than the previous one, and he needs this lower one, for what the Jew requires to be able to organize, build, and maintain his definitive world rule, is the lowering of the racial level of the other peoples, so that in the end he, as the only one racially pure, is enabled to rule over all of them. This is *the* lowering of the races, the effects of which we can still see today in a number of peoples on this earth. We know that the Hindus in India are one such people, a mixture of the superior Aryan immigrants and the original dark black population, and that this people today bears the consequences; for it is also the slave people of a race that may appear to us in many points to be almost a second Jewry.

A further problem is the problem of the physical debilitation of all races, i.e., the Jew strives to do away with anything that he knows is somehow strength-producing, that has a muscle-building effect, and above all to eliminate anything that he knows will, under certain conditions, keep a people so healthy that it will decide not to tolerate in its midst criminals against the people, i.e., pests and parasites present in the community of the people, but rather under certain circumstances to punish them with death, and this is his greatest fear and worry; for even the heaviest bolts of the most secure prison are not so heavy, and the prison itself is not so secure that a few million ultimately couldn't burst it open. Only one bolt can never be raised, and that is death, and the Jew is most afraid of this, and he yearns for the abolition of this barbaric punishment everywhere where he still lives as a parasitic people and seeks its ruthless employment everywhere where he is already master. [Lively applause.]

And he has excellent means at his disposal for the debilitation of bodily strength. First of all he controls business, *the* business that is nothing less than the provision of food and other necessary articles of daily use; he organizes it and uses it to hold back these articles from daily life when necessary, in order to make them more expensive, on the one hand, but also to withdraw them in order to produce the means of physical debilitation that has always been most effective: famine. And so we see them organize on a large scale, from [the biblical] Joseph in Egypt to [Walther] Rathenau[7] of today. Everywhere we see behind these organizations not a striving to make possible the provision of food by means of a splendid organization, but rather by this means to gradually *create* famine. We also know that as a politician he never had reason or cause to fear this famine. On the contrary, whenever the Jew appears in political parties, famine and misery become the fertile soil on which he can begin to thrive. He wishes for it, and therefore he doesn't think of alleviating the social misery. For this is, of course, the bed in which he truly thrives.

Hand in hand with this goes a struggle against the health of the people. . . .

The Jew Corrupts Culture and Seeks Domination

Finally he reaches for his last means: the destruction of the entire culture, of everything that we consider absolutely indispensable in a state that wants to be known as a state with its own culture. Here perhaps the effects of his activities are least evident, but here the effects are actually most dreadful. We are familiar with his activities in the arts, how painting today is becoming a grotesque caricature of everything that we call true inner feeling. [Lively agreement.] . . .

He operates in literature just as he does in painting, sculpture, and music. Here, of course, he has a great resource. He is the publisher and, above all, editor of more than 95 percent of all newspapers that are printed. He uses this power; and anyone who has become such a monster of an antisemite as I am [Laughter.] can smell out where the Jew begins, when he picks up the paper, [Laughter.] and recognizes already from the front page that again this is not one of *us*, but rather that one of *those* people is behind it. [Laughter.] We know very well that all these puns and contortions only serve to cover over the inner hollowness of his soul, to obscure the fact that the man has no emotional perception and experience, and for his lack of true soul he substitutes bombast, filled with clichés, verbal gyrations, and figures of speech that seem absurd, and from the start it is all cautiously explained the he doesn't understand them himself and hasn't had a sufficient educational background. [Laughter.] . . .

Our theaters, the places that Richard Wagner once wanted to have darkened in order to produce the ultimate degree of seriousness and solemnity, in which he wanted to have works performed that he was ashamed to call "plays" and described instead as "sacred dramas," the place that was meant to be the final exaltation, the redemption of the individual from all his misery and affliction, but also from all the rottenness that, unfortunately, is present in life, the place that is intended to raise the individual into a realm where the air is purer—what has become of it? Today it is a place where you must feel ashamed to enter, with fear that someone might see you as you were going in. [Very true.] . . . [T]he theater has become the breeding place of vice and shamelessness, and now a thousand times worse is that new invention that resulted perhaps from a brilliant flash of genius, and which the Jew was immediately able to transform into the dirtiest business that one could imagine: the moving picture. [Stormy approval and applause.] At first one could attach the highest hopes to these brilliant inventions. The easy disseminator of deep knowledge among a whole people, a whole world. And what has become of it? It is now the disseminator of the greatest rubbish and the greatest shamelessness. And so the Jew continues to operate. For him there is no spiritual perception, and just as his patriarch Abraham had pimped for his own wife, so he finds it not unusual today if he pimps for young girls, and through the centuries we can encounter him everywhere, in North America and in Germany, in Austria-Hungary, and throughout the Orient, as a dealer in human wares, and it cannot be denied, the greatest defender of Jews cannot deny the fact, that all these dealers in white slavery are *exclusively* Jews. One can come up with material here that is horrible. For the Germanic sensibility there would be only one punishment possible here: the punishment would be death—for people who cruelly exploit something that to a million others means the greatest happiness or the greatest misfortune, people who conceive of this merely as a business, a product. But to those Jews love is nothing but a business by which they can earn money. At any time they are ready to destroy the happiness of some marriage or other, if only thirty pieces of silver can be gotten out of it. [Stormy bravos and applause.] . . .

Here too we observe: the same Jew . . . mocks religion, inserts himself everywhere, destroys everywhere, and can never provide a substitute. . . .

If then the Jew destroys the state from these three great standpoints, i.e., the moral conception of work, the national purity of a people, and its inner life as the third, so that he undermines the capacity to form and maintain the state, then he also begins to act externally and sets his axe to the authority of reason in the state and replaces the authority of reason with the authority of the majority of the masses, and he knows very well that this majority will dance to his tune, because he possesses the means to direct them: he has the press, not perhaps to *register* public opinion, but to *falsify* it, and he knows how to make public opinion useful for him through the roundabout way of the press, and he thus can control the *state* alongside public opinion. The authority of the great sponge of the majority, led by the Jew, replaces the authority of reason and intellect, [until] he becomes a dictator [or as] today in Russia . . . a few Jewish millionaires [rule]. . . .

. . . He is a Jew, who works with only one burning idea in mind: how shall I raise my people up to become the master race; and when we see, for example, in the Jewish periodicals, how it is laid down that every Jew is obliged absolutely and everywhere, to enter into the struggle against all antisemites, whoever and wherever they may be, then we can only conclude that every German, whatever and wherever he may be, becomes an antisemite. [Strong bravos and extended applause.] . . . [O]ne thing has become clear to us: to free our economy from these clamps it is necessary to take up the fight against their source, and to organize the political struggle of the masses against their [Jewish] oppressors. [Stormy applause.] . . .

[Reforming Germany] must go hand in hand with the struggle against the opponent of all social amelioration: Judaism. Here too we know very well that scientific knowledge can only be a preliminary task, and that with this knowledge the organization must come that one day will turn into action, and this action remains fixed and unalterable for us. It is the removal of the Jews from our people, [Strong, lengthy applause!] not because we wouldn't grant them their existence, we congratulate the rest of the world on their visit, [Much laughter.] but because for us the existence of our own people is much more important than that of an alien race. [Bravos.] And here we are convinced that [beyond] this scientific antisemitism. . . . it must be our concern to awaken, whip up, and incite the instinctual feelings against the Jews in our people. . . .

[Some people say that before 1914] we never heard anything about the Jew. . . . But that does not mean that he wasn't there. . . . For we haven't had this [antisemitic] movement only since the war, rather it has existed as long as there have been Jews. If you go back in Jewish history and read that the Jews exterminated by the sword the original tribes in Palestine, you can imagine that an antisemitism existed as logical reactions, and it has existed the whole time until today. . . . [Strong bravos and clapping.][8]

Mein Kampf, *1924*

Many of the views expressed in Hitler's speech "Why Are We Antisemites?" reappear in *Mein Kampf*.

The Jew offers the most powerful contrast to the Aryan. . . . Despite all their seemingly intellectual qualities the Jewish people are without true culture, and especially without a culture of their own. What Jews seem to possess as culture is the property of others, for the most part corrupted in their hands.

In judging the Jewish position in regard to human culture, we have to keep in mind their essential characteristics. There never was—and still is—no Jewish art. The Jewish people made no original contribution to the two queen goddesses of all arts: architecture and music. What they have contributed is bowdlerization or spiritual theft. Which proves that Jews lack the very qualities distinguishing creative and culturally blessed races. . . .

The first and biggest lie of Jews is that Jewishness is not a matter of race but of religion, from which inevitably follow even more lies. One of them refers to the language of Jews. It is not a means of expressing their thoughts, but of hiding them. While speaking French a Jew thinks Jewish, and while he cobbles together some German verse, he merely expresses the mentality of his people.

As long as the Jew is not master of other peoples, he must for better or worse speak their languages. Yet as soon as the others have become his servants, then all should learn a universal language (Esperanto for instance), so that by these means the Jews can rule more easily. . . .

For hours the black-haired Jewish boy lies in wait, with satanic joy on his face, for the unsuspecting girl whom he disgraces with his blood and thereby robs her from her people. He tries by all means possible to destroy the racial foundations of the people he wants to subjugate.

But a people of pure race conscious of its blood can never be enslaved by the Jew; he remains forever a ruler of bastards.

Thus he systematically attempts to lower racial purity by racially poisoning individuals.

In politics he begins to replace the idea of democracy with the idea of the dictatorship of the proletariat.

He found his weapon in the organized Marxist masses, which avoid democracy and instead help him to subjugate and govern people dictatorially with his brutal fists.

Systematically he works toward a double revolution, in economics and politics.

With the help of his international contacts he enmeshes people who effectively resist his attacks from within in a net of external enemies whom he incites to war, and, if necessary, goes on to unfurling the red flag of revolution over the battlefield.

He batters the national economies until the ruined state enterprises are privatized and subject to his financial control.

In politics he refuses to give the state the means for its self-preservation, destroys the bases of any national self-determination and defense, wipes out the faith in leadership, denigrates the historic past, and pulls everything truly great into the gutter.

In cultural affairs he pollutes art, literature, theatre, befuddles national sentiment, subverts all concepts of beauty and grandeur, of nobleness and goodness, and reduces people to their lowest nature.

Religion is made ridiculous, custom and morals are declared outdated, until the last props of national character in the battle for survival have collapsed. . . .

Thus the Jew is the big rabble-rouser for the complete destruction of Germany. Wherever in the world we read about attacks on Germany, Jews are the source, just as in peace and during the war the newspapers of both the Jewish stock market and the Marxists systematically incited hatred against Germany. Country after country gave up its neutrality and joined the world war coalition in disregard of the true interest of the people.

Jewish thinking in all this is clear. The Bolshevization of Germany, i.e., the destruction of the German national people-oriented intelligentsia and thereby the exploitation of German labor under the yoke of Jewish global finance are but the prelude for the expansion of the Jewish tendency to conquer the world. As so often in history, Germany is the turning point in this mighty struggle. If our people and our state become the victims of bloodthirsty and money-thirsty Jewish tyrants, the whole world will be enmeshed in the tentacles of this octopus. If, however, Germany liberates itself from this yoke, we can be sure that the greatest threat to all humanity has been broken.[9]

NOTES

1. George L. Mosse, ed. *Nazi Culture*, trans. Salvator Attansio et al. (New York: Grosset and Dunlap, 1965), xxxviii.

2. Quoted in Alan Bullock, *Hitler: A Study in Tyranny* (New York: Harper Torchbooks, 1964), 400.

3. *Hitler's Secret Conversations, 1941-1944*, trans. Norman Cameron and R. H. Stevens, with an introductory essay by H. R. Trevor-Roper (New York: Farrar, Straus and Young, 1953), 28.

4. Quoted in Lucy Dawidowicz, *The War against the Jews, 1933-1945* (New York: Holt, Rinehart and Winston, 1975), 21.

5. Quoted in Uriel Tal, "Consecration of Politics in the Nazi Era," in *Judaism and Christianity under the Impact of National Socialism*, ed. Otto Dov Kulka and Paul R. Mendes-Flohr (Jerusalem: Historical Society of Israel, 1987), 70.

6. Jews in central Europe in the early modern period who served rulers as ministers of finance, army suppliers, personal bankers, and so forth; a famous one was Joseph Süss Oppenheimer, 1698-1737, who was known as Jud Süss, the subject of a 1940 Nazi antisemitic film by that name.

7. A German-Jewish industrial magnate, organizer of German raw material allocation in World War I, minister of reconstruction and then foreign minister of the Weimar Republic until he was murdered by antisemitic thugs in 1922.

8. From "Hitlers 'Grundlegende' Rede über den Antisemitismus," ed. Reginald H. Phelps, *Vierteljahrhefte für Zeitgeschichte*, 16 (1968): 390-420, trans. Robert K. Kramer of Manhattan College especially for this volume.

9. Excerpted from Marvin Perry et al., *Sources of the Western Tradition*, vol. 2, *From the Renaissance to the Present*, 5th ed., trans. Theodore H. von Laue (Boston: Houghton Mifflin, 2003), 361-362.

TWENTY

Nazi Racial Culture: The Corruption of the Intellect

"Racial thought and its consequences are fundamental to the whole cultural drive of the Third Reich," according to George Mosse. "Once this has been understood, everything else will follow."[1] Biology was the discipline that was most contaminated by Nazi racial ideology. Most of Germany's biologists, nearly two-thirds of whom were party members, welcomed the new "political biology" and "national biology." Far from being coerced by the regime, "Scientists themselves chose to place their work in the service of racial biology and racial policy [of genocide and "resettlement" of Eastern Europe]," says German historian Ute Deichmann.[2] Nor were they loath to participate in pitiless SS-sponsored experiments on concentration camp prisoners in their quest of a "deliberate, scientifically founded race policy" to ensure the "racial improvement of Volk and race" and the "elimination" of "genetically inferior people."[3] "Racial eugenics," "racial hygiene," and "racial science" were taught at every level of the educational system. Instruction in biology was intended to strengthen German students' will to fight against the racial deterioration of the German Volk and inculcate the lesson that great states and empires fall because they allow anti-eugenic racial mixing to prevail, what Hitler endlessly warned against as "blood-poisoning." The young would thus learn, presumably, the truth of Hitler's adage that "All that is not race is trash."

Pursuant to Hitler's oft-quoted pronouncement in *Mein Kampf*, "The state is only a means to the end of preserving the existence of the race," Nazi racial ideology dictated both policy and cultural life in the Third Reich. The Hereditary Health Law decreed by Hitler in July 1933 prescribed sterilization of "less valuable" members of the Volk, those whose racial profile indicated that their offspring were likely to be physically or mentally deformed. In 1939 the regime instituted the "euthanasia" program—the first organizational step on the road to mass murder—that authorized the killing of the mentally and physically handicapped. Side by side with the biology teacher as one of the Volkish professions that was to rebuild the Reich was the German physician, eulogized as the "biological soldier." Physicians—nearly half of them held party membership and many became SS doctors—were the guardians of the health of the eternal Volk. They engaged in sterilization, euthanasia, hideous medical experiments on concentration camp inmates, and mass murder.

In 1935 the Nuremberg laws and a series of decrees based on Nazi racial ideology deprived Jews of their citizenship, reducing them to outcasts. Thousands of

Jewish doctors, lawyers, artists, musicians, and professors were barred from practicing their professions, and Jewish members of the civil service were dismissed. Marriage or sexual encounters between Germans and Jews were forbidden and subject to brutal punishment and humiliation. Universities, schools, restaurants, pharmacies, hospitals, theatres, museums, and athletic facilities were gradually closed to Jews, who were viewed as an "anti-race." As a rule, German academic, business, and clerical elites did not protest. Indeed, many welcomed and applauded the Nazi edicts. Traditional German elites collaborated with the Nazis in developing and implementing the racial policies that degraded Jews, robbed them of their livelihoods and property, and eventually culminated in genocide.

Hermann Gauch

"Non-Nordics are more or less equal to the animals," 1939

Believing that the struggle of racial forces occupied the center of world history, Nazi ideologists tried to strengthen the racial consciousness of the German people. Numerous courses in "racial science" introduced in schools and universities emphasized the superiority of the "Nordic" (German Aryan) soul and the worthlessness of Jews. The University of Berlin offered a "scientific" course, University Course 736, on "The History of the Jewish Menace."[4] The following excerpt, crude and spurious as it is, from Herman Gauch's New Foundations of Racial Science (1939) illustrates National Socialist thinking that was propagated by scholars, scientists, and schoolteachers. Thus was scientific learning in Germany corrupted and rendered complicitous in the Holocaust.

The mixture of races . . . causes and promotes diseases. It is a breach of the laws of order in the universe, a crime against the future generation, manslaughter and murder.

We come to the conclusion that all the better developed characteristics are typical of the Nordic body and the Nordic soul. . . . Non-Nordics are more or less equal to the animals or they form a . . . link to them. *The non-Nordic thus occupies an intermediate position between the Nordic and the animal and ranks next to the man-apes.* He is therefore not a hundred percent human being. . . . He might be compared with the Neanderthal man, but better and more accurate is the description: "sub-man." . . .

The Nordic and the non-Nordic races have not a single characteristic in common: We are not justified, therefore, in speaking of a "human race." As a matter of fact there are actually some animals which have Nordic characteristics, such as the faithfulness of the dog, which is lacking in the non-Nordic. . . .

Nordic man is therefore the creator of all culture and civilization. The salvation and preservation of the Nordic man alone will save and preserve culture and civilization. Lasting success can, of course, be achieved only through the unification of the whole Nordic humanity of the Germanic countries and a number of other strongly Nordic areas.[5]

Jakob Graf

"How We Can Learn to Recognize a Person's Race," 1935

Jakob Graf was a schoolteacher and author of textbooks on heredity and "racial biology," which were required subjects in school curricula. He presented history as the creative dominance of the Aryans—tall, long-headed, fair-skinned, light-eyed, and blond—that lasted "as long as they kept their race pure," from the ancient Greeks to the Germans of his day. He designed assignments to teach pupils "to recognize a person's race" at a glance, from one of which the following is excerpted. Items that are not reproduced here direct pupils to write descriptions of each race, analyze art and literature for illustrations of race, and study the "racial soul" in order to see how it "harmonizes" with a person's physical features. Teaching simplified racism at the schoolchild level served to diffuse it widely in German society.

Racial Homework

3. What are the expressions, gestures, and movements which allow us to make conclusions as to the attitude of the racial soul? . . .

9. Observe people whose special racial features have drawn your attention, also with respect to their bearing when moving or when speaking. Observe their expressions and gestures.

10. Observe the Jew: his way of walking, his bearing, gestures, and movements when talking.

11. What strikes you about the way a Jew talks and sings?

12. What are the occupations engaged in by the Jews of your acquaintance?

13. What are the occupations in which Jews are not to be found? Explain this phenomenon on the basis of the character of the Jew's soul.

14. In what stories, descriptions, and poems do you find the psychical character of the Jew pertinently portrayed? ("The Jew in the Thistles" from Grimm's Fairy Tales; *Debit and Credit* by Gustav Freytag; *Ut mine Stromtid* [in German dialect about the revolution of 1848] by Fritz Reuter; *The Hunger Pastor* by Wilhelm Raabe; *The Merchant of Venice* by Shakespeare.) Give examples.[6]

A German Mother

"Remember that the Jews are children of the Devil and human murderers," 1938

Hitler wrote in *Mein Kampf,* "The crown of the racial state's entire work of education and training must be to burn the racial sense and racial feeling into the instinct and the intellect, the heart and the brain of youth entrusted to it. No boy and no girl must leave school without having been led to an ultimate realization of the necessity and essence of blood purity." And to Hermann Rauschning, who later fled the regime and tried to alert the world to the Nazi danger, he described the end product of racial education: "My pedagogy is hard. Weakness must be stamped out. . . . I want a violent, domineering, undismayed, cruel youth."[7] The molding of the mind of German youth began in the crib, when the child was exposed to Hitlerian idolatry in the form of fairy tales depicting the messianic Führer heaven-sent to protect the infants of Germany and kill the Bolshevik-Jewish ogre. Children's inculcation included the full range of Christian antisemitic myths, such as this selection from the elementary school curriculum, in which a peasant mother, standing before a roadside shrine to Christ, indoctrinates her three children with Jew-hatred.

Children, look here! The Man who hangs on the Cross was one of the greatest enemies of the Jews of all time. He knew the Jews in all their corruption and meanness. Once he drove the Jews out with a whip, because they were carrying on their money dealings in the Church. He called the Jews killers of men from the beginning. By that He meant that the Jews in all times have been murderers. He said further to the Jews: Your father is the Devil! Do you know, children, what that means? It means that the Jews descend from the Devil. And because they descend from the Devil, they live like devils. So they commit one crime after another. Because this man knew the Jews, because He proclaimed the truth to the world, He had to die. Hence, the Jews murdered Him. They drove nails through his hands and feet and let Him slowly bleed. In such a horrible way the Jews took their revenge. And in a similar way they have killed many others who had the courage to tell the truth about the Jews. Always remember these things, children. When you see the Cross, think of the terrible murder by the Jews on Golgotha. Remember that the Jews are children of the Devil and human murderers.[8]

Fritz Brennecke

The Nazi Primer: Official Handbook for Schooling the Hitler Youth, 1937

Officially, the co-opting of German youth, male and female, began in public school with the child at age six, continued as a *Pimpf* (cub) at age ten in the *Jungvolk,* and age fourteen in the *HitlerJugend* (*HJ,* Hitler Youth) headed by Baldur von Schirach. Its ideological indoctrination was rife with antisemitism and even anti-Christianity. A secret *Hitler Youth Leaders' Manual* of 1938 specified that Christianity and communism, both founded by Jews, were one and the same. The material included ribald songs ridiculing Christianity and its "dirty little Jew."

The Hitler Youth gave the regime a tight ideological and institutional grip on the mind and body of the young. It was the principal source of recruits for the SS and *Waffen-SS* (the armed SS trained and equipped for military operations and intended ultimately to replace the regular army). Under agreements between Schirach and Himmler, the *HJ* became "the adolescent SS" and an essential part of "the SS State." At the Nuremberg trials, where Schirach was tried and sentenced to twenty years, Chief Prosecutor William Jackson summed up, "It was this wretched man who perverted millions of innocent German children. . . . [He] trained them in legions for service in the *SS* and *Wehrmacht,* and delivered them up to the Party as fanatic, unquestioning executors of its will. . . . insuring that [they] grew up rabid anti-Semites . . . to bully Jews. . . . He morally corrupted [the youth] and prepared them for the perpetration of every atrocity."[9] Children and youth were reduced to "human raw material" to be used and used up like any other resource available to the regime.

Excerpts follow from the 1937 *Handbook.* Although it often quotes or paraphrases *Mein Kampf,* the work is restrained and seemingly rational in its exposition of what the curriculum should inculcate in the mind of youth. Its "scientific" and "objective" tone suggests that there could be no question or argument about the ideas and policies it advocates.

The most significant and most efficacious realities in the life of a people are "Blood and Soil." Whoever recognizes their binding force and effects in history can also take part in shaping the future. To foster the building up of a political will in the Hitler Youth organization according to the National Socialist outlook on life is, therefore, the task of this little handbook. . . .

Times gone by have ignored the obvious unlikeness of men, or have consciously acted contrary to better knowledge. . . . Even in our day the fact is shown many times that certain men have no feeling for race honor or race shame. The many hybrids resulting from unions with Germans of black troops occupying the Rhineland[10] and of Jews are tragic witnesses of the fact. Even those occupying the highest places in government during the "System Time" [the Weimar Republic] consciously closed their eyes to the facts of race.

Even today the racial ideas of National Socialism have implacable opponents. Free Masons, Marxists, and the Christian church join hands in brotherly accord on this point. The worldwide order of Free Masons conceals its Jewish plans for ruling the world behind the catchword "Mankind" or "Humanity." Masonry can take as much credit for its effort to bring Jews and Turks into the fold as does Christianity itself. Marxism has the same goal as Free Masonry. In this case, to disguise its real intentions the slogan "Equality, Liberty and Fraternity" is preached. Under Jewish leadership Marxism intends to bring together everyone "who bears the face of man."

The Christians, above all the Roman Church, reject the race idea with the citation "before God all men are equal." All who have the Christian belief, whether Jews, bush niggers, or whites, are dearer to them and more worthwhile than a German who does not confess Christianity. . . .

. . . Now what distinguishes the Nordic race from all others? It is uncommonly gifted mentally. It is outstanding for truthfulness and energy. Nordic men for the most part possess, even in regard to themselves, a great power of judgement. They incline to be taciturn and cautious. They feel instantly that talking too loud is undignified. They are persistent and stick to a purpose when once they have set themselves to it. Their energy is displayed not only in warfare but also in technology and in scientific research. They are predisposed to leadership by nature.

We . . . shape the life of our people and our legislation according to the verdicts of the teachings of genetics. . . . That is one more reason for our belief: A Jew both in Germany and in all other countries remains only a Jew. He can never change his race by centuries of residence with other people, as he often asserts, but just as often contradicts by his own actions.

Inheritance is in the long run always victorious over environmental influences. All arguments and political demands which are founded on the belief in the power of environment are therefore false and weak. . . .

. . . Some 400 of the 1000 mental diseases alone are definitely known to be inheritable. . . . The more serious of the hereditary diseases, especially the mental diseases, make their carriers completely unsuited for living. They . . . become of little value to the community. The less worthy multiply without restraint and are continually spreading their hereditary sufferings. . . .

. . . Germany today has to reckon with some 1,000,000 feeble-minded, 250,000 hereditary mental defectives, 90,000 epileptics and 40,000 hereditary bodily defectives.

Most of these congenitally diseased and less worthy persons. . . . cannot take care of themselves and must be maintained and cared for in institutions. This costs the state enormous sums yearly. . . . Out of a real humanitarianism for the afflicted and the strongest feeling of responsibility to our people as a whole the National Socialist government has taken legal steps to prevent a further, unrestricted spreading of the more serious hereditary diseases. . . .

Intermarrying with races of foreign blood is as dangerous for the continuance and existence of a people as inheritable internal defects. The German people have direct contact only with one type of foreign people: with the Jews. So for us fostering race is one and the same thing as a defensive warfare against mind and blood contamination by the Jews. The extent to which Germans and Jews cross each other's paths scarcely needs to be presented today. The Jewish hegemony in the cultural and intellectual life of the last few decades has brought the disrupting and disturbing character of this people to the attention of all Germans.

The first opposition measures of the National Socialists must, therefore, aim to remove the Jews from the cultural and economic life of our folk. Numerous laws have laid the bases for this. . . .

The number of Jews in the German Reich is generally given as 500,000. This figure includes, however, only Jews of the Mosaic faith. The Jew has always attempted to disguise himself by changing his name and faith so that the proportion of Jews is actually much higher. An official publication estimates that the number of real Jews, not of the Mosaic faith, is about 300,000 and that the hybrids number about 775,000. The number of those not having German blood in the German Reich would, according to this report, amount to almost 1,555,000. This figure reveals the extent of the Jewish invasion into our folk. At the same time the large number of hybrids is a sad indication of the absence of racial instincts in the past. Racial pride and a feeling of racial shame were first re-awakened by National Socialism. But racial intermixings have also been forbidden legally. The "law for the protection of German blood and of German pride of October 15, 1935" imposes very severe punishments upon those of German blood who unite with foreign races, and states precisely what proportion of non-German blood causes a person to lose his status as a German.

Wiping out of the less worthy and selection of the best are the means for raising and maintaining the racial values of our people.[11]

Johannes Stark

"The Jewish spirit has little aptitude for creative activity in the sciences," 1934

According to Alfred Rosenberg, a leading Nazi antisemite and ideologue, the Jews were "arch-materialists." It was absolutely necessary "in our science" to be Germans and National Socialists, and to avoid any science that "came from the Jew."[12] In the generation before 1933 and the Nazi regime, about a quarter of German physicists and mathematicians—among them Albert Einstein—were Jews. Hitler, who had a phobia against science, is reported to have informed the distinguished physicist Max Planck, "If the dismissal of Jewish scientists means annihilation of contemporary German science, then we shall do without science for a few years." Two Nobel laureates in physics, Philipp Lenard, who won in 1906, and Johannes Stark (1874–1961), the winner in 1919, were Nazi enthusiasts since 1924 and lifetime antisemites who worked tirelessly to substitute "Aryan science" or "German physics" for "Jewish physics," which was equated with Einstein's theory of relativity. To them Hitler was a "natural scientist who searches for Truth according to empirical means."[13] The danger to German science was not, they said, from Jewish "blood" but from Jewish "mentality," such as infected the non-Jew Max Planck in the creation of quantum mechanics, and they operated from the Lenard Institute, a Nazi think tank, to combat that mentality. Regarded as cranks by their colleagues in the 1920s, Lenard and Stark came into their own in the Nazi period but were countered effectively if passively by Planck and energetically by Max von Laue, himself a Nobel laureate in 1912 and a man of great moral courage. His fame seems to have shielded him from the regime, despite his dismissal of "Aryan physics" and his defense of Jewish colleagues. To the "Aryans," Einstein's theory of relativity was, as Lenard said, "a Jewish fraud";[14] Lenard and Stark equated "Jewish science" with theory, abstraction, materialism, and complexity, whereas "German science" was "spiritual" and "organic," springing from experiment and observation. In the following excerpt from his exposition of Nazi science, *Nationalsozialismus und Wissenschaft* (National Socialism and Science), published in 1934 by the Nazi Party press, Stark exemplifies the distortion and irrationality of a scientific mind and temperament infected with antisemitism.

The slogan has been coined, and has been spread particularly by the Jews, that science is international. It refers not so much to science as such as to scientific researchers and demands a special position in the nation for them. They ought not to be considered from a national point of view, but are to be evaluated strictly on the merits of their scientific activity without regard to their ethnic origin. According to this concept, Jewish scientists ought to be inviolable even in the National Socialist state and should be allowed to continue to exert a standard-setting influence. From the National Socialist side, in opposition to this view, it must be insisted upon with all possible emphasis that in the National Socialist state, even for the scientist, the duty to the nation stands above any and all other obligations. The scientist, too, must consider himself a member and a servant of the nation. He does not exist only for himself or even for his science. Rather, in his work he must serve the nation first and foremost. For these reasons, the leading scientific positions in the National Socialist state are to be occupied not by elements alien to the Volk but only by nationally-conscious German men.

But aside from this fundamental National Socialist demand, the slogan of the international character of science is based on an untruth, insofar as it asserts that the type and the success of scientific activity are independent of membership in a national group. Nobody can seriously assert that art is international. It is similar with science. Insofar as scientific work is not merely imitation but actual creation, like any other creative activity it is conditioned by the spiritual and characterological endowments of its practitioners. Since the individual members of a people have a common endowment, the creative activity of the scientists of a nation, as much as that of its artists and poets, thus assumes the stamp of a distinctive Volkish type. No, science is not international; it is just as national as art. This can be shown by the example of Germans and Jews in the natural sciences.

Science is the knowledge of the uniform interconnection of facts; the purpose of natural science in particular is the investigation of bodies and processes outside of the human mind, through observation and, insofar as possible, through the setting up of planned experiments. The spirit of the German enables him to observe things outside himself exactly as they are, without the interpolation of his own ideas and wishes, and his body does not shrink from the effort which the investigation of nature demands of him. The German's love of nature and his aptitude for natural science are based on this endowment. Thus it is understandable that natural science is overwhelmingly a creation of the Nordic-Germanic blood component of the Aryan peoples. Anyone who, in [Philipp] Lenard's classic work *Grosse Naturforscher* [Great Investigators of Nature], compares the faces of the outstanding natural scientists will find this common Nordic-Germanic feature in almost all of them. The ability to observe and respect facts, in complete disregard of the "I," is the most characteristic feature of the scientific activity of Germanic types. In addition, there is the joy and satisfaction the German derives from the acquisition of scientific knowledge, since it is principally this with which he is concerned. It is only under pressure that he decides to make his findings public, and the propaganda for them and their commercial exploitation appear to him as degradations of his scientific work.

The Jewish spirit is wholly different in its orientation: above everything else it is focused upon its own ego, its own conception, and its self-interest—and behind its egocentric conception stands its strong will to win recognition for itself and its interests. In accordance with this natural orientation the Jewish spirit strives to heed facts only to the extent that they do not hamper its opinions and purposes, and to bring them into such a connection with each other as is expedient for effecting its opinions and purposes. The Jew, therefore, is the born advocate who, unencumbered by regard for truth, mixes facts and imputations topsy-turvy in the endeavor to secure the court decision he desires. On the other hand, because of these characteristics, the Jewish spirit has little aptitude for creative activity in the sciences because it takes the individual's thinking and will as the measure of things, whereas science demands observation and respect for the facts.

It is true, however, that the Jewish spirit, thanks to the flexibility of its intellect, is capable, through imitation of Germanic examples, of producing noteworthy accomplishments, but it is not able to rise to authentic creative work, to great discoveries in the natural sciences. In recent times the Jews have frequently invoked the name of Heinrich Hertz as a counter-argument to this thesis. True, Heinrich Hertz made the great discovery of electromagnetic waves, but he was not a full-blooded Jew. He had a German mother, from whose side his spiritual endowment may well have been conditioned. When the Jew in natural science abandons the Germanic example and engages in scientific work according to his own spiritual particularity, he turns to theory. His main object is not the observation of facts and their true-to-reality presentation, but the view which he forms about them and the formal exposition to which he subjects them. In the interest of his theory he will suppress facts that are not in keeping with it and likewise, still in the interest of his theory, he will engage in propaganda on its behalf. Only his theory is valid for him, and in the face of doubts he demands a faith in his theory as if it were a dogma. The dogmatic zeal and propagandistic drive of the Jewish scientist leads him to report on his achievements not only in scientific journals but also in the daily press and on lecture tours. The phenomenon, for example, of Jews pushing themselves prominently to the foreground at scientific congresses, such as the gatherings of German natural scientists and physicians, can be explained in the same way.[15]

Julius Streicher

Jews as International Conspirators and Ritual Murderers, 1930s

Julius Streicher (1885–1946) was the most conspicuous antisemitic demagogue in the Nazi movement; he gloried in the title of "Scourge of the Jews" and "Number One Nazi Jew Baiter." Streicher was born into a pious, lower middle class, Catholic family in Bavaria and in childhood lived in Deggendorf village, the scene of a shrine to a purported host desecration incident and massacre of Jews in 1338 that was celebrated in an annual religious festival until the 1990s. Such medieval Christian antisemitic motifs abound in Streicher's speeches and journalism rather than modern "racial" ones. Ritual murder was at the core of his antisemitic phobia, and many issues of his newspaper *Der Stürmer* (The Attacker, 1923–1945) repeated and embellished the myth—a good illustration of traditional antisemitism merging with Nazi, racial antisemitism. His weekly specialized in lurid articles and pornographic cartoons of hideous-looking Jews enticing, torturing, and butchering children, draining their blood and mixing it with matzohs and wine, and praying that all Gentiles will speedily die. Typical of Streicher's use of the ritual murder weapon is his 1935 speech to a mass meeting of the Anti-Jewish World League, when he warned of the pending "mass murder" planned by the "whip-swinging" Jews, what would be "the greatest ritual murder of all times" and the prelude to "Jewish domination not just in Germany but final Jewish domination in the whole world." "Golgotha [the site of Jesus's crucifixion] has not yet been avenged," he declaimed, explaining that the Jews are thereby a "criminal people" who commit "desecrations of churches, of usury, of ritual murder, etc."[16] These crimes were made incumbent upon Jews by the teachings of the Talmud.

Satanization of the Jews was another medieval avatar to Streicher, who was given to quoting its foundation text in the Gospel of John (8:42–47) and pronouncing a dire future for the Jews: "This satanic race has no right to exist." In a 1925 speech, Streicher was perhaps the first Nazi to draw the inference of genocide: since "for thousands of years the Jew has been destroying the nations. . . . [W]e can annihilate the Jews."[17] "Jewish" medicine—insulin, salvorsin, Wassermann tests—doctors, research, and science were, said Streicher, key elements of the Jewish world conspiracy that employed abortion, venereal disease, homosexuality, and ritual murder to destroy the Aryans. Streicher was tried and executed by the Nuremberg Tribunal, "[f]or his 25 years of speaking, writing, and preaching hatred of the Jews. . . . Such was the poison Streicher injected into the minds of thousands of Germans which caused them to follow the National Socialist policy of Jewish persecution and extermination."[18] The Tribunal had identified over fifty passages in *Der Stürmer* that demanded extermination of the Jews; Streicher had certainly contributed to the creation of the genocidal racial consensus.

The first selection from *Der Stürmer* deals with ritual murder. While Streicher was a simpleminded oaf and mocked for his crudity by the more sophisticated party leaders, his lucubrations on supposed Jewish criminality and ritual murder were prototypical of Nazi culture and propaganda and were shared by the leadership from Hitler and Himmler on down. His medieval and Lutheran antisemitism exemplifies the relationship between Nazi anti-Jewish ideology and traditional religious expressions of antisemitism, which they built upon. The excerpts below are typical of Streicher's demagogic style.

(A) "Jewish Murder Plan against Gentile Humanity Exposed: The Murderous People," 1934

. . . The Jews are under a terrible suspicion the world over. Who does not know this, does not understand the Jewish problem. Anyone who merely sees the

Jews, as Heinrich Heine . . . described them, "a tribe which secures its existence with exchange and old trousers, and whose uniforms are long noses," is being misled. But anyone who knows the monstrous accusation which has been raised against the Jews since the beginning of time, will view these people in a different light. He will begin to see not only a peculiar, strangely fascinating nation, but criminals, murderers, and devils in human form. He will be filled with holy anger and hatred against these people.

The suspicion under which the Jews are held is murder. They are charged with enticing Gentile children and Gentile adults, butchering them and draining their blood. They are charged with mixing this blood into their matzos' unleavened bread and using it to practice superstitious magic. They are charged with torturing their victims, especially the children, and during this torture they shout threats, curses, and cast spells against the Gentiles. This systematic murder has a special name. It is called Ritual Murder.

The knowledge of Jewish ritual murder is thousands of years old. It is as old as the Jews themselves. The Gentiles have passed the knowledge of it from generation to generation, and it has been passed down to us through writings. It is known of throughout the nation. Knowledge of ritual murder can be found even in the most secluded rural villages. The grandfather told his grandchildren, who passed it on to his children, and his children's children, until we have inherited the knowledge today.

It is also befalling other nations. The accusation is immediately raised loudly, anywhere in the world, where a body is found which bears the marks of ritual murder. Historically, the accusation is raised only against the Jews. Hundreds and hundreds of other races, tribes, and races attempted to accuse them of the planned murder of children for religious purposes. All nations have hurled this accusation against the Jews, and many great men have confirmed the accusation. Dr. Martin Luther writes in his book *The Jews and Their Lies:* "They stabbed and pierced the body of the young boy Simon of Trent. They have also murdered other children. . . . The sun never did shine on a more bloodthirsty and revengeful people as they, who imagine themselves to be the people of God, and who desire to and think they must murder and crush the heathen. Jesus Christ, the Almighty Preacher from Nazareth, spoke to the Jews: 'Ye are of your father the devil, and the lusts of your father ye will do. He was a murderer from the beginning.'"

The Struggle of **Der Stürmer**

The only newspaper in Germany, yes, in the whole world, which often screams the accusation of ritual murder into the Jewish face is *Der Stürmer.* For more than ten years *Der Stürmer* has led a gigantic battle against Judaism. . . .

. . . It is our duty to frustrate the gigantic Jewish murder plot against humanity. It is our duty to brand this nation before the whole world, to uncover its crimes, and to render it harmless. It is our duty to free the world from this national pest and parasitic race.

(B) "The Murder of the 10-year-old Gertrud Lenhoff in Quirschied (Saarpfalz)," 1937

The Jews are our MISFORTUNE!

[Cannibalism is an intrinsic part of Judaism, for] the numerous confessions made by the Jews show that the execution of ritual murders is a law to the Talmud Jew. The former Chief Rabbi (and later monk) Teofiti[19] declares, F[or] I[nstance], that the ritual murders take place especially on the Jewish Purim (in memory of the Persian murders) and Passover (in memory of the murder of Christ).

The instructions are as follows: The blood of the victims is to be tapped by force. On Passover, it is to be used in wine and matzos; thus, a small part of the blood is to be poured into the dough of the matzos and into the wine. The mixing is done by the Jewish head of the family.

The procedure is as follows: the family head empties a few drops of the fresh and powdered blood into the glass, wets the fingers of the left hand with it and sprays (blesses) with it everything on the table. The head of the family then says: "Dam Izzardia chynim heroff dever Isyn porech harbe hossen maschus pohorus" (Exodus 7:12 [there is no such citation]) ("Thus we ask God to send the ten plagues to all enemies of the Jewish faith."). Then they eat, and at the end the head of the family exclaims: "Sfach, chaba, moscho kol hagoym!" ("May all Gentiles perish as the child whose blood is contained in the bread and wine!")

The fresh (or dried and powdered) blood of the slaughtered is further used by young married Jewish couples, by pregnant Jewesses, for circumcision, and so on. Ritual murder is recognized by all Talmud Jews. The Jew believes he absolves himself thus of his sins.

(C) "The Pan-Jewish Worldwide Attack: Secret Plans against Germany Revealed: The Jewish World Conference," 1933

The "Rotterdam Courant," a Dutch news service, released the following interesting item to the world press on 19 June 1933. The so-called world economic conference is still in session in London. It is a conference with a lot of talk and little action. The Jews however have decided to use the conference for their purposes. They announced on 15 July a Jewish World Conference.

The purpose of the conference is to make decisions and provide guidelines directed against National Socialist Germany. These decisions and guidelines are to be brought to the world economic conference. At the same time, the Jewish conference is to agree on international Jewish policies. The organizers are the Jewish finance lords of England, the Anglo-Jewish Industry and Trade Federation. The conference will be organized by the Jewish attorney Samuel Volkmeyer from America and the Jewish big industrialist Lord Melchett of England.

All the leading Jews of the world will come together. The leading rabbis (they are the political leaders of World Jewry) and the Jewish millionaires and billionaires, the bank and stock exchange leaders, the heads of trusts and major Jews in commerce. These are the Jews of whom Walther Rathenau wrote . . . "Three hundred men, all of whom know each other, determine the history of the world. Nothing happens against their will. They are the true rulers, the real uncrowned kings."

These three hundred men want to continue and intensify Pan-Jewry's boycott war against Germany. They will attempt to fight Germany until it bends to their will or is forced to its knees. They will stop at nothing. They will lie and slander, and continually attempt to incite the whole world against Germany. Every means a Jewish brain can think of will be used. The Jews know that Germany's victory in its domestic and international struggle for freedom means the end for Pan-Jewry. . . .

EXTERMINATE THEM!

The Jew was so sure of his cause in 1897 that he could write in the *Protocols:*

> Even if a spiritual hero should arise in the enemy's camp and make war against us, he will be defeated. The newcomer cannot stand against an experienced warrior. The battle between us and him would be pitiless, waged in a manner never before seen in the world. The spiritual hero would be too late.

The Jew miscalculated. The spiritual hero did not come too late. He took up battle with Pan-Jewry and won the victory. The world knows the name of this hero. He is Adolf Hitler, the Führer of the German freedom movement. The Jew sank under his blows in the dust. Now he sees the enormous danger he faces. He has been uncovered, his criminal plans have been discovered, and a battle is coming like the world has never seen. World Jewry faces Adolf Hitler. World Jewry faces Germany. The Jews will fight without pity. We must also fight without pity against Pan-Jewry. The Jewish people is the people of the Devil [another allusion to the Gospel of John 8:42–47]. It is a people of criminals and murderers. The Jewish people must be exterminated from the face of the earth.[20]

Ernst Hiemer

Der Giftpilz *(The Poisonous Mushroom)*, 1938

Der Giftpilz is a typical example of the scurrilous writings addressed to all age groups that flooded Germany after 1933. It was written in 1938 by Ernst Hiemer, editor in chief of *Der Stürmer* and Streicher's principal lieutenant from 1934 to the end of the regime in 1945; he testified as a witness for the defense at the Nuremberg trial of Streicher. The book instructs schoolchildren how to recognize the menace and danger of "the Jew" by the stereotypical caricature of Jewish physical features that are presented in the text as well as by its vicious cartoons. In addition to branding the Jew as race defiler and abuser of little children, *Der Giftpilz* teaches that the He-brew Bible permits Jews to commit any and all crimes, depicts Jews as exploiters of the workers, as murderers, and as a poisonous mushroom—an image that has a particular resonance with German folklore.

[Karl]

"It is almost noon," he [the classroom teacher] said, "now we want to summa-rize what we have learned in this lesson. What did we discuss?"

All children raise their hands. The teacher calls on Karl Scholz, a little boy on the first bench. "We talked about how to recognize a Jew."

"Good! Now tell us about it!"

Little Karl takes the pointer, goes to the blackboard and points to the sketches.

"One usually recognizes a Jew by his nose. The Jewish nose is crooked at the end. It looks like the figure 6. Therefore it is called the "Jewish Six." Many non-Jews have crooked noses, too. But their noses are bent, not at the end but further up. Such a nose is called a hook nose or eagle's beak. It has nothing to do with a Jewish nose."

"Right!" says the teacher. "But the Jew is recognized not only by his nose. . . ." The boy continues. The Jew is also recognized by his lips. His lips are usually thick. Often the lower lip hangs down. That is called "sloppy." And the Jew is also recognized by his eyes. His eyelids are usually thicker and more fleshy than ours. The look of the Jew is lurking and sharp.

Then the teacher goes to the desk and turns over the blackboard, on its back is a verse. The children recite it in chorus:

From a Jew's countenance—the evil devil talks to us,

The devil, who in every land—is known as evil plague.

If we shall be free of the Jew—and again will be happy and glad,

Then the youth must struggle with us—to subdue the Jew devil.

[Inge]

Inge sits in the reception room of the Jew doctor. She has to wait a long time. She looks through the journals which are on the table. But she is [much] too nervous to read even a few sentences. Again and again she remembers the talk with her mother. And again and again her mind reflects on the warnings of her leader of the BDM [League of German Girls, parallel to the male Hitler Youth]: "A German must not consult a Jew doctor! And particularly not a Ger-man girl! Many a girl that went to a Jew doctor to be cured, found disease and disgrace!"

When Inge had entered the waiting room, she experienced an extraordi-nary incident. From the doctor's consulting room she could hear the sound of crying. She heard the voice of a young girl: "Doctor, doctor leave me alone!"

Then she heard the scornful laughing of a man. And then all of a sudden it became absolutely silent. Inge had listened breathlessly.

"What may be the meaning of all this?" she asked herself and her heart was pounding. And again she thought of the warning of her leader in the BDM.

Inge was already waiting for an hour. Again she takes the journals in an endeavor to read. Then the door opens. Inge looks up. The Jew appears. She screams. In terror she drops the paper. Frightened she jumps up. Her eyes stare into the face of the Jewish doctor. And this face is the face of the devil. In the middle of this devil's face is a huge crooked nose. Behind the spectacles two criminal eyes. And the thick lips are grinning. A grinning that expresses: "Now I got you at last, you little German girl!"

And then the Jew approaches her. His fleshy fingers stretch out after her. But now Inge has her wits. Before the Jew can grab hold of her, she hits the fat face of the Jew doctor with her hand. Then one jump to the door. Breathlessly Inge runs down the stairs. Breathlessly she escapes the Jew house.

[Three Pimpfs]

The pimpf [Hitler Youth cub, age 10-14] so far has not said anything. Suddenly he stops. Then he grasps his two friends by the arm and pulls them away. They stop in front of a billboard. They read a large poster. It says Julius Streicher makes an address in the People's Hall about "The Jews are our misfortune."

"That is where we go!" shouts Konrad, "I wanted to hear him speak for a long time." "I have heard him once before at a meeting two years ago," says Erich. "Do tell us all about it!" the two pimpfs beg.

The Hitler youth recounts: "The meeting was overcrowded. Many thousands of people attended. To begin with, Streicher talked of his experiences in the wars of struggle, and of the tremendous achievements of the Hitler Reich. Then he began to talk about the Jewish question. All he said was so clear and simple that even we boys could follow it. Again and again he told about examples taken from life. At one time he talked most amusingly and cracked jokes, making all of us laugh. Then again he became most serious, and it was so quiet in the hall that one could hear a needle drop. He talked of the Jews and their horrible crimes. He talked of the serious danger which Judaism is for the whole world.

'Without a solution of the Jewish question there will be no salvation of mankind.'

That is what he shouted to us. All of us could understand him. And when, at the end, he shouted the 'Sieg-Heil' for the Führer, we all acclaimed him with tremendous enthusiasm. For two hours Streicher spoke at that occasion. To us it appeared to have been but a few minutes."[21]

NOTES

1. George L. Mosse, ed. *Nazi Culture*, trans. Salvator Attansio et al. (New York: Grosset and Dunlap, 1965), 60.

2. Ute Deichmann, *Biologists under Hitler*, trans. Thomas Dunlap (Cambridge, Mass.: Harvard University Press, 1996), 271.

3. Quoted in Deichmann, *Biologists under Hitler*, 323.

4. Gregor A. Ziemer, *Education for Death: The Making of the Nazi* (London: Oxford University Press, 1941), 190.

5. From Hermann Gauch, *New Foundations of Racial Science*, trans. V. Ogilvie, "Education under Hitler," *Friends of Europe*, 17 (December 1934): 59-60; a periodical published in London by German anti-Nazis in exile.

6. From Mosse, *Nazi Culture*, 80-81.

7. Hermann Rauschning, *The Voice of Destruction* (New York: G. P. Putnam's Sons, 1940), 251-252.

8. From Gregory Paul Wegner, *Anti-Semitism and Schooling under the Third Reich* (London: Routledge Falmer, 2002), 162.

9. International Military Tribunal, *Trial of the Major War Criminals*, 42 vols., (Nuremberg, 1947-1949), 19: 1399, 1112, 1196, 1658, on the CD-ROM *Nuremberg War Crimes Trials* (Seattle: Aristarchus Knowledge Industries, 1995); volume numbers correspond to the original publication, pagination does not.

10. Under the treaty of Versailles, Allied troops were to occupy the Rhineland for fifteen years—it ended in 1930; the French army deployed units recruited in its African colonies; the "hybrids" were persecuted by the Nazi regime.

11. From Fritz Brennecke, *The Nazi Primer: Official Handbook for Schooling the Hitler Youth*, trans. Harwood L. Childs (New York: Harper & Brothers, 1938), 4, 7-10, 20, 48, 56, 59, 62-63, 68-72, 77-81, 84.

12. Quoted in Mosse, *Nazi Culture*, 78.

13. Quoted in Claudia Koonz, *The Nazi Conscience* (Cambridge, Mass.: Belknap Press of Harvard University Press, 2003), 202.

14. In 1944 Gauleiter (Nazi regional party leader) Joseph Wagner denounced relativity as a "Jewish" and therefore non-Aryan term that he would not employ because it hampered scientific research, technological application, and the war effort.

15. From Mosse, *Nazi Culture*, 205-208.

16. Office of the United States Counsel for Prosecution of Axis Criminals, *Nazi Conspiracy and Aggression*, 8 vols. and 2 supplements (Washington, D.C.: U.S. Government Printing Office, 1946-1948), 8: 21, document M-33.

17. Ibid., 11, document M-13.

18. *Nazi Conspiracy and Aggression, Opinion and Judgment*, vol. unnumbered, 380, 385 on the CD-ROM.

19. More accurately, Neofito, the putative "Moldavian ex-rabbi" whose life and work remain obscure. First published in part in 1803 and in various languages in the nineteenth century, the bogus tome was much used, by the Vatican among others, as an infallible "source" for ritual murder and other supposed Jewish crimes.

20. (A) *Der Stürmer*, special issue no. 1, May 1934 in Randall L. Bytwerk, *Julius Streicher: The Man Who Persuaded a Nation to Hate Jews* (New York: Cooper Square Press, 2001), 199-201. (B) *Der Stürmer*, April 1937, Nuremberg document 2699-PS, trans. in *Nazi Conspiracy and Aggression* (Washington, D.C.: U.S. Government Printing Office, 1947), 5: 372-373. (C) *Der Stürmer*, no. 34, July 1933, trans. Randall L. Bytwerk; downloaded from www.calvin.edu/academic/cas/gpa/ds6.htm.

21. Nuremberg document 1778-PS, *Nazi Conspiracy and Aggression*, 4: 358-360.

TWENTY-ONE

The Jew in Nazi Wartime Propaganda

The Nazi regime was very sensitive to public opinion and was constantly engaged in surveying, sampling, and manipulating it. Propaganda as much as terror generated the consensus of loyalty and allegiance that emerged in Germany by the summer of 1933, and although modified and shifting over the years, it endured until the spell was broken by Hitler's suicide in 1945.The principal figure in the shaping of Nazi propaganda, both before and during the war, was Joseph Goebbels (1897–1945), the Minister of Propaganda and Popular Enlightenment.

Goebbels was born into a devoutly Catholic, lower middle class family in Rheyt, an industrial town in the Rhineland of Germany; small, crippled, and deformed, and always sickly and frail, Goebbels was rejected for military service in World War I. The valedictorian of his secondary school and an omnivorous reader, Goebbels was enabled by his parents' frugality and a Catholic organization's scholarship to attend the universities of Bonn, Freiburg, Würzburg, Munich, and Heidelberg, where he earned his doctorate in literature and Germanistics in 1921. Joining the Nazi Party in 1924, Goebbels supported Hitler's faction in party disputes and became Gauleiter (regional party leader) of Berlin in 1926; he was credited with having "captured Berlin for the movement." It is not clear how Goebbels became an antisemite or whether he actually believed the Aryan racial theories and the antisemitic ideology or simply used them as instruments of propaganda and power manipulation. Frustration as an unemployed Ph.D. and unpublished poet and novelist is the backdrop of his earliest vicious antisemitic pronouncements. Goebbels's antisemitism seems to have emanated from his idolatrous attachment to Hitler (whom he exalted as "the creative instrument of fate and deity") and his reading of Houston Stewart Chamberlain and many other such antisemitic authors. Cynical, nihilistic, opportunistic, devoid of any inner conviction except in the quest for power and domination, Goebbels recognized antisemitism's political potential.

Goebbels had a genius for propaganda, which in his hands was persuasive lying and manipulative deception; in 1930 Hitler made him coordinator of Nazi propaganda for the national political campaigns and elections. Goebbels early recognized the potential of the radio and used it himself with great demagogic effectiveness. Never outgrowing his adolescent adulation for Hitler, Goebbels was the principal creator of the Hitler myth, the cult of the infallible Führer and savior of Germany. In 1933 Hitler made Goebbels Minister of Propaganda and Popular Enlightenment with authority over press, radio, film, and theater. Within a short time Dr. Goebbels, as he insisted on being called, eliminated "Jewish" and "Negro" elements from music, literature, art, and theatre. His propaganda presented the invasion of Soviet Russia as a war imposed on Germany by Bolshevik Russia in alliance with "plutocratic" Britain, a conspiracy orchestrated by the real rulers of those countries, "the Jews," who are bent on world domination and the destruction of Germany. Goebbels was instrumental in launching "the burning of the [Jewish] books" on May 10, 1933; the pogrom of November 9, 1938, known as *Kristall-nacht;* the mobilization for "total war" following the Stalingrad defeat in 1943; and the suppression of the army officers' attempt to assassinate Hitler on July 20, 1944. Central though he was, there is no basis for the claim made by the discredited David Irving (see page 283) that Goebbels was "the mastermind of the Third Reich," that he was responsible for the Holocaust, which he implemented behind Hitler's back, without his knowledge and against his will.

Joseph Goebbels

"The Jews Are to Blame," 1941

Goebbels took the initiative in 1941 to impose on Jews the infamous yellow badge— a "hygienic prophylactic." When some citizens of Berlin expressed opposition to the stigmatizing badge, Goebbels castigated their "sentimentality" in the article excerpted below, "The Jews Are to Blame," which was published in the party weekly, *Das Reich.* The article is typical of Goebbels's antisemitic fulminations in its vocabulary and phrasing as well as in creating new myths and repeating old ones, most notably that the Jews ignited this war as they had in 1914. A keen, secret reader of *Das Reich* and Goebbels's weekly articles was Victor Klemperer (see page 156), a forcibly retired professor of Romance literature and linguistics and victim of Nazi persecution as a "non-Aryan Christian"; he drew many examples from Goebbels of Orwellian "easy-speak"—circumlocutions, euphemisms, every kind of linguistic device to delude readers—for a post-war book analyzing Nazi totalitarian language and propaganda.

The historic responsibility of world Jewry for the outbreak and widening of this war has been proven so clearly that it does not need to be talked about any further. The Jews wanted war, and now they have it. But the Führer's prophecy of 30 January 1939 to the German Reichstag is also being fulfilled: If international finance Jewry should succeed in plunging the world into war once again, the result will be not the Bolshevization of the world and thereby the victory of the Jews, but rather the destruction of the Jewish race in Europe.

We are seeing the fulfillment of the prophecy. The Jews are receiving a penalty that is certainly hard, but more than deserved. World Jewry erred in adding up the forces available to it for this war, and now is gradually experiencing the destruction that it planned for us, and would have carried out without a second thought if it had possessed the ability. It is perishing according its own law: "An eye for an eye, a tooth for a tooth."

Every Jew is our enemy in this historic struggle, regardless of whether he vegetates in a Polish ghetto or carries on his parasitic existence in Berlin or Hamburg or blows the trumpets of war in New York or Washington. All Jews by virtue of their birth and their race are part of an international conspiracy against National Socialist Germany. They want its defeat and annihilation, and do all in their power to bring it about. That they can do nothing inside the Reich is hardly a sign of their loyalty, but rather of the appropriate measures we took against them.

One of these measures is the institution of the yellow star that each Jew must wear. We wanted to make them visible as Jews, particularly if they made even the least attempt to harm the German community. It is a remarkably humane measure on our part, a hygienic and prophylactic measure to be sure that the Jew cannot infiltrate our ranks unseen to sow discord.

As the Jews first appeared several weeks ago on the streets of Berlin graced with their Jewish star, the initial reaction of the citizens of the Reich capital was surprise. Only a few knew that there were still so many Jews in Berlin. Everyone suddenly found someone in the neighborhood who seemed like a harmless fellow citizen, who perhaps complained or criticized a bit more than normal, and whom no one had thought to be a Jew. He had concealed himself, mimicked his surroundings, adopting the color of the background, adjusted to the environment, in order to wait for the proper moment. Who among us had any idea that the enemy was beside him, that a silent or clever auditor was attending to conversations on the street, in the subway, or in the lines outside cigarette shops? There are Jews one cannot recognize by external signs. These are the most dangerous. It always happens that when we take some measure against the Jews, English or American newspapers report it the next day. Even today the Jews still have secret connections to our enemies abroad and use these not only in their own cause, but in all military matters of the Reich as well. The enemy is in our midst. What makes more sense than to at least make this plainly visible to our citizens? . . .

This is an elementary principle of racial, national, and social hygiene. They will never give us rest. If they could, they would drive one nation after another into war against us. Who cares about their difficulties, they who only want to force the world to accept their bloody financial domination? The Jews are a parasitic race that feeds like a foul fungus on the cultures of healthy but ignorant peoples. There is only one effective measure: cut them out.

How stupid and thoughtless are the arguments of the backward friends of the Jews in the face of a problem that has occupied mankind for millennia! How they would gape if they could ever see their dear Jews in power! But that would be too late. That is why it is the duty of a national leadership to take all necessary measures to keep such a thing from happening. There are differences between people just as there are differences between animals. Some people are good, others bad. The same is true of animals. The fact that the Jew still lives among us is no proof that he belongs among us, just as a flea is not a household pet simply because it lives in a house. When Mr. Bramsig or Mrs. Knöterich feel pity for an old woman wearing the Jewish star, they should also remember that a distant nephew of this old woman by the name of Nathan Kaufmann sits in New York and has prepared a plan by which all Germans under the age of 60 will be sterilized. They should recall that a son of her distant uncle is a warmonger named Baruch or Morgenthau or Untermayer who stands behind Mr. Roosevelt, driving him to war, and that if they succeed, a fine but ignorant U.S. soldier may one day shoot dead the only son of Mr. Bramsig or Mrs. Knöterich. It will all be for the benefit of Jewry, to which this old woman also belongs, no matter how fragile and pitiable she may seem. . . .

Therefore, we must say again and yet again:

1. The Jews are our destruction. They started this war and direct it. They want to destroy the German Reich and our people. This plan must be blocked.

2. There are no distinctions between Jews. Each Jew is a sworn enemy of the German people. If he does not make his hostility plain, it is only from cowardice and slyness, not because he loves us.

3. The Jews are to blame for each German soldier who falls in this war. They have him on their conscience, and must also pay for it.

4. If someone wears the Jewish star, he is an enemy of the people. Anyone who deals with him is the same as a Jew and must be treated accordingly. He earns the contempt of the entire people, for he is a craven coward who leaves them in the lurch to stand by the enemy.

5. The Jews enjoy the protection of our enemies. That is all the proof we need to show how harmful they are for our people.

6. The Jews are the enemy's agents among us. He who stands by them aids the enemy.

7. The Jews have no right to claim equality with us. If they wish to speak on the streets, in lines outside shops or in public transportation, they should be ignored, not only because they are simply wrong, but because they are Jews who have no right to a voice in the community.

8. If the Jews appeal to your sentimentality, realize that they are hoping for your forgetfulness, and let them know that you see through them and hold them in contempt.

9. A decent enemy will deserve our generosity after we have won. The Jew however is not a decent enemy, though he tries to seem so.

10. The Jews are responsible for the war. The treatment they receive from us is hardly unjust. They have deserved it all.[1]

Antisemitic Indoctrination of the German Soldier

Jews and Bolsheviks as Devils, 1941–1943

Accepting the claims and assertions made in their memoirs and autobiographies by German generals after World War II, many Germans maintained that the *Wehrmacht* (the German armed forces) was an apolitical professional fighting force that shunned Nazi ideology and race hatred and faithfully lived up to the traditional laws and rules of war; according to such apologists it was solely Heinrich Himmler's SS that was responsible for the extermination of Jews. It is now clear that such claims blaming all or most criminality on the "black coats" of the SS serves as a glib "alibi" for the *Wehrmacht* and Germany:[2] Units of the German army joined the SS in rounding up Jews and participated in mass murder. Recently historians have also shown that the regular army—junior officers in particular who had been indoctrinated in the Hitler Youth and Labor Front and a quarter to a third of whom were Nazi Party members—far from being apolitical, was imbued with the Nazi ideology, and that many German officers and soldiers, succumbing to Nazi indoctrination, viewed the war, particularly on the eastern front, as a titanic struggle against evil and subhuman Jewish-led Bolsheviks who threatened the very existence of the German Volk. In 1939 the German High Command issued a leaflet to company officers to instruct their men that the two principal aims of the approaching war were "1. Wiping out all after-effects of the Jewish influence. . . . 2. The struggle against World Judaism [which] we fight the way one would fight a poisonous parasite . . . the plague of all peoples."[3] The following excerpts from SS headquarters, German generals, and letters written by soldiers bear out the conclusion of Omer Bartov:

> It is on the issue of genocide that the German military surely comes out worse than any other modern army. This is both because the army itself actively pursued a policy of mass killing of Russians, and because it was an essential instrument in the realization of the "Final Solution." The attempt to differentiate between the *Wehrmacht* and the SS, between the fighting at the front and the death camps in the rear, presents a wholly false picture of the historical reality. . . . [T]he army was involved in the implementation of the "Final Solution" at every conceivable level, beginning with the conquest of the areas which contained the highest concentration of Jewish population, through rendering logistical and manpower support to the *Einsatzgruppen* [SS murder units] and the death camp administrations, to the bitter determination with which it resisted the final and inevitable defeat of the Third Reich at a time when the rate of the industrial killing of millions of human beings was at its height. The *Wehrmacht* was thus a crucial factor in the most horrendous crime perpetrated by any nation in modern history.[4]

The first excerpt, part of a tract issued by SS headquarters, vividly illustrates the mythical quality of Nazi ideology.

Just as night rises up against the day, just as light and darkness are eternal enemies, so the greatest enemy of world-dominating man is man himself. The
sub-man—that creature which looks as though biologically it were of absolutely the same kind, endowed by Nature with hands, feet and a sort of brain,
with eyes and mouth—is nevertheless a totally different, a fearful creature, is
only an attempt at a human being, with a quasi-human face, yet in mind and
spirit lower than any animal. Inside this being a cruel chaos of wild, unchecked
passions: a nameless will to destruction, the most primitive lusts, the most
undisguised vileness: A sub-man—nothing else! . . . Never has the sub-man
granted peace, never has he permitted rest. . . . To preserve himself he needed
mud, he needed hell, but not the sun. And this underworld of sub-men found
its leader: the eternal Jew![5]

> ["Information for Troops" distributed to regular army units used similar lan-
> guage.]

Anyone who has ever looked at the face of a red commissar knows what
the Bolsheviks are like. Here there is no need for theoretical expressions. We
would insult the animals if we described these mostly Jewish men as beasts.
They are the embodiment of the Satanic and insane hatred against the whole
of noble humanity. The shape of these commissars reveals to us the rebellion
of the *Untermenschen* [submen] against noble blood. The masses, whom they
have sent to their deaths [in this war against Germany] by making use of all
means at their disposal such as ice-cold terror and insane incitement, would
have brought an end to all meaningful life, had this eruption not been dammed
at the last moment.[6]

> [In his Order of the Day of October 10, 1941, Field Marshal Walter von
> Reichenau, commander of the Sixth Army, appealed to his men in the lan-
> guage of Nazi racial ideology; Hitler was so impressed with this "excellent"
> proclamation that he called for its distribution to all front-line units of the
> *Ostheer* (eastern army). In August Reichenau had been angered by the inter-
> vention of Ernst Tewes, a Catholic army chaplain, and two or three others
> trying to stop the shooting of Jewish children in the Ukrainian town of Belaya
> Tserkov; but "All we managed to save were shot" within two days and Tewes
> was posted to a more dangerous area.][7]

SECRET!
Subject: Conduct of Troops in Eastern Territories.
Regarding the conduct of troops towards the Bolshevistic system, vague ideas
are still prevalent in many cases. The most essential aim of war against the
Jewish-Bolshevistic system is a complete destruction of their means of power
and the elimination of Asiatic influence from the European culture. In this
connection the troops are facing tasks which exceed the one-sided routine of
soldiering. The soldier in the eastern territories is not merely a fighter according to the rules of the art of war but also a bearer of ruthless national ideology
and the avenger of bestialities which have been inflicted upon Germans and racially related nations.

Therefore the soldier must have full understanding for the necessity of a severe but just revenge on subhuman Jewry. The Army has to aim at another purpose, i.e. the annihilation of revolts in the hinterland which, as experience proves, have always been caused by Jews. . . .

. . . Being far from all political considerations of the future, the soldier has to fulfill two tasks:

1. *Complete annihilation of the false Bolshevistic doctrine of the Soviet State and its armed forces.*

2. *The pitiless extermination of foreign treachery and cruelty* [of guerillas] *and thus the protection of military personnel in Russia.*

This is the only way to fulfill our historical task to liberate the German people once for ever from the Asiatic-Jewish danger.[8]

[The Prussian-German tradition of "the unpolitical soldier" resulted in military commanders who were morally apathetic, political yes-men. Brilliantly trained, they attained the highest degree of military proficiency, but no more than a narrowly technical and blinkered professionalism. Field Marshall Erich von Manstein, the most gifted military strategist of World War II, exemplified their blindness in the readiness with which he—like almost all his fellow commanders—issued orders pursuant to carrying out Hitler's infamous Commissar Order of June 6, 1941 (ordering immediate liquidation of all captured Communist Party political liaisons to the Red Army), his "Night & Fog Decree" of December 12, 1941 (requiring the "disappearance into the night and fog" of anyone suspected of resistance or sabotage), and others like them, many of which used virtually identical wording. A British military court sentenced Manstein to eighteen years imprisonment but he was released in 1952. In November 1941, as commander of the Eleventh Army, Manstein issued the following order.]

Since 22 June [1941, the onset of the German invasion of Soviet Russia] the German Volk is in the midst of a battle for life and death against the Bolshevik system. This battle is conducted against the Soviet army not only in a conventional manner according to the rules of European warfare. . . .

Judaism constitutes the mediator between the enemy in the rear and the still fighting remnants of the Red Army and the Red leadership. It has a stronger hold than in Europe on all key positions of the political leadership and administration, it occupies commerce and trade and further forms cells for all the disturbances and possible rebellions.

The Jewish-Bolshevik system must be eradicated once and for all. Never again may it interfere in our European living space.

The German soldier is therefore not only charged with the task of destroying the power instrument of this system. He marches forth also as a carrier of a racial conception and as an avenger of all the atrocities which have been committed against him and the German people.

The soldier must show understanding for the harsh atonement of Judaism, the spiritual carrier of the Bolshevik terror.[9]

[And in that same month, Colonel-General Hermann Hoth also interpreted the war as a struggle between racial superiors and inferiors; the American military tribunal sentenced Hoth to fifteen years.]

It has become increasingly clear to us this summer [of 1941], that here in the East spiritually unbridgeable conceptions are fighting each other: German sense of honor and race, and a soldierly tradition of many centuries, against an Asiatic mode of thinking and primitive instincts, whipped up by a small number of mostly Jewish intellectuals: fear of the knout [whip used for flogging], disregard of moral values, leveling down, throwing away of one's worthless life.

More than ever we are filled with the thought of a new era, in which the strength of the German people's racial superiority and achievements entrust it with the leadership of Europe. We clearly recognize our mission to save European culture from the advancing Asiatic barbarism. We now know that we have to fight against an incensed and tough opponent. This battle can only end with the destruction of one or the other; a compromise is out of the question.[10]

[The frontline soldier was affected by ideological propaganda.]

I have received the "Stürmer" [Julius Streicher's crudely antisemitic newspaper (see page 182)] now for the third time. It makes me happy with all my heart. . . . You could not have made me happier. . . . I recognized the Jewish poison in our people long ago; how far it might have gone with us, this we see only now in this campaign. What the Jewish regime has done in Russia, we see everyday, and even the last doubters are cured here in view of the facts. We must and we will liberate the world from this plague, this is why the German soldier protects the Eastern Front, and we shall not return before we have uprooted all evil and destroyed the center of the Jewish-Bolshevik "world-do-gooders."[11]

[In October 1942 the Army High Command (OKH) re-iterated these ideas in the following order directed to the officer corps.]

Every officer must be filled with the conviction that it is first of all the influence of the Jews which hinders the German people in realising its claims for living space and status in the world and forces our people for the second time to turn against a world of enemies with the blood of our best sons. Therefore the officer must have an unambiguous, completely uncompromising position regarding the Jewish question. There is no difference between so-called decent Jews and others.[12]

[A year later, October 1943, Himmler, in his notorious speech on "the page of glory" to high SS officers at Posen, expressed the same sentiments as army documents, practically word for word, indicating that if the *Wehrmacht* and SS had once been rivals for power they had become collaborators in genocide, differing somewhat in means but not ends.]

I mean the clearing out of the Jews, the extermination of the Jewish race. It's one of those things it is easy to talk about. "The Jewish race is being exterminated," says one Party member, "that's quite clear; it's in our program; elimination of the Jews, and we're doing it, exterminating them." And then there come 80 million worthy Germans and each one has his decent Jew. Of course, the others are vermin, but this one is an A-1 Jew. Not one of all those who talk this way has witnessed it, not one of them has been through it. Most of you must know what it means when 100 corpses are lying side by side, or 500–1000. To have stuck it out and at the same time apart from exceptions caused by human weakness to have remained decent fellows, that is what has made us hard. This is a page of glory in our history which has never been written and is never to be written, for we know how difficult we should have made it for ourselves, if with bombing raids, the burden and deprivations of war we still had Jews today in every town as secret saboteurs, agitators, and trouble mongers.[13]

NOTES

1. Downloaded from German Propaganda Archive, http://www.calvin.edu/academic/cas/gpa, trans. Randall L. Bytwerk.

2. Quoted in Omer Bartov, *The Eastern Front, 1941-45, German Troops and the Barbarisation of Warfare* (New York: St. Martin's Press, 1986), 182 n. 121.

3. Bartov, *The Eastern Front*, 94.

4. Omer Bartov, *Germany's War and the Holocaust: Disputed Histories* (Ithaca: Cornell University Press, 2003), 14.

5. Quoted in Norman Cohn, *Warrant for Genocide* (New York: Harper and Row, 1968), 124.

6. Quoted in Bartov, *The Eastern Front*, 83.

7. Quoted in Doris L. Bergen, "German Military Chaplains in the Third Reich," in Omer Bartov and Phyllis Mack, *In God's Name: Genocide and Religion in the Twentieth Century* (New York: Berghahn Books, 2001), 125; of about a thousand chaplains in the German army, fewer than ten engaged in any kind of resistance or opposition to the Holocaust.

8. Nuremberg document D-411, International Military Tribunal, *Nazi Conspiracy and Aggression*, 8 vols. and 2 supplements (Washington, D.C.: U.S. Government Printing Office, 1946-1948), 7: 51-53.

9. Quoted in Omer Bartov, *Hitler's Army: Soldiers, Nazis, and War in the Third Reich* (New York: Oxford University Press, 1992), 130.

10. Quoted in Bartov, *Hitler's Army*, 130-131.

11. Quoted in Bartov, *Hitler's Army*, 163.

12. Quoted in Bartov, *The Eastern Front*, 94.

13. International Military Tribunal, *Nuremberg War Crimes Trials*, CD-ROM (Seattle: Aristarchus Knowledge Industries, 1995), 3: 1468-1469 (Nuremberg document PS-1919).

TWENTY-TWO

The Holocaust (Shoah)

The Nazis' "Final Solution of the Jewish Question" aimed to destroy European Jewry to the last man, woman, and child. The task of implementing the Final Solution was given to Heinrich Himmler and the SS, and they fulfilled their grisly duties with fanaticism and bureaucratic efficiency. In exterminating the Jewish people, the Nazis believed they were righteous and courageous and serving a higher good—the defense of the sacred Volk. Regarding themselves as idealists who were writing a glorious chapter in the history of Germany, the SS tortured and murdered with immense dedication and efficiency.

Special units of SS—the *Einsatzgruppen,* trained for mass murder—followed on the heels of the German army into Russia. Entering captured villages and cities, they rounded up Jewish men, women, and children, herded them to execution grounds, and slaughtered them with machine-gun and rifle fire at the edge of open trenches, which sometimes were piled high with thousands of victims, including severely wounded people, who would suffocate to death when the pit was filled with earth. Aided by Ukrainian, Lithuanian, and Latvian auxiliaries, *Volksdeutsche* (ethnic Germans living in the east), and contingents from the Romanian army, the *Einsatzgruppen* massacred some 1.3 million Jews. It was the boast of SS-Colonel Karl Jäger, commander of *Einsatzkommando* 3 (strike force) of about 250 men, that "careful planning" enabled him to lead five such actions per week and shoot some 130,000 Jews in Lithuania from June 22 to December 1, 1941. Units of the *Wehrmacht* (regular armed forces) actively participated in the roundups of Jews and sometimes in the shootings.

In Poland, where some 3.3 million Jews lived, the Germans established ghettos in the larger cities. Jews from all over the country were crammed into these ghettos, which were sealed off from the rest of the population. The German administration deliberately curtailed the food supply, and many Jews died of malnutrition, disease, and beatings.

The mass killings by *Einsatzgruppen* posed problems for the Germans. These murders were too public, whereas the Germans wanted to keep the Final Solution as secret as possible. Furthermore, the face-to-face killing of civilians, including women and children, was often too hard on the psyche of the personnel charged with carrying out such orders. (They could refuse to obey such orders, and those few who did were not punished in any significant way.) To overcome these difficulties, the Germans built death camps in Poland designed to murder Jews in gas chambers.[1] With the aid of collaborators in occupied lands, Jews from all over Europe were rounded up—for "resettlement," they were told. Jammed into sealed cattle cars, eighty or a hundred to a car, the victims traveled sometimes for days, without food or water, choking from the stench of vomit and excrement and shattered by the crying of children. Disgorged at the concentration camps, they entered "another planet." SS doctors quickly inspected the new arrivals, "the freight," as they referred to them. Rudolf Höss, the commandant of Auschwitz—the most notorious of the murder factories—described the procedure with clinical detachment (see page 211). Those who could work were "selected"; all the rest, obviously children, babies, and pregnant women, were immediately herded naked into the death chamber—shower rooms, they were told. The corpses, covered with blood and excrement and intertwined with each other, were piled high to the ceiling. To make way for the next group, the *Sonderkommando*, a squad of Jewish prisoners, emptied the gas chambers of the corpses and removed gold teeth, which, along with the victims' hair, eyeglasses, and clothing, were carefully collected and catalogued for the war effort and for German civilians. (The expropriation of Jewish property throughout Europe helped keep Germans prosperous until the last year of the war and strengthened their ties to the Nazi regime.) Later the bodies were burned in crematoria specially constructed by civilian contractors, such as Topf & Sons of Erfurt. The chimneys belched black smoke, and the stench of burning flesh permeated the entire region. Between 1.1 and 1.5 million people died in Auschwitz—90 percent of them Jews. Non-Jewish victims included Romani and Sinti, political prisoners, and Soviet prisoners of war.

Auschwitz was more than a murder factory. It also provided the German industrial giant I. G. Farben (one of about a hundred German firms that exploited Jewish workers in camps and ghettos), which operated a factory adjoining the camp, with slave laborers, Jewish and non-Jewish. The working pace at the factory and the ill-treatment by guards and civilian foremen were so brutal, reported a physician and inmate, that "while working many prisoners suddenly stretched out flat, turned blue, gasped for breath, and died like beasts."[2]

Auschwitz also allowed the SS to shape and harden themselves according to the National Socialist creed. A survivor recalls seeing SS men and women amuse themselves with pregnant inmates. The unfortunate women were "beaten with clubs and whips, torn by dogs, dragged by the hair, and kicked in the stomach with heavy German boots. Then, when they collapsed, they were thrown into the crematory—alive."[3] By systematically overworking, starving, beating, terrorizing, and degrading the inmates, by making them live in filth—according to the tactic of "excremental assault" that "swiftly turned [men] into stinking, repulsive skeletons"[4]—and sleep sprawled all over each other in tiny cubicles, the SS deliberately sought to strip prisoners of all human dignity, to make them appear and behave as "subhumans," and even to make them believe that they were "subhuman," as the National Socialist ideology asserted. The SS relished their absolute power over the inmates; it was proof of their Aryan superiority and elite status.

The SS were often ideologues committed to racist doctrines, which, they believed, were supported by the laws of biology. They were true believers driven by a utopian vision of a new world order founded on a Social Darwinist fantasy of racial hierarchy and eternal struggle. To realize this mythic vision of ultimate good, the Jews, the source of all evil, had to be destroyed; the defense of the fatherland and the "race" required the elimination of the Jews. Other SS, and many of their numerous volunteers and collaborators, including municipal policemen and military personnel, were simply ordinary people doing their duty as they had been trained, following orders the best way they knew how. They were morally indifferent bureaucrats, concerned with techniques and effectiveness, and careerists and functionaries seeking to impress superiors with their ability to get the job done. Such people quickly adjusted to the routines of mass murder. Thus, as Konnilyn Feig observes, the thousands of German railway workers "treated the Jewish cattle-car transports as a special business problem that they took pride in solving so well."[5] The German physicians who selected Jews for the gas chambers were concerned only with the technical problems and efficiency, and those doctors and scientists who performed unspeakable medical experiments on Jews viewed their subjects as laboratory animals, as the following correspondence of an I. G. Farben official with Commandant Höss testifies:

> In contemplation of experiments of a new soporific drug we would appreciate your procuring for us a number of women. . . . We propose to pay not more than 170 marks a head. If agreeable, we will take possession of the women. We need approximately 150. . . . Received the order of 150 women. Despite their emaciated condition, they were found satisfactory. . . . The tests were made. All subjects died. We shall contact you on the subject of a new load.[6]

The German industrialists who worked Jewish slave laborers to death considered only cost effectiveness in their operations. So, too, did the firms that built the gas chambers and the furnaces, whose durability and performance they guaranteed. An eyewitness reports that engineers from Topf & Sons experimented with different combinations of corpses, deciding that "the most economical and fuel-saving procedure would be to burn the bodies of a well-nourished man and an emaciated woman or vice versa together with that of a child, because, as the experiments had established, in this combination, once they had caught fire, the dead would continue to burn without any further coke being required."[7] Commandant Höss, who exemplified the bureaucratic mentality, noted that his gas chambers were more efficient than those used at Treblinka, because they could accommodate far more people and the use of Zyklon-B fumigant gas avoided awkward delays in starting up diesel motors. The Germans were so concerned with efficiency and cost that— to conserve ammunition or gas and not slow down the pace from the time victims were ordered to undress until they were hurried into the chambers—toddlers were taken from their mothers and thrown live into burning pits or mass graves.

There have been many massacres during the course of world history. And the Nazis murdered many non-Jews in concentration camps and in reprisals for acts of resistance. What is unprecedented about the Holocaust was the Nazis' determination to murder without exception every single Jew who came within their grasp, and the fanaticism, ingenuity, cruelty, and systematic way—mass murder—with which they pursued this goal to the last hour of the war.

The Holocaust was the fulfillment of Nazi racial theories. Believing that they were cleansing Europe of worthless life and a dangerous race that threatened Germany, Nazi executioners performed their evil work with dedication, assembly-line precision, and moral indifference—a gruesome testament to human irrationality and wickedness. Using the technology and bureaucracy of a modern state, the Germans killed approximately 6 million Jews: some two-thirds of the Jewish population of Europe. About 1.5 million of the murdered were children; almost 90 percent of Jewish children in German-occupied lands perished. Tens of thousands of entire families were wiped out without a trace. Centuries-old Jewish community life and culture vanished, never to be restored. Burned into the soul of the Jewish people was a wound that could never entirely heal. Written into the history of Western civilization was an episode that would forever cast doubt on the Enlightenment conception of human goodness, rationality, and the progress of civilization. The following excerpts show how deeply Nazi mythology—the Jews as racial degenerates, global conspirators, satanic evil-doers—penetrated the consciousness of Germans carrying out the Final Solution.

Chaim A. Kaplan

Scroll of Agony: *The Warsaw Ghetto, 1939–1941*

Chaim Aron Kaplan was born in Russia in 1880. He received both a Jewish talmudic and a secular education. An educator and writer, he founded a pioneer Hebrew school and was its principal for forty years in Warsaw, to which he had moved around 1900. He contributed frequently to Hebrew and Yiddish periodicals and edited Hebrew textbooks for children. In 1921 Kaplan visited the United States and in 1936 he stayed in Palestine with his two children who had emigrated earlier; his intention to settle in Palestine was thwarted by personal problems and he returned to Poland. In 1941, when he could have procured a visa, he decided to stay in Warsaw to record Jewish persecution in his diaries for posterity. Written in Hebrew, Kaplan's diary is a magnificent example of contemporary history written in the direst of circumstances when his life was in danger and he was virtually starving. He describes the German conquest of Poland, the relationship of Poles and Jews, and the death agony of the Jewish community in the Warsaw ghetto, a story punctuated by the Germans' systematic brutality in inflicting persecution, torture, starvation, deportations, and death. As seen in the excerpts that follow, Kaplan is at his most brilliant in dissecting the motives and ultimate aims of "the German barbarians" who "seek to steal [the liberty] of mankind." Not all of the diary, running from September 1939 to August 1942, survived the war. Kaplan was deported to Treblinka where he and his wife were murdered in December 1942 or January 1943.

October 28, 1939.

In the eyes of the conquerors we are outside the category of human beings. This is the Nazi ideology, and its followers, both common soldiers and officers, are turning it into a living reality. Their wickedness reaches the heights of human cruelty. These people must be considered psychopaths and sadists, because normal people are incapable of such abominable acts. There are army officers whose greatest pleasure is to lie in wait for bearded Jews on Nalewki Street, to attack them, and to cut off half their beards. The unfortunate Jew is afraid to oppose this, lest his opposition be considered a crime for which he will be punished. Jews are pulled out of lines and beaten for no reason. . . .

Our tragedy is not in the humane or cruel actions of individuals, but in the plan in general, which shows no pity toward the Jews. We are certain that this census is being taken for the purpose of expelling "nonproductive elements." And there are a great many of us now. No one knows whose lot will be drawn and therefore sorrow is on every face. We are caught in a net, doomed to destruction. . . .

November 11, 1939.

. . . This is not the eve of destruction, but destruction itself. Our personal degradation is calamitous, and material impoverishment is bound up in our degradation. The entire administrative machinery is geared toward this end. Everywhere—"no Jews allowed." Czarism used to do this, but without sadism. With all its savagery, it had laws which it was careful to obey; there were certain limitations to its persecutions. Beyond such a point it is no longer "law" but barbarity, and Czarism refrained from barbarity. Not so the unclean Nazi! Everything is permitted him; he has no restrictions. That shame which keeps one from sinning has abandoned him. On the contrary, cruelty to Jews is a national *mitzvah* [Hebrew for commandment or good deed]. He who causes them the most suffering is the most praiseworthy. And so we are trodden upon like mud in the streets. And the upright, ordinary Jew asks himself and his fellows-in-distress: Is there no justice in the world?

Just as darkness rules the streets of Warsaw, so does it dominate our minds. The conqueror depletes the spirit along with more material things. Every spark of light is a potential breach in the kingdom of darkness of bestial Nazism; therefore everything that ties us to the democratic world is denied us. . . .

December 25, 1939.

. . . The principles of Nazism are not, after all, terribly original. The nullification of all hitherto accepted ideals was adopted from Bolshevism. The starling did not visit the crow for nothing, but because they are two of a kind. They share an ideological affinity, which becomes one at the first opportunity.

Nor did Nazism carry on original work in the field of hatred toward the Jewish people. They merely plowed more deeply, fertilized the field and its seeds, so that it would yield new, flourishing crops. Nazism found the primeval matter of religious hatred all prepared as a heritage of the Middle Ages. It merely reinforced it with economic hatred, in which it mixed various drugs— bits of ideology from Nietzsche, from Houston Stewart Chamberlain, and from other bigots and racists. . . .

February 9, 1940.

. . . In the mind of the Führer. . . . [t]here is no remedy for the Jews but "Krepieren" [to croak, die like animals]. But the Jews refuse "Krepieren." It appears to me that the Führer is mistaken, as were Pharaoh, Nebuchadnezzar, and Haman.

March 10, 1940.

The gigantic catastrophe which has descended on Polish Jewry has no parallel, even in the darkest periods of Jewish history. First, in the depth of the hatred. This is not just hatred whose source is in a party platform, and which was invented for political purposes. It is a hatred of emotion, whose source is some psychopathic malady. In its outward manifestations it functions as physiological hatred, which imagines the object of hatred to be unclean in body, a leper who has no place within the camp.

The masses have absorbed this sort of qualitative hatred. Their limited understanding cannot grasp ideological hatred; psychology is beyond them and they are incapable of understanding it. They have absorbed their masters' teachings in a concrete, corporeal form. The Jew is filthy; the Jew is a swindler and an evildoer; the Jew is the enemy of Germany, who undermines its existence; the Jew was the prime mover in the Versailles Treaty, which reduced Germany to nothing; the Jew is Satan, who sows dissension between one nation and another, arousing them to bloodshed in order to profit from their destruction. These are easily understood concepts whose effect in day-to-day life can be felt immediately.

But the founders of Nazism, and the party leaders, created a scientific ideology on deeper foundations. They have a complete doctrine which analyzes the Jewish spirit inside and out. Judaism and Nazism are two world outlooks, neither of which is compatible with the other, and for this reason they cannot live together. For two thousand years Judaism has left its imprint, culturally and spiritually, on nations of the world. It stood like a rock, blocking the spread of German paganism whose teaching was different and whose culture was carved out of a different source. Two kings cannot use one crown. Either humanity would be Judaic, or it would be idolatrous-German. Up until now it was Judaic. Even Catholicism is a daughter of Judaism, and the child of its spirit, and is therefore afflicted with the shortcomings it inherited from its mother. The new world which Nazism will fashion is directed toward primitive idolatry with all of its attitudes. It is therefore ready to fight Judaism to the finish.[8]

Hermann Graebe

The Slaughter of "Untermenschen" *in Ukraine, 1942*

While the regular German army penetrated deeply into Soviet Russia, special SS units, the *Einsatzgruppen,* rounded up Jews, often entire villages and families, for mass executions. In massacring the Jews, the SS believed that they were ridding Europe of *Untermenschen* (subhumans) that threatened the German Volk and Aryan races. Hermann Graebe, a German construction engineer, saw such mass butchery in Dubno, Ukraine. He gave a sworn affidavit before the International Military Tribunal at Nuremberg, where the Allies tried the major German war criminals after World War II. Graebe had joined the Nazi Party in 1931 but later renounced his membership, and during the war he rescued Jews from the SS. Graebe was the only German citizen to volunteer to testify at the Nuremberg trials, an act that brought him the enmity of his compatriots. Socially ostracized, Graebe emigrated to the United States, where he lived until his death at the age of 85 in 1986. Following is Graebe's affidavit.

On October 5, 1942, when I visited the building at Dubno, my foreman told me that in the vicinity of the site, Jews from Dubno had been shot in three large pits, each about 30 metres long and 3 metres deep. About 1,500 persons had been killed daily. All the 5,000 Jews who had still been living in Dubno before the pogroms were to be liquidated. As the shooting had taken place in his presence, he was still much upset.

Thereupon, I drove to the site accompanied by my foreman and saw near it great mounds of earth, about 30 metres long and 2 metres high. Several trucks stood in front of the mounds. Armed Ukrainian militia drove the people off the trucks under the supervision of an SS man. The militia acted as guards on the trucks and drove them to and from the pit. All these people had the regulation yellow patches on the front and back of their clothes, and thus could be recognized as Jews.

My foreman and I went directly to the pits. Nobody bothered us. Now I heard rifle shots in quick succession from behind one of the earth mounds. The people who got off the trucks—men, women and children—had to undress upon the orders of the SS man, who carried a riding or dog whip. They had to put down their clothes in fixed places, sorted according to shoes, top clothing and underclothing. I saw a heap of shoes of about 800 to 1,000 pairs, a great pile of underlinen and clothing.

Without screaming or weeping, these people undressed, stood around in family groups, kissed each other, said farewells, and waited for a sign from another SS man, who stood near the pit, also with a whip in his hand. During the fifteen minutes I stood near I heard no complaint or plea for mercy. I watched a family of about eight persons, a man and a woman both about fifty with their children of about one, eight and ten, and two grown-up daughters of about twenty and twenty-nine. An old woman with snow-white hair was holding the one-year-old in her arms and singing to it and tickling it. The child was cooing with delight. The couple was looking on with tears in their eyes. The father was holding the hand of a boy about ten years old and speaking to him softly; the boy was fighting his tears. The father pointed to the sky, stroked his head, and seemed to explain something to him.

At that moment the SS man at the pit shouted something to his comrade. The latter counted off about twenty persons and instructed them to go behind the earth mound. Among them was the family which I have mentioned. I well remember a girl, slim and with black hair, who, as she passed close to me, pointed to herself and said "23." I walked around the mound and found myself confronted by a tremendous grave. People were closely wedged together and lying on top of each other so that only their heads were visible. Nearly all had blood running over their shoulders from their heads. Some of the people shot were still moving. Some were lifting their arms and turning their heads to show that they were still alive. The pit was already two-thirds full. I estimated that it already contained about 1,000 people.

I looked for the man who did the shooting. He was an SS man, who sat at the edge of the narrow end of the pit, his feet dangling into the pit. He had a tommy-gun on his knees and was smoking a cigarette. The people, completely naked, went down some steps which were cut in the clay wall of the pit and clambered over the heads of the people lying there, to the place to which the SS man directed them. They lay down in front of the dead or injured people; some caressed those who were still alive and spoke to them in a low voice.

Then I heard a series of shots. I looked into the pit and saw that the bodies were twitching or the heads lying motionless on top of the bodies which lay before them. Blood was running from their necks. I was surprised that I was not ordered away, but I saw that there were two or three postmen in uniform nearby. The next batch was approaching already. They went down into the pit, lined themselves up against the previous victims and were shot.

When I walked around the mound, I noticed another truckload of people which had just arrived. This time it included sick and infirm persons. An old, very thin woman with terribly thin legs was undressed by others who were already naked, while two people held her up. The woman appeared to be paralyzed. The naked people carried the woman around the mound. I left with my foreman and drove back in my car to Dubno.

On the morning of the next day, when I again visited the site, I saw about thirty naked people lying near the pit—about 30 to 50 metres away from it. Some of them were still alive; they looked straight in front of them with a fixed stare and seemed to notice neither the chilliness of the morning nor the workers of my firm who stood around. A girl of about 20 spoke to me and asked me to give her clothes and help her to escape. At that moment we heard a fast car approach and I noticed that it was an SS detail. I moved away to my site. Ten minutes later we heard shots from the vicinity of the pit. The Jews still alive had been forced to throw the corpses into the pit, then they had themselves to lie down in this to be shot in the neck.[9]

Y. Pfeffer

The Concentration Camp Routine:
Daily Brutalization and Humiliation, 1940s

The concentration camp and killing center at Majdanek, near Lublin in Poland, was set up in 1941, initially to produce military supplies. It quartered fifty thousand or more prisoners and by war's end at least two hundred thousand victims had been murdered there. On November 3, 1943, the SS celebrated a "harvest festival" by machine-gunning eighteen thousand Jews at the edge of ditches the victims had dug. Despite great economic need and labor shortages, none of the concentration or so-called labor camps was productive or profitable: The ideology put so high a priority on the annihilation of the Jews that the war effort and economic efficiency simply did not count. In 1946 a Jewish survivor of Majdanek, Y. Pfeffer, described the camp's daily routine in the hellish world created by the SS and Nazi ideology.

You get up at 3 AM. You have to dress quickly, and make the "bed" so that it looks like a matchbox. For the slightest irregularity in bed-making the punishment was 25 lashes, after which it was impossible to lie or sit for a whole month.

Everyone had to leave the barracks immediately. Outside it is still dark—or else the moon is shining. People are trembling because of lack of sleep and the cold. In order to warm up a bit, groups of ten to twenty people stand together, back to back so as to rub against each other.

There was what was called a washroom, where everyone in the camp was supposed to wash—there were only a few faucets—and we were 4,500 people in that section (no. 3). Of course there was neither soap nor towel or even a handkerchief, so that washing was theoretical rather than practical. . . . In one day, a person there became a lowly person indeed.

At 5 AM we used to get half a litre of black, bitter coffee. That was all we got for what was called "breakfast." At 6 AM—a headcount (*Appell* in German). We all had to stand at attention, in lines, according to the barracks, of which there were 22 in each section. We stood there until the SS men had satisfied their game-playing instincts by "humorous" orders to take off and put on caps. Then they received their report, and counted us. After the headcount—work.

We went in groups—some to build railway tracks or a road, some to the quarries to carry stones or coal, some to take out manure, or for potato-digging, latrine-cleaning, barracks—or sewer—repairs. All this took place inside the camp enclosure. During work the SS men beat up the prisoners mercilessly, inhumanly and for no reason.

They were like wild beasts and, having found their victim, ordered him to present his backside, and beat him with a stick or a whip, usually until the stick broke.

The victim screamed only after the first blows, afterwards he fell unconscious and the SS man then kicked at the ribs, the face, at the most sensitive parts of a man's body, and then, finally convinced that the victim was at the end of his strength, he ordered another Jew to pour one pail of water after the other over the beaten person until he woke and got up.

A favorite sport of the SS men was to make a "boxing sack" out of a Jew. This was done in the following way: Two Jews were stood up, one being forced to hold the other by the collar, and an SS man trained giving him a knock-out. Of course, after the first blow, the poor victim was likely to fall, and this was prevented by the other Jew holding him up. After the fat, Hitlerite murderer had "trained" in this way for 15 minutes, and only after the poor victim was completely shattered, covered in blood, his teeth knocked out, his nose broken, his eyes hit, they released him and ordered a doctor to treat his wounds. That was their way of taking care and being generous.

Another customary SS habit was to kick a Jew with a heavy boot. The Jew was forced to stand to attention, and all the while the SS man kicked him until he broke some bones. People who stood near enough to such a victim, often heard the breaking of the bones. The pain was so terrible that people, having undergone that treatment, died in agony.

Apart from the SS men there were other expert hangmen. These were the so-called Capos. The name was an abbreviation for "barracks police." The Capos were German criminals who were also camp inmates. However, although they belonged to "us," they were privileged. They had a special, better barracks of their own, they had better food, better, almost normal clothes, they wore special red or green riding pants, high leather boots, and fulfilled the functions of camp guards. They were worse even than the SS men. One of them, older than the others and the worst murderer of them all, when he descended on a victim, would not revive him later with water but would choke him to death. Once, this murderer caught a boy of 13 (in the presence of his father) and hit his head so that the poor child died instantly. This "camp elder" later boasted in front of his peers, with a smile on his beast's face and with pride, that he managed to kill a Jew with one blow.

In each section stood a gallows. For being late for the headcount, or similar crimes, the "camp elder" hanged the offenders.

Work was actually unproductive, and its purpose was exhaustion and torture.

At 12 noon there was a break for a meal. Standing in line, we received half a litre of soup each. Usually it was cabbage soup, or some other watery liquid, without fats, tasteless. That was lunch. It was eaten—in all weather—under the open sky, never in the barracks. No spoons were allowed, though wooden spoons lay on each bunk—probably for show, for Red Cross committees. One had to drink the soup out of the bowl and lick it like a dog.

From 1 PM till 6 PM there was work again. I must emphasize that if we were lucky we got a 12 o'clock meal. There were "days of punishment"—when lunch was given together with the evening meal, and it was cold and sour, so that our stomach was empty for a whole day.

Afternoon work was the same: blows, and blows again. Until 6 PM.

At 6 there was the evening headcount. Again we were forced to stand at attention. Counting, receiving the report. Usually we were left standing at attention for an hour or two, while some prisoners were called up for "punishment parade"—they were those who in the Germans' eyes had transgressed in some way during the day, or had not been punctilious in their performance. They were stripped naked publicly, laid out on specially constructed benches, and whipped with 25 or 50 lashes.

The brutal beating and the heart-rending cries—all this the prisoners had to watch and hear.[10]

Terrence Des Pres

Degradation by "Excremental Assault," 1941–1945

The Nazi imperative to humiliate and degrade Jews took many forms; perhaps the worst was what Terrence des Pres characterized as "excremental assault," which caused prisoners more mental torment than hunger or the perpetual prospect of death. For the Germans to murder millions of Jews, it was necessary to prove to themselves that their victims were subhumans unworthy of life by immersing them in filth and stench. As the commandant of Treblinka, Franz Stangl, famously explained, it was necessary to inflict all the cruelty and humiliation to dehumanize the inmates in order "[t]o condition those who actually had to carry out the policies, . . . [t]o make it possible for them to do what they did." In the camps it was impossible to wash oneself or stay clean, part of a system designed to crush the spirit of prisoners and reduce them to animaldom. Several instances drawn from the memoirs of camp survivors appear below.

> [The horror began in the deportation trains, in the boxcars with eighty to a hundred people crammed in.]

The temperature started to rise, as the freight car was enclosed and body heat had no outlet. . . . The only place to urinate was through a slot in the skylight, though whoever tried this usually missed, spilling urine on the floor. . . . When dawn finally rose . . . we were all quite ill and shattered, crushed not only by the weight of fatigue but by the stifling, moist atmosphere and the foul odor of excrement. . . . There was no latrine, no provision. . . . On top of everything else, a lot of people had vomited on the floor. We were to live for days on end breathing these foul smells, and soon we lived in the foulness itself.

[Conditions at Auschwitz were typical of the deliberate, systematic deprivation that overwhelmed inmates.]

At the outset the living places, the ditches, the mud, the piles of excrement behind the blocks, had appalled me with their horrible filth. . . . And then I saw the light! I saw that it was not a question of disorder or lack of organization but that, on the contrary, a very thoroughly considered conscious idea was behind the camp's existence. They had condemned us to die in our own filth, to drown in mud, in our own excrement. They wished to abase us, to destroy our human dignity, to efface every vestige of humanity, to return us to the level of wild animals, to fill us with horror and contempt toward ourselves and our fellows. . . . But from the instant when I grasped the motivating principle . . . it was as if I had been awakened from a dream. . . . I was not going to become the contemptible, disgusting brute my enemy wished me to be.

[Disease was an inevitable and deliberate concomitant factor.]

Everybody in the block had typhus . . . it came to Bergen Belsen in its most violent, most painful, deadliest form. The diarrhea caused by it became uncontrollable. It flooded the bottom of the cages, dripping through the cracks into the faces of the women lying in the cages below, and mixed with blood, pus and urine, formed a slimy, fetid mud on the floor of the barracks.

[The latrines were designed to make lavatory functions into personal crises and unmitigatedly defiling.]

There was one latrine for thirty to thirty-two thousand women and we were permitted to use it only at certain hours of the day. We stood in line to get into this tiny building, knee-deep in human excrement. As we all suffered from dysentery, we could rarely wait until our turn came, and soiled our ragged clothes, which never came off our bodies, thus adding to the horror of our existence by the terrible smell which surrounded us like a cloud. We squatted on these planks like birds perched on a telegraph wire, so close together that we could not help soiling one another.

[The sadistic guards often refined the cruelty of immersion in feces by tossing the soup bowls into latrines and forcing prisoners to retrieve them; prisoners afraid to resort to the latrines at night, which was forbidden and exposed them to being "beaten, knocked down, and trampled" by the guards, felt compelled to use their eating utensils instead.]

The first days our stomachs rose up at the thought of using what were actually chamber pots at night. But hunger drives, and we were so starved that we were ready to eat any food. That it had to be handled in such bowls could not be helped. During the night, many of us availed ourselves of the bowls secretly. We were allowed to go to the latrines only twice each day. How could we help it? No matter how great our need, if we went out in the middle of the night we risked being caught by the SS, who had orders to shoot first and ask questions later.

[The nightly task of emptying the overflowing latrines gave more opportunities for ideologically inspired sadism.]

The location was slippery and unlighted. Of the thirty men on this assignment, an average of ten fell into the pit in the course of each night's work. The others were not allowed to pull the victims out. When the work was done and the pit empty, then and only then were they permitted to remove the corpses.

[The death marches, of which there were many, especially as the war came to an end, provide variations on the theme of excremental assault, since pausing to relieve oneself or for any other reason meant death.]

Urine and excreta poured down the prisoners' legs, and by nightfall the excrement, which had frozen to our limbs, gave off its stench. We were really no longer human beings in the accepted sense. Not even animals, but putrefying corpses moving on two legs.[11]

Rudolf Höss, Commandant of Auschwitz

A. On the Necessity to Murder Jewish Children
B. Assembly Line Mass Murder, 1946

The belief that Jews possessed superhuman powers of destruction and domination was a crucial component of historic antisemitism. This kind of fear and phobia can be traced back to the Middle Ages and has taken many bizarre forms; it is the psychological substratum of such documents as the *Protocols of the Learned Elders of Zion*. It has often generated an imperative sense that the Jews must be destroyed before they destroy society, that the fewer the Jews are the more dangerous they are, that the more assimilated Jews are the more dangerous, and so on through a series of irrational permutations. In 1940, Nicholas Berdyaev, the Russian scholar in exile, acknowledged with shame what he called his fellow Christians' "mystical fear of the Jews." One climactic instance of the German fear of the Jews as a fundamental motive for the Holocaust was reported in his memoir *Kaputt* by the Italian war correspondent Curzio Malaparte, who spent considerable time in Cracow, Poland, at the headquarters of Hans Frank (later tried and executed as a war criminal): "The *leitmotiv* of fear, of German cruelty as a result of that fear, had become the principal keynote of my entire war experience. . . . That which drives the Germans to cruelty, to deeds most coldly, methodically and scientifically cruel is fear. Fear of the oppressed, the defenseless, the weak, the sick; fear of women and of children, fear of the Jews."[12]

The first document testifies to how fear translates into aggression and cruelty. It is an excerpt from the pre-trial interrogation at the International Military Tribunal of Rudolf Höss, commandant at Auschwitz, who was summoned as a witness; he explains why Heinrich Himmler, the head of the SS, ordered him to kill Jewish children.

A. Testimony of Rudolf Höss taken at Nürnberg, Germany, on
1 April 1946, 1430 to 1730 by Mr. Sender Jari and Lt. Whitney Harris.
Also present: Mr. George Sackheim, Interpreter; Pilani A. Ahuna,
Court Reporter.

A. On the Necessity to Murder Jewish Children

QUESTION BY MR. JARI TO THE INTERPRETER:

Q Do you swear that you will fully and truly interpret the testimony from German to English and English to German?

A I do.

QUESTIONS BY MR. JARI TO THE WITNESS THROUGH THE INTERPRETER:

Q What is your name?

A Rudolf Höss.

Q Do you swear that you will tell the whole truth before God?

A I do. . . .

Q You told me . . . that [Reichführer-SS Heinrich] Himmler had explained to you that every Jew irrespective of sex, or age, was a danger to the German people?

A Yes.

Q Are you sure it was after the Russian campaign had started [that you met with Himmler]?

A No, it was before the Russian campaign had started.

Q Then it couldn't have been in July?

A I cannot remember the exact month, but I know for sure it was before the date that the Russia campaign was launched.

Q Where did you meet him?

A In his office on Prince Albert Street 8.

Q Who else was present?

A I was alone.

Q What reasons did he give for this order?

A I don't recall his exact words, but the meaning was that the Führer had given the order for the final solution of the Jewish problem.

Q What does final solution mean?

A That means the extermination; that's the way he stated it.

Q You state it as meaning the extermination?

A Yes. . . .

Q And did he tell you anything else? Did you go there immediately after your talk with him on your tour of inspection?

A No, at first I returned to Auschwitz. He explained to me that it was not his habit to discuss such matters with inferiors; however, this case was so important and of such great significance that he had decided to explain to me his reasons and they were as follows: he said to me that if the extermination of

Jewry did not take place at this time the German people would be eliminated by the Jews.

Q Did he explain to you how the Jews would be able to eliminate the German people?

A No.

Q What other reasons did he give?

A That was the reason. He had planned originally to dispatch a higher ranking officer to Auschwitz to continue this extermination action, but reconsidered because he felt that it would only be a cause of friction between myself as the Camp Commandant and the higher ranking officer in charge of the exterminations. Therefore, he gave me the order. In addition to that the fact that I was supposed to treat this as top secret matter and not discuss it with anybody was explained. All the instructions such as procedure and orders I was to receive from the RSHA [Reich Security Main Office] through [Adolf] Eichmann. . . .

Q When the people arrived in Auschwitz, there was a railroad station within the camp already, wasn't there?

A Yes.

Q They were unloaded, and were they marched?

A In this railroad station there was a side track. The people stepped down from the train, discarded their baggage and were then examined by doctors and sorted.

Q Who were the doctors? What kind of doctors did you use?

A The SS camp physicians.

Q According to what principles were they sorted out?

A According to the principles of whether they were fit for work or not.

Q Now you say a trainload consisted on the average of 2,000 people. How many doctors did you have assigned to check on each trainload?

A There were always two doctors on duty.

Q How many trains arrived daily?

A The largest number of trains that ever arrived in one day were five. This was in 1944 during the Hungarian action.

Q But on the average how many trains arrived daily?

A Two.

Q 4,000 people?

A Yes.

Q And two doctors examined them?

A Yes, they filed by them.

Q So the examination really never took place; they just had a look?

A Yes.

Q And according to which plan was the decision taken?

A According to the order as to whether or not a man or a woman was strong and healthy.

Q And what about the children? Were all the children killed?

A That depended upon their stature. Some of the 15 and 16-year old children also went to work, if they were strong.

Q In other words, children below 15 were exterminated.

A Yes.

Q Just because of Himmler's order?

A Yes.

Q And because they were dangerous to the German people?

A Yes.

Q So a child of three or four years old was dangerous to the German people.

A No, it isn't quite that way. I should have elaborated perhaps a little more on my statement before of Himmler's explanation. He said the German people would not have carried rights unless the Jewish people were now exterminated.

Q So that is really a confirmation of what you said. The German people could not rise at all because of the four-year old Jewish children.

A Yes.

B. *Assembly Line Mass Murder, 1946*

The following document is excerpted from Höss's affidavit for the International Military Tribunal at Nuremberg; he summarizes his Nazi career and describes the Auschwitz death process as he had designed it. He was returned to Poland for trial, where he was executed in 1947.

I have been constantly associated with the administration of concentration camps since 1934, serving at Dachau until 1938; then as Adjutant in Sachsenhausen from 1938-5/1/1940, when I was appointed Commandant of Auschwitz. I commanded Auschwitz until 12/1/1943, and estimate that at least 2.5 million victims were executed and exterminated there by gassing and burning, and at least another half million succumbed to starvation and disease making a total dead of about 3 million [historians now estimate 1.1 to 1.5 million deaths at Auschwitz]. This figure represents about 70-80% of all persons sent to Auschwitz as prisoners, the remainder having been selected and used for slave labor in the concentration camp industries; included among the executed and burned were approximately 20,000 Russian prisoners of war (previously screened out of prisoner-of-war cages by the Gestapo) who were delivered at Auschwitz in *Wehrmacht* [regular army] transports operated by regular *Wehrmacht* officers and men. The remainder of the total number of victims included about 100,000 German Jews, and great numbers of citizens, mostly Jewish, from Holland, France, Belgium, Poland, Hungary, Czechoslovakia, Greece, or other countries. We executed about 400,000 Hungarian Jews alone at Auschwitz in the summer of 1944.

Mass executions by gassing commenced during the summer of 1941 and continued until fall 1944. I personally supervised executions at Auschwitz until

12/1/1943 and know by reason of my continued duties in the Inspectorate of Concentration Camps, WVHA, that these mass executions continued as stated above. All mass executions by gassing took place under the direct order, supervision, and responsibility of RSHA [Reich Security Main Office]. I received all orders for carrying out these mass executions directly from RSHA.

The "final solution" of the Jewish question meant the complete extermination of all Jews in Europe. I was ordered to establish extermination facilities at Auschwitz in 6/1941. At that time there were already in the general government [of Poland under Nazi rule] three other extermination camps; Belzek, Treblinka and Wolzek. These camps were under the *Einsatzkommando* of the Security Police and SD [Security Service]. I visited Treblinka to find out how they carried out their exterminations. The Camp Commandant at Treblinka told me that he had liquidated 30,000 in the course of one-half year. He was principally concerned with liquidating all the Jews from the Warsaw Ghetto. He used monoxide gas and I did not think that his methods were very efficient. So when I set up the extermination building at Auschwitz, I used Cyclon B, which was a crystallized Prussic Acid which we dropped into the death chamber from a small opening. It took from 3 to 15 minutes to kill the people in the death chamber depending upon climatic conditions. We knew when the people were dead because their screaming stopped. We usually waited about one-half hour before we opened the doors and removed the bodies. After the bodies were removed our special commandos took off the rings and extracted the gold from the teeth of the corpses. This gold was melted down and brought to the Chief Medical Office of the SS at Berlin.

Another improvement we made over Treblinka was that we built our gas chambers to accommodate 2000 people at one time, whereas at Treblinka their 10 gas chambers only accommodated 200 people each. The way we selected our victims was as follows: we had two SS doctors on duty at Auschwitz to examine the incoming transports of prisoners. The prisoners would be marched by one of the doctors who would make spot decisions as they walked by. Those who were fit for work were sent into the Camp. Others were sent immediately to the extermination plants. Children of tender years were invariably exterminated since by reason of their youth they were unable to work. Still another improvement we made over Treblinka was that at Treblinka the victims almost always knew that they were to be exterminated and at Auschwitz we endeavored to fool the victims into thinking that they were to go through a delousing process. Of course, frequently they realized our true intentions and we sometimes had riots and difficulties due to that fact. Very frequently women would hide their children under the clothes but of course when we found them we would send the children in to be exterminated. We were required to carry out these exterminations in secrecy but of course the foul and nauseating stench from the continuous burning of bodies permeated the entire area and all of the people living in the surrounding communities knew that exterminations were going on at Auschwitz.

We received from time to time special prisoners from the local Gestapo office. The SS doctors killed such prisoners by injections of benzene. Doctors had orders to write ordinary death certificates and could put down any reason at all for the cause of death.

From time to time we conducted medical experiments on women inmates, including sterilization and experiments relating to cancer. Most of the people who died under these experiments had been already condemned to death by the Gestapo [for trying to escape, etc.].[13]

NOTES

1. Some 2.5 million to 3 million Jews were gassed in Nazi death factories built in Poland—Chelmno, Treblinka, Sobibor, Belzec, Lublin, Majdanek, and Auschwitz-Birkenau, the largest; statistical estimates range from 5.2 to 6.9 million total victims, the higher calculations reflecting research since opening of archives in Eastern Europe; in more recent years historians like Omer Bartov have begun to examine casualty totals in smaller towns and villages where murders and expulsions were carried out on local initiatives, such as Buczacz, a multiethnic Galician town.

2. Quoted in Joseph Borkin, *The Crime and Punishment of I. G. Farben* (New York: Free Press, 1978). 143.

3. Gisella Perl, *I Was a Doctor at Auschwitz* (New York: International Universities Press, 1948), 80.

4. The survivor Alexander Donat, quoted in Terrence Des Pres, *The Survivor: An Anatomy of Life in the Death Camps* (New York: Oxford University Press, 1976), 54; chap. 3 is entitled "Excremental Assault," 51-71.

5. Konnilyn G. Feig, *Hitler's Death Camps* (New York: Holmes & Meier, 1979), 37.

6. Quoted in Erich Kahler, *The Tower and the Abyss* (New York: George Braziller, 1957), 74-75.

7. Filip Müller, *Eyewitness in Auschwitz: Three Years in the Gas Chambers* (New York: Stein and Day, 1979), 100.

8. From Chaim A. Kaplan, *Scroll of Agony: The Warsaw Diary of Chaim A. Kaplan*, trans. and ed. Abraham I. Katsh (New York: Macmillan, 1965), 59-60, 67-68, 91-92, 118, 129-130.

9. Nuremberg document PS-2992, *Nazi Conspiracy and Aggression* (Washington, D.C.: U.S. Government Printing Office, 1946), 5: 696-699.

10. From Yehuda Bauer, *A History of the Holocaust* (New York: Franklin Watts, 1982), 211-13.

11. Excerpts from survivor diaries and memoirs as quoted in Des Pres, *The Survivor*, 53-63.

12. Curzio Malaparte, *Kaputt*, trans. Cesare Foligno (New York: Dutton, 1946), 91.

13. Document A: excerpted from *The "Final Solution" in the Extermination Camps and the Aftermath*, vol. 12 of *The Holocaust: Selected Documents in Eighteen Volumes*, ed. John Mendelsohn and Donald S. Detwiler (New York: Garland, 1982), 56, 74, 80-82, 90-92, 114. Document B: Nuremberg Document 3868-PS: Affidavit of Rudolf Franz Ferdinand Hoess, 4/5/1946; Military Tribunal. Volume XXXIII. *Documents and Other Material in Evidence* (Nuremberg: IMT, 1949), 277-279.

PART THREE

Contemporary

After 1945 antisemitism declined in Europe but it did not disappear. It was discredited by the genocide of the Continent's Jews and muted because there were so few Jews to fasten on. In recent years the exacerbation of the Arab-Israeli conflict has generated a resurgence of antisemitism in Europe, even among polite circles. The Israeli military campaign in the spring of 2002 in the West Bank in response to repeated suicide bombings that killed and mutilated hundreds of Israeli citizens resulted in a rash of antisemitic incidents in Europe. In several countries—Ukraine, Greece, Holland, Belgium, Germany, Britain, and France—cemeteries were vandalized, Holocaust memorials defaced, synagogues torched, buses transporting Jewish schoolchildren stoned, and Jews beaten. Some 360 crimes against Jews and Jewish institutions were reported in France, where the violence was most severe. It is likely that Muslim extremists were responsible for most of the violence, but antisemitic attitudes were not limited to people of Middle Eastern descent. In demonstrations held in many European cities in support of the Palestinians, Israelis were equated with Nazis, Prime Minister Ariel Sharon with Hitler, and the Israeli flag was burned. At times crowds shouted, "Death to the Jews!" In past decades the most virulent expressions of antisemitism were confined almost exclusively to the fringe groups of the extreme Right that idolized Hitler and revered the Nazi past. Now representatives of the Left—the Greens, trade unionists, socialists, and student organizations—actively participated in the demonstrations and denounced Israel in venomous language.

What is most distressing is the way the press and intellectuals, who previously glossed over the Israeli casualties of suicide bombers, were quick to condemn Israel, often sinking into the ordure of antisemitism. Thus a cartoon in the Italian newspaper *La Stampa* depicted a baby Jesus in the manger looking at an Israeli tank and saying, "Don't tell me they want to kill me again." The Vatican daily *L'Osservatore Romano* said that Israel was engaging in "aggression that turns into extermination." Accepting as true the grotesque Palestinian fabrication that a massacre had taken place at Jenin, the press in several countries accused the Israeli army of engaging in genocide. Supposedly the scene of "a massacre of hundreds of innocents," in actuality, 52 Palestinians, most of them armed, and 26 Israeli soldiers were killed in ten days of hard street fighting that had followed a series of suicide bombings, one of which in Netanya killed 29 Israelis and injured 140, all of it downplayed in the European media. Several British authors rejected Israel's right to exist, and José Saramago, a Nobel laureate in literature, felt it appropriate to "compare what is happening in the Palestinian territories with Auschwitz."[1]

In Muslim lands antisemitism is pervasive and vicious, routinely employing Christian and Nazi myths, which most westerners now regard as repulsive. Widely circulated, the *Protocols of the Learned Elders of Zion,* among several other rabidly antisemitic texts of Western origin and all readily available, is often referred to as an authoritative source for Jewish aims. Mainstream and official Arab publications endorse the myths of an international Jewish conspiracy, ritual murder, and Holocaust denial. The demonization of the Jews, which made the Holocaust possible, shapes the perception of millions of people in Islamic lands.

TWENTY-THREE

The Catholic Church Confronts Its Antisemitic Past

For nearly two millennia the Roman Catholic Church was the bearer of a hateful antipathy for Jews and Judaism that has its roots in the New Testament and Church Fathers. The Catholic documents on Jews and Judaism that follow were not issued until decades after World War II and represent a radical break with tradition, inconceivable under previous popes. In many but not all ways they alter historic Catholic theology and teaching.

They were anticipated by one dramatic incident in the reign of Pope Pius XI (1924–1939). In his sermon to Belgian pilgrims on September 6, 1938, Pius quoted from the missal "an awe-inspiring text": "*Sacrificium patriarchae nostri Abrahae*" (The Sacrifice of Our Patriarch Abraham), and commented, "Note that Abraham is called our patriarch, our ancestor. Anti-Semitism is not compatible with the thought and the sublime realization expressed in this text. It is a deplorable movement, a movement in which we, as Christians, must have no part." Sobbing, he went on: "No, it is not possible for Christians to take part in anti-Semitism. . . . [A]nti-Semitism is inadmissible. We are spiritually Semites." Pius XI's encyclical, incomplete and unissued at his death, *Humani Generis Unitas* (The Unity of the Human Race) very effectively condemned German and Italian racism as a fundamental violation of the unity of the human race, but he still remained trapped in ancient anti-Judaism and reiterated the theology of deicide and supersession, and so, "this unhappy people, destroyers of their own nation, whose misguided leaders had called down upon their own heads a Divine malediction, [were] doomed . . . to perpetually wander over the face of the earth."[2]

The Second Vatican Council, 1962–1965

Nostra Aetate *(In Our Time), 1965*

Nostra Aetate was promulgated by Pope Paul VI (1963–1978) on October 28, 1965, but is the posthumous gift of Pope John XXIII (1958–1963), who had summoned the Second Vatican Council. It is the first document in the history of the Catholic Church to speak affirmatively of the Jews that is doctrinally binding. There is some expression of gratitude and an understanding that without its Jewish foundations, the Church could not stand. It mitigates rather than annuls the historically malevolent accusation of deicide, stating that the crucifixion "cannot be charged against all the Jews, without distinction, then alive, nor against the Jews of today." There is no recognition of Christian guilt for religious antisemitism and its baleful effects over the centuries, but it was in the mind of many of the American and Western European bishops as the document went through its several drafts, by which it was weakened in some respects though strengthened in others. Despite some shortcomings, *Nostra Aetate* was a theological breakthrough and inaugurated a revolution in Catholic-Jewish relations that continues in later documents. Following is the portion that deals with the Jews, section 4 of the "Declaration on the Relationship of the Church to Non-Christian Religions."

As this Sacred Synod searches into the mystery of the Church, it remembers the bond that spiritually ties the people of the New Covenant to Abraham's stock.

Thus the Church of Christ acknowledges that, according to God's saving design, the beginnings of her faith and her election are found already among the Patriarchs, Moses and the Prophets. She professes that all who believe in Christ—Abraham's sons according to faith—are included in the same Patriarch's call, and likewise that the salvation of the Church is mysteriously foreshadowed by the chosen people's exodus from the land of bondage. The Church, therefore, cannot forget that she received the revelation of the Old Testament through the people with whom God in His inexpressible mercy concluded the Ancient Covenant. Nor can she forget that she draws sustenance from the root of that well-cultivated olive tree onto which has been grafted the wild shoot, the Gentiles. Indeed, the Church believes that by His cross Christ Our Peace reconciled Jews and Gentiles, making both one in Himself.

The Church keeps ever in mind the words of the Apostle about his kinsmen: "Theirs is the sonship and the glory and the covenants and the law and the worship and the promises; theirs are the fathers and from them is the Christ according to the flesh" (Rom 9:4-5), the Son of the Virgin Mary. She also recalls that the Apostles, the Church's mainstay and pillars, as well as most of the early disciples who proclaimed Christ's Gospel to the world, sprang from the Jewish people.

As Holy Scripture testifies, Jerusalem did not recognize the time of her visitation, nor did the Jews, in large number, accept the Gospel; indeed not a few opposed its spreading. Nevertheless God holds the Jews most dear for the sake of their Fathers; He does not repent of the gifts He makes or of the calls He issues—such is the witness of the Apostle. In company with the Prophets and the same Apostle, the Church awaits that day, known to God alone, on which all peoples will address the Lord in a single voice and "serve him shoulder to shoulder" (Soph 3:9).

Since the spiritual patrimony common to Christians and Jews is thus so great, this Sacred Synod wants to foster and recommend that mutual understanding and respect which is the fruit, above all, of biblical and theological studies as well as of fraternal dialogues.

True, the Jewish authorities and those who followed their lead pressed for the death of Christ; still, what happened in His passion cannot be charged against all the Jews, without distinction, then alive, nor against the Jews of today. Although the Church is the new people of God, the Jews should not be presented as rejected or accursed by God as if this followed from the Holy Scriptures. All should see to it, then, that in catechetical work or in the preaching of the word of God they do not teach anything that does not conform to the truth of the Gospel and the spirit of Christ.

Furthermore, in her rejection of every persecution against any man, the Church, mindful of the patrimony she shares with the Jews and moved not by political reasons but by the Gospel's spiritual love decries hatred, persecutions, displays of anti-Semitism, directed against Jews at any time and by anyone.

Besides, as the Church has always held and holds now, Christ underwent His passion and death freely, because of the sins of men and out of infinite love, in order that all may reach salvation. It is, therefore, the burden of the Church's preaching to proclaim the cross of Christ as the sign of God's all-embracing love and as the fountain from which every grace flows.[3]

Vatican Commission for Religious Relations with the Jews

Notes on the Correct Way to Present the Jews and Judaism in Preaching and Catechesis in the Roman Catholic Church, *1985*

The *Notes* is a much more determined, uncompromising, and empathetic document than *Nostra Aetate* of twenty years earlier: it goes to the root of historical antisemitism in Christian misinterpretation and misapplication of the New Testament beginning as early as the second century; it affects teaching and preaching from Sunday school and daily Mass to the seminaries for training priests; it accepts much of the New Testament scholarship of the last half century; it interprets the crucifixion as essentially a Roman affair; and it depicts Judaism of the first century as a vital religion, not trapped in legalism, materialism, or other of the ancient stereotypes. The *Notes* makes the crucial point that anti-Jewish feeling and thought in the New Testament were not part of Jesus's teaching and conduct but were imported from a later age when the Gospels were written and edited. The anti-Judaism reflected in the Gospels was a response to the conflict—after the time of Jesus—between the nascent church and its Jewish parentage.

Preliminary Considerations

On March 6, 1982, Pope John Paul II [1978-2005] told delegates of episcopal conferences and other experts, meeting in Rome to study relations between the Church and Judaism:

You yourselves were concerned, during your sessions, with Catholic teaching and catechesis regarding Jews and Judaism. . . . We should aim, in this field, that Catholic teaching at its different levels, in catechesis to children and young people, presents Jews and Judaism, not only in an honest and objective manner, free from prejudices and without any offenses, but also with full awareness of the heritage common to Jews and Christians.

* * *

The effective use of these means [*Nostra Aetate*, 4, and the 1967 *Guidelines and Suggestions* for implementing it] presupposes the thorough formation of instructors and educators in training schools, seminaries and universities. . . .

I. Religious Teaching and Judaism

1. In *Nostra Aetate*, 4, the Council speaks of the "spiritual bonds linking" Jews and Christians and of the "great spiritual patrimony" common to both, and it further asserts that "the Church of Christ acknowledges that, according to the mystery of God's saving design, the beginning of her faith and her election are already found among the patriarchs, Moses and the prophets."

2. Because of the unique relations that exist between Christianity and Judaism—"linked together at the very level of their identity" (John Paul II, March 6, 1982)—relations "founded on the design of the God of the Covenant" (*ibid.*)—the Jews and Judaism should not occupy an occasional and marginal place in catechesis: their presence there is essential and should be organically integrated.

3. This concern for Judaism in Catholic teaching has not merely a historical or archeological foundation. As the Holy Father said in the speech already quoted, after he had again mentioned the "common patrimony" of the Church and Judaism as "considerable": "To assess it carefully in itself and with due awareness of the faith and religious life of the Jewish people *as they are professed and practiced still today* can greatly help us to understand better certain aspects of the life of the Church" (italics added). It is a question then of *pastoral* concern for a still living reality closely related to the Church. The Holy Father has stated this permanent reality of the Jewish people in a remarkable theological formula, in his allocution to the Jewish community of West Germany at Mainz, on November 17, 1980: ". . . the people of God of the Old Covenant, which has never been revoked. . . ."

4. Here we should recall the passage in which the *Guidelines and Suggestions* (1) tried to define the fundamental condition of dialogue: "respect for the other as he is," knowledge of the "basic components of the religious tradition of Judaism," and again learning "by what essential traits the Jews define themselves in the light of their own religious experience" (*Introd.*). . . .

8. The urgency and importance of precise, objective and rigorously accurate teaching on Judaism for our faithful follows too from the danger of anti-Semitism which is always ready to reappear under different guises. The

question is not merely to uproot from among the faithful the remains of anti-Semitism still to be found here and there, but much rather to arouse in them, through educational work, an exact knowledge of the wholly unique "bond" (*Nostra Aetate*, 4) which joins us as a Church to the Jews and to Judaism. In this way, they would learn to appreciate and love the latter, who have been chosen by God to prepare the coming of Christ and have preserved everything that was progressively revealed and given in the course of that preparation, notwith-standing their difficulty in recognizing in him their Messiah. . . .

II. Relations between the Old and New Testament

[Part II is concerned to establish that Christian interpretation of the Old Testament in no way undermines God's covenant with the Jewish people. The Old Testament is a shared heritage that is equally precious and valid for Jews and Christians. The New Testament does not replace the Old, for in many respects it "does no more than resume" its revelation and must be "read in the light of" Hebrew scripture. "Attentive to the same God who has spoken, hanging on the same word," Christians and Jews "have to witness to one same meaning and one common hope in Him who is the master of history."]

III. Jewish Roots of Christianity

12. Jesus was and always remained a Jew; his ministry was deliberately limited "to the lost sheep of the house of Israel." Jesus is fully a man of his time, and of his environment—the Jewish Palestinian one of the first century, the anxieties and hopes of which he shared. This cannot but underline both the reality of the incarnation and the very meaning of the history of salvation, as it has been revealed in the Bible.

13. Jesus' relations with biblical law and its more or less traditional interpretations are undoubtedly complex, and he showed great liberty toward it. . . . But there is no doubt that he wished to submit himself to the law, that he was circumcised and presented in the Temple like any Jew of his time, that he was trained in the law's observance. He extolled respect for it and invited obedience to it. The rhythm of his life was marked by observance of pilgrimages on great feasts, even from his infancy. The importance of the cycle of the Jewish feasts has been frequently underlined in the Gospel of John.

14. It should be noted also that Jesus often taught in the Synagogues and in the Temple, which he frequented as did the disciples even after the Resurrection. He wished to put in the context of synagogue worship the proclamation of his Messiahship. But above all he wished to achieve the supreme act of the gift of himself in the setting of the domestic liturgy of the Passover, or at least of the paschal festivity. This also allows of a better understanding of the "memorial" character of the Eucharist.

15. Thus the Son of God is incarnate in a people and a human family. This takes away nothing, quite the contrary, from the fact that he was born for all men (Jewish shepherds and pagan wise men are found at his crib) and died for

all men (at the foot of the cross there are Jews, among them Mary and John, and pagans like the centurions). Thus he made two peoples one in his flesh. . . .

16. His relations with the Pharisees were not always or wholly polemical. Of this there are many proofs. . . .

17. Jesus shares, with the majority of Palestinian Jews of that time, some pharisaic doctrines: the resurrection of the body; forms of piety, like alms-giving, prayer, fasting and the liturgical practice of addressing God as Father; the priority of the commandment to love God and our neighbor. (This is so also with Paul who always considered his membership of the Pharisees as a title of honor.)

18. Paul also, like Jesus himself, used methods of reading and interpreting Scripture and of teaching his disciples which were common to the Pharisees of their time. This applies to the use of parables in Jesus' ministry, as also to the method of Jesus and Paul of supporting a conclusion with a quotation from Scripture.

19. . . . An exclusively negative picture of the Pharisees is likely to be inaccurate and unjust. If in the Gospels and elsewhere in the New Testament there are all sorts of unfavorable references to the Pharisees, they should be seen against the background of a complex and diversified movement. Criticisms of various types of Pharisees are moreover not lacking in rabbinical sources. "Phariseeism" in the pejorative sense can be rife in any religion. It may also be stressed that, if Jesus shows himself severe toward the Pharisees, it is because he is closer to them than to other contemporary Jewish groups.

20. All this should help us to understand better what St. Paul says about the "root" and the "branches." The Church and Christianity, for all their novelty, find their origin in the Jewish milieu of the first century of our era, and more deeply still in the "design of God" (*Nostra Aetate*, 4), realized in the patriarchs, Moses and the prophets (*ibid.*), down to its consummation in Christ Jesus.

IV. The Jews in the New Testament

21. [Part IV urges stringent care in interpreting critical passages in the Gospels to "avoid appearing to arraign the Jewish people as such," pointing out that the term "the Jews," depending on context, is better understood as "the leaders of the Jews" or "the adversaries of Jesus" than as the entire people. It states that "The Gospels are the outcome of long and complicated editorial work," and quotes the Vatican document *Dei Verbum* (The Word of God) on the three stages of composition: "The sacred authors wrote the four Gospels, selecting some things from the many which had been handed on by word of mouth or in writing, reducing some of them to a synthesis, explicating some things in view of the situation of their Churches, and preserving the form of proclamation, but always in such fashion that they told us the honest truth about Jesus."]

A. Hence it cannot be ruled out that some references hostile or less than favorable to the Jews have their historical context in [later] conflicts between the nascent Church and the Jewish community. Certain controversies reflect Christian-Jewish relations long after the time of Jesus.

To establish this is of capital importance if we wish to bring out the meaning of certain Gospel texts for the Christians of today.

All this should be taken into account when preparing catechesis and homilies for the last weeks of Lent and Holy Week.

B. It is clear on the other hand that there were conflicts between Jesus and certain categories of Jews of his time, among them Pharisees, from the beginning of his ministry.

C. There is moreover the sad fact that the majority of the Jewish people and its authorities did not believe Jesus—a fact not merely of history but of theological bearing, of which St. Paul tries hard to plumb the meaning.

D. This fact, accentuated as the Christian mission developed, especially among the pagans, led inevitably to a rupture between Judaism and the young Church, now irreducibly separated and divergent in faith, and this state of affairs is reflected in the texts of the New Testament and particularly in the Gospels. There is no question of playing down or glossing over this rupture; that could only prejudice the identity of either side. Nevertheless it certainly does not cancel the spiritual "bond" [invoked by *Nostra Aetate*]. . . .

F. There is no putting the Jews who knew Jesus and did not believe in him, or those who opposed the preaching of the apostles, on the same plane with Jews who came after or those of today. If the responsibility of the former remains a mystery hidden with God, the latter are in an entirely different situation. [Vatican II's declaration on *Religious Liberty* is invoked, that all must be free and unrestrained to act in accordance with their conscience and beliefs.] This is one of the bases—proclaimed by the Council—on which Judaeo-Christian dialogue rests.

22. The delicate question of responsibility for the death of Christ must be looked at from the standpoint of the conciliar declaration *Nostra Aetate*, 4 and of *Guidelines and Suggestions* (III). [These and other documents are quoted to the effect that Jesus's suffering must not be blamed on *all* the Jews of that time, still less on Jews living today; that Jesus's suffering and death were providential in expiation of all men's sins; and that "the Jews should not be presented as repudiated or cursed by God, as if such views followed from the holy Scriptures."]

V. The Liturgy

[Part V acknowledges Christian indebtedness to Jewish liturgy, both in form and content.]

VI. Judaism and Christianity in History

25. The history of Israel did not end in 70 AD [with the Roman conquest and destruction of the Temple]. It continued, especially in a numerous diaspora which allowed Israel to carry to the whole world a witness—often heroic—of

its fidelity to the one God and to "exalt him in the presence of all the living" (Tobit 13:4), while preserving the memory of the land of their forefathers at the heart of their hope (Passover *Seder*).

Christians are invited to understand this religious attachment which finds its roots in biblical tradition, without however making their own any particular religious interpretation of this relationship.

The existence of the state of Israel and its political options should be envisaged not in a perspective which is in itself religious, but in their reference to the common principles of international law.

The permanence of Israel (while so many ancient peoples have disappeared without trace) is an historic fact and a sign to be interpreted within God's design. We must in any case rid ourselves of the traditional idea of a people *punished*, preserved as a *living argument* for Christian apologetic. It remains a chosen people, "the pure olive on which were grafted the branches of the wild olive which are the Gentiles" (John Paul II, March 6, 1982, alluding to Rom 11:17-24). We must remember how much the balance of relations between Jews and Christians over two thousand years has been negative. We must remind ourselves how the permanence of Israel is accompanied by a continuous spiritual fecundity, in the rabbinical period, in the Middle Ages and in modern times, taking its start from a patrimony which we long shared, so much so that "the faith and religious life of the Jewish people, as they are professed and practiced still today, can greatly help us to understand better certain aspects of the life of the Church" (John Paul II, March 6, 1982). Catechesis should on the other hand help in understanding the meaning for the Jews of the extermination during the years 1939-1945, and its consequences.

26. Education and catechesis should concern themselves with the problem of racism, still active in different forms of anti-Semitism. The Council presented it thus: "Moreover, (the Church), mindful of her common patrimony with the Jews and motivated by the Gospel's spiritual love and by no political considerations, deplores the hatred, persecutions and displays of anti-Semitism directed against the Jews at any time and from any source" (*Nostra Aetate*, 4). The *Guidelines* comment: "The spiritual bonds and historical links binding the Church to Judaism condemn (as opposed to the very spirit of Christianity) all forms of anti-Semitism and discrimination, which in any case the dignity of the human person alone would suffice to condemn."

Conclusion

27. Religious teaching, catechesis and preaching should be a preparation not only for objectivity, justice, and tolerance but also for understanding and dialogue. Our two traditions are so related that they cannot ignore each other. Mutual knowledge must be encouraged at every level. There is evident in particular a painful ignorance of the history and traditions of Judaism, of which only negative aspects and often caricature seem to form part of the stock ideas of many Christians.

That is what these notes aim to remedy. This would mean that the Council text and *"Guidelines and Suggestions"* would be more easily and faithfully put into practice.[4]

We Remember: A Reflection on the Shoah, *1998*

Expressing repentance for the past and hope for the future, *We Remember: A Reflection on the Shoah,* which was ten years in the making, directs Catholics to wrestle with the immense evil of the *Shoah*—to come to an understanding of its history and to ponder how crimes on such a scale could occur in Christian civilization. *We Remember* also has implications for Catholic education, requiring that the Holocaust be seriously addressed in its programs and curricula, urging study and reflection, both on the centuries of Christian denigration of Judaism and the historic misunderstanding of the Church's nature and teaching.

Yet *We Remember* has met with much criticism from Jews and Catholics alike. It distinguishes sharply between historic Christian anti-Judaism and Nazi racist, "neopagan" antisemitism, as two radically different phenomena that were essentially unconnected with each other; most historians deny that proposition and conclude that the traditional Christian teaching of contempt served as a seedbed for all forms of modern antisemitism, including Nazism. Second, critics maintain that the document's contention that anti-Judaism had no real bearing on the Holocaust is historically inaccurate and detracts from the Church's effort to confront squarely the greatest evil of modern history. Third, *We Remember* distinguishes between the Church as a sacred and blameless institution and its members at all levels, many of whom bear responsibility for the sin of antisemitism. This distinction is a traditional principle of Catholic theology but ignores the fact that contempt for Jews and Judaism was woven into the teaching and preaching of the Church from the Church Fathers on. Fourth, *We Remember* ignores Christian perpetrators of the *Shoah*—virtually all the planners of genocide and the actual murderers had been baptized—largely confining itself to blaming those Christians who did nothing, the bystanders, and praising those heroic few who helped. Fifth, what has generated the most faultfinding is *We Remember's* very favorable presentation of Pope Pius XII (1939–1958) for having saved many Jews, when his wartime conduct has come under attack by historians, who differ widely in their assessment of his wartime role, a subject rendered more contentious in recent years by the Vatican's initiation of the process of his canonization. Pius did not remain entirely "silent" but said little and quite late; he excommunicated no fascist or Nazi qua fascist or Nazi, and he excommunicated no one for persecuting Jews, but excommunicated communists en masse. The historical verdict on Pius XII awaits the opening of the Vatican's secret archives (they were recently opened but only to 1939).

Despite the criticism, the issuance of *We Remember* testifies to great progress in Catholic-Jewish relations since Vatican II. In conferences and dialogues, Jewish and Catholic clergy, scholars, and officials work closely to promote good ties between the faiths. Pope John Paul II was a pivotal figure in the improvement of relations between Catholics and Jews. It is likely that his commitment to this project stemmed in part from his experiences with Jews. He grew up with Jewish friends and was not contaminated by the antisemitism that was so pervasive in his native Poland; during World War II he lived in Krakow, where with great personal courage he helped individual Jews and witnessed Nazi persecution and street violence against them, as well as the destruction of the Krakow ghetto in 1943. After a decade in which Pope John Paul II had frequently spoken forcefully in condemnation of antisemitism past and present, opened the Vatican archives of the papal inquisition (the Holy Office), inaugurated diplomatic relations with Israel, as pope visited for the first time in history a synagogue (he chose the great synagogue of Rome), and beatified Father Bernhard Lichtenberg, the priest who prayed publicly for the well-being of the Jews from his pulpit at St. Hedwig's Cathedral in Berlin and was martyred by the Nazis—it may confidently be said that the Catholic-Jewish dialogue has reached the stage of more convergence than divergence. In March 2000 John Paul II made a memorable pilgrimage to Israel, where he again expressed his great anguish over what Jews have suffered and he prayed at the Western Wall, the holiest site in Judaism. *We Remember,* excerpted below, opens with a statement by Pope John Paul II.

Letter of Pope John Paul II, 1998

On numerous occasions during my pontificate I have recalled with a sense of deep sorrow the sufferings of the Jewish people during the Second World War. The crime which has become known as the *Shoah* remains an indelible stain on the history of the century that is coming to a close.

As we prepare for the beginning of the third millennium of Christianity, the Church is aware that the joy of a jubilee is above all the joy that is based on the forgiveness of sins and reconciliation with God and neighbor. Therefore she encourages her sons and daughters to purify their hearts through repentance of past errors and infidelities. She calls them to place themselves humbly before the Lord and examine themselves on the responsibility which they too have for the evils of our time.

It is my fervent hope that the document *We Remember: A Reflection on the Shoah,* which the Commission for Religious Relations with the Jews has prepared . . . will indeed help to heal the wounds of past misunderstandings and injustices. May it enable memory to play its necessary part in the process of shaping a future in which the unspeakable iniquity of the *Shoah* will never again be possible. May the Lord of history guide the efforts of Catholics and Jews and all men and women of good will as they work together for a world of true respect for the life and dignity of every human being, for all have been created in the image and likeness of God.

I. The Tragedy of the *Shoah* and the Duty of Remembrance

The twentieth century is fast coming to a close, and a new millennium of the Christian era is about to dawn. The 2000th anniversary of the birth of Jesus Christ calls all Christians, and indeed invites all men and women, to seek to discern in the passage of history the signs of divine providence at work as well as the ways in which the image of the Creator in man has been offended and disfigured.

This reflection concerns one of the main areas in which Catholics can seriously take to heart the summons which Pope John Paul II has addressed to them in his apostolic letter *Tertio Millennio Adveniente* (The Advent of the Third Millennium):

> It is appropriate that, as the second millennium of Christianity draws to a close, the Church should become more fully conscious of the sinfulness of her children, recalling all those times in history when they departed from the spirit of Christ and his Gospel and, instead of offering to the world the witness of a life inspired by the values of faith, indulged in ways of thinking and acting which were truly forms of counter-witness and scandal.

This century has witnessed an unspeakable tragedy which can never be forgotten: the attempt by the Nazi regime to exterminate the Jewish people, with the consequent killing of millions of Jews. Women and men, old and young, children and infants, for the sole reason of their Jewish origin, were persecuted and deported. Some were killed immediately, while others were degraded, ill-treated, tortured, and utterly robbed of their human dignity, and then murdered. Very few of those who entered the camps survived, and those who did remained scarred for life. This was the *Shoah*. It is a major fact of the history of this century, a fact which still concerns us today.

Before this horrible genocide, which the leaders of nations and Jewish communities themselves found hard to believe at the very moment when it was being mercilessly put into effect, no one can remain indifferent, least of all the Church, by reason of her very close bonds of spiritual kinship with the Jewish people and her remembrance of the injustices of the past. The Church's relationship to the Jewish people is unlike the one she shares with any other religion. However, it is not only a question of recalling the past. The common future of Jews and Christians demands that we remember, for "there is no future without memory." History itself is *memoria futuri* [a memory of the future].

In addressing this reflection to our brothers and sisters of the Catholic Church throughout the world, we ask all Christians to join us in meditating on the catastrophe which befell the Jewish people and on the moral imperative to ensure that never again will selfishness and hatred grow to the point of sowing such suffering and death. Most especially we ask our Jewish friends, "whose terrible fate has become a symbol of the aberrations of which man is capable when he turns against God," to hear us with open hearts.

II. What We Must Remember

While bearing their unique witness to the Holy One of Israel and to the Torah, the Jewish people have suffered much at different times and in many places. But the *Shoah* was certainly the worst suffering of all. The inhumanity with which the Jews were persecuted and massacred during this century is beyond the capacity of words to convey. All this was done to them for the sole reason that they were Jews.

The very magnitude of the crime raises many questions. Historians, sociologists, political philosophers, psychologists, and theologians are all trying to learn more about the reality of the *Shoah* and its causes. Much scholarly study still remains to be done. But such an event cannot be fully measured by the ordinary criteria of historical research alone. It calls for a "moral and religious memory" and, particularly among Christians, a very serious reflection on what gave rise to it.

The fact that the *Shoah* took place in Europe, that is, in countries of long-standing Christian civilization, raises the question of the relation between the Nazi persecution and the attitudes down the centuries of Christians toward the Jews.

III. Relations between Jews and Christians

The history of relations between Jews and Christians is a tormented one. His Holiness Pope John Paul II has recognized this fact in his repeated appeals to Catholics to see where we stand with regard to our relations with the Jewish people. In effect, the balance of these relations over 2,000 years has been quite negative.

At the dawn of Christianity, after the crucifixion of Jesus, there arose disputes between the early Church and the Jewish leaders and people who, in their devotion to the law, on occasion violently opposed the preachers of the Gospel and the first Christians. In the pagan Roman Empire, Jews were legally protected by the privileges granted by the emperor, and the authorities at first made no distinction between Jewish and Christian communities. Soon, however, Christians incurred the persecution of the state. Later, when the emperors themselves converted to Christianity, they at first continued to guarantee Jewish privileges. But Christian mobs who attacked pagan temples sometimes did the same to synagogues, not without being influenced by certain interpretations of the New Testament regarding the Jewish people as a whole. "In the Christian world—I do not say on the part of the Church as such—erroneous and unjust interpretations of the New Testament regarding the Jewish people and their alleged culpability have circulated for too long, engendering feelings of hostility toward this people." Such interpretations of the New Testament have been totally and definitively rejected by the Second Vatican Council.

Despite the Christian preaching of love for all, even for one's enemies, the prevailing mentality down the centuries penalized minorities and those who were in any way "different." Sentiments of anti-Judaism in some Christian quarters and the gap which existed between the Church and the Jewish people led to a generalized discrimination, which ended at times in expulsions or attempts at forced conversions. In a large part of the "Christian" world, until the end of the eighteenth century those who were not Christian did not always enjoy a fully guaranteed juridical status. Despite that fact, Jews throughout Christendom held on to their religious traditions and communal customs. They were therefore looked upon with a certain suspicion and mistrust. In times of crisis such as famine, war, pestilence, or social tensions, the Jewish minority was sometimes taken as a scapegoat and became the victim of violence, looting, even massacres.

By the end of the eighteenth century and the beginning of the nineteenth century, Jews generally had achieved an equal standing with other citizens in most states and a certain number of them held influential positions in society. But in that same historical context, notably in the nineteenth century, a false and exacerbated nationalism took hold. In a climate of eventful social change, Jews were often accused of exercising an influence disproportionate to their numbers. Thus there began to spread in varying degrees throughout most of Europe an anti-Judaism that was essentially more sociological and political than religious.

At the same time, theories began to appear which denied the unity of the human race, affirming an original diversity of races. In the twentieth century, National Socialism in Germany used these ideas as a pseudoscientific basis for a distinction between so-called Nordic-Aryan races and supposedly inferior races. Furthermore, an extremist form of nationalism was heightened in Germany by the defeat of 1918 and the demanding conditions imposed by the victors, with the consequence that many saw in National Socialism a solution to their country's problems and cooperated politically with this movement.

The Church in Germany replied by condemning racism. The condemnation first appeared in the preaching of some of the clergy, in the public teaching of the Catholic bishops, and in the writings of lay Catholic journalists. Already in February and March 1931, Cardinal Bertram of Breslau, Cardinal Faulhaber and the bishops of Bavaria, the bishops of the province of Cologne, and those of the province of Freiburg published pastoral letters condemning National Socialism, with its idolatry of race and of the state. The well-known Advent sermons of Cardinal Faulhaber in 1933, the very year in which National Socialism came to power, at which not just Catholics but also Protestants and Jews were present clearly expressed rejection of the Nazi antisemitic propaganda. In the wake of the *Kristallnacht*, Bernhard Lichtenberg, provost of Berlin cathedral, offered public prayers for the Jews. He was later to die at Dachau and has been declared blessed.

Pope Pius XI too condemned Nazi racism in a solemn way in his encyclical letter *Mit Brennender Sorge*, which was read in German churches on Passion Sunday 1937, a step which resulted in attacks and sanctions against members of the clergy. Addressing a group of Belgian pilgrims on September 6, 1938, Pius XI asserted: "Antisemitism is unacceptable. Spiritually, we are all Semites." Pius XII, in his very first encyclical, *Summi Pontificatus*, October 20, 1939, warned against theories which denied the unity of the human race and against the deification of the state, all of which he saw as leading to a real "hour of darkness."

IV. Nazi Antisemitism and the Shoah

Thus we cannot ignore the difference which exists between antisemitism, based on theories contrary to the constant teaching of the Church on the unity of the human race and on equal dignity of all races and peoples, and the longstanding sentiments of mistrust and hostility that we call *anti-Judaism*, of which, unfortunately, Christians also have been guilty.

The National Socialist ideology went even further, in the sense that it refused to acknowledge any transcendent reality as the source of life and the criterion of moral good. Consequently, a human group, and the state with which it was identified, arrogated to itself an absolute status and determined to remove the very existence of the Jewish people, a people called to witness to the one God and the law of the covenant. At the level of theological reflection we cannot ignore the fact that not a few in the Nazi Party not only showed aversion to the idea of divine providence at work in human affairs, but gave proof of a definite hatred directed at God himself. Logically such an attitude also led to a rejection of Christianity and a desire to see the Church destroyed or at least subjected to the interests of the Nazi state.

It was this extreme ideology which became the basis of the measures taken first to drive the Jews from their homes and then to exterminate them. The *Shoah* was the work of a thoroughly modern neopagan regime. Its antisemitism had its roots outside of Christianity, and in pursuing its aims, it did not hesitate to oppose the Church and persecute her members also. But it may be asked whether the Nazi persecution of the Jews was not made easier by the anti-Jewish prejudices imbedded in some Christian minds and hearts. Did anti-Jewish sentiment among Christians make them less sensitive or even indifferent to the persecutions launched against the Jews by National Socialism when it reached power?

Any response to this question must take into account that we are dealing with the history of people's attitudes and ways of thinking, subject to multiple influences. Moreover, many people were altogether unaware of the "final solution" that was being put into effect against a whole people; others were afraid for themselves and those near to them; some took advantage of the situation; and still others were moved by envy. A response would need to be given case by case. To do this, however, it is necessary to know what precisely motivated people in a particular situation.

At first the leaders of the Third Reich sought to expel the Jews. Unfortunately, the governments of some western countries of Christian tradition, including some in North and South America, were more than hesitant to open their borders to the persecuted Jews. Although they could not foresee how far the Nazi hierarchs would go in their criminal intentions, the leaders of those nations were aware of the hardships and dangers to which Jews living in the territories of the Third Reich were exposed. The closing of borders to Jewish emigration in those circumstances, whether due to anti-Jewish hostility or suspicion, political cowardice, or shortsightedness, or national selfishness, lays a heavy burden of conscience on the authorities in question.

In the lands where the Nazis undertook mass deportations, the brutality which surrounded these forced movements of helpless people should have led [witnesses] to suspect the worst. Did Christians give every possible assistance to those being persecuted and in particular to the persecuted Jews?

Many did, but others did not. Those who did help to save Jewish lives, as much was in their power, even to the point of placing their own lives in danger, must not be forgotten. During and after the war, Jewish communities and Jewish leaders expressed their thanks for all that had been done for them, including what Pope Pius XII did personally or through his representatives to save hundreds of thousands of Jewish lives. Many Catholic bishops, priests, religious, and laity have been honored for this reason by the state of Israel.

Nevertheless, as Pope John Paul II has recognized, alongside such courageous men and women, the spiritual resistance and concrete action of other Christians was not that which might have been expected from Christ's followers. We cannot know how many Christians in countries occupied or ruled by the Nazi powers or their allies were horrified at the disappearance of their Jewish neighbors and yet were not strong enough to raise their voices in protest. For Christians, this heavy burden of conscience of their brothers and sisters during the Second World War must be a call to penitence.

We deeply regret the errors and failures of those sons and daughters of the Church. We make our own what is said in the Second Vatican Council's declaration *Nostra Aetate*, which unequivocally affirms: "The Church . . . mindful of her common patrimony with the Jews, and motivated by the Gospel's spiritual love and by no political considerations, deplores the hatred, persecutions, and displays of antisemitism directed against the Jews at any time and from any source."

We recall and abide by what Pope John Paul II, addressing the leaders of the Jewish community in Strasbourg in 1988, stated: "I repeat again with you the strongest condemnation of antisemitism and racism, which are opposed to the principles of Christianity." The Catholic Church therefore repudiates every persecution against a people or human group anywhere, at any time. She absolutely condemns all forms of genocide as well as the racist ideologies which give rise to them. Looking back over this century, we are deeply saddened by the violence that has enveloped whole groups of peoples and nations. We recall in particular the massacre of the Armenians, the countless victims in Ukraine in the 1930s, the genocide of the Gypsies, which was also the result of racist ideas, and similar tragedies which have occurred in America, Africa, and the Balkans. Nor do we forget the millions of victims of totalitarian ideology in the Soviet Union, in China, Cambodia, and elsewhere. Nor can we forget the drama of the Middle East, the elements of which are well known. Even as we make this reflection, "many human beings are still their brothers' victims."

V. Looking Together to a Common Future

Looking to the future of relations between Jews and Christians, in the first place we appeal to our Catholic brothers and sisters to renew the awareness of the Hebrew roots of their faith. We ask them to keep in mind that Jesus was a descendant of David; that the Virgin Mary and the apostles belonged to the Jewish people; that the Church draws sustenance from the root of that good olive tree on to which have been grafted the wild olive branches of the gentiles; that the Jews are our dearly beloved brothers, indeed in a certain sense they are "our elder brothers."

At the end of this millennium the Catholic Church desires to express her deep sorrow for the failures of her sons and daughters in every age. This is an act of repentance (teshuvah), since as members of the Church we are linked to the sins as well as the merits of all her children. The Church approaches with deep respect and great compassion the experience of extermination, the *Shoah* suffered by the Jewish people during World War II. It is not a matter of mere words, but indeed of binding commitment. *"We would risk causing the victims of the most atrocious deaths to die again if we do not have an ardent desire for justice, if we do not commit ourselves to ensure that evil does not prevail over good as it did for millions of the children of the Jewish people. . . . Humanity cannot permit all that to happen again."*

We pray that our sorrow for the tragedy which the Jewish people has suffered in our century will lead to a new relationship with the Jewish people. We wish to turn awareness of past sins into a firm resolve to build a new future in which there will be no more anti-Judaism among Christians or anti-Christian sentiment among Jews, but rather a shared mutual respect as befits those who adore the one Creator and Lord and have a common father in faith, Abraham.

Finally, we invite all men and women of good will to reflect deeply on the significance of the *Shoah*. The victims from their graves and the survivors through the vivid testimony of what they have suffered have become a loud voice calling the attention of all of humanity. To remember this terrible experience is to become fully conscious of the salutary warning it entails: The spoiled seeds of anti-Judaism and antisemitism must never again be allowed to take root in any human heart.[5]

NOTES

1. For this and much else of a similar nature, Peter Pulzer, "The New Antisemitism: Or When Is a Taboo Not a Taboo," in *A New Antisemitism? Debating Judaeophobia in 21st-Century Britain*, ed. Paul Iganski and Barry Kosmin (London: Profile Books, 2003), 95; Gabriel Schoenfeld, "Israel and the Anti-Semites," *Commentary*, June 2002.

2. Georges Passelecq and Bernard Suchecky, *The Hidden Encyclical*, trans. Steven Rendall (New York: Harcourt Brace, 1997), 138 for the sermon, 246-259 for the draft encyclical.

3. From *The Documents of Vatican II*, ed. Walter M. Abbott (New York: Herder and Herder, 1966), 663-667.

4. From *More Stepping Stones to Jewish-Catholic Relations*, ed. Helga Croner (New York: Paulist Press, 1985), 220-232. Most biblical and other citations have been deleted.

5. From *Catholics Remember the Holocaust* (Washington, D.C.: Secretariat for Ecumenical and Interreligious Affairs, National Conference of Catholic Bishops, 1998), 43, 47-55. Quotations within *We Remember* are statements of John Paul II.

TWENTY-FOUR

Protestant Churches Confront Their Antisemitic Past

The extermination of European Jewry has compelled the Christian churches to confront a dire heritage—centuries of denigration of Judaism and Jews that made the Holocaust possible. Perhaps, because of its connection to Germany, the Lutheran Church has been most forward in confronting the issue but has had the greatest difficulty in doing so. As Franklin Littell said, "Christianity had in recent years experienced no greater shame than that symbolized by the fact that the Nazis could reissue Martin Luther's attacks on the Jews without gloss or amendment";[1] indeed, inspired by *Kristallnacht,* the Lutheran bishop of Thuringia and member of the Nazi Party since 1930, Martin Sasse, published excerpts from Luther's fulminations and prefaced them with an enthusiastic introduction citing Luther and Hitler as Germany's greatest antisemites. In 1939 Sasse was a prime mover in founding the Institute for the Study and Eradication of Jewish Influence on German Church Life as a research center at the venerable University of Jena. Its membership included some fifty theology professors, several of them renowned, and numerous graduate students, bishops, and pastors. It issued a great many commercially successful publications in large numbers, including its "de-Judaized" New Testament, a de-Judaized hymnal, and a catechism from which all Hebrew words like Amen, Hallelujah, and Hosannah were purged. Walter Grundmann—professor of New Testament, Nazi Party member, and director of the Institute—proclaimed in 1942, at the Holocaust's zenith, that "a healthy Volk must and will reject Judaism in every form. This fact is justified for and through history. Should someone be upset about Germany's attitude toward Judaism, Germany has the historical justification and historical authorization for the fight against Judaism on its side."[2] After the war almost all the institute's members remained unrepentant, their careers and prestige were unimpaired, and they tried to preserve the institute, asserting that it had been established to defend Christianity against Nazism, that its members had been persecuted by the regime, and that overcoming "Jewishness" remained an essential Christian goal.

Immediately after the war, Protestant clergy could not bring themselves to admit very much wrongdoing or they confined themselves to abstractions. They invoked the example of the Confessing Church and the Barmen Declaration of 1934 as examples of effective resistance against the Nazi regime, but such claims do not stand up to examination.[3] The Confessing Christians were adamant in their opposition to the "German Christians," Nazi zealots who accounted for somewhat more than a third of the eighteen thousand Protestant clergy and, initially with the backing of Hitler, acquired dominant positions at all levels of the German Evangelical Church; they largely succeeded in consolidating a Reich church under a Reich bishop that was incorporated into the party and regime: "The Church must enter completely into the Third Reich, . . . be coordinated into the rhythm of the National Revolution, . . . fashioned by the ideas of Nazism," averred one pastor. "Christ has come to us through Adolf Hitler," declared another. The German Christians demanded a "racially pure," "German peoples' Church" that was rid of the Old Testament "with its Jewish morality and stories of cattle dealers and concubines"; they wanted a church based on a de-Judaized New Testament purified of "the theology of Rabbi Paul," and inspired by a "heroic" and "Aryan" rather than "crucified Jesus."[4] Such churchmen were chagrined in 1935 when Heinrich Himmler rejected their petition seeking membership in the SS for theology students and pastors; a year later many of them protested Nazi Party orders removing swastikas from church newspaper mastheads and altars—insisting that to the faithful it was an inspiring symbol. To some observers the German Christians, with their Nazified theology, violent antisemitism and anti-communism, strutting in SA brown uniforms "with the swastika on our breast and the cross in our heart," were a logical outcome of traditional conservative, nationalistic Lutheranism. The declaration of German Christian leaders in November 1941 (see below) is typical of its allegiance to the Nazi regime.

Led by Dietrich Bonhoeffer and Martin Niemöller, the Confessing Christians (accounting for less than a third of the Protestant pastors, while another third remained "neutral") vigorously opposed such encroachments of the state on the sphere of the church; this included condemnation of the "Aryan paragraph" that barred Christians of Jewish descent or married to Jews from the clergy and administrative positions in the church.[5] Other than resistance to such state encroachment on the church's domain, only a few Confessing Christians criticized particular state policies, such as the euthanasia program, but they did not oppose the state and never defended the Jews or protested their persecution. In this, as their Swiss Calvinist mentor Karl Barth relentlessly brought to their attention and urged them to overcome, they were gravely handicapped by the Lutheran theology of the two kingdoms, the spiritual, the realm to which the church confined itself, and the temporal, the realm of the state, where legality, power, and coercion prevailed and the church did not intervene to criticize, constrain, or oppose. Thus, as Claudia Koonz concluded, the church "never quite surrendered and never really resisted."[6]

The "German Christian" Leaders

Declaration of Allegiance, November 1941

The declaration followed the German invasion of Soviet Russia in June, the decree of September imposing the wearing of the yellow badge on Jews, and the onset in October of systematic deportation of German Jews to concentration camps in the east. It was not possible for the authors of the declaration to be unaware of the persecution being suffered by the Jews in their midst. The declaration typifies the German Christian movement's subservience to the regime, its Nazi antisemitic ideology, and its obliviousness to the most fundamental Christian teachings. Regarded contemptuously by the regime, the German Christians never woke up to the fact that in the Nazi Party's view, "National Socialism and Christianity are irreconcilable," and that after "this successful war" Hitler intended a final solution for the churches.

The German National Socialist Leadership has irrefutably proved by numerous documents that this war in its world-wide dimensions has been hatched by the Jews. It has therefore taken internal and external decisions and measures against Jewry that are indispensable for the safeguarding of German life.

As members of the community of the German nation the undersigned German Evangelical Provincial Churches and their Presidents are in the frontline of this historic defensive affair, which *inter alia* necessitated the Reich Police regulations of marking the Jews [with the Star of David] as the born enemies of the world and the Reich. Dr. Martin Luther, too, after bitter experience, demanded the strictest measures against the Jews and their expulsion from German territories.

From the crucifixion of Christ to our own day the Jews have combated Christianity and abused or falsified it in pursuance of their selfish goals. By Christian baptism nothing is changed in the racial peculiarities of a Jew, nor in his national characteristics or his biological being. The German Evangelical Church has to preserve and support the religious life of fellow Germans. Christians of Jewish race have no room and no right in it.

The . . . German Evangelical Churches and their Presidents have therefore annulled each and all intercourse with Jewish Christians. They are determined not to tolerate any influence of the Jewish mind on German religious and ecclesiastical life.[7]

Evangelical Church of Germany Council

Stuttgart Declaration of Guilt, October 1945

After the war the Confessing Church's tenacious defense of the church against Nazi encroachment in the ecclesiastical sphere was embellished by conservative churchmen, consciously and wrongly, to have included opposition to Nazi ideology and practice, including the deification of Hitler, imperialist wars and annexations, antisemitism, and the mass murder of Jews, Slavs, and Romany. They cultivated three myths: that they were ignorant of the crimes of the regime, that their resistance was widespread and sustained, that they were victims of both the Nazis and the Allies. They were willing to confess and repent before God but not, as one pastor

urged, "earthly judges" or those against whom the crimes and offenses were committed; this would avert "any loss of dignity before the enemy," by which the pastor meant the Jews, other victims, and the Allies. This was what Bonhoeffer had
rejected as "cheap grace," and stemmed from Luther's teaching of the universal
sinfulness and guilt of mankind and "salvation by faith alone."[8] In 1945 the Provisional Council, the governing body of the re-named "Evangelical Church in Germany" (EKD, mostly Lutheran but including Calvinist Reform and Union churches),
issued the Stuttgart "Declaration of Guilt," a profoundly moving pronouncement
that was inspired by the heroic leader of the "Confessing Church," Niemöller. Yet
the Stuttgart declaration did not so much as mention Jews and their mass extermination. Reactions to the declaration in Germany were negative and outraged. Letters to the editor and editorials focused on German suffering and excoriated the Allied occupation, dubbed the Allies un-Christian hypocrites, lambasted Niemöller as
a traitor, accused all of Europe of a long history of anti-German attitudes, repeated
old myths about Leftists and Jews stabbing Germany in the back in World War I, dis-
paraged democracy, and compared the horrors of twelve to thirteen million Germans displaced by the Red Army and vengeful Poles and Czechs from the eastern
territories to the Holocaust. Or, as Bishop Theophil Wurm, one of the signers of the
declaration, wrote in his "Letter to the Christians of England" in December 1945:
"To pack the German people into a still narrower space [than under the 1919 Versailles treaty], to cut off as far as possible the material basis of their very existence,
is no different, in essentials, from Hitler's plan to stamp out the existence of the
Jewish race."[9] Wurm also equated the Allied fire bombing of German cities with
Nazi genocide, attacked denazification measures, and complained about the "in-
discriminate" arrest of Nazi Party members (including his son, who had joined in
1922). The lengthy 1946 memorandum "The Guilt of the Others" by Hans Asmussen, a distinguished theologian and head of the EKD's chancellery, also distorted
the facts of recent German history and the meaning of the Nazi era, and even laid
the groundwork for Holocaust denial.

The Council of the Protestant Church in Germany welcomes representatives
of the World Council of Churches to its meeting on October 18-19, 1945 in
Stuttgart.

   We are all the more thankful for this visit, as we know ourselves to be
with our people in a great community of suffering, but also in a great solidarity of guilt. With great anguish we state: through us has endless suffering been brought to many peoples and countries. What we have often borne
witness to before our congregations, we now declare in the name of the whole
Church. We have for many years struggled in the name of Jesus Christ against
the spirit which found its terrible expression in the National Socialist regime
of tyranny, but we accuse ourselves for not witnessing more courageously, for
not praying more faithfully, for not believing more joyously, and for not lov-
ing more ardently.

   Now a new beginning can be made in our churches. Grounded on the

Holy Scriptures, directed with all earnestness toward the only Lord of the Church, they now proceed to cleanse themselves from influences alien to the faith and to set themselves in order. Our hope is in the God of grace and mercy that He will use our churches as His instruments and will give them authority to proclaim His word, and in obedience to His will to work creatively among ourselves and among our people.

That in this new beginning we may become wholeheartedly united with the other churches of the ecumenical fellowship fills us with deep joy.

We hope in God that through the common service of the churches the spirit of violence and revenge which again today tends to become powerful may be brought under control in the whole world, and that the spirit of peace and love may gain the mastery, wherein alone tortured humanity can find healing.

So in an hour in which the whole world needs a new beginning we pray: "Veni Creator Spiritus."

[Signed by Bishop Wurm, Pastors Asmussen and Niemöller, and six other churchmen.][10]

Synod of the Evangelical Church in Germany

Statement on the Jewish Question, Berlin-Weissensee, 1950

"The Ten Points of Seelisberg," promulgated by the International Council of Christians and Jews in 1947, also neglected to mention the Holocaust, but it is a milestone document for it attacked traditional Christian prejudices and seems to have had a positive impact on German Protestant theologians. A year later, 1948, the EKD's Council issued a similarly limited "Message Concerning the Jewish Question." It condemned antisemitism but defeated its purpose by its supersessionism, triumphalism, and conversionism, and is a classic instance of how anti-Judaism, of which the authors remained prisoners, can still serve as the "necessary preparation" for antisemitism. One clergyman gave apt if bizarre expression to the authors' theological position when he said, "Antisemitism is justified but this antisemitism must remain within biblically set limits."[11] Bishop Wurm remained dissatisfied with the 1948 "Message," however, and urged that it include reference to "the way Jewish literati, since the days of Heinrich Heine, sinned against the German people by mocking all that is sacred and how in many areas the peasants suffered as a result of Jewish profiteers" as well as the Allies' "hand[ing] the reins of power to the Jews who have returned" in quest of revenge; thus did Bishop Wurm, a fervent admirer of the antisemitic Wilhelmine court preacher Adolf Stöcker (see page 105), exhibit the antisemitic stereotypes he never ceased to harbor.[12] However, in 1950, by which time the fact of Israel reborn began to register theologically, the Berlin-Weissensee synod of the EKD forthrightly renounced supersessionsim.

We believe in the Lord and Savior, who as a person came from the people of Israel. . . .

We believe God's promise to be valid for his Chosen People even after the crucifixion of Jesus Christ.

We state that by omission and silence we became implicated before the God of mercy in the outrage which has been perpetrated against the Jews by people of our nation. . . .

We ask all Christians to disassociate themselves from all antisemitism and earnestly to resist it, whenever it stirs again, and to encounter Jews and Jewish Christians in a brotherly spirit.

We ask the Christian congregations to protect Jewish graveyards within their areas if they are unprotected.

We pray to the Lord of mercy that he may bring about the Day of Fulfillment when we will be praising the triumph of Jesus Christ together with the saved Israel.[13]

The Church Council of the Evangelical Lutheran Church in America

"Declaration of the Evangelical Lutheran Church in America to the Jewish Community," April 18, 1994

It was not until the 1960s and 1970s that EKD churchmen renounced or drastically modified its mission for the conversion of the Jews in favor of dialogue and mutual respect; it took until 1980, at the Rhineland synod of the EKD, before missionary-conversionist activity to the Jews was condemned explicitly. By then the EKD had long joined the World Council of Churches and was a frequent participant in international and ecumenical organizations. The "Report of a Consultation on 'The Oneness of God'" under Lutheran World Federation auspices in Oslo in 1975 was more searching and wide ranging than any document that had emerged in Germany: "Lutherans and other Christians are painfully aware of the fact that Christianity has for 19 centuries been a source of anti-Semitic thought and action. We cannot confess our guilt of involvement in the Holocaust in the 1940s without committing ourselves to action that will prevent the repetition of such a tragedy [in the Middle East]."

A milestone for American Protestant denominations was the 1987 statement by the General Assembly of the Presbyterian Church (USA), "A Theological Understanding of the Relationship between Christians and Jews." It reads in part:

[Over many centuries] the church misused portions of the New Testament as proof texts to justify a heightened animosity toward Jews. For many centuries, it was the church's teaching to label Jews as "Christ-killers" and a "deicide race." This is known as the "teaching of contempt." Persecution of Jews was at times officially sanctioned, and at other times indirectly encouraged or at least tolerated. Holy Week became a time of terror for Jews. . . .

It is painful to realize how the teaching of the church has led individuals and groups to behavior that has tragic consequences. It is agonizing to discover that the church's "teaching of contempt" was a major ingredient that made possible the monstrous policy of annihilation of Jews by Nazi Germany.[14]

A fundamental obstacle for Lutherans was the founder. In 1964 the Lutheran World Federation's Department of World Mission met in Denmark and issued "The Church and the Jewish People"; although with regard to antisemitism it acknowledged that "we [Lutherans] confess our own peculiar guilt, and we lament with shame the responsibility which our church and her people bear for this sin," the document reiterated the traditional theology that Christianity had superceded Judaism and also sanctioned the Christian mission to convert the Jews. It took until 1969 to agree on Section 4, "On the Theology of the Church's Relation to Judaism," but it was still not possible to repudiate Luther's baleful antisemitic works because, according to a participant, "genuine harm would be done" to the church by any statement that implied a linkage between Luther and Hitler; hence, the document is limited to stating that the challenge of the Jewish people's continuing existence "proved to be too much for him," that his response to their presence "overstepped the bounds" of human authority.[15] There was a breakthrough in 1971 when the Metropolitan New York Synod of the Lutheran church "repudiated the antisemitic writings of Dr. Martin Luther." The Lutheran World Federation addressed this subject in various meetings, and in a 1984 statement issued by its international assembly declared that "We cannot accept or condone the violent verbal attacks that the Reformer has made against the Jews." With the document below issued in 1994, the Lutheran community in the United States addressed the antisemitism of its founder.

In the long history of Christianity there exists no more tragic development than the treatment accorded the Jewish people on the part of Christian believers. Very few Christian communities of faith were able to escape the contagion of anti-Judaism and its modern successor, anti-Semitism. Lutherans belonging to the Lutheran World Federation and the Evangelical Lutheran Church in America feel a special burden in this regard because of certain elements in the legacy of the reformer Martin Luther and the catastrophes, including the Holocaust of the twentieth century, suffered by Jews in places where the Lutheran churches were strongly represented.

The Lutheran communion of faith is linked by name and heritage to the memory of Martin Luther, teacher and reformer. Honoring his name in our own, we recall his bold stand for truth, his earthy and sublime words of wisdom, and above all his witness to God's saving Word. Luther proclaimed a gospel for people as we really are, bidding us to trust a grace sufficient to reach our deepest shames and address the most tragic truths.

In the spirit of that truth-telling, we who bear his name and heritage must with pain acknowledge also Luther's anti-Judaic diatribes and the violent recommendations of his later writings against the Jews. As did many of Luther's own companions in the sixteenth century, we reject this violent invective, and yet more do we express our deep and abiding sorrow over its tragic effects on subsequent generations. In concert with the Lutheran World Federation, we particularly deplore the appropriation of Luther's words by modern anti-Semites for the teaching of hatred toward Judaism or toward the Jewish people in our day.

Grieving the complicity of our own tradition within this history of hatred, moreover, we express our urgent desire to live out our faith in Jesus Christ with love and respect for the Jewish people. We recognize in anti-Semitism a contradiction and an affront to the Gospel, a violation of our hope and calling, and we pledge this church to oppose the deadly working of such bigotry, both within our own circles and in the society around us. Finally, we pray for the continued blessing of the Blessed One upon the increasing cooperation and understanding between Lutheran Christians and the Jewish community.[16]

The General Convention of the Episcopal Church of America

Resolution of the General Convention No. D055, July 22, 1997

The Episcopal Church's formal apology to the Jews in 1997 for 1,900 years of Christian prejudice and persecution in word and in deed was initiated by the Episcopal priest Bevan Stanley. The statement was drafted by an Episcopal layman, the attorney Timothy Bingham. On his mother's side he is of Jewish descent, and remembers as a boy being terrorized by the assertion of his Episcopal priest that unless one believed in Jesus, one was doomed to eternal damnation and hellfire. Once the draft was presented and approved "with great enthusiasm" by the highest Episcopal authority in the United States (its phraseology had been seriously weakened in committee but was restored to the original wording at the 800-member national convention largely through the dogged persistence and compelling argumentation of Father Stanley), it continues to be presented in formal ceremonies for acceptance to individual churches. While the resolution, excerpted below, owes much to the example of the conciliar document of 1965, *Nostra Aetate,* it goes considerably beyond it in offering an apology and seeking forgiveness, although with the understanding that forgiveness can come only from God. In Bingham's words, "Many Christians don't realize the extent of harm perpetrated on the Jews by the official Christian church." He hopes "this resolution leads to reconciliation, so that Christians and Jews see each other as true co-equals who happen to have different covenants with the same God."

WHEREAS, the General Convention adopted the following resolution,
NOW, THEREFORE, we [the official representatives] present the following resolution to [the specific synagogue]:
Resolved, The House of Bishops concurring, that this 72nd General Convention reaffirms the Episcopal Church's commitment to interfaith cooperation

and dialogue with our sisters and brothers of the Jewish faith; and be it further *Resolved*, That we commend the Evangelical Lutheran Church in America for the leadership it has given in this area and more particularly its 1994 *Declaration to the Jewish Community*; and be it further *Resolved*, That we acknowledge, with regret, our acts of moral blindness and outright prejudice, throughout history and today, that we have contributed to the abuse and mistreatment of Jews.
Adopted by the House of Deputies 7/22/97.
Concurred by the House of Bishops.[17]

Jewish Responses to Christian Overtures

Some Jewish organizations like the Anti-Defamation League and the American Jewish Committee were quick to respond favorably to *Nostra Aetate*. They helped initiate Jewish-Christian dialogue groups, participated in joint ventures to implement *Nostra Aetate* and subsequent Vatican documents, and maintained liaison with the Vatican and national hierarchies to urge and plan further steps in Jewish-Christian understanding and dialogue. Jewish religious groups were much slower and reluctant to enter the field. Some skeptics note that the Church still makes universalist claims, such as the *"Dominus Jesus": On the Unity and Salvific Universality of Jesus Christ and the Church* (2000) that reasserts the claim that salvation is to be attained only within the Catholic Church. Some Jewish groups and individuals express misgivings about harsh pronouncements in the Vatican press about Israel, the unwillingness or inability to admit historic responsibility upon the part of the Church and its clergy for historic antisemitism, and the defense of the wartime Pope Pius XII in his "silence" and seeming indifference to the plight of the Jews. Others insist that there is no basis for Jewish-Christian dialogue; the biblical scholar Jacob Neusner argues that the two religions represent "different people talking about different things to different people."[18] Reform and Conservative Jewry have been remarkably forthcoming in participating at the grassroots in Jewish and Holocaust studies programs in Catholic colleges; in sharing festivals in churches and synagogues; and in conducting book discussions, sponsoring speakers, and organizing exhibits.

The first full-fledged response by a group of Jewish thinkers to the developments in Christian denominations occurred in 2000 with the publication of "*Dabru Emet: A Jewish Statement on Christians and Christianity*." *Dabru Emet* is Hebrew for "speak truth," and alludes to Zechariah 8:16: "Speak the truth to one another, render true and perfect justice in your gates." Rabbi Irving Greenberg, one of its signers, wrote that *Dabru Emet* is "the most positive affirmation [of Christianity] ever made by a committed Jewish group." Rabbi James Rudin, also actively engaged in Jewish-Christian dialogue, objected that "Christianity and Christian teachings over the centuries created the seedbed for Nazism to grow in," that on the Holocaust *Dabru Emet* "lets Christian teaching off too easily." For lack of space, only the opening passage and the eight themes that guide its exposition are presented here:

In recent years, there has been a dramatic and unprecedented shift in Jewish and Christian relations. Throughout the nearly two millennia of Jewish exile,

Christians have tended to characterize Judaism as a failed religion or, at best, a religion that prepared the way for, and is completed in, Christianity. In the decades since the Holocaust, however, Christianity has changed dramatically. An increasing number of official Church bodies, both Roman Catholic and Protestant, have made public statements of their remorse about Christian mistreatment of Jews and Judaism. These statements have declared, furthermore, that Christian teaching and preaching can and must be reformed so that they acknowledge God's enduring covenant with the Jewish people and celebrate the contribution of Judaism to world civilization and to Christian faith itself.

We believe these changes merit a thoughtful Jewish response. Speaking only for ourselves—an interdenominational group of Jewish scholars—we believe it is time for Jews to learn about the efforts of Christians to honor Judaism. We believe it is time for Jews to reflect on what Judaism may now say about Christianity. As a first step, we offer eight brief statements about how Jews and Christians may relate to one another.

Jews and Christians Worship the Same God
Jews and Christians Seek Authority from the Same Book
Christians Can Respect the Claim of the Jewish People upon the Land of Israel
Jews and Christians Accept the Moral Principles of Torah
Nazism Was Not a Christian Phenomenon
The Humanly Irreconcilable Difference between Jews and Christians Will Not Be
    Settled until God Redeems the Entire World as Promised in Scripture
A New Relationship between Jews and Christians Will Not Weaken Jewish Practice
Jews and Christians Must Work Together for Justice and Peace[19]

NOTES

1. Franklin H. Littell, *The Crucifixion of the Jews* (1975; reprint, Macon, Ga.: Mercer University Press, 1996), 104.

2. Quoted in Susannah Heschel, "When Jesus Was an Aryan," in *In God's Name: Genocide and Religion in the Twentieth Century,* ed. Omer Bartov and Phyllis Mack (New York: Bergbahn Books, 2001), 80.

3. The oppositional wing of the Confessing Church sent a private letter to Hitler in June 1936, stating, "When blood, race, nationality, and honor are thus raised to the rank of qualities that guarantee eternity, the Evangelical Christian is bound, by the First Commandment, to reject the assumption. When the 'Aryan' human being is glorified, God's word bears witness to the sinfulness of all men. When, within the National Socialist compass of life, an anti-Semitism is forced on the Christian that binds him to hatred of the Jew, the Christian injunction to love one's neighbor still stands. . . . The Evangelical conscience, which shares the responsibility for the people and the government, is most heavily burdened by the fact that there are still concentration camps in Germany—which describes itself as a country in which justice is administered—and that the measures and actions of the State police are exempt from any judicial control." Quoted in Matthew D. Hockenos, *A Church Divided: German Protestants Confront the Nazi Past* (Bloomington: Indiana University Press, 2004), 32. The great majority of Lutherans were unwilling to follow the lead of these courageous clergy.

4. Quotations in John S. Conway, *The Nazi Persecution of the Churches* (New York: Basic Books, 1968), 46, 48, 52.

5. The Confessing Church originated 1933-1934 when Pastors Dietrich Bonhoeffer and Martin Niemöller (famous World War I submarine captain) initiated opposition within the Lutheran church against "the Aryan paragraph"; Bonhoeffer was murdered by the Nazis in 1945, Niemöller spent 1937-1945 in concentration camps.

6. Claudia Koonz, *Mothers in the Fatherland: Women, the Family, and Nazi Politics* (New York: St. Martin's Press, 1987), 263.

7. From Conway, *The Nazi Persecution of the Churches*, 262.

8. Quoted in Hockenos, *A Church Divided*, 70.

9. Quoted in Hockenos, *A Church Divided*, 108.

10. From Hockenos, *A Church Divided*, 187, appendix 4.

11. Quoted in Hockenos, *A Church Divided*, 229, n. 57.

12. Quoted in Hockenos, *A Church Divided*, 151.

13. From Hockenos, *A Church Divided*, 199, appendix 8.

14. Quoted in Daniel Jonah Goldhagen, *A Moral Reckoning* (New York: Knopf, 2002), 231.

15. Harold H. Ditmanson, ed., *Stepping-Stones to Further Jewish-Lutheran Relationships: Key Lutheran Statements* (Minneapolis: Fortress Press, 1990), 21.

16. Retrieved from a website dedicated to Jewish-Christian relations: www.jcrelations.com

17. Reproduced from a copy provided by Timothy W. Bingham of New Haven, Connecticut, March 12, 2003.

18. Quoted by Frank Kermode in his review of Harold Bloom, *Jesus and Yahweh*, in *New York Review of Books*, 52, 19 (Dec. 1, 2005): 42.

19. *Dabru Emet* appeared in *The New York Times*, Sept. 20, 2000, 37; it can be downloaded from www.beliefnet.com. Also see the collection of essays, Tikva Frymer-Kensky, Peter Ochs, and David Sandmel, eds., *Christianity in Jewish Terms* (Boulder, Colo.: Westview Press, 2000).

TWENTY-FIVE

Antisemitism in the Soviet Union and the New Russia

Joseph Stalin, the absolute ruler of the Soviet Union 1928–1953, was an utterly cruel persecutor of the Jewish minority. His antisemitism was a pathological obsession that can be traced to traditional Russian Orthodox prejudice that was reinforced by his seminary training in his native Georgia, his exposure to tsarist Russian culture when it was punctuated by pogroms, a Marxist ideological hostility, and his fierce rivalry with other Bolshevik leaders of Jewish origin (notably Leon Trotsky) who surpassed him in intellect and personal magnetism. In the last decade of Stalin's totalitarian rule, observes Amir Weiner, "The Jew was thought of as an inherently alien organism, which people wished to see removed from their midst"; he concludes that "The Soviet regime and citizen may not have possessed the exterminatory impulse and institutions that made the Nazi regime unique. But after the war, they displayed a willingness to discuss and operate on the very same [racial] assumptions as their arch enemy, if only temporarily."[1]

The Kremlin barred recognition of the genocidal treatment meted out to Jews by the Nazi invaders; such efforts as the *Red Book,* intended to detail Jewish exploits as soldiers and partisans in the war, were denounced as "Jewish chauvinism" and never allowed to see the light of day in the Soviet Union.[2] After 1945, reports and monuments commemorated the suffering of the population as a whole and made no mention of the Jewish agony. Commemoration of massacres, such as that of Babi Yar in the outskirts of Kiev, where the Germans murdered, according to their records, 33,771 Jews in two days in September 1941, if held at all, rarely mentioned the Jewish victims. The years of German occupation and propaganda in the Soviet Union had profound effects in grafting onto a traditional popular antisemitism the Nazi brand of racial antisemitism. Racial-nationalist criteria seeped more and more into Soviet conceptions of internal enemies, groups, and nationalities, the Jews above all.[3] To Stalin the Jew remained a Jew, the eternal alien and "cosmopolitan," "unreceptive" to socialism as to Marxism, and immune to re-education as the new Soviet man: ineluctably his genes, as well as his history and traditions, disqualified him.[4] In the years immediately after the war all the stereotypes about Jews since tsarist times reappeared, buoyed by racist references in official propaganda and popular prejudice.

Three events in particular revealed the lethal antisemitic direction taken by Stalin: the trial and execution of the chief members of the Jewish Anti-Fascist Committee; the trial and execution in Czechoslovakia of communist party officials, most of them Jews; and the "Doctors' Plot," in which physicians, most of them Jews, were accused of murdering party officials.

In the spring of 1942, the communist regime approved the formation of the Jewish Anti-Fascist Committee (JAC), hoping that it would raise money and galvanize support for the Soviet war effort, particularly the need to open up a second front, from Jews in the West. Indeed when two representatives of the JAC visited the United States on a five-month tour in 1943 (they also spent some time in Mexico, Canada, and Britain), they were warmly received by American Jews and were eminently successful in raising money and rousing moral support for the Soviet cause—from start to finish the JAC was under close supervision by state security officials.

Chaired by the famed director of the Moscow Yiddish Theater, Solomon Mikhoels, and including many Jewish intellectuals and Yiddish writers, the committee grew in prominence and became a voice for Soviet Jewry. It initiated a lively newspaper, *Eynikkayt* (Unity), that celebrated things Jewish, broadcast the committee's activities, and while extolling Stalin as Jewry's great benefactor, felt secure enough to complain of unfair treatment of Jews and urged greater recognition of Jewish contribution to the war effort. The JAC collected documents and data relevant to the German persecution of Jews and growing antisemitism, which it tried to publish. Holding that "the central idea of the whole book is the idea that the Germans made war on the USSR only as an attempt to wipe out the Jews," Soviet authorities refused publication of this record compiled principally by Ilya Ehrenburg, a renowned journalist and novelist, and Vasily Grossman, the most famous battlefield correspondent of the war. *The Black Book: The Ruthless Murder of Jews by German-Fascist Invaders Throughout the Temporarily-Occupied Regions of the Soviet Union and in the Death Camps of Poland during the War of 1941–1945* was eventually published in English in New York in 1981 but never appeared in the Soviet Union.[5]

The Cold War and the establishment of the state of Israel in 1948, which had an electrifying effect on Soviet Jewry, led Stalin to question the loyalty of Soviet Jews. Ironically, Soviet Russia played a decisive role in Israel's birth: it supported the 1947 UN resolution, quickly extended diplomatic recognition in May 1948, and permitted satellite Czechoslovakia to sell military equipment critical for the War of Independence, but then switched sides. Becoming increasingly paranoid that Jews would betray him, Stalin launched a vicious antisemitic campaign. Already in January 1948, he had ordered the assassination of Solomon Mikhoels—death due to a car accident was the official explanation. In September 1948, Golda Meier, head of the first Israeli embassy to the Soviet Union, arrived in Moscow and was greeted by huge crowds when she attended synagogue for Sabbath services and even larger crowds on the High Holy Days. Convinced that Soviet Jews were contaminated with Zionism, Stalin declared that "every Jew is a nationalist and an agent of American intelligence"[6] and he was as determined to destroy Yiddish culture—the source of Jewish identity—in the USSR and Eastern Europe as he was to conduct another brutal purge. Many Jews were arrested and fired from their positions of authority and prestige in the arts, journalism, medicine, and the party;

societies of Yiddish writers and Yiddish language publications (including *Eynikkayt*) were terminated; the JAC was disbanded and many of its members, several of them prominent Yiddish writers, were arrested and charged with being members of a bourgeois nationalist organization and agents of the United States. Preparations for a public show trial went on in the deepest secrecy for nearly three years but were canceled because the defendants rejected "misstatements and distortions" by the court officers, recanted their "confessions," and remained unbroken in spirit despite torture and solitary confinement; and the documentary "evidence"—mostly from the JAC's archives—was largely useless to the prosecution. The defendants were stripped of their medals earned during the war and thirteen were condemned to death and secretly executed on August 12, 1952, what came to be commemorated as the "Night of the Murdered Poets." Relatives of the executed Jews, who were not told of the fate of their loved ones, were charged with being the kin of traitors to the motherland and exiled for ten years to forbidden regions in the east.

During and after the secret trial Soviet propaganda bombarded the public with tales of "criminal nationalist Jews" and a vast "Judeo-Zionist" plot. In 1955, two years after Stalin's death, the Supreme Court of the USSR concluded that the case against the committee members had been "falsified" and repealed the sentences posthumously "because there was no substance to the charges against them." This meant that the case was "closed" but without rehabilitating the victims, which did not occur until 1956 and not fully until 1989. The trial transcript remained secret until 1994.

Stalin's antisemitic and anti-Zionist campaign was exported to the satellite countries, where it effected an astounding purge of Eastern European communist leaders from 1948 to 1953. In November 1952, fourteen high members of the Czech communist party were accused of conspiring to undermine communist rule. Eleven of the fourteen defendants were Jews, including Rudolf Slansky, former head of the party. Emphasizing the defendants' Jewish ancestry, the prosecution denounced them as "Zionist adventurers." The media in other satellite countries also attacked them. Radio Bucharest broadcast ominously: "We also have criminals among us, Zionist agents and agents of international Jewish capital. We shall expose them and it is our duty to exterminate them."[7] Slansky and his codefendants were hanged.

In early 1952 fifteen physicians—"the terrorist group of saboteur doctors"— more than half of them Jews, were arrested, accused of having killed the prominent Soviet ideologist Andrei Zhdanov in 1948 and plotting to poison other high Kremlin officials. When this was revealed to the public in January 1953, there was an intense press campaign and many local grassroots meetings demanding further inquiry and punishment for "rootless cosmopolitans," "persons without identity," "passportless wanderers," and the like. Concurrently, there was the gradual unveiling of what purported to be a huge conspiracy of intellectuals, Jews, soldiers, industrial managers, high party members, and leaders of non-Russian republics and satellite countries, with all the trappings of a new general purge and Great Terror as in the 1930s. The doctors' public show trial was scheduled to start in mid-March 1953 and was intended to pave the way for massive deportations of Soviet Jews to

Siberia. Some writers argue—on the basis of claims of access to the KGB archives—that Stalin was embarked on his own Final Solution that would have resulted in mass murder of Jews. Whatever Stalin planned, it was all cut short by his death on March 5. In the weeks that followed the Kremlin announced that it had all been a mistake, that the doctors were falsely accused and were the victims of torture, that there had been numerous "legal violations by the state security forces," and that such abuses were widespread.[8] This process culminated in Nikita Khrushchev's famous secret speech of 1956 denouncing Stalin's crimes, but it was "de-Stalinization" effected by a Stalinist and entailed no denunciation of antisemitism. The demonization of the Jews persisted in popular attitudes despite the release and rehabilitation of the doctors—indeed, this was seen as proof of the Jews' insidious power and influence. The Yiddish schools, newspapers, theaters, and publishing centers were not revived, and the number of Jewish cultural institutions and synagogues continued to shrink. Why try to revive a "dead culture"? asked a party ideological chief.[9]

Following Israel's victory in the Six-Day War in 1967, Soviet antisemitic propaganda, using Nazi-like language and caricatures, increasingly demonized the Jewish people, condemning Zionism as fascist and racist, Judaism as a wicked religion, and Jews as a criminal and conspiratorial people, as the excerpts below from Soviet writers and propagandists illustrate. Equating Jews with Nazism became a common theme in Soviet propaganda: "[T]he Zionists were the ones who taught Hitler cruelty. A perusal of his book *Mein Kampf* will reveal the passion with which Hitler quoted from the *Protocols of the Elders of Zion* and how zealously he implemented all the wicked formulas contained in this program of the Jews for the seizure of gold and power, for the future control of the subjugated nations, etc. He just replaced the Jews with the Germans."[10] For many years Soviet Jews who sought to immigrate to Israel, the refuseniks, were imprisoned, fined, and accused of participating in the "Zionist-fascist-imperialist conspiracy" against the "Socialist Camp." It took until October 1991, at a ceremony marking the fiftieth anniversary of Babi Yar, before President Mikhail Gorbachev denounced antisemitism, the first time in history that a Russian leader had done so. Gorbachev put an end to official antisemitism, but the new freedom under glasnost saw the appearance of many antisemitic publications and parties. This popular antisemitism was as virulently aggressive and more blatantly racist than in previous decades; part of it is a revival, despite three generations of state atheism and government suppression of religion, of Orthodox Christian antisemitism. In spite of the dissidents' movement and the struggle for human rights, antisemitism remains deeply rooted in Russia and in the former Soviet republics.[11]

Parallel developments have occurred in Ukraine, a former Soviet republic and one of the classic lands of lethal antisemitism. A Ukrainian university, the Interregional Academy of Personnel Management (MAUP), has more than fifty thousand students enrolled in several campuses across the country. Under its president, Georgy Tschokin, MAUP has been a center of antisemitic propaganda for several years. It hosts international antisemitic conferences and publishes two journals, *Personnel* and *Personnel Plus,* which contain much antisemitic material in pseudo-scholarly garb and students are forced to subscribe. The American white supremacist and antisemite David Duke "teaches" there and was awarded a doctorate for a thesis on "Zionism." He was a leading participant in MAUP's conference in June 2005 on "Zionism: Threat to World Peace." Tschokin identifies himself approvingly with Iranian President Ahmadinejad's demand that Israel be "wiped off the map" and in his statements combines traditional Christian antisemitism with "anti-Zionism":

> We'd like to remind that the Living God Jesus Christ said to Jews two thousand years ago: "Your father is a devil!" . . . Zionism in 1975 was acknowledged by General Assembly of UNO as the form of racism and race discrimination, that, in the opinion of the absolute majority of modern Europeans, makes the most threat to modern civilization. Israel is the artificially created state (classic totalitarian type). . . . Their end is known, and only the God's true will rescue all of us. We are not afraid, as God always together with his children![12]

In the early twenty-first century many antisemitic incidents have occurred in Ukraine and efforts have been made to prevent Jewish organizations from operating there and to ban Jewish publications. Several members of the government condemned MAUP's activities and called for enforcement of the laws against religious and racial incitement; in June 2006 the minister of education closed seven of its campuses. It remains far short, however, of President Viktor Yushchenko's claim of "zero tolerance" of antisemitism in Ukraine.[13]

Ruth Okuneva

"Anti-Semitic Notions: Strange Analogies," 1980s

The following excerpts from various works of Soviet propaganda were compiled by Ruth Okuneva, a Russian historian who emigrated to Israel in 1981. Okuneva demonstrated how closely the themes of Soviet antisemitism replicated statements of the Black Hundreds, a notorious antisemitic movement in tsarist Russia, and the statements of Nazi ideologists as well as those of medieval antisemites.

The chief strategic aim of the Zionist movement is the establishment of its domination of the world.

* * *

Their obsession with the idea of world domination is the primary cause of the crimes which humanity has witnessed.

* * *

. . . [A] group of people appeared who profess a doctrine which alleges that they have been chosen by God to dominate the world.

*   *   *

"To sow poison and demoralization," i.e., to corrupt and destroy society, to deceive the peoples . . . the Zionists could not do this without having control of the most powerful propaganda apparatus—the mass media. That is why their first objective is always to take control of newspapers and magazines, telegraph agencies, publishing houses, radio and television, the entire industry of the word. In this pursuit they have already achieved a great deal.

*   *   *

Zionism is fascism. . . . The basic content of Zionism is anticommunism, implacable hostility to the Soviet Union and other socialist countries, to the international revolutionary movement, and to all the anti-imperialist forces of today.

*   *   *

If we review the Torah from the standpoint of modern civilization and progressive Communist morality, it proves to be an unsurpassed textbook of bloodthirstiness and hypocrisy, treachery, perfidy, and licentiousness—of every vile human quality.

*   *   *

The peculiarities of the Jewish religion are hatred of mankind, preaching genocide, cultivating a love of power, and glorifying criminal means of achieving power.

*   *   *

The chauvinistic idea of world domination has been particularly repulsive; formulated in the "Holy Scriptures," it has been reflected in their prayers.

*   *   *

[I]n official abstracts of the prescripts of Judaism, repeated emphasis is given to the "exclusiveness" of the Jews, their innate superiority to the *goyim* [Hebrew for Gentiles], their right to world domination.

*   *   *

"God's chosen people" have their own laws, their own sphere, their own destiny, whereas the despised *goyim* are suited only to be "tools with the power of speech," slaves.

*   *   *

The Jews want to have slaves, but the slaves must not be Jews.

*   *   *

The teachings of Judaism are pervaded with hatred for work and contempt for the man who spends his day in toil. The entire ideology of Judaism is not imbued with the idea of work, but with a narrow practicality, the means for making a profit, a mania for silver, the spirit of egoism, and the craving for money.

* * *

The Talmud teaches that one is forbidden to steal only from a *khaver* (a fellow-man). One is permitted to take everything from anyone else (the *goyim*), because God has reserved all non-Jewish wealth for the Jews.[14]

Judicial Proceedings against Members of the Jewish Anti-Fascist Committee, 1948–1952

Excerpts from the trial record of members of the JAC follow.

Soon after the Jewish Anti-Fascist Committee was organized, its directors, under the cover of carrying out the tasks assigned to the committee, began to unfurl a program of nationalistic activity and established contact with Jewish nationalistic organizations in America. . . .

In May 1943, Lozovsky, under the pretext of intensifying propaganda about the achievements of the USSR and about the struggle with fascism, obtained permission for Mikhoels and Fefer to go to the United States. He assigned them to establish personal contact with Jewish nationalistic circles in the United States in a struggle against the Soviet state. Before they left for America, Mikhoels and Fefer . . . collected a number of materials about industry in the USSR, which they conveyed to the Americans. While in the United States, Mikhoels and Fefer established ties with representatives of Jewish nationalists—with the millionaire Rosenberg, . . . with the Zionist leader Weizmann, and with others to whom they provided slanderous information about the situation of Jews in the USSR. . . .

Upon their return to the USSR in late 1943, Mikhoels and Fefer informed Lozovsky and their other confederates about the criminal conspiracy with Jewish nationalists in the United States. Carrying out Rosenberg's assignment, Mikhoels, Fefer, Epshteyn, and Shimeliovich, with the knowledge and consent of their accomplices, drafted a letter to the Soviet government in which they raised the question of settling Jews in the Crimea and creating a Jewish republic there. . . . In the letter, [they] slandered the national policy of the Communist Party and the Soviet government, asserting that anti-Semitism was supposedly flourishing in the USSR, that the Jewish population in the USSR was not being "properly settled," that the "Jewish question" was not resolved, and that the Jewish masses of "all the countries of the world" would provide material assistance in building a Jewish republic.

. . . [A] significant portion of the materials sent to the United States by the leaders of the Jewish Anti-Fascist Committee were secret and contained state secrets.

During their stay in the USSR from 1943-1946, the American journalists Goldberg and Novick, who were Jewish nationalists, were provided by Lozovsky and Fefer with broad opportunities to gather information of interest to them. Lozovsky arranged for intelligence agent Goldberg to receive secret materials about . . . the economies of Latvia, Lithuania, and Estonia and also secret materials that Lozovsky received from Scientific Research Institute 205 about British foreign policy. Furthermore, Lozovsky assigned Fefer to accompany Goldberg to the Baltic region and Ukraine, where Goldberg, with Fefer's assistance, contacted local Jewish nationalists and through them also received secret information about the economy and culture of the Soviet Union.

In pursuit of the criminal goal of struggling against the national policy of the party and the Soviet government, [members of the JAC], at the direction of Jewish nationalistic circles in the United States, launched a broad campaign of propaganda among the Jewish population in the USSR and abroad, using for these purposes the newspaper *Eynikkayt*, . . . the publishing house Deremes, Yiddish literary anthologies, the Jewish theater, and the Office of Jewish Culture of the Ukrainian Academy of Sciences.

. . . [These media] spread the notion that the Jews as a nation are separate and different and the false thesis of the exceptional nature of the Jewish people as a people who . . . supposedly had made exceptional contributions in labor and science.

Idealizing the distant past, they extolled biblical images in a nationalistic spirit and spread the idea of a "fraternal" unity of Jews the world over transcending class and based solely on "shared blood," in doing so joining ranks with bourgeois nationalists in the United States, Palestine, and other countries. . . .

A vivid example of how the leaders of the Jewish Anti-Fascist Committee joined ranks with Jewish nationalists in the United States is . . . the so-called *Black Book*. . . . In this book the Jews are set off in a category separate and opposed to other peoples; the contribution of the Jews to world civilization is exaggerated; attention is paid exclusively to the losses borne by the Jews during the Second World War; and the idea is presented that fascism supposedly represented a threat to the Jews alone, and not to all peoples and to world civilization. As a result . . . nationalistic elements among the Jews began turning to the Jewish Anti-Fascist Committee with requests to send them to Palestine, to organize volunteer military units to fight on the side of the State of Israel, together with a great number of slanderous complaints about the infringement of Jews' rights allegedly taking place in various parts of the country. . . .

Broadening the functions of the Jewish Anti-Fascist Committee without permission, its leaders engaged in getting housing and jobs for Jewish settlers sent to Birobydzhan[15] and for Jews returning from evacuation, and finding employment for Jews in the formerly [German-] occupied parts of Ukraine and the Crimea. All of these criminal anti-Soviet activities by the leaders of the Jewish Anti-Fascist Committee attest to the fact that the Jewish Anti-Fascist Committee was transformed into a center of nationalistic activity and espionage. . . .

In meetings with . . . Goldberg, [Bergelson] provided him with information about Birobydzhan.

[The Court Record continues with the indictments of the remaining fourteen accused and death sentences for all but one.][16]

The Doctors' Plot

"beasts in the guise of physicians," 1953

In January 1953 the Soviet Union announced that "a Zionist terrorist gang" of Soviet Jewish doctors had conspired with Americans and Britons to murder high Soviet officials. Stalin intended to stage a show trial as an excuse for rounding up and resettling Jews in the east as he had done with other ethnic groups considered to be threats to the Marxist state. After Stalin's death two months later the case was dropped. In the interval, however, the Soviet press engaged in vicious anti-Jewish tirades as exemplified by the following excerpt from the journal *Krokodil.*

The Soviet people were filled with anger and indignation by the monstrous crimes perpetrated by the terrorist gang of physician-saboteurs exposed by the state security organs of the Soviet Union.

There is no limit to the despicable baseness of these cruel monsters who hide behind the noble title of doctor and defile the sacredness of science. An investigator has established that the group of murderous doctors planned through detrimental treatment to do away with prominent Soviet figures. Taking advantage of their position as doctors, the criminals made deliberately incorrect diagnoses and thereby killed their patients through improper "treatment."

The base murderers thus did away with such leading statesmen as A. A. Zhdanov and A. S. Shcherbakov.

The criminals have confessed that they incorrectly diagnosed Comrade A. A. Zhdanov's illness. Concealing his real condition—a myocardial infarction—they prescribed a regimen that was contraindicated in that serious condition, thereby killing him. An inquest has revealed that the criminals also shortened the life of Comrade A. S. Shcherbakov; they improperly administered powerful medication, prescribed a regimen that was ruinous to the patient's health, and thereby drove him to his death.

These beasts in the guise of physicians pursued unmistakably subversive purposes. The criminals tried their hardest to undermine the health of leading military figures, in order to weaken the defense of the Soviet Union. They tried to disable Marshals A. M. Vasilevsky, L. A. Govorov, and I. S. Konev, General of the Army A. M. Shtemenko, Admiral G. I. Levchenko, and others.

The subversive activity of the group of murderous physicians was directed by the hand of imperialist warmongers. The criminals had sold out [and] served the interests of American and British intelligence services.

Most of this villainous gang, including Professors Vovsi, B. Kogan, Feldman, Greenstein, Etinger, and others, were connected with the international Jewish bourgeois-nationalistic Joint organization, founded by the American intelligence services purportedly to provide material to Jews in other countries. Under the direction of the American intelligence services, this organization actually carries on large-scale espionage, terrorist, and other subversive activities in a number of countries, including the Soviet Union. During the investigation, prisoners admitted to having received instructions from the American Zionist Joint organization "to exterminate prominent leaders of the USSR." Other members of the terrorist group (Vinogradov, M. Kogan, Yegorov) turned out to be long-standing agents of the British intelligence services.[17]

Letter to the Attorney General to Investigate Jews, 2004

There was a resurgence of antisemitism in the wake of the socio-economic crisis—generating much resentment, rather like Germany after World War I—that marked the demise of the Soviet Union in 1989–1990. Nationalists attacked the "Bolshevik Jews" as responsible for the revolution of 1917 and the totalitarian tyranny; communists condemned the Jews for undermining the state and engineering its downfall. A poll indicated that 42 percent of Russians believed that Jews were too powerful and influential, and 28 percent wanted the tsarist Pale of Settlement—a kind of super-ghetto—revived.

In the last few years Holocaust denial has grown greatly in Russia, called by one scholar "the world center of denial." It is propagated on the Internet, where at least four websites are dedicated to Holocaust denial and fraudulent "revisionist histories" and videos, much of the material being imported, but increasingly indigenous articles appear; Russia also sees the publication of enormous quantities of antisemitic books of all kinds that are widely available in Russian bookstores. A documentary film on antisemitism in Russia, produced by the Moscow Human Rights Bureau, *The Shadow of the Swastika,* explores the rise of the neo-Nazi ideology among the young and ultra-Right groups in a country that suffered enormously from Nazism and played a decisive role in its defeat.

The letter excerpted below was sent by a group of nationalist members of the Duma and newspaper and magazine editors to the Russian attorney general. It was drawn up by members of the Rodina (motherland) Party in 2004 and demanded that all Jewish organizations in Russia be disbanded because they are extremist bodies and are bent on world domination; they engage in the "illegal propagation of Jewish national and religious extremism." One source of their ire was the "oligarchs," buccaneering capitalist entrepreneurs, many of them Jews, who profited enormously in the 1990s from privatization of former Soviet industries such as oil, electricity, and communications; subsequently, many of them are in exile or jail. Rodina takes the line that the Jews are themselves to blame for antisemitism. Some months earlier the Moscow district prosecutor initiated an investigation of the umbrella group, the Congress of Jewish Religious Communities and Organizations of

Russia, for issuing the *Shulkhan Arukh* of Rabbi Joseph Caro in Russian translation; that sixteenth-century codification of Jewish law—the most widely used and authoritative code for Orthodox Jews throughout the Diaspora for 450 years—was condemned as supposedly requiring Jews to ill-treat and discriminate against Gentiles and to indulge in criminal rituals; these are the same allegations repeatedly leveled against Jewish religious texts since the twelfth century, like the attacks on the Talmud by Eisenmenger (see page 49). Strong protests at home and abroad induced the prosecutor to cancel the investigation, fully vindicating the Congress' right, according to the chief rabbi, to publish Jewish works; nevertheless, Caro's book remains a subject of attack in the Rodina letter. Russian authorities received many letters, one reportedly having five thousand signatures, in support of the accusations and the letter. A few members of the Duma protested and President Vladimir Putin said he felt shamed by the letter, but a third of the public said they felt no shame whatsoever.

Jewish Joy, Russian Tears

Dear Mr. Attorney General:

[The letter begins with the complaint that in 2003 there were sixty-some criminal investigations for "inciting inter-ethnic hatred."]

Who is shouting, "Stop, thief!"?

The overwhelming majority of these cases are initiated by Jewish activists or organizations, who charge their defendants with "antisemitism." But the overwhelming majority of those accused and convicted are Russian patriots. . . . The major problem that must be elucidated in these investigations and trials is this: do the sharply negative assessments of the Jews by Russian patriots correspond in essence to the truth about the Jews . . . or do they not? . . . We can assure you, Mr. Attorney General, that on these matters there exists a large quantity of universally recognized facts and sources from around the world, on the basis of which it is possible to draw the indisputable conclusion that the Russian patriots' negative assessments of typical Jewish qualities and actions with respect to non-Jews correspond to the truth, since these actions are not chance occurrences, but are prescribed in Judaism and have been practiced for two millennia. Thus, the incriminating statements and publications made by patriots against the Jews constitute self-defense. . . .

The Morality of Jewish Fascism

To corroborate this, we draw your attention to the *Kitsur* [i.e., abbreviated] *Shulkhan Arukh* book officially published in Moscow in 2001. . . . This is a condensed version of the Jewish law code, the *Shulkhan Arukh*, compiled several centuries ago on the basis of the Talmud and required in practice to this day.[18] In the introduction to the book it is frankly acknowledged that. . . . some regulations of the Judaic code of behavior are insulting to the non-Jewish population of Russia, but [they have been deleted]. . . . However, even in this expurgated publication we find the following provisions:

* In the "Laws about idolatry" it is stated that "it is forbidden to use the

figure of two crossed sticks, which they worship." That is to say, Christianity is considered a variety of idolatry. . . .

* The instruction on seeing a "house of idolatry" (i.e., place of Christian worship) is to pronounce a curse on it. . . .

* "The Jewess ought not to help non-Jews with childbirth." . . .

* "It is forbidden to surrender a Jew into the hands of a non-Jew, whether the matter has to do with the Jew's life or his property; and it does not matter whether this is done by some action or by words; and it is forbidden to report him or to point out the places where he has hidden his property." . . . We imperatively request that it be noted that this concerns the behavior prescribed for Jews in the context of investigations and trials.

One of the 13 major principles of Judaism is the requirement that they must await a Jewish world ruler who will appoint Jews to rule over the other peoples of the world: "I believe unconditionally in the arrival of the mashiakh [messiah], and, although his coming may be delayed, nevertheless each day I await him."

In the teachings of the Orthodox Church this expected Jewish ruler of the world is identified with the Antichrist, against whom Jesus Christ warned (John 5:43[?]), as did the Apostle Paul (2 Thess. 2), and the holy Church Fathers. This is an important and integral part of Orthodox teachings. . . .

We believe that on the basis of this one official Jewish publication alone the law-enforcement agencies should, in accordance with article 282 of the Criminal Code of the Russian Federation, suppress the propagation of a religion that, among the Jews, incites hatred towards the rest of the "Russian population." This is especially so if we look at [additional passages of] the *Shulkhan Arukh.* . . .

* "It is forbidden to save them [non-Jews] when they are close to death. For example, when you see that one of them has fallen into the sea, do not rescue him, even if he wants to pay. . . . It is permitted to test medicine on [non-Jews] to see whether or not it is effective." . . .

* "When a Jew has robbed a non-Jew and they force the Jew to take an oath, then he must in his heart proclaim his oath invalid, because he has been forced to take it." Note: this again concerns the behavior of Jews during investigations and trials! . . .

* "It is permitted to kill a traitor anywhere, even in our time. It is permissible to kill him, before he manages to make a denunciation to the authorities [and thus cause 'bodily or monetary loss, no matter how small'] . . . and anyone who is the first to kill gets merit." . . .

Provocateurs and Haters of Humanity

It should be noted that even the last prescriptions for killing remain today not only theory, but also practice. Thus, the former chairman of Kharkov's Jewish community E. Khodos published proofs showing that members of the Jewish Chabad movement carried out the 1990 murder of a priest-Jew [a convert]. . . . But the authorities in the Russian Federation were not interested in such evidence. Criminals are supposed to be sought only among "Russian anti-semites."

We would like to emphasize that anti-Jewish actions throughout the world are constantly staged by Jews themselves as a way of provoking punitive mea-sures against patriots. The best-known case in Russia is that of Arkady Norin-sky, who in 1988 sent out antisemitic leaflets in the name of Pamyat [a fanati-cally nationalistic, antisemitic organization] in order to impel the authorities to suppress it. . . . It was only after [discovery of millions of copies] that the provocation was uncovered.

Among recent incidents, one may recall a strange series of acts of vandal-ism that took place in 1998-1999. On the night of 13 May 1998, in Moscow, an explosion occurred at a synagogue, damaging a wall. The same day "a burn-ing canister of gasoline" was placed not far from the synagogue in Otradny. In Irkutsk "a Jewish cemetery was desecrated." . . . of course the uproar in the world media was loud and all of them put the blame, without any evidence, on some sort of Russian Nazis.

But when shortly after that, in 1999, a synagogue in Birobydzhan [see note 15] was destroyed, it was established in court that the Jews themselves had hired a man to do this, but the democratic media kept silence.

On the basis of the laws and practices of Jewish behavior cited above, it is easy to understand that Jews living among all other peoples have notoriously experienced "antisemitism," i.e., resistance against this kind of Judaic morality. For this very reason, Jews did not enjoy equal rights in Christian states and at-tained it only as a result of anti-monarchist bourgeois revolutions. Thus in the Russian Empire, the Jews, after unsuccessful attempts by the tsarist govern-ment at making them "like everybody else," lost their equality [*sic*] in the nine-teenth century, not because they were Jewish by blood . . . since the empire was multinational; not because they were not Christians . . . since the Muslims and Buddhists and others were not Christians; but because the Jewish religion was anti-Christian and misanthropic reaching the point of ritual murder. Many ex-amples of this ritual extremism were proven and documented in courts [in the nineteenth century].

To all this, one may add the words of the Prayer of Shefokh, in which the Jews on the eve of their Passover issue a call to their "G-d" "to exterminate from heaven" all other peoples.

Jewish Aggressiveness as a Form of Satanism

The spiritual cause of this hatred of humankind is explained in the Gospels in the words of Christ regarding the Jewish priests who rejected the Son of God: "Your father is the devil and you choose to carry out your father's desires. He was a murderer from the beginning. . . ." (John 8:44).

This elucidation of Judaic aggressiveness as a form of Satanism is gener-ally accepted in the Orthodox Church. Well-known philosopher-intellectuals who cannot be suspected of antisemitism expressed it. [Several examples sup-posedly show that] the Jews who rejected Christ became the "laboratory for all sorts of spiritual vices, poisoning the world and particularly Christian humanity"; that the Jew who rejects Christianity, "betrays himself and easily falls under the power of dark forces."

This unfortunately is what happened with the larger part of the Jewish people (in contrast to its smaller part, converted to Christianity). But they do not want to recognize this and believe that that statement of the truth by Christ and after Him by Orthodox Christians is "insulting" to the Jews. Jewish plaintiffs frequently direct their charge of "antisemitism" against this essential part of the Orthodox doctrine itself, demanding that it be banned.

But we cannot agree with banning the Orthodox concept of history as the struggle of the forces of good (on the side of the Church) against the forces of evil (the side opposed to the religion that prepares for the reign of Antichrist).

Following the precepts of the Fathers of the Orthodox Church, we also cannot accept the false understanding of tolerance imposed on us as humility in the face of sin, evil, heresies, and in this case of Satanism. A Christian must, precisely out of respect for the image of God placed in each person and for the sake of saving his soul, frankly indicate to Jews their dangerous deviation from the truth into Satanism. It is this that, from a Christian point of view, constitutes the manifestation of true love for humanity, whereas the "tolerant" indulgence of heresies and Satanism only contributes to their spiritual demise and, under their onslaught, to that of their many victims. . . .

This "real Jewish chauvinism" [quoting Hannah Arendt's definition of Jewish chosenness] and the aggressive spirit of the *Shulkhan Arukh* clearly revealed themselves in the course of the destruction of the USSR and the postcommunistic reforms in our country, and were expressed in the illegal appropriation of state property [privatization under Boris Yeltsin] as "goods with no owner," and also in the composition of the new ruling group. "The government is full of Jews," acknowledged Rabbi Adolf Shayevich. Thus, their influence on the life of the country proved to be completely disproportionate to their numbers . . . to the detriment of the interests of all the other peoples of the country and especially the Russian people who formed the state.

The Jewish Revolution

The well-known Jewish publicist L. Radzikhovsky calls this a "democratic-capitalist revolution" and says: "The Jewish and Jewish-oriented intelligentsia constituted in Russia one of the chief carriers of Western liberal ideology and became the ideologists of this revolution." Therefore, "Jews have greater weight in Russian politics and business than in the politics and business of any other Christian country." This he calls the "good luck of the Jews." . . .

"For the first time in thousands of years, since the moment the Jews settled in Russia, we have acquired real power in this country," states another Jewish writer. . . . [Others] emphasize that the destructive and self-interested policy of the Jewish oligarchs degrades the Russian people and provokes the hostility of the Russian people toward the Jews. . . .

We request that the attorney general's office regard [such statements] as admission of Jewish responsibility for the current aggravation of the Russo-Jewish conflict.

This is essential, given the fact that in order to retain the illegally seized "un-owned" state property and their power, the ruling oligarchs conduct a policy aimed at bringing about the decay of the people's morals and the extinction of spiritual values, attempting to turn the people into an animal mass without faith or tradition. . . .

Among other numerous examples of the extinction of spiritual values we must draw attention . . . to the policy of the [Jewish] Minister of Culture who now leads a government agency and its television program, "The Cultural Revolution," in which Russian patriotism and Orthodox traditions are regularly degraded. It propagandizes obscenity and the idea that "sex is the engine of culture." All protests of the Russian community against the outrageous and, in essence, provocative activity of this "chief man of culture in the country" have proven futile.

Moreover, for their attacks the minister and his associates have the central channels of Russian television at their disposal, while the Orthodox patriots, who are on the defensive, have the tiny print runs [of publications], for which they are investigated and brought to trial. . . . [But the Orthodox patriot will] protect his people and things sacred to them. The example of this was given by Christ Himself, who by the whip banished from the temple the merchants who had profaned it.

What Is Permissible to Whom?

In comparison with the statements of the accused Russian patriots, much more aggressive statements by Jews regarding non-Jews are printed in Jewish newspapers published in the Russian Federation. For example, in the organ of the Russian Jewish Congress, an Israeli Knesset deputy . . . called for the forcible expulsion of the Palestinians from Israel. Accordingly, the Palestinians . . . in violation of UN Security Council resolutions! . . . are not only thrown out of their homeland (4 million refugees [*sic*]), but their activists are murdered along with their families. This is what the *Shulkhan Arukh* looks like when adopted as the state policy of Israel.

And the Jews of the Russian Federation support it. The Russian Jewish Congress states that one of its aims is "to conduct actions of solidarity with the people of Israel, political lobbying in the interest of Israel." . . .

Jewish communities all over the world are engaged in similar "political lobbying" in the interest of international Jewry to the detriment of the interests of the countries of their residence, and particularly the USA. That state has become an instrument for the attainment of the global aims of Jewry. And they try to mask this by slapping the charge of antisemitism (i.e., alleged racial hatred) on all those who do not agree with their morality, their activities, their wars.

But such an inversion of concepts is a crude forgery, as should be clear to any impartial judge. One can say that the whole democratic world today finds itself under the financial and political control of international Jewry. . . . And we do not want our Russia, against whose revival a permanent preventive war without rules is being conducted, to be among such unfree countries.

Therefore, we, both in order to protect our fatherland and out of self-defense, are forced to turn to you, Mr. Attorney General, with the imperative request that within the shortest period you verify the outrageous facts presented above and, if they are confirmed, . . . officially to institute proceedings for the prohibition in our country of all Jewish religious and national associations as extremist. We also request that persons responsible for making available to these associations state and municipal property, privileges, and state financing, be called to account, regardless of the posts they occupy.

[Signed by nine authors, almost all of them newspaper editors, "the representatives of the orthodox-patriotic public," plus more than five hundred signatories, including nineteen deputies to the Duma.][19]

NOTES

1. Amir Weiner, "When Memory Counts: War, Genocide, and Postwar Soviet Jewry," in *Crimes of War: Guilt and Denial in the Twentieth Century,* ed. Omer Bartov, Atina Grossman, and Mary Nolan (New York: New Press, 2002), 215, 192.

2. Proposed by Ilya Ehrenburg and Vasily Grossman in 1944, it was condemned as "bragging" and allowed to appear in small part only in 1948 as *Parzinasakia druzhba.* It is virtually impossible to find in the very few libraries where it is supposed to be available.

3. Vasily Grossman, *Life and Fate,* trans. Robert Chandler (New York: Harper and Row, 1985), 576-581.

4. Amir Weiner, *Making Sense of War: The Second World War and the Fate of the Bolshevik Revolution* (Princeton: Princeton University Press, 2001), 195, 198.

5. Trans. John Glad and James S. Levine (New York: Holocaust Publications and Schocken Books, 1981).

6. Quoted in Joshua Rubenstein and Vladimir P. Naumov, eds., *Stalin's Secret Pogrom: The Postwar Inquisition of the Jewish Anti-Fascist Committee,* trans. Laura E. Wolfson (New Haven, Conn.: Yale University Press, 2001), 62.

7. Quoted in Rubenstein and Naumov, *Stalin's Secret Pogrom,* 61.

8. Quoted in Nicolas Werth, "A State against Its People," in *The Black Book of Communism: Crimes, Terror, Repression,* Stéphan Courtois et al., trans. Jonathan Murphy and Mark Kramer (Cambridge, Mass.: Harvard University Press, 1999), 253.

9. Quoted in Bernard Wasserstein, *Vanishing Diaspora: The Jews in Europe since 1945* (Cambridge, Mass.: Harvard University Press, 1996), 184.

10. L. Dimerski-Tsigelman, "The Attitude toward Jews in the USSR" in *Anti-Semitism in the Soviet Union: Its Roots and Consequences,* ed. Theodore Freedman (New York: Anti-Defamation League of B'nai B'rith, 1984), 85.

11. See Werth, "A State against its People," 242-260.

12. Ukraine University of Hate. "A Backgrounder on MAUP," Nov. 3, 2006; down-

loaded from ADL website, http://www.ADL.org/main_Anti_Semitism_International/maup_ukraine.htm.

13. From the Anti-Defamation League's website, www.ADL.org, "Ukraine University Schooling in Anti-Semitism," Dec. 2, 2005.

14. From Ruth Okuneva, "Anti-Semitic Notions: Strange Analogies," in Freedman, *Anti-Semitism in the Soviet Union*, 272, 281, 285, 287, 291-294.

15. Reflecting Stalin's ideas of nationality at the time and an attempt to solve the "Jewish question" and sap the appeal of Zionism and settlement in Palestine under the British Mandate, Birobydzhan was a Kremlin scheme that emerged in 1928 to settle Jews in this remote area of Siberia, which was eventually to become "a Jewish autonomous republic." With an extremely inhospitable climate and poor soil, and much propaganda but little assistance, the settlement floundered and two-thirds of its Jewish settlers left by 1938. The American Joint Distribution Committee supplied agricultural machinery and training until prohibited by the suspicious Soviet government. Birobydzhan's growth was checkmated by the Purge Trials of the 1930s, when it was declared "not for normal Soviet citizens" and the secret police took control; mounting antisemitism undermined its Yiddish culture and institutions. After 1945 there was a brief revival, but in 1948 most of its Yiddish writers and Jewish politicians were arrested and executed, part of the "conspiracy" of the Jewish Anti-Fascist Committee to create an anti-Soviet "national deviationist" culture. Today there is very little that is Jewish about the "Soviet Zion"; perhaps three thousand of its quarter-million citizens are Jewish.

16. From Rubenstein and Naumov, *Stalin's Secret Pogrom*, 486-489.

17. From Freedman, *Anti-Semitism in the Soviet Union*, 532-533.

18. The work alluded to is not Joseph Caro's treatise but a partial nineteenth-century summary by a Hungarian, Rabbi Shlomo Ganzfried, who was concerned to refute Reform Judaism; it was not nearly so authoritative or as widely used as Caro's. In any event the text refers to idolatry/idolaters, which have always been treated by the rabbis as a great danger and temptation. Chief Rabbi Berel Lazar stated to the prosecutor that "the book does not incite national and religious hatred. At issue were entries involving responsibilities of a Jew vis-à-vis idol worshipers, not non-Jews." In reporting the case's dismissal he said, "We showed that the attacks were baseless and stemmed from the poor translation of the original text. For example, it does not say that a Jewish midwife should not help a non-Jewish woman deliver her child, but an idol worshipper. . . . We brought examples from other halachic [legal] literature to prove this, and we showed . . . that Jewish doctors and midwives in Russian hospitals and in Jewish hospitals don't discriminate according to such an idea"—from http://jihadwatch.org/dhimmiwatch/archives/006841.php. It is true that earlier rabbinical works had very harsh things to say about Christians/Christianity—not unexpectedly by victims of Christian persecution—but, as we have seen in Menachem Ha-Me'iri (see page 50), most of these came to be recognized as obsolete and were discarded, and began to be replaced by a theory of religious toleration.

19. The Rodina letter was made available to us by Dr. Ilya A. Altman, Vice-President of the Russian Holocaust Foundation in Moscow, and translated for this volume by Tatyana Gourov of New York. The many citations, giving the letter a legal scholarly air, have been deleted.

TWENTY-SIX

The Lingering Appeal of Nazism in Germany

With the disclosure of the Third Reich's crimes against humanity, Nazism was widely discredited in the decades following World War II. Nevertheless, a small core of un-repentant Nazis continued to harbor xenophobic and racist views and looked back nostalgically on Hitler and the Nazi era, although changing conditions within Germany made them reluctant to express these attitudes publicly. In recent years extreme right-wing and neo-Nazi groups have emerged in Germany (and Austria), often attracting unemployed or under-employed youths and skinheads prone to violence. Their angry hatred has been directed at foreign-born laborers and their families dwelling in Germany, particularly Turks, whom they regard as parasites and inassimilable aliens, and Jews, the traditional target of the radical Right. These groups circulate Nazi propaganda and memorabilia and at times desecrate and vandalize Jewish cemeteries, synagogues, and Holocaust memorials, and they commit other violent acts, particularly against immigrants. Monitored by the government and opposed by the great majority of Germans, these right-wing hoodlums do not constitute a threat to German democracy.

Ingo Hasselbach

Führer–Ex: Memoirs of a Former Neo-Nazi, 1996

The rebellious son of members of the communist elite in East Germany, Ingo Hasselbach spent much of his adolescence in jail for petty crimes. After sharing a prison cell with the former Dresden Gestapo chief and hearing the old man blame Germany's division and weakness on the stale, but still emotionally appealing, myth of a global Jewish conspiracy, Hasselbach formed East Germany's first neo-Nazi party upon his release in 1988. Over the next five years, first in the East and then in the newly unified Germany, he led a violent, extremist group that engaged in street violence and organized and indoctrinated a small, but tightly organized, cadre. The neo-Nazi movement's activities increased dramatically after unification, as splinter groups in the East and the West knitted together and began to plan terrorist attacks against foreigners and leftist opponents.

After confronting the human cost of the movement's activities—the firebombing of foreign refugee hostels in Solingen and Mölln—Hasselbach underwent a change of heart. He abandoned neo-Nazi dogmas, including Holocaust denial, after he and his brother Jens began to analyze the assertions of the deniers. At threat to his life, he publicly broke off neo-Nazi activities in 1993 and dedicated himself to working with German youths to steer them away from hatred and violence. The following selection from *Führer-Ex* details the depth of organization of the neo-Nazi movement, sheds light on its support network within Germany, Austria, and beyond, describes the violent groundwork deemed necessary for the creation of a "Fourth Reich," and indicates the tenacity of antisemitic ideology.

As the founder of the former East Germany's first neo-Nazi political party, I'd been the main contact for several American far-right organizations in Europe and one of the main distributors of their propaganda. Before I got out of the Movement in 1993, I organized teach-ins, ran paramilitary camps, and indoctrinated young people at marches and meetings.

I began developing right-wing extremist ideas in 1987, when I was nineteen years old and sitting in an East German prison for shouting "the Wall must fall!" in a public place. When I got out, I began working secretly with a small militant group opposed to the Communist government. . . .

. . . Those looking for a new Führer saw me as a pure "blond beast" risen from the ashes of the Iron Curtain, and, along with the drug of never-ending rebellion, I began to crave the fix of power I got from handing out hate literature, planning attacks, and standing at the head of hundreds of other equally angry young people, egging them on, pushing them further over the edges of decency.

I made contact with a flourishing international network of neo-Nazis and racist movements and began building up caches of weapons and starting paramilitary camps. Like the extremists in America, the common attitude we shared was a hatred for the government (especially federal government agents), a belief that our freedoms and traditions as white men (or, as we said, Aryans) were being infringed on by a multicultural society, and a general anti-Semitism that held that the Jews ran a conspiracy that emanated from New York and Washington.

While most of these ideas could have come from European anti-Semitic tracts from before World War II, they didn't. Virtually all of our propaganda and training manuals came from right-wing extremist groups in Nebraska and California. Such materials are legal to print in the United States under the First Amendment. In Germany they are not, under the Constitution passed after the defeat of the Third Reich.

We also received illegal materials from our friends in Nebraska—the world headquarters of the NSDAP/AO, the successor to the original National Socialist German Workers' Party, or Nazi Party—like a U.S. Army training manual entitled *Explosives and Demolitions*, which has since been copied and circulated (still with the TOP SECRET stamp across the title page) to thousands of right-wing extremists all over Europe. A computer program we received from the NSDAP/AO, entitled "A Movement in Arms," described how to build bombs and wage a war of right-wing terrorism against a democratic government. Before I quit, I'd become the leader of an NSDAP/AO terrorist cell, taking my orders directly from Lincoln, Nebraska.

I'd had plenty of contact with America. But it was an America populated by men who hated their country and found the swastika a more appealing symbol than the Statue of Liberty, who saw great affinities between their Founding Fathers and Adolf Hitler. It was an America oddly obsessed with Germany and the Third Reich. . . .

I began the slow and difficult process of getting out of the Movement after the fatal firebombing in 1992 of a Turkish family in the city of Mölln in northern Germany by two young men in the middle of the night. It had killed two young girls and the grandmother of one of the girls. My group had had nothing to do with the attack, but for the first time the deadly potential of our rhetoric was driven home to me. The police investigation showed that the perpetrators had connections with and had received propaganda from a group like mine in Hamburg, as well as from an American neo-Nazi group. . . .

. . . Morally, I was just as responsible as anyone who planted a fuse or drove a truck with explosives in it—because my messages of hatred against the larger society influenced who knows how many potentially violent young men. The first step for me in rejoining the civilized world was realizing that. . . .

[Hasselbach describes the movement's contacts with old Nazis still loyal to Hitler and Nazi Party principles.]

While the backbone of our organization was young men in their teens and twenties, we also got many visits from older people. . . . They often provided us with propaganda from the Third Reich that they'd carefully saved at home. These old Nazis—some from the SS, others from the Wehrmacht—would speak about the principles of National Socialism in a way that made the concepts seem real and immediate. They could convey an enthusiasm for the SS, Hitler, and the Cause that simply could not be duplicated by someone who had not lived through the time.

These were not "important" Nazis, by and large, but that didn't matter. They were the living embodiment of not only Nazi glory but *German* glory. I came to realize then how fully Hitler had succeeded in merging the concepts of nationalism and Nazism in Germany and what a benefit that was to us. . . .

One man who came to us had belonged to the SS Leibstandarte, the elite SS bodyguards who were always around Adolf Hitler. This man educated us about race, about the system of National Socialism and its entire program, about everything. He was still completely fixated on Hitler. . . .

[The old SS man] began our race education by making us aware of the racial characteristics of others. We started to pay attention to the size of everyone's head, the shades of color in their eyes, the shape of their hands. We learned to recognize the typical features of a Jew. For example, [he] taught us that a short back of the hand is typical for Jews and that a Jew will never have a straight body. Such things.

For the neo-Nazis, the Jew was still the main enemy. There was more violence against foreigners simply because Jews were harder to find. You would not see any recognizable Jews nowadays in the street. I thought I'd met a few people who were Jews—I wondered about it and tried to check the signs—but I couldn't be sure. There were hardly any Jews left in Germany, so we got little chance to practice our knowledge. But our Movement was always about the past and the future more than the present. It was important to learn about the racial characteristics of Jews in order to be able to understand the original Nazism, the history of our Movement, and it was also important for the future, when we might need to spot and segregate Jews again. The present was merely a stepping-stone between the Third and Fourth Reichs. . . .

If we really needed money badly, a telephone call to a well-to-do "friend" was all it took. One time there was a transport problem: one call, and the next day I had 5,000 marks in hand to buy a car.

This money was the gift of an elderly woman whose husband had been very influential in the National Socialists but had died during the war. These Nazi widows were usually well off because they got pensions from the State; in the case of the more fervent ones, their husbands had usually been rather high-ranking Nazis, and, as pensions were based on rank, this made them very rich indeed. It is an irony of the West German system that the widows of resistance fighters often didn't get any pension at all, while the widows of SS generals lived in luxury.

These old ladies all treated Michael Kühnen with great respect. He'd stop by their meetings, which would take place in individual homes or rented rooms, where they'd always serve coffee and lots of sweet cakes; the atmosphere was dainty. . . .

Kühnen would stop by to shake the old ladies' hands and to gossip with them about their health and the Jews. And they would gawk like a movie star was in their presence, for they knew Kühnen was the Führer of the Movement, even if he wasn't their Führer, because that title would forever remain in the hands of their girlhood passion—Adolf Hitler, the *Führer!* In return, Kühnen had a deep respect for these militant Nazi widows. Partly because of this, he founded an organization called the HNG—the Help Organization for National Prisoners—to give old Nazi widows something useful to do: take care of young neo-Nazis sitting in prison.

The HNG was explicitly devoted to the rights and comforts of imprisoned neo-Nazis. . . .

These Nazi widows send prisoners food and cigarettes and keep them supplied with propaganda material. In dark moments, they encourage them to hang on so they can fight the Jew another day. The HNG also publishes a monthly newsletter, the *HNG News*, which is distributed to all "political prisoners"—

only neo-Nazis, not Communists, of course—to keep them abreast of all the goings-on in the scene. . . . [T]hese old ladies were actually ideologically harder and more ruthless than most neo-Nazis of my generation.

In their youth, they had been hard-core Nazis, and they held stubbornly to this ideology. Bitterness and old age had only further hardened their love of the Führer and hatred of the Jews. A meeting with them was no ordinary coffee klatch. When these women began to gossip, they would talk about Auschwitz— or rather, the "Auschwitz lie"—and about the Jews and foreign pigs and Communists who should all be kicked out of Germany.

But first and always, they talked about Jews. Hatred of Jews was their deepest conviction, and Jews were their favorite topic of conversation. I don't think I ever talked about Jews as much as with these venomous little old ladies.

But they didn't just talk. They distributed propaganda and Holocaust denial literature and they had a distinct advantage in that they were inconspicuous. They also worked as secret agents and spies for the Movement. They did come under surveillance, and about once a year some action was taken against the HNG. But usually the authorities would simply take the propaganda material away from an HNG member and tell her to stop passing it out in the future. It was a tough call for the cops because one couldn't very well put old ladies behind bars, though many of them really belonged there.

For one thing, they also held big meetings in which they would give speeches not directly calling for arson. But they might say, "It's about time something is done against foreigners, something our cowardly, corrupt democratic government in Bonn has neither the will nor the morality to do. . . ." Officially they would oppose the bombings and fires, while praising the young men who set foreigners' shelters on fire as being brave and patriotic in a land of cowardly democrats and multicultural mongrels.

And eventually they would express regret that they had to fight foreigners instead of the Jews. They'd say, "Nowadays there are only the foreigners, it is important to fight them . . . but we should not forget the Jews! We should not forget the Jews," they would always add, hopefully. . . .

Somehow, it seemed more natural for young people to have these beliefs. I know that sounds crazy. But it is a uniquely sinister sensation to be sitting next to an eighty-year-old woman who is eating a piece of cake and dribbling coffee onto her blouse, and saying, "We absolutely should desecrate more Jewish cemeteries this month." And somehow I hated them for trying to incite a young person like me to do such things. . . .

[Military training and ideological indoctrination were cardinal concerns of the movement.]

By far the most serious war games I observed were in Austria. They were organized by . . . trainers from the Austrian Federal Army, the Bundesheer. I went as an observer for the north German neo-Nazis. We took video cameras so we could film their camp for our own training exercises. What I saw in Austria made me realize that our exercises had all been childish games.

The exercises were held in Langleuren, a town where the far-right Austrian Freedom Party was very strong. The Austrian trainees arrived on Friday evening and practiced until Sunday afternoon—without sleep. It was total round-the-clock paramilitary training. During the day they practiced target shooting, grenade attacks, and laying explosives.

At night more specialized training took place. Night marches were accompanied by hand-to-hand combat in the dark and training in the art of silent killing. . . .

. . . What was unusual were the straw dummies used for the killing exercises. These were all dressed as concentration camp inmates, with striped uniforms and yellow Jewish stars on their breasts.

The Austrians would line up a row of these macabre scarecrows, and by the end of the practice there'd be little left of them. They practiced shooting them, stabbing them, and then, when they were mostly destroyed, putting them into a pile and blowing them up with grenades or timed charges.

The sadistic nostalgia for concentration camp tortures could hardly have been lost on anyone, but everyone participated cheerfully, taking the costumes as an amusing joke.

"Jews die!" a row of troops would scream as they led a bayonet charge against the scarecrows or shot them. Before blowing them up, there was simply mechanical efficiency, because it was a purely "technical" operation and they were clocking one another. They seemed to have an infinite supply of these striped concentration camp uniforms. I have no idea where they got them. . . .

The basic requirement for indoctrination was youth. We accepted older members, of course, but far fewer and treated them differently. It was assumed that if you joined an organization like ours when you were over, say, twenty-two, you were aware of what the Movement's history and implications were. You had at the very least the foundation of hatred and loyalty, a basic understanding of who the enemy was and why you wanted to fight him. This is not to say that older members weren't indoctrinated—in the Movement it was a permanent, ongoing process; you were never too old to indoctrinate or be indoctrinated but we focused on indoctrinating teenagers. . . .

. . . We taught them about Germany in their grandparents' era, Germany the last time it had been a great power in the world—and we gave them a map of Europe at the time.

Together we'd look at the map showing Germany in 1937 and Germany today, and I'd say, "Look at the Poles, they took this from us . . . the Czechs took this . . . and Austria too belonged to the German Reich. All this is gone. It was stolen, taken unlawfully from us Germans." You inflamed the recruit's feeling of injustice. And you began to draw all the strings connecting everything to the Jews. The land was gone because the Jews had stabbed Germany in the back in the First World War and then created the lie of the Holocaust in the Second. We'd begin to spend a lot of time on the *results* of the Holocaust lie, even before proving it was a lie. That way you first established Jewish guilt and made the idea suspect without having to confront the evidence. The Holocaust myth was simply a way to weaken Germans, as well as how the Jews had swindled Germany into financing the State of Israel.

And you could watch a fourteen-year-old quickly develop a total feeling of injustice. This could have been someone who'd never thought about the Jews before, and in a way that was even better, because he'd had no time to develop perspective or counter-arguments.

What you wanted was a fresh tablet upon which to write. With the exception of someone whose grandparents had been concentration camp guards and who had been a ruthless Jew-hating Nazi from the cradle on, anyone who had thought much about the Holocaust before you got to him was basically disqualified from indoctrination. We didn't want to waste our time on him because he'd have too many questions in his head, too many doubts. But if you took a real blank slate and you worked on him, the result would often be someone who was soon filled with hate and prepared to either commit violent acts or at least express his anger in some other way. . . .

[Later my brother Jens and I] talked about Thies Christophersen's book *The Auschwitz Lie*, one of the central texts of our belief—or should I say disbelief?—system. The former German SS concentration camp guard and now Danish citizen wrote that in Auschwitz the prisoners had been allowed to go out every day after work to go to a brothel, for example, or, if they liked, they could stay in and listen to beautiful music in "their rooms." He should know, he wrote, because he had been a guard there. Even hard-core neo-Nazis sometimes privately laughed at Christophersen's book. Most of us argued that concentration camps had existed and had been harsh, only that there had been no mass murder and no gassing. Christophersen maintained that Auschwitz had been like a hotel, complete with swimming pools to cool off in during the summer. . . .

Now we realized that Christophersen had never even been inside the main camp at Auschwitz where the Jews were because he admits it in the book. He had been in the part of the camp reserved for professional criminals and political prisoners, which was completely separate from the main camp, where the Jews and the Gypsies were being murdered. . . .

But the *Leuchter Report* was even more important because it claimed to refute technically and scientifically the possibility that mass annihilation had taken place at Auschwitz between 1942 and 1945. It relied not just on the account of an old man but on the word of an "outside expert," an American engineer named Fred Leuchter who supposedly had built gas chambers in the United States, the only country in the world that still executed people with a cyanide solution similar to that used by the Nazis at Auschwitz.

. . . Jens and I examined *The Leuchter Report* in detail. We saw that it was written in a ridiculous style and that the evidence didn't seem scientific except in the most superficial way. . . . Leuchter wrote that he had proved from soil and water samples that cyanide gas had not been present at Auschwitz. But he had collected the samples from areas where there had been no gassing or burning of corpses. More important, the entire premise of the "experiment" was absurd, since the gas residues would have had fifty years to disperse into the groundwater; of course he hadn't found any.

Jens and I were shocked at how shoddy and absurd this cornerstone text of the Movement actually was. The secret was that nobody ever looked at it in detail. It was simply a prop, useful for dazzling a young person eager to hear that Germans were not, in fact, guilty of the worst crime in history. A neo-Nazi could thump his hand on the report and say, "Look, here an American engineer, a disinterested expert, has determined that the so-called gassings were a lie. . . ."

I tried bringing these things up with some of my Kamerads, but they didn't want to hear them. They were happy with their view of the world. Afterward I often asked myself why I had not sat down sooner and read this thing thoroughly. The answer was that I had not wanted to. I had seen in National Socialism something both humanitarian and heroic. In order to maintain this view, I'd had to look the other way from the truth.

Much later, I found out that Christophersen had once been videotaped saying that he had told lies about Auschwitz in order to protect the Germans—to free them from guilt. He hadn't realized that the camera team filming the interview was from a normal television station; he'd thought they were Kamerads filming for internal use. He'd said it very matter-of-factly, as an afterthought, something like "Hey, pals, I only did all this in order to help Germany, of course it all happened but it's better to forget about it." He later said that the film crew had tricked him and put words into his mouth.

These conversations and readings with Jens were the first concrete steps I took toward freeing myself from the ideology that had held me in its grasp and that I had used to grab others and reel them into the Movement.[1]

NOTE

1. From Ingo Hasselbach, *Führer-Ex* (New York: Random House, 1996), vii-x, 106-108, 148-151, 212-213, 243-244, 332-334.

TWENTY-SEVEN

Neo-Nazi Antisemitism in the United States: A Radical Fringe

With regard to the scourge of antisemitism, the United States has long been regarded as "exceptional," that antisemitism was rarely more than a nuisance, that it was weaker there than anywhere else, that it had little or no legal, institutional, or ideological basis. In more recent decades, the traditional judgment and perception have been subject to some qualification by Leonard Dinnerstein, Michael Dobkowski, and Robert Michael, among others. Christian or religious antisemitism took root with the colonists and has often inspired suspicion and fear of Jews, for the image of the Jews deriving from Christianity helped to determine the perception of Jews in a secularized world. Recent historians take note of the Populist movement of agrarian and worker discontent, one strand of which was belligerently antisemitic. One Populist leader, Ignatius Donnelly (1831–1901), was a flaming antisemitic demagogue who authored the bestselling antisemitic novel *Caesar's Column* and the party's 1892 platform; according to Donnelly's litany, Jews are haters of mankind and lecherous, unpatriotic, avaricious, secretive and conspiratorial, and crave power and domination. Thomas Watson (1856–1922), the party's presidential candidate in 1904, was elected to the Georgia legislature, the U.S. Congress, and in 1920 the Senate; a demagogic orator and writer, violently anti-black, anti-Catholic, and antisemitic, Watson stirred up fear and hatred against Leo Frank—who was falsely accused of murder and lynched in 1915—as a sexual pervert and part of "the gigantic conspiracy of Big Money" victimizing farmers and workers. The demagogic radio priest Father Charles Coughlin (1891–1979) declaimed against Jews as communists and international bankers, serialized the *Protocols,* admired Hitler and Mussolini, attacked the "British-Jewish-Roosevelt conspiracy" when World War II began, and was not finally censored by the Catholic Church until 1942. The Depression of 1929 brought a new wave of antisemitism, as did World War II (which some decried as the "Jews' war" supposedly because it was fought in behalf, variously, of American Jews, "World Jewry," or "Bolshevik Russia"). In August 1940, 42 percent of those polled said Jews had too much power; the number increased to 58 percent in June 1945. Ironically, in 1936 the editors of *Fortune* magazine, after reviewing the directors of leading American business institutions, including banking and finance, concluded that Jews were underrepresented in the corporate

world and that there was "no basis whatever for the suggestions that Jews monopo-
lize U.S. business and industry."[1] Fear of communist infiltration, beginning with
the Red Menace of the 1920s and continuing intermittently to the end of the Cold
War in 1989, also fostered the phobia that Jews were dangerous conspirators in
the service of a foreign power. Antisemitic stereotypes remained sufficiently strong
in America until the early 1960s to exclude Jews from social clubs and residential
areas and resorts, and to hinder their entrance into universities and the professions.
Nevertheless, John Higham's conclusion remains valid and compelling: "No decisive event, no deep crisis, no powerful social movement, no great individual is associated primarily" with antisemitism in the United States.[2]

American Jews aware of Jewish history regard the United States as a promised
land, a land of freedom and opportunity little blemished by antisemitic barriers and
excesses. At the present time the fringe groups that embrace and spout antisemitic
myths are usually neo-Nazis. Scorned by the general public and monitored by the
government, they represent no real threat to Jewish life and institutions. The following documents reveal the paranoia, hate, mythical thinking, and attraction to conspiracy theories that drive these American antisemites.

William L. Pierce

The Turner Diaries, 1978

The Turner Diaries, written by Andrew Macdonald, pseudonym of William L. Pierce
(1933–2002), purports to be a "novel," but is, instead, a manifesto of hate and call
for race war and genocide. It sold a quarter-million copies, although it was never reviewed in mainstream media or sold in standard bookstores. Pierce earned a Ph.D.
at the University of Colorado and taught physics for a time at Oregon State University. He joined the American Nazi Party in the 1960s, then the National Socialist White People's Party, and became the leading figure in the National Alliance
based in Washington, D.C. Pierce is idolized by neo-Nazi and other hate groups
like "The Order," and his book is reported to have been gospel truth to Timothy
McVeigh and the rationale for the bombing of the Federal Building in Oklahoma
City in 1995. The book's ideological underpinning plainly is racism, and the author
is obsessed with racial mixture and issues of racial degeneration and inferiority. In
the author's view, all non-whites are criminal offenders against nature's racial laws,
but Jews, because of their alliance with blacks, are the greatest menace. Only by
extinguishing the Jews can the white race be restored. As in Hitler's pathological
metaphors, the Jews are a "cancer" that has to be rooted out. The "Organization"
struggles against the Jewish-infected U.S. government. The emerging regime and
dominant ideology in the *Diaries* are clearly Nazi.

Predictably, Holocaust denial is another feature of *The Turner Diaries.* Thus it is
reported that German POWs were tortured en masse into confessing to war crimes,
as was the treacherously kidnapped Adolf Eichmann.[3] Gas chambers never existed,

only "propaganda that has worked so well for them in the past" in winning public sympathy and hiding their crimes. Rather than being victims, it was the Jews in 1939 who declared war on Germany.

Following are excerpts from *The Turner Diaries.* In the opening scene "Organization" members are watching television coverage of the building they had blown up, the first step in the "Great Revolution" to liberate the country from Jewish domination.

All day yesterday and most of today we watched the TV coverage of rescue crews bringing the dead and injured out of the building. It is a heavy burden of responsibility for us to bear, since most of the victims of our bombs were only pawns who were no more committed to the sick philosophy of the System [the same term in Nazi propaganda for the Weimar Republic] than we are.

But there is no way we can destroy the System without hurting many thousands of innocent people—no way. It is a cancer too deeply rooted in our flesh. And if we don't destroy the System before it destroys us—if we don't cut this cancer out of our living flesh—our whole race will die. . . .

And is this not the key to the whole problem? The corruption of our people by the whole Jewish-liberal-democratic-egalitarian plague which afflicts us is more clearly manifested in our soft-mindedness, our unwillingness to recognize the harder realities of life, than in anything else.

Liberalism is an essentially feminine, submissive worldview. Perhaps a better adjective is infantile. It is the world view of men who do not have the moral toughness, the spiritual strength to stand up and do single combat with life, who cannot adjust to the reality that the world is not a pink-and-blue, padded nursery in which the lions lie down with the lambs and everyone lives happily ever after.

Nor should spiritually healthy men of our race even *want* the world to be like that, if it could be so. That is an alien, essentially Oriental [read Jewish] approach to life, the world view of slaves rather than of free men of the West.

But it has permeated our whole society. Even those who do not consciously accept the liberal doctrines have been corrupted by them. Decade after decade the race problem in America has become worse. But the majority of those who wanted a solution, who wanted to preserve a White America, were never able to screw up the courage to look the obvious solutions in the face.

All the liberals and the Jews had to do was begin screeching about "inhumanity" or "genocide," and most of our people who had been beating around the edges of a solution took to their heels like frightened rabbits. Because there was never a way to solve the race problem which could be "fair for everybody," or which everyone concerned could be politely persuaded into accepting without any fuss or unpleasantness, they kept trying to evade it, hoping that it would go away by itself. And the same has been true of the Jewish problem and the eugenics problem and a thousand related problems. . . .

I am sorry, of course, for the millions of White people, both here and in

Russia, who died—and who have yet to die before we have finished—in this war to rid ourselves of the Jewish yoke. But innocents? I think not. Certainly that term should not be applied to the majority of adults.

After all, is not man essentially responsible for his condition—at least, in a collective sense? If the White nations of the world had not allowed themselves to become subject to the Jew, to Jewish ideas, to the Jewish spirit, this war would not be necessary. We can hardly consider ourselves blameless. We can hardly say we had no choice, no chance to avoid the Jew's snare. We can hardly say we were not warned.

Men of wisdom, integrity, and courage [i.e., antisemites] have warned us over and over again of the consequences of our folly. And even after we were well down the Jewish primrose path, we had chance after chance to save ourselves—most recently 52 years ago [in World War II] when the Germans and the Jews were locked in struggle for the mastery of central and eastern Europe.

We ended up on the Jewish side in that struggle, primarily because we had chosen corrupt men as our leaders. And we had corrupt leaders because we valued the wrong things in life. [There follows an exposition that Nature does not accept excuses or mistakes in questions of survival of the race, and the like.] We must look at our situation collectively, in a race-wide sense. We must understand that our race is like a cancer patient undergoing drastic surgery in order to save his life. There is no sense in asking whether the tissue being cut out is "innocent" or not. That is no more reasonable than trying to distinguish the "good" Jews from the bad ones—or, as some of our thicker-skulled "good ol' boys" still insist on trying, separating the "good niggers" from the rest of their race. . . .

Your day is coming, Jews, your day is coming. [The Organization launches its genocidal race war:]

So we decided to preempt. We struck first, but not at the government's forces. We fired all our missiles from Vandenberg [air force base, the Organization having infiltrated the armed forces] (except for half-a-dozen targeted on New York) at two targets: Israel and the Soviet Union. As soon as our missiles had been launched, RC [a command headquarters] announced the news to the Pentagon via a direct telephone link. The Pentagon, of course, had immediate confirmation from its own radar screens, and it had no choice but to follow up our salvo with an immediate and full-scale nuclear attack of its own against the Soviet Union, in an attempt to knock out as much of the Soviet retaliatory potential as possible.

The Soviet response was horrendous, but spotty. They fired everything they had left at us, but it simply wasn't enough. Several of the largest American cities, including Washington and Chicago, were spared.

What the Organization accomplished by precipitating this fateful chain of events is fourfold: First, by hitting New York and Israel, we have completely knocked out two of world Jewry's principal nerve centers, and it should take them a while to establish a new chain of command.

Second, by forcing them to take a decisive action, we pushed the balance of power in the U.S. government toward the military leaders. For all practical purposes, the country is now under a military government. . . .

Within 24 hours after we hit Tel Aviv and half-a-dozen other Israeli targets, hundreds of thousands of Arabs were swarming across the borders of occupied Palestine. Most of them were civilians, armed only with knives or clubs, and Jewish border guards mowed down thousands of them, until their ammunition was exhausted. The Arabs' hatred, pent up for 45 years, drove them on—across mine fields, through Jewish machine-gun fire, and into the radioactive chaos of burning cities, their single thought being to slay the people who had stolen their land, killed their fathers, and humiliated them for two generations. Within a week the throat of the last Jewish survivor in the last *kibbutz* and in the last smoking ruins of Tel Aviv had been cut. [Its ruins remain "too radioactive for human habitation."]

[The Russians have attacked the Jews in a similar way.] In the ruins of Moscow and Leningrad during the first few days the people rounded up all the Jews they could get their hands on and hurled them into burning buildings or onto burning heaps of debris.

And anti-Jewish riots have broken out in London, Paris, Brussels, Rotterdam, Bucharest, Buenos Aires, Johannesburg, and Sydney. The governments of France and the Netherlands, both rotten to the core with Jewish corruption, have fallen, and the people are settling scores in the towns and villages throughout those countries.

It's the sort of thing which happened time after time in the Middle Ages, of course—every time the people had finally had their fill of the Jews and their tricks. Unfortunately, they never finished the job, and they won't this time either. I'm sure the Jews are already making their plans for a comeback, as soon as the people have calmed down and forgotten. The people have such short memories!

But *we* won't forget! That alone is enough to insure that history will not repeat itself. No matter how long it takes us and no matter what lengths we must go, we'll demand a final settlement of the account between our two races. If the Organization survives this contest, no Jew will—anywhere. We'll go to the uttermost ends of the earth to hunt down the last of Satan's spawn.

["Turner" waxes philosophical:] I regret that I won't be around to participate in the final success of our revolution, but I am happy I have been allowed to do as much as I have. . . . [O]f all the billions of men and women of my race who have lived, I will have been able to play a more vital role than all but a handful of them in determining the ultimate destiny of mankind. What I will do today will be of more weight in the annals of the race than all the conquests of Caesar and Napoleon—if I succeed. [His mission was successful but fatal to him, one of the "Martyrs" celebrated thereafter, as in Nazi Germany, on November 9. The Organization having destroyed the System and finalized genocide worldwide, "the principal centers of world Jewish power [were] annihilated" and Hitler's aims at last fulfilled.][4]

The Canard of Ritual Murder in Cincinnati

"All Christian Parents: The Safety of Your Children Is at Stake!" 1980s

Some contemporary antisemites continue to employ the centuries-old myth of ritual murder, as is evidenced by this anonymous flier that was circulated in Cincinnati in the 1980s. However, this myth is no longer believed or endorsed by members of the elite or the various Christian churches. Indeed, thinking people simply dismiss it as the ranting of vulgar Jew-baiters.

The Arnold S. Leese cited in the flier as a great authority was actually a psychopathic veterinarian and vicious antisemite who spent most of World War II in a British prison as a security risk. Paranoid about "the Jewish menace," that the Jews were out to dominate the world and destroy the Aryan race, Leese was a devotee of Hitler from the early 1920s and an "Imperial Fascist"; he anticipated the Nazis, apparently the first to advocate "extermination" of the Jews by "lethal chamber," and also in proposing that they all be shipped off to Madagascar. His book on ritual murder that is touted in the flier, like all his writings and antisemites' generally, is full of lies and myths.

PUBLIC NOTICE
ALL CHRISTIAN PARENTS:
THE SAFETY OF YOUR CHILDREN IS AT STAKE!
BEWARE!!!

The persistent rumors concerning the Jews' practice of a pagan form of "Human Sacrifice" known as "Ritual Murder" have unfortunately been proven true. Arnold S. Leese has published a book titled, *Jewish Ritual Murder*, which proves beyond a shadow of a doubt that the Jews are now, and have been for centuries, practicing the murder of little Christian children in order to use their blood in religious ceremonies of the Jewish Synagogue.

HERE IS THE UNFORTUNATE STORY:

WHEN—At this time of the year just before the Jewish Holy Day of Passover (April 16 to 23) fanatic Jews run the streets in a crazed search for Christian Blood!

WHO—Their favorite victims are young male children whom they take a fiendish delight in crucifying and bleeding white in the image of our Savoir [*sic*] whom they murdered so long ago.

WHY—Because according to secret Jewish ritual (which they will of course deny) they must have Christian Blood to mix with the dough of their Ceremonial Passover Bread. They believe that only by partaking of the blood of your children will they assure their own entrance into their heaven.

PROOF—The court records of all Europe are filled with well documented cases where the Jews were caught and convicted; nearly fifty such cases have been brought to trial in the last century alone. The Jewish arguments against the accusation are all more or less worthless; for example that all the accusations are brought by "Anti-Semites." How could anyone help being "anti-Semitic" if he knew that the Jews murder little Christian children and use their blood in pagan rituals. For further proof we suggest that you read Arnold S. Leese's book *Jewish Ritual Murder.*

FOR YOUR CHILDREN'S SAKE!

CAN YOU AFFORD TO SAY "THAT IT'S NOT TRUE."

Distributed as a public service by The American Committee for the Unfortunate Truth About Our Jewish Brothers.[5]

Raphael S. Ezekiel

The Racist Mind, *1995*

In *The Racist Mind,* social psychologist Raphael S. Ezekiel, who interviewed Klansmen and neo-Nazis and attended their gatherings, analyzed the mindset of white American racists, particularly their attachment to crude antisemitic myths. Excerpted below are the author's accounts of discussions he had with Klansmen regarding their feelings about Jews and his attendance at a meeting of "The Aryan Nations."

The discussion, first with Dave and then with Lennie, went on for several hours. Arthur's eyes bored into me steadily the entire time. He sat, smoldering and angry. Several times he took a knife from his pocket, being sure that I noticed, and stroked its long blade. When I asked Lennie what he would do if the movement came to power, Arthur suddenly erupted with words of deep violence: "*Castrate all the men, sterilize all the women, and chain them in the backyard like dogs!*"

His voice had been sudden, guttural, and level. "What I'd like to do," he went on, "whites ever once get into power, that would be the thing to do: Castrate the males, Jewish and nigger males, castrate them and sterilize the females, chain them in the yard like dogs."

Dave Holland grinned and said, "Nice man."

I laughed and said, "Arthur and I have a friendly relationship."

Holland added, "That's one thing about it, buddy, he lets you know where you stand."

"Yeah," I said, "that was kind of subtle. Now, quite what did that mean?"

"I sit here," Arthur said, "and thought about it a little bit, that's what I'd like to do."

"Well," I said, "I guess I'll have to ask you, Arthur, how come?"

"Yeah," he answered. "I think they're behind communism and I think the Holocaust is a hoax. They're out to destroy the Aryan race. Like Dave said and like Lennie said, they're backing the niggers because niggers aren't smart enough, aren't wealthy enough, to hack the communist movement in America.

Which I think started, the nigger part of it started with Martin Luther King, and now continues with Jesse Jackson, Hosea Williams. And what it says in the Bible, in Saint John, chapter eight, I think it starts in verse thirty-six, it says, you are of your father the devil and of him you will do, he was a murderer from the beginning, abide not in the truth because there is no truth in it. And it goes on to say, the Jews. And Jesus was speaking to the Jews. And I think they're the children of the Devil."

"Literally?"

"Yeah. Literally."

"So," I asked, "like, you and I are just absolutely different?"

"Absolutely different! As different as Karl Marx and Adolf Hitler."

"Well," I pointed out, "they were both human beings, that's all."

"I don't know," Arthur said. "I don't feel the Jews are a race. I don't feel that the Jews are a race of human beings."

"Another species of animal?" I asked.

"Lot more along the lines of a *leech*." he answered. "Or a *maggot*."

"How long," I asked, "have you rejoiced in this belief?"

"I guess most of my adult life. As long as I can remember, from a small child."

"Did your daddy and mommy teach you that?"

He said no—said that he just woke up and realized what was going on in the world. I asked whether he had ever seen a Jew, and Arthur said he had seen plenty of them. I asked where, and he replied, "Sitting around, they're around—oh, not that many, quite a few, they're around. I saw them in delis and bakeries, in Atlanta."

"And you looked," I inquired, "and you said, 'Wow, you're a devil'?"

"No," he said, "I just believe in the Bible, what the Bible says about Jews."

. . . He said, "I believe it's just what I came to believe. I think God instilled me with it, the feelings I feel and the beliefs I feel toward Jews." . . .

I told them I was curious about something. "When you talk about black people," I pointed out, "you say 'nigger.' When you talk about Jews when I'm not in the room, what do you call them?"

Arthur answered at once and in a flat voice: "'Kike.'" Then he spat out: "'Finks!' 'Leech!' 'Maggot!'"

I asked what kind of word he would use ninety percent of the time.

"Just 'Jew' or 'kike,' you know, simple as that."

We talked awhile about a theory Lennie offered, that Jews were related to goats. A bit later I tried out on them my observation that Jews, whom they hated, committed few violent crimes. Arthur croaked out: "They crucified Christ! . . . And if we only knew how many babies have been aborted since abortion was invented, then we would know practically how many Jews in modern day [are murderers]. . . . Jews engineered and invented abortion from the very beginning, when it was first invented. . . . I'm sure there's a lot more Jews that's murderers than there are whites. And the Jews also crucified Christ!"

I wanted to check a few things out with the pair of them—just which crimes had the Jews committed? Lennie quickly added the two World Wars to the crucifixion. I asked whether the Jews had created the American Revolution, and he became unsure of himself. I felt we might be getting past the party line. Eagerly I asked whether the Jews had created the Civil War.

"The treasurer of the Confederacy!" Arthur cried out.

"Judah Benjamin," I supplied for him.

"He was Jewish," Arthur went on. "He ran off and went up north with the money, and that's what caused them to lose the Civil War." I knew Arthur was badly misinformed here. But it is rare to get a Klansman trying to talk logically about stuff he hasn't been taught, so I asked some more questions about history. Lennie, sure of most things, just didn't know about the American Revolution and thought that by the War of 1812 I was referring to the 1898 war with Spain. "No," I told him, "the war with England in 1812."

"No," Lennie said, "I don't know about that."

"Was Andrew Jackson a Jew?" I asked him.

"I really don't know that, either," Lennie said.

I persevered: "Was Abraham Lincoln a Jew?"

Lennie said that he was assassinated by a Jew. . . .

"I think John Wilkes Booth, I think it was a Jewish conspiracy, even way back then. And they assassinated Lincoln so he couldn't send [blacks] back [to Africa]. Because they knew then how it was going to be today. They had it planned out, and perceived in their minds." . . .

[In the following excerpt, Ezekiel describes a gathering in Idaho of "The Aryan Nations."]

We enter the anteroom with its hanging flags of the Northern European nations; most of the militants in attendance use the peculiar Christian Identity religion as a major organizing tool, and Identity preaches that the true Israel-ites (the "Aryans") founded the Northern European nations after their expul-sion from Palestine. It preaches that the Aryans are called now by their heav-enly white Father to world domination, to rule over the dark subhuman races, and to a struggle to death with Satan's nonhuman children, the Jews.

. . . Our walk down this path of banners takes us alongside walls of Aryan Nations art, pictures drawn perhaps by prisoners and mailed in (the organi-zation and most like it maintain a highly active correspondence with prison populations). In each drawing, a youth of Nordic bearing, a young man with high cheekbones, plunges a spear or a sword into the belly of a serpent or a dragon; each of the impaled animals is identified by a six-pointed Star of David and the hammer-and-sickle of Communism. Between two of these pictures hangs a framed, idealized portrait of the face of Adolf Hitler. He is noble and suffering; shining black hair and strong cheekbones surround deep, gleaming eyes. The intent eyes demand our attention.

. . . [T]he altar is dominated by an upright Roman sword, the symbol of the organization and its version of the Cross. This sword, this Cross, bears a swastika at its hilt. A memorial wreath to Rudolf Hess, Hitler's lieutenant who had died not long before, stands beside the altar.

The speeches begin and run through the day. . . .

The first speaker . . . complains about the use of condoms [and] attacks what he calls "AIDS groups." The second speaker, a retired military officer [declared that] since the Russian Revolution, 140 million people had been slain "by the Jew Talmudic Communists."

Every evil, he tells us, comes from money. "And behind money is the Zionist Talmudic Jew." The Federal Reserve System, he tells us, is a private system owned by eight banks, all of them Jewish, four of them foreign; his list includes Warburg, Lazard Fréres, Rothschild, Kuhn-Loeb, and Chase Manhattan. We must get rid of the Federal Reserve System and of the income tax. We must repudiate the national debt.

"We must," he goes on, "tell the people at the top: There will be treason trials! You will be strung from the trees!"

The room explodes in loud applause. Cries of *"Hail Victory!"* [English for the Nazi shout, *Sieg Heil.*] Cries of *"White Power!"*

The immigration since 1900 has been alien, he tells us, alien in every way, not Christian. The country was not set up to be pluralistic. He tells us "nigger jokes"—jokes about "nigger preachers," "nigger churches." Americans, he notes, are lazy in their thinking, apathetic, listening to TV, but awakening, beginning to avoid the dangers of Zionism. Back in 1902, he tells us, the international Zionists decided to destroy the four nations that must he destroyed if the Jews are to control the world: Russia, Germany, the United States, and Canada. They set aside $2 billion for that purpose, the financing coming from Jews in America. Lenin's plan is on schedule, the encirclement of the United States. In 1943, forty-seven U.S. students, forty-five of them Jews, were sent to Russian schools and came back charged to infiltrate American schools; the results, he points out, are visible in the Vietnam protests.

We need, he tells us, free enterprise, respect for the family, and the end of integration. We see around us treason. "The men behind the Iron Curtain would not be afraid to fight, those who have seen their families slaughtered by the Jew Talmudic Communists."

He recites for us much of a heroic ode by Byron, winding up at its dramatic description of one man's sacrifice: "We need men at the gap! *Who will stand at the gap with me?*"

The crowd explodes in cries of *"Hail Victory! Hail Victory! Hail Victory! White Power! White Power!"*

The old officer is followed to the pulpit by a Canadian organizer who has been observing the trial in Canada of a Canadian white racist [Ernst Zündel] who disseminates claims that the Holocaust did not occur. The strangest part of his talk comes at the beginning. Details of the Holocaust, for this movement, are lies invented by the Jews to gain leverage over non-Jews. . . . The gas chambers were just delousing chambers. . . .

[H]e points out that twenty-one Jews were behind the French Revolution, the Russian Revolution, and both world wars. What is to be done? "The Order chaps . . ." he says, referring to the terrorist cell that assassinated Alan Berg [a Jewish talk-show host], and robbed armored cars, "the Order chaps were very *sincere* men. They *tried.*" There is loud applause. "They lacked security," he goes on, "but they tried and that's what we all should do. Our vision must be victory. *Hail Victory!*"

The audience cries its echo: *"Hail Victory!"*

A Klan leader speaks next. He is neatly dressed, as usual, and his thin mustache is neatly trimmed. A prissy fellow, he pastors at an Identity church in the South and leads one of the largest Klans. . . .

. . . There is a real war in the world, he tells us; the seed of the white race is at war with the seed of the Serpent, the Bolshevik. "We will win or we will bend our backs for all eternity." The Jew has a natural propensity to destroy the morals and the children we love, he tells us. There is eternal warfare between the offspring of the Lord and the offspring of the Serpent. "They hate us, they hate our Father, they hate our culture, they hate our music, they hate our children." They are the Antichrist, he declares. The hatred will not go away just because we ignore it; it will go on until Christ returns. . . .

The children of Satan, he reports, are in rebellion against Christ. They want to change us. They hate us because we love our nation, our morals, our families. We look at what has happened in the last twenty-five or thirty years—the abortions, the homosexuality, the race mixing. We can see that the idea of the Jews is to change us; that the United States will be ruled by God or by tyrants.

We in the United States, he goes on, have joined the rebellion against God, have joined the evil empire. The average church at this time sees nothing wrong with race mixing, with homosexuality. But the Bible, he reminds us, "does not say *convert* the homos, have dialogue with the queers. The Bible says to *execute* them!"

Loud applause greets this statement.[6]

NOTES

1. Jeffrey Herf, *The Jewish Enemy: Nazi Propaganda during World War II and the Holocaust* (Cambridge, Mass.: Harvard University Press, 2006), 79-82.

2. Quoted in Albert S. Lindemann, *Esau's Tears* (Cambridge: Cambridge University Press, 1997), 253.

3. The Nazi SS officer who coordinated the deportation of Jews to the death camps; he was kidnapped in Argentina by Israeli agents. After a lengthy trial in Jerusalem, intended to establish a historical record of the Holocaust, he was executed in 1962.

4. From Andrew Macdonald, *The Turner Diaries* (New York: Barricade Books, 1978, 2nd ed., 1996), 35, 42-43, 62, 106, 111, 118, 190-191, 195-199, 202, 209.

5. From Jacob R. Marcus, ed., *The Jew in the American World, A Source Book* (Detroit: Wayne State University Press, 1996), 509-510.

6. From Raphael S. Ezekiel, *The Racist Mind: Portraits of American Neo-Nazis and Klansmen* (New York: Viking, 1995), 18-19, 22-23, 40-44.

TWENTY-EIGHT

Holocaust Denial:
A Neo-Nazi Mythology

The documents in this volume treat classic antisemitic myths: the Jews as agents of Satan out to destroy Christendom or international conspirators out to dominate the modern world; the Jews as ritual murderers; the Jews as exploiting Shylocks and capitalists; and the Jews as racial inferiors corrupting Aryan blood and European culture. In recent decades antisemites and neo-Nazis have manufactured a new myth, that of Holocaust denial. According to this myth, the Germans had no policy of extermination. Rather, the Jews invented the Holocaust to gain world sympathy for Zionism and to wrest enormous indemnity payments from innocent Germans. Using their putative capacity for conspiracy, financial power, political influence, and control over the media, say the deniers, Jews have managed to dupe the world.

Holocaust denial, which flies in the face of all documentary evidence, including the testimony of eyewitnesses, survivors, perpetrators, and bystanders, demonstrates anew the fragility of human reason and the seemingly limitless capacity of the mind to embrace the most grotesque beliefs. It is still another illustration of the power of Jew-hatred to drag the mind into the murky waters of the irrational.

David Irving's Failed Libel Suit

The Verdict of Justice Charles Gray, 2000

In his numerous books on World War II, published by respectable houses, British historian David Irving sought to cleanse Hitler's image and to relativize Nazi war crimes—in his view they were no worse than the deeds committed by the Allies: for example, the firebombing of Dresden. Initially, Irving did not deny the Holocaust, maintaining that it was Goebbels or Himmler who, unknown to Hitler ordered the extermination of the Jews. But increasing association with Holocaust deniers and the far Right (and a more than latent antisemitism) led him to accept the deniers' position. He began to argue that Jews were not systematically slaughtered in accordance with the policy and directives of the Third Reich and that no Jews were murdered in gas chambers. He simply dismissed the eyewitness testimony of Jewish survivors, whom he categorized as liars, psychiatric cases, and extortionists.

Irving sued Deborah Lipstadt and her publisher, Penguin Books, for libel, because in *Denying the Holocaust: The Growing Assault on Truth and Memory* (1993) she labeled him a "dangerous spokesperson for Holocaust denial," who bends historical evidence "until it conforms with his ideological leanings and political agenda." Irving maintained that Lipstadt, holder of the Dorot Chair in Modern Jewish and Holocaust Studies at Emory University in Atlanta, Georgia, had tarnished his reputation, making it difficult for him to publish, that he was a victim of an organized international campaign—"a global Jewish endeavor"—to discredit and silence him. The case was tried in London in early 2000. Several distinguished authorities were employed to analyze Irving's writings and speeches to produce evidence of his fascist inclinations and his willful distortion of history. Irving represented himself in what he liked to call a "David and Goliath struggle." He also consistently portrayed himself as a defender of free speech against the forces of censorship. Both sides agreed to dispense with a jury and to leave the decision to Justice Charles Gray. England's tough libel law required that Lipstadt and Penguin prove that their charges against Irving were true.

Lipstadt's barrister, Richard Rampton, told the court that Irving "is a falsifier of history. To put it bluntly, he is a liar. . . . Mr. Irving has used many different means to falsify history: invention, misquotation, suppression, distortion, manipulation and—not least—mistranslation. But all these techniques have the same ultimate effect: falsification of the truth." Irving's association with neo-Nazis, white supremacists, and the racist British National Party, said Rampton, tells us a great deal about his character. He quoted Irving's words before a Canadian audience in September 1991 in which he said that Auschwitz is "baloney, . . . a legend. I say quite tastelessly, in fact, that more women died in the back of Edward Kennedy's car at Chappaquiddick than ever died in a gas chamber at Auschwitz. . . . There are so many survivors going around, in fact, the number increased as the years go past, which is biologically very odd. . . . I'm going to form an association of Auschwitz survivors of the Holocaust, and other liars, or the ASSHOLS." Rampton accused Irving of "feeding and encouraging the most cynical anti-Semitism" in his audiences when delivering speeches.

Richard Evans, professor of modern history at Cambridge University who, assisted by two doctoral students, had spent two years evaluating Irving's books, testified that he was startled by the "sheer depth of duplicity" that he found in Irving's treatment of the Holocaust and was "shocked" by his standard of scholarship. He labeled as antisemitic Irving's numerous speeches in which he placed responsibility for the Holocaust on the behavior of the Jews themselves. In one instance Irving had declared it entirely possible that an elderly Jewish lady might have tattooed herself in order to gain reparations as a concentration camp survivor. (Jews not immediately gassed and retained as slave labor had an identification number tattooed on their forearms.)

Robert Jan van Pelt, professor of architecture at the University of Waterloo in Canada, and, with Debórah Dwork, co-author of *Auschwitz, 1270 to the Present* (1996), discussed the "massive amount of evidence" documenting the gas chambers: the drawings of German architects; German documents showing huge quantities of Zyklon-B gas shipped to the death camps; reports by escaped inmates; eyewitness accounts immediately after liberation, including those of the *Sonderkommando*—Jewish prisoners selected to work in the crematoria; Polish forensic investigations conducted in 1945–1946; the confessions immediately after the war of German personnel at the camp; and American aerial photography. Van Pelt told the court that he was "absolutely certain" that between 1942 and 1944 at least a million people perished in Auschwitz's gas chambers.

Professors Peter Longerich of the University of London and Christopher Browning of the University of North Carolina prepared reports on the systematic murder of Europe's Jews by firing squads and gas chambers. Under cross-examination by Rampton concerning this evidence, Irving conceded that the firing-squad mass killings of Jews on Soviet territory was both systematic and known and approved by Hitler, that Chelmno was a permanent camp using gas vans (he had earlier claimed that it was merely "experimental"), and that Polish Jewry "vanished from sight" in the camps, where they met an "ugly" fate and "perished," but he refused to concede that they died there in gas chambers.

Professor Hajo Funke of the Free University of Berlin told the court that Irving was expelled from Germany in 1993 because the authorities were unwilling to "further tolerate his use of Germany as a playground for his right-wing extremism." Irving had been a principal speaker for the extremist and antisemitic German People's Union (DVU) since the 1980s. With his "star" status at the DVU annual rallies, said Funke, Irving had publicly identified himself with an organization that "propagates racial hatred." Funke related how Irving attended a small gathering in a hotel in Munich on April 20, 1990, in which guests toasted Adolf Hitler on his 101st birthday. Irving has been banned from Germany (and Austria, Italy, Canada, and Australia). A video was shown to the court of a meeting addressed by Irving where booted skinheads were chanting "Sieg Heil." Irving suggested that the skinheads had been bribed to attend and shout these slogans.

Irving argued that the so-called gas chambers were used for fumigating corpses, hair, and clothing infected with typhus lice. He dismissed as "worthless" the testimony provided by survivors who arrived at Auschwitz in cattle cars and survived the "selections" that sent those deemed unfit to work to the gas chambers. These accounts, he said are "a matter for psychiatric evaluation"—in short, the survivors had made it all up. He also rejected the testimony given after the war by Nazi personnel at Auschwitz, for British officers "had ways of making people talk." And he suggested that the drawings of the Auschwitz gas chambers by Nazi architects were forgeries.

Ruling for the defendants, Penguin Books and Deborah Lipstadt, Justice Gray, in a damning judgment, declared that Irving was indeed a Holocaust denier who falsified history to fit his antisemitic, pro-Hitler, and neo-Nazi outlook. The verdict was a triumph for justice. The evidence presented by the defense and Justice Gray's scathing indictment of Irving's views demolished Irving's reputation as a historian. By demonstrating the neo-Nazi and racist mindset of deniers and their self-conscious manipulation and distortion of the historical record in order to buttress ideological prejudices, the case should also relegate the deniers to the status of Hitler apologists and racists and their writings to Goebbels-like rubbish. No doubt the deniers, inveterate antisemites and admirers of the Third Reich, will continue with their hate mongering, but hopefully the crushing and humiliating defeat of their star "historian" will cause their audience to diminish.[1] Excerpts from Justice Gray's judgment follow.

13.9 [T]he Defendants have selected nineteen instances where they contend that Irving has in one way or another distorted the evidence. Having considered the arguments, which I have summarised at some length, I have come to the conclusion that the criticisms advanced by the Defendants are almost invariably well-founded. For whatever reason (and I shall consider later the question of Irving's motivation), I am satisfied that in most of the instances cited by the Defendants Irving has significantly misrepresented what the evidence, objectively examined, reveals.

13.10 . . . I should bear in mind that the criticisms which the Defendants make of Irving's historiography are supported by the evidence of historians of the greatest distinction. . . .

13.27 . . . I was unconvinced by the strenuous efforts made by Irving to refute the sinister interpretation placed by the Defendants on Hitler's pronouncements on the Jewish question from late 1941 onwards. . . .

13.29 In my view consideration of the context requires an objective historian to take into account such matters as Hitler's history of anti-semitism; the importance in the Nazi ideology of achieving racial purity; the attacks on Jews and their property before the outbreak of war; the policy of deporting Jews and the systematic programme, approved by Hitler, of shooting Jews in the East. So considered, I am satisfied that most, if not all, of the pronouncements by Hitler which are relied on by the Defendants do bear the sinister connotation which they put on them. To take but one example, when Hans Frank [head of the General Government of Poland] said on 16 December 1941 that he had been told in Berlin "liquidate [the Jews] yourselves," I am satisfied that the evidence strongly supports the conclusion that he was reporting what Hitler had said to the Gauleiter [regional party leaders] on 12 December and that Hitler had indeed given instructions for the liquidation of the Jews. That after all is what the evidence suggests happened on an ever-increasing scale in the following months. Irving's claim that Frank was telling his audience [in Cracow, Poland] what he had told the authorities in Berlin (and not the other way round) appears to me to be wholly untenable. . . .

13.31 It is my conclusion that the Defendants are justified in their assertion that Irving has seriously misrepresented Hitler's views on the Jewish question. He has done so in some instances by misinterpreting and mistranslating documents and in other instances by omitting documents or parts of them. In the result the picture which he provides to readers of Hitler and his attitude towards the Jews is at odds with the evidence.

Auschwitz

13.68 When the trial started, it appeared from Irving's written statement of case that he was adhering to the position often adopted in his speeches about Auschwitz, namely that no gas chambers were commissioned or operated at the camp and that in consequence no Jew lost his or her life in chambers there.

13.69 As I have already observed . . . , in the course of the trial Irving modified his position: he accepted that there was at least one gas chamber (or "cellar") at Auschwitz, albeit used solely or mainly for the fumigation of clothing. He also accepted that gassing of Jews had taken place at the camp "on some scale." He did not indicate on what scale. Irving firmly denied the claim advanced by van Pelt that 500,000 Jews were killed in morgue 1 of crematorium 2. The case for the Defendants on the other hand was, as I have said, that almost one million Jews were put to death in the gas chambers of Auschwitz.

13.70 In these circumstances the central question which, as it appears to me, falls to be determined is whether or not the evidence supports the Defendants' contention that the number of deaths ran into hundreds of thousands or whether Irving is right when he claims that the killing by gas was on a modest scale. . . .

13.72 The case for the Defendants . . . is that there exists what van Pelt described as a "convergence" of evidence which is to the ordinary, dispassionate mind overwhelming that hundreds of thousands of Jews were systematically gassed to death at Auschwitz, mainly by the use of hydrogen cyanide pellets called Zyklon-B. I have set out . . . the individual elements which make up that convergence of evidence. . . .

13.75 . . . [I]t appears to me that the cumulative effect of the documentary evidence for the genocidal operation of gas chambers at Auschwitz is considerable.

13.76 . . . Few and far between though they may be, documents do exist for which it is difficult to find an innocent explanation. . . . As to [Gestapo head Heinrich] Müller's letter about the incineration capacity of the ovens . . . it does not seem to me that, despite its unusual features, a dispassionate historian would dismiss it out of hand, as did Irving, as a forgery. Van Pelt believed it to be genuine. . . . I accept the reasoning of van Pelt. If the Müller document is authentic, it is further cogent evidence of genocidal gassing because the capacity to which Müller refers cannot have been needed to incinerate those who succumbed to disease . . .

13.77 Whilst I acknowledge that the reliability of the eye-witness evidence is variable, what is to me striking about that category of evidence is the similarity of the accounts and the extent to which they are consistent with the documentary evidence. The account of, for example, [*Sonderkommando*] Tauber, is so clear and detailed that, in my judgment, no objective historian would dismiss it as invention unless there were powerful reasons for doing so. Tauber's account is corroborated by and corroborative of the accounts given by others. . . . The evidence of other eye-witnesses . . . would in my view appear credible to a dispassionate student of Auschwitz. There is no evidence of cross-pollination having occurred. It is in the circumstances an unlikely explanation for the broad similarity of the accounts in this category.

13.78 My conclusion is that the various categories of evidence do "converge" in the manner suggested by the Defendants. I accept their contention which I have summarised [earlier]. My overall assessment of the totality of the evidence that Jews were killed in large numbers in the gas chambers at Auschwitz is that it would require exceedingly powerful reasons to reject it. Irving has argued that such reasons do exist.

13.79 The reason why Irving initially denied the existence of gas chambers at Auschwitz was, as has been seen, *The Leuchter Report* [see page 270]. I have summarised in some detail the findings made by Leuchter. . . . I have also set out . . . the reasons why van Pelt on behalf of the Defendants dismissed *The Leuchter Report* as flawed and unreliable. Those reasons were put to Irving in cross-examination. It is a fair summary of his evidence to say that he accepted the validity of most of them. . . . Conclusion: Having considered the various arguments advanced by Irving to assail the effect of the convergent evidence relied on by the Defendants, it is my conclusion that no objective, fair-minded historian would have serious cause to doubt that there were gas chambers at Auschwitz and that they were operated on a substantial scale to kill hundreds of thousands of Jews. . . .

13.95 . . . [I]t appears to me to be incontrovertible that Irving qualifies as a Holocaust denier. Not only has he denied the existence of gas chambers at Auschwitz and asserted that no Jew was gassed there, he has done so on frequent occasions and sometimes in the most offensive terms. By way of examples, I cite his story of the Jew climbing into a mobile telephone box-cum-gas chamber; his claim that more people died in the back of Kennedy's car at Chappaquiddick than died in the gas chambers at Auschwitz; his dismissal of the eye-witnesses *en masse* as liars or as suffering from a mental problem; his reference to an Association of Auschwitz Survivors and Other Liars or "ASS-HOLS," and the question he asked of Mrs. Altman how much money she had made from her tattoo. . . .

13.101 It appears to me to be undeniable that most, if not all, of the statements set out [earlier] reveal clear evidence that, in the absence of any excuse or suitable explanation for what he said or wrote, Irving is anti-semitic. His words are directed against Jews, either individually or collectively, in the sense that they are by turns hostile, critical, offensive and derisory in their references to Semitic people, their characteristics and appearances. A few examples will suffice: Irving has made claims that the Jews deserve to be disliked; that they brought the Holocaust on themselves; that Jewish financiers are crooked; that Jews generate anti-semitism by their greed and mendacity; that it is bad luck for Mr. Wiesel to be called 'Weasel'; that Jews are amongst the scum of humanity; that Jews scurry and hide furtively, unable to stand the light of day; that Simon Wiesenthal has a hideous, leering evil face; and so on.[2] . . .

13.105 The inference which in my judgment is clearly to be drawn from what Irving has said and written is that he is anti-semitic.

13.106 I have concluded that the allegation that Irving is a racist is also established for broadly analogous reasons. This is unsurprising for anti-semitism is a form of racism. . . .

13.114 The evidence supports the claim that Irving has associated with several extreme right-wing organisations in the US. He has a close and long-standing relationship with the Institute of Historical Review. . . . It is an avowedly revisionist organisation whose membership undoubtedly includes many from the extreme right wing. Irving agreed that the membership of the IHR includes "cracked anti-semites." The evidence indicates that Irving is also associated with the National Alliance. I accept the Defendants' case. . . . In my view Irving cannot fail to have become aware that the National Alliance is a neo-Nazi and anti-semitic organisation. The regularity of Irving's contacts with the National Alliance and its officers confirms Irving's sympathetic attitude towards an organisation whose tenets would be abhorrent to most people. . . .

13.136 . . . I return to the central issue of Irving's historiography. As I have already held, the passages in *Denying the Holocaust* of which Irving complains include as an important part of their defamatory sting the meaning that he has deliberately falsified and distorted the historical evidence because he is an apologist for and a partisan of Hitler and on that account is intent on exonerating him. . . .

13.162 It is not difficult to discern a pattern [in Irving's frequent association with extremist and neo-Nazi organizations and individuals]. . . . Over the past fifteen years or so, Irving appears to have become more active politically than was previously the case. He speaks regularly at political or quasi-political meetings in Germany, the United States, Canada and the New World. The content of his speeches and interviews often displays a distinctly pro-Nazi and anti-Jewish bias. He makes surprising and often unfounded assertions about the Nazi regime which tend to exonerate the Nazis for the appalling atrocities which they inflicted on the Jews. He is content to mix with neo-fascists and appears to share many of their racist and anti-semitic prejudices. The picture of Irving which emerges from the evidence of his extra-curricular activities reveals him to be a right-wing pro-Nazi polemicist. In my view the Defendants have established that Irving has a political agenda. It is one which, it is legitimate to infer, disposes him, where he deems it necessary, to manipulate the historical record in order to make it conform with his political beliefs.

13.163 Having reviewed what appear to me to be the relevant considerations, I return to the issue which I defined [earlier as Irving's motivation]. I find myself unable to accept Irving's contention that his falsification of the historical record is the product of innocent error or misinterpretation or incompetence on his part. When account is taken of all the considerations set out . . . above, it appears to me that the correct and inevitable inference must be that for the most part the falsification of the historical record was deliberate and that Irving was motivated by a desire to present events in a manner consistent with his own ideological beliefs even if that involved distortion and manipulation of historical evidence. . . .

13.167 . . . The charges which I have found to be substantially true include the charges that Irving has for his own ideological reasons persistently and deliberately misrepresented and manipulated historical evidence; that for the same reasons he has portrayed Hitler in an unwarrantedly favourable light, principally in relation to his attitude towards and responsibility for the treatment of the Jews; that he is an active Holocaust denier; that he is anti-semitic and racist and that he associates with right wing extremists who promote neo-Nazism.

XIV. Verdict

14.1 It follows that there must be judgment for the Defendants.[3]

NOTES

1. In November 2005 Irving was arrested in Austria on the accusation of Holocaust denial for two speeches he gave there in 1989; refused bail, in February 2006 he pleaded guilty and was sentenced to three (of a possible ten) years in prison under the 1992 law that makes it a crime when anyone "denies, grossly plays down, approves or tries to excuse the National Socialist genocide or other National Socialist crimes against humanity in a print publication, in broadcast or other media." Irving conceded that "I made a mistake when I said there were no gas chambers at Auschwitz" and is reported to have acknowledged that the Nazis had systematically slaughtered Jews; two days afterward in a prison interview, he stated that Jews exaggerated the number of deaths in the camps and that Jews, who have been hated for millennia, "bear blame for what happened," and he added to a reporter of the London *Independent* that "Jews will see a second Holocaust in 20 to 30 years." His lawyer appealed the sentence. *The New York Times*, Feb. 21, 2006, A11; Simon Wiesenthal Center, *Response*, 27 (Spring 2006): 3.

2. Elie Wiesel (1929-), survivor of Auschwitz, Nobel Peace Prize laureate in 1986, author of *Night* and other works on the Holocaust; Simon Wiesenthal (1908-2005), Holocaust survivor, author of autobiographical *The Sunflower*, and relentless tracker of war criminals to bring them to trial.

3. Excerpted from the Judgment in the High Court of Justice, 1996-I-1113, Queen's Bench Division, Before: The Hon. Mr. Justice Gray, April 11, 2000. The decision in its entirety was placed on the Internet, http://wood.ccta.gov.uk/courtser/judgemen, from which these excerpts are taken. Section and paragraph numbers are retained from the original; minor errors of spelling, omitted words, and so forth have been corrected.

TWENTY-NINE

African American Antisemitism: The Nation of Islam

According to a 1998 study by the Anti-Defamation League, antisemitism is four times stronger among African Americans than it is among the rest of the population; it is nearly twice as strong among black leaders than the rank and file, and stronger among the young and educated than the black population at large. Another survey in 2002 found that 35 percent of African American respondents held strongly antisemitic views. In the past, however, there was sufficient commonality between blacks and Jews, two oppressed peoples, to work together. In the 1950s and 1960s, various Jewish organizations and numerous Jews acting individually joined with blacks in the civil rights struggle. The American Jewish Congress and the Anti-Defamation League collaborated with the NAACP to challenge discrimination in the courts. Attorney Jack Greenberg, head of the Legal Defense Fund of the NAACP, was instrumental in assisting Thurgood Marshall to win the 1954 case of *Brown v. Board of Education of Topeka, Kansas,* that ended the legal basis of public school segregation. Jewish labor leaders contributed their organizational skills to the movement, and probably more than half the lawyers representing civil rights workers were Jews. Jews donated more than half the money raised by civil rights organizations. They were also active in the front lines—the freedom rides, sit-ins, and protest marches—constituting about two-thirds of the white Freedom Riders traveling in the South in the summer of 1961 to promote desegregation and probably half the summer volunteers in the black voter registration drive in Mississippi in 1964. Many of the participants were rabbis and yarmulkes—"freedom hats" as they were called—became something of a symbol of the struggle. Two Jewish volunteers, Andrew Goodman and Michael Schwerner, were murdered with James Chaney, a black, by racists in Mississippi. In that same year, seventeen white rabbis were jailed with Dr. Martin Luther King, Jr., in St. Augustine, Florida, for participating in an anti-segregation demonstration. Jewish participation in the cause of black civil rights started earlier and was significantly greater than that of any other definable white group. So obvious was the partnership that Mississippi Senator Theodore Bilbo, a spokesman for white supremacists, declared, "The niggers and the Jews of New York are working hand in hand."[1]

While Jews could identify with an oppressed minority, profound differences between the two groups ultimately served to pull them apart. The socio-economic status of Jews in recent decades and their historical experience in America were far different from that of blacks. Jews achieved extraordinary success in American society, whereas a significant percentage of blacks remained mired in poverty. And whereas in the 1960s and after the barriers to Jewish advancement had been reduced to only an occasional stumbling block, blacks, despite considerable progress, continued to struggle against enormous obstacles, including the psychological legacy of slavery, segregation, lynching, sharecropping, and the ongoing bigotry of white Americans. Having themselves climbed out of poverty and utilized public education to full advantage, Jews would become impatient with a black underclass mired in welfare, illiteracy, and illegitimacy. "Why can't they lift themselves up the way we did?" would become an all-too-common, but naive, response of middle-class Jews to the cruel plight of the ghetto poor.

Thus even during the years that Jews and African Americans were forging a successful alliance, friction, and even hostility, existed between the two groups. Like other Christians, blacks were exposed to the negative image of Jews found in the New Testament and perpetuated directly or indirectly from the pulpit. And Jews were not unaffected by the anti-black sentiments that pervaded American society. As Jews and blacks rubbed shoulders in northern cities, particularly after World War II, additional causes for tension emerged. Blacks accused Jewish landlords of rent gouging, Jewish storeowners of selling shoddy merchandise at high prices and not hiring blacks, and Jewish housewives of demeaning black domestics. And Jews, like other whites, were troubled by the influx of blacks into their neighborhoods. Generally Jews were less opposed to integrated neighborhoods and schools than other definable white groups, and, unlike some white ethnics, they never resorted to violence to keep blacks out. Nevertheless, like other whites, many Jews, citing black crime and decaying schools, fled, often to the growing suburbs. The riots that devastated several American cities in the 1960s and 1970s caused many Jews to retreat from their espousal of black causes. The scenes, graphically depicted on television, of blacks trashing shops, many of them owned by Jews, and carting away stolen merchandise exacerbated feelings about black criminality. And in subsequent years, the rapid deterioration of formerly Jewish working-class and middle-class neighborhoods now inhabited predominately by blacks and the proliferation of urban black street crime, whose victims not infrequently were Jews, led more and more Jews to sympathize less with the plight of the black underclass.

But what really split the alliance of blacks and Jews was the growing influence of black militants who rebelled against integration and called for black nationalism and "Black Power." In their denunciation of whites, militants increasingly singled out Jews as the principal enemy of black people. When these militants postured with weapons, praised violence as liberating, and engaged in antisemitic rhetoric, they seemed like black fascists to Jews. When they defended the burning and looting in the cities as guerrilla warfare against oppressors and colonizers, Jews, like other Americans, saw them as wild-eyed fanatics who threatened American society.

The Historical Research Department of the Nation of Islam

The Secret Relationship between Blacks and Jews, *1991*

The Nation of Islam (NOI) went far to sunder the alliance. Minister Louis Farrakhan, the current leader of NOI, is an arch-conspiricist and antisemite who has used Jew-hatred as a demagogic instrument of mass mobilization. Beginning in 1984, he indulged in vituperative antisemitic demagoguery, dredging up every element of traditional antisemitism: Jews as deicides, Satan's apostles armed with super-human powers, capitalist exploiters, communist revolutionaries, global conspira-tors, ritual murderers, and poisoners of non-Jews. Farrakhan said that 85 percent "of the people of earth are victimized by a small clique who use their power and knowledge to manipulate the masses against the best interests of the people." Jews have a "stranglehold" on the American government. "Murder" is planted "in the hearts of Jews across the nation and across the world." Once Jewish control was limited to the ghetto, but now "you are our managers, you are our agents. You run the institutions quietly behind the scenes. You pull the strings where education is concerned. You're the scriptwriters. You're the Hollywood promoters. . . ." Jewish doctors infect black children with diseases and conduct AIDS research on blacks. "Jewish control of black organizations has to be busted up and broken." "The same group of people" developed capitalism and communism. According to Farrakhan, Jewry is inauthentic and illegitimate: "This Caucasian who claims to be the Jew, Is-rael, has been masquerading as the chosen of God. . . . The real Israel . . . is the black man and woman of America and the world." Farrakhan sees himself, and is seen by his followers, as the new Moses leading the new chosen people against the modern "Pharaoh," the Jews who dominate and exploit African-Americans.[2]

To his classic demagogic armory, Farrakhan added a new weapon, the myth that the Jews originated and dominated the four-hundred year Atlantic slave trade, profited immensely from it, owned a disproportionate number of slaves, and were the cruelest and most oppressive masters. In 1991 *The Secret Relationship Between Blacks and Jews* was published anonymously—like the *Protocols,* with which it has much in common—under NOI's imprint. The volume purports to provide the evi-dence that Jews were the guilty initiators, organizers, and beneficiaries of the slave system. It was prepared by the Historical Research Department of the Nation of Islam, an unknown entity that published nothing before or since. *Secret Relationship* maintains that Jews are a criminal people who, in past centuries, united "in an un-holy coalition of kidnappers and slave makers," from which they gained their "im-mense wealth." Jews abused and raped black women "with abandon" and used liquor to demoralize American Indians and black Africans. The authors of *Secret Re-lationship* proudly boast that the Jews have been found out. In an interview with the *Amsterdam News* (January 8, 1994), Farrakhan stated that Jews "have never admitted until recently that they were involved in the slave trade. They put it on the Gentiles. They put it on the Arabs, but they never came out publicly until we published that book and said that they were involved." In fact, *Secret Relationship* has provided absolutely nothing new—neither new information nor new insights into the four-century Atlantic slave economy. That Jews were both slave traders and slave owners is long known and well known, but for students of slavery Jewish involvement was only of the slightest importance because they were bit players. In comparison to Muslims, Catholics, Protestants, and black Africans, Jews were only marginally involved in slavery, either as traders or owners.

In *Jews and the American Slave Trade,* Saul S. Friedman tellingly demolishes the libel that Jews were a major factor in the slave trade:

> There were 697,681 slaves in America in 1790, 1,538,022 slaves in 1820. According to official census records, Jews owned 209 slaves in 1790, 701 in 1820. During the formative years of the United States . . . when the importation and sale of Africans was at its peak *Jews owned less than three-one hundredths of a percent, 0.03 percent of all the slaves in America.*
>
> Only a handful of Jews . . . figured prominently in the transport of slaves across the Atlantic and even their participation is relatively small. Actual British government shipping records show that Jewish owners accounted for less than 2 percent of all slaves imported into . . . North America in the eighteenth century. . . . [N]one of the 200 illegal slavers operating off the coast of Cuba after [the slave trade became] illegal in 1808 were Jews. . . . Jews played no role in the import of more than one million African slaves to Brazil in the nineteenth century. At no time were Jews among the major slave holders, planters, magnates, or traders in what was to become the United States. . . . According to public records, only one Jew . . . ever served as an overseer on a plantation.[3]

Over the four centuries of the Atlantic slave trade, Jews accounted for less than 2 percent of the six hundred thousand Africans brought to the United States and considerably less than 1 percent of the about ten million slaves who went to other areas of the New World. In a review of Eli Faber's *Jews, Slaves, and the Slave Trade* published in the *American Historical Review* (June 2000), David Eltis wrote that a recently published database contains the "names of 31,260 individual owners of transatlantic slave ventures. Eighty-four of these names are linked to fifty or more voyages and only one of this 'elite group' has any possible Jewish connection." David Brion Davis, America's leading authority on the institution of slavery, comments on Jewish involvement: "It is easy enough to point to a few Jewish slave traders in Amsterdam, Bordeaux, or Newport. But far from indicating that Jews constituted a major force behind the exploitation of Africa, inquiry shows that these merchants were highly exceptional, far outnumbered by Catholics and Protestants who flocked to share the great bonanza. . . . [H]istory would have been the same with or without Jewish slave traders and planters."[4]

The message of the authors of *Secret Relationship* to black people is clear: It was the Jews who oppressed us in the past and continue to oppress us today. Hence they seem to take a perverse delight in listing any Jew who was in some way linked to the Atlantic slave trade. Conversely, they simply ignore evidence that points to a different conclusion. The tactic of singling out the Jew as bearing a special guilt for the terrible iniquities inflicted on blacks is classic antisemitism, and like other accusations hurled at Jews by antisemites, this one is equally absurd.

In NOI's bookstores, *The Secret Relationship* keeps close company with the *Protocols of the Learned Elders of Zion, The Hoax of the Twentieth Century* by a leading Holocaust denier, *The International Jew* by Henry Ford, *The Jews and Their Lies* by Martin Luther, and other antisemitic classics. It is strange that *Secret Relationship,* "the Bible of the new anti-Semitism," is sold by the Institute of Historical Review, the leading Holocaust denial organization. It is stranger yet that Farrakhan and NOI leaders hobnob willingly with white supremacists such as Thomas Metzger formerly of the KKK and founder of the White Aryan Resistance, and Matt Hale, head of the World Church of the Creator, who, utilizing NOI "research," declares, "European Whites did not bring the slaves to America. On the contrary, it was the Asiatic Jews who brought them here (as Louis Fahrakhan [*sic*] has also pointed out)."[5]

Referring to the 1980s, Farrakhan said "I was vicious in those days," and so he was, and despite some mellowing, so he remained. His retreat from his antisemitic campaign reflects the tactical calculation that, in the United States at least, it is not possible to rev up a mass movement simply on the basis of demagogic Jew-hatred, no matter how ferocious the tirades, no matter how tumultuous the applause in packed lecture halls. In any event, neither he nor the NOI[6] has retracted the lies and distortions that abound in *Secret Relationship.* This section begins with excerpts from *Secret Relationship* and concludes with two black spokesmen, one a Farrakhan clone who provides the most extreme example of black antisemitism, the other a distinguished scholar who refutes it.

[By our research] Jews have been conclusively linked to the greatest criminal endeavor ever undertaken against an entire race of people . . . a crime against humanity . . . the Black African Holocaust. They were participants in the entrapment and forcible exportation of millions of Black African citizens into the wretched and inhuman life of bondage for the financial benefit of Jews. The effects of this unspeakable tragedy are still being felt among the peoples of the world at this very hour.

Deep within the recesses of the Jewish historical record is the irrefutable evidence that the most prominent of the Jewish pilgrim fathers used kidnapped Black Africans disproportionately more than any other ethnic or religious group in New World history and participated in every aspect of the international slave trade. The immense wealth of Jews, as with most of the White colonial fathers, was acquired by the brutal subjugation of Black Africans purely on the basis of skin color . . . a concept unfamiliar to Moses. Now, compiled for the first time, the Jewish sources reveal the extent of their complicity in Black slavery in the most graphic of terms.

Until now, the facts herein were known only to a few. Most have always assumed the relationship between Blacks and Jews has been mutually supportive, friendly and fruitful . . . two suffering people bonding to overcome hatred and bigotry to achieve success. But history tells an altogether different story. This report will focus on the hidden history of Blacks and Jews from the Jewish historical record. . . .

. . . In 1350, Spain began a series of conversion drives to convert all Jews in Spain to Christianity, and in unprecedented numbers, and with little resistance, the Jews converted. This rush to mass conversion [was] an event, unparalleled in Jewish history. . . .

. . . Some fifty thousand Jews chose to convert rather than leave their land and their riches.

Contrary to popular notions, those who left were not refugees searching for religious freedom but entrepreneurs looking for economic opportunities. When they fled, they brought few Torah scrolls and even fewer copies of the Jewish holy book Talmud with them. . . .

The majority fled south and eastward to North Africa and to centers like Salonika, Constantinople, Aleppo and Damascus; while others sought and found refuge in the Netherlands where they "established synagogues, schools, cemeteries and a high level of wealth and culture." Most escaped "with considerable sums of money." Though scattered throughout the globe by political, economic and religious circumstances, they would reunite later in an unholy coalition of kidnappers and slave makers. . . .

The Jewish Caribbean presence began in earnest with Columbus' initial foray into the region. With these early Jewish colonists the economic motivation for the exploitation of millions of Black Africans was introduced to the Western Hemisphere. The strategy seemed simple enough . . . wealth would be amassed through a plantation economy driven by sugar cane. . . . [T]he history of the industry became entwined with the western migration of the Jews. They were primarily the financiers and merchants and in a few cases they were also the plantation masters. Jews from Portugal, Holland, England and all over Europe advantaged themselves through the domination of the commerce of these island regions, particularly in sugar.

Jewish slave traders procured Black Africans by the tens of thousands and funneled them to the plantations of South America and throughout the Caribbean. There remains no documented trace of protest over this behavior . . . it was a purely commercial venture with which Judaism did not interfere. Whether the local influence was Portuguese, Dutch or English, the Black man and woman fared the same. In Curaçao in the seventeenth century, as well as in the British colonies of Barbados and Jamaica in the eighteenth century, Jewish merchants played a major role in the slave trade. In fact, in all the American colonies, whether French (Martinique), British, or Dutch, Jewish merchants frequently dominated. . . .

With the help of the Jewish slave traders, Blacks poured in. . . . [T]he Jewish share in overall trade was disproportionately large. . . . This dominance of trade by the Jewish community made them the most prominently poised of any group to exploit the slave markets. . . .

. . . Jewish entrepreneurs ventured west and formed the commercial base which made possible the settlement of the New World. . . . Jews, as an elementary fact, participated in the process by which millions of African citizens were enslaved and murdered. . . .

The earliest Jewish settlements were established in Newport, Rhode Island and New York where there were numerous Jewish slaveholders long before and right through the American Revolution. Jews adapted to the business climate of colonial North America and operated with the same skill they had demonstrated in the island regions to the south and accepted Black slavery without question. In the North before 1800 and in the South all through the colonial period, slaves were stocked as commodities by Jewish merchants. Countless thousands of Africans were brought here in colonial times as slaves by Jewish merchant-shippers and in the South Jews began to enter the planter class in substantial numbers.

The New York- and Newport-area Jews had established a highly efficient trans-Atlantic shipping operation. Jews who settled in North Africa with access into the African mainland arranged with African tribal traitors for the transport of Blacks to the Atlantic coast for sale to the New World merchant-shippers. . . .

It should be made very plain at this point that even until the Civil War era, Jews as a community never interfered with the practice of slavery or registered any reservation about its dehumanizing effects. When some colonies had proposed high tariffs on the importation of slaves, intending to discourage the slave trade, Jewish merchants . . . protested, for they "were among those who wished to see the traffic continue." Slavery was a business concern mitigated only by the bottom line. Regionally, one can discern no difference in attitude or philosophy of the Jews with regard to *non Jewish* human bondage. . . .

Jews were indistinguishable from other White Americans in their attitudes and treatment of Blacks! When "King Cotton" dominated the South, Jews began to enter the planter class in substantial numbers. Slave-dealing was an extremely profitable business. . . . Plantation supply became the bread and butter Jewish enterprise with their goods of all descriptions keeping the Southern slave economy in motion.

At no time did Southern Jews feel tainted by the slave trade and they were found at every level of the slavocracy. . . .

. . . The Civil War and the slavery issue caused no great moral convulsion among the Jews of America. By this time the total population of the United States was estimated to be 31,443,321 and Jews numbered about 150,000. So many of their fortunes were founded and maintained on the backs of the African that only a tiny fraction of Jews, North or South, spoke for his freedom. . . .

The slavery debate raged across the country but no Jewish leaders in the Old South "ever expressed any reservations about the justice of slavery or the rightness of the Southern position." Jewish clergy did not even discuss *Black* slavery until 1860, and then primarily in support of it. . . .

Black men, women and children fell victim by the tens of millions to the slave traders and slave makers. As chattel, the African was unaccounted for in many a transaction and hidden within a substantial smuggling commerce. Given the evidence presented of the mercantile capabilities of the Jews and their concurrent indifference to African humanity, one might fairly assert that they are accountable for many of these murders. Certainly, one could justifiably argue that in places such as Surinam,[7] Curaçao, Barbados and other slave depots under their control, a majority of the murders of Black hostages were committed by Jews or their agents. To quantify, however, is a most difficult proposition. Tens of millions suffered and died . . . how many tens of how many millions is the question. . . .

[Rather than the toll of some 15 million accepted by scholars, *Secret Relationship* places the] number of Africans killed . . . closer to 100 million murder victims. The actual figures are staggering, and as key operatives in the enterprise, Jews have carved for themselves a monumental culpability in slavery—and the holocaust. . . .

During the 14th and 15th centuries, European Jews were dominant as shippers, navigators, cartographers and traders piloting the seas and exploring for new trade routes and sources of commerce. Their money backed many exploratory forays and their equipment and supplies filled many of the ships' holds. By the time they settled in the New World they had acquired hundreds of vessels to ferry their goods through the Caribbean and South American settlements and on to Europe. The Jews, in fact, were the largest ship chandlers in the entire Caribbean region and owned warehouses with inventories to outfit the largest sailing vessels and to make ship repairs. It was written of the Curaçao traders, that "nearly all the navigation . . . was in the hands of the Jews."

Sugar came out and kidnapped Africans went in . . . an extremely profitable arrangement for the Jews involved in the trade. Slave shipping itself brought an immense return and there was no comparable endeavor for the profiteer. . . .

The holds of the holocaust ships were indescribably filthy and the ship owners assumed a high death rate in transport and some of the survivors were close to death on arrival. . . .

All of the following "Chosen People" are confirmed to have participated in the Black African slave trade. According to *their* own literature, each one is a prominent historical figure and most are highly regarded and respected by Jews themselves. Even the most prominent of Jewish Americans never voiced any reservation whatsoever about this practice. [There follow 100 pages of biographical sketches of some 450 Jews who were involved in the slave system, with the assurance that further research will add many more to this rogues gallery.][8]

Khallid Abdul Muhammed

". . . *You're from the Synagogue of Satan,*" *1993*

Reproduced in *The New York Times* by the Anti-Defamation League, Khallid Abdul Muhammed's hate speech at Kean College on November 29, 1993, gave him instant notoriety. At the time Khallid (occasionally spelled as Khalid) was a representative of Farrakhan and national spokesman of the Nation of Islam. Black organizations at various colleges continued to extend him invitations and audiences often cheered his venomous references to Jews. Below are excerpts from the speech delivered at Kean College; the sequence of the passages has been rearranged since the original remarks are turgid and disordered.

Brothers and sisters . . . the so-called Jew, and I must say so-called Jew, because you're not the true Jew. You are Johnny-come-lately-Jew, who just crawled out of the caves and hills of Europe just a little over 4,000 years ago. You're not from the original people. You are a European strain of people who crawled around on your all fours in the caves and hills of Europe, eatin' Juniper roots and eatin' each other.

*   *   *

Who are the slumlords in the black community? The so-called Jew. . . . Who is it sucking our blood in the black community? A white imposter Arab and a white imposter Jew. Right in the black community, sucking our blood on a daily and consistent basis. They sell us pork and they don't even eat it themselves. A meat case full of rotten pork meat, and the imposter Arab and the imposter white Jew, neither of them eat it themselves. A wall full of liquor keeping our people drunk and out of their head, and filled with the swill of the swine, affecting their minds. They're the blood suckers of the black nation and the black community. Professor Griff was right, when he spoke here . . . and when he spoke in the general vicinity of Jersey and New York, and when he spoke at Columbia Jew-niversity (*sic*) over in Jew (*sic*) York City. He was right.

*   *   *

The DeBeers mines, Oppenheimer, our people, our brothers and sisters in South Africa, hundreds of them lose their lives. Sometime thousands in those mines. Miles underground, mining diamonds for white Jews. That's why you call yourself Mr. Rubenstein, Mr. Goldstein, Mr. Silverstein. Because you been stealing rubies and gold and silver all over the earth. That's why we can't even wear a ring or a bracelet or a necklace without calling it Jew-elry. We say it real quick and call it jewelry, but it's not jewelry, it's Jew-elry, 'cause you're the rogue that's stealing all over the face of the planet earth.

*   *   *

You see everybody always talk about Hitler exterminating 6 million Jews. That's right. But don't nobody ever ask what did they do to Hitler? What did they do to them folks? They went in there, in Germany, the way they do everywhere they go, and they supplanted, they usurped, they turned around and a German, in his own country, would almost have to go to a Jew to get money. They had undermined the very fabric of the society. Now he was an arrogant no-good devil bastard, Hitler, no question about it. He was wickedly great. Yes, he was.

He used his greatness for evil and wickedness. But they are wickedly great too, brother. Everywhere they go, and they always do it and hide their head.

*   *   *

We don't owe the white man nothin' in South Africa. He's killed millions of our women, our children, our babies, our elders. We don't owe him nothing in South Africa. If we want to be merciful at all, when we gain enough power from God Almighty to take our freedom and independence from him, we give him 24 hours to get out of town, by sundown. That's all. If he won't get out of town by sundown, we kill everything white that ain't right [inaudible] in South Africa. We kill the women, we kill the children, we kill the babies. We kill the blind, we kill the crippled, [inaudible], we kill 'em all. We kill the faggot, we kill the lesbian, we kill them all. You say why kill the babies in South Africa? Because they gonna grow up one day to oppress our babies, so we kill the babies. Why kill the women? They, they . . . because they lay on their back, they are the military or the army's manufacturing center. They lay on their back and reinforcements roll out from between their legs. So we kill the women too. You'll kill the elders too? Kill the old ones too. Goddamit, if they in a wheel-chair, push 'em off a cliff in Cape Town. Push 'em off a cliff in Cape Town, or Johannesburg, or [inaudible], or Port Sheppston or Durban, how the hell you think they got old. They old oppressing black people. I said kill the blind, kill the crippled, kill the crazy. Goddamn, and when you get through killing 'em all, go to the goddam graveyard and dig up the grave and kill 'em, goddam, again. 'Cause they didn't die hard enough. They didn't die hard enough. And if you've killed 'em all and you don't have the strength to dig 'em up, then take your gun and shoot in the goddam grave. Kill 'em again. Kill 'em again, 'cause they didn't die hard enough.

*   *   *

We found out that the Federal Reserve ain't really owned by the Federal Government. . . . But it ain't owned by the Federal Government. The Federal Reserve is owned by, you just touched on it a little while ago. (Jews.) It's owned by the Jews.

*   *   *

Brother, I don't care who sits in the seat at the White House. You can believe that the Jews control that seat, that they sit in from behind the scenes. They control the finance, and not only that, they influence the policy-making.

*   *   *

No white Jews ever in bondage in Egypt for 400 years. You're not the chosen people of God. Stop telling that lie. Let's go a little further with this. Many of you put out the textbooks. Many of you control the libraries. Lie-braries. NBC, ABC, CBS, you don't see nothin' or makes sure we don't see. Warner Brothers, Paramount, huh? Hollywood, period.

* * *

But [they] also are most influential in newspaper, magazine, print media and electronic media.

These people have had a secret relationship with us. They have our entertainers in their hip pocket. In the palm of their hand. I should say. They have our athletes in the palm of their hand.

Many of our politicians are in the palm of the white man's hand, but in particular, in the palm of the Jewish white man's hand.

* * *

The Jews have told us, the so-called Jews have told us, ve [*sic*] ve, ve suffer like you. Ve, ve, ve, ve marched with Dr. Martin Luther King, Jr. Ve, ve, ve were in Selma, Alabama. Ve, ve were in Montgomery, Alabama. Ve, ve were on the front line of the civil rights marches. Ve have always supported you. But let's take a look at it. The Jews, the so-called Jews, what they have actually done, brothers and sisters, is used us as cannon fodder.

* * *

Go to the Vatican in Rome, when [*sic*] the old, no-good Pope, you know that cracker. Somebody need to raise that dress up and see what's really under there.[9]

Henry Louis Gates, Jr.

"Black Demagogues and Pseudo-Scholars," 1992

Henry Louis Gates, Jr., the W. E. B. Du Bois Professor of Humanities and head of the Afro-American Studies Department at Harvard, has drawn praise for his condemnation of black antisemitism. In an essay entitled "Memoirs of an Anti-Anti-Semite," he explained that he took a public stand "because those black intellectuals I most admire—Cornel West, Patricia Williams, Manning Marable, Marian Wright Edelman, Martin Kilson, Bell Hooks—insisted by argument and by their example, that it was important to do so. I did it because they showed that being anti-Semitic is not a way of being problack." In the op-ed piece he published in *The New York Times* (July 20, 1992), Gates discussed the seriousness of this new antisemitism, which, he said, is "in large part the province of the better educated classes" and is deliberately "engineered and promoted" by leaders seeking to capitalize on African American resentment.

During the past decade, the historic relationship between African-Americans and Jewish Americans—a relationship that sponsored so many of the concrete advances of the civil rights era—showed another and less attractive face. While anti-Semitism is generally on the wane in this country, it has been on the rise among black Americans. A recent survey finds that not only are blacks twice as likely as whites to hold anti-Semitic views but—significantly—that it is among the younger and more educated blacks that anti-Semitism is most pronounced.

The trend has been deeply disquieting for many black intellectuals. But it is something most of us, as if by unstated agreement, simply choose not to talk about. At a time when black America is beleaguered on all sides, there is a strong temptation simply to ignore the phenomenon or treat it as something strictly marginal. And yet to do so would be a serious mistake. As the African-American philosopher Cornel West has insisted, attention to black anti-Semitism is crucial, however discomfiting, in no small part because the moral credibility of our struggle against racism hangs in the balance. When the Rev. Jesse Jackson, in an impassioned address to the World Jewish Congress on July 7, condemned the sordid history of anti-Semitism, he not only went some distance toward retrieving the once abandoned mantle of the Rev. Dr. Martin Luther King Jr.'s human statesmanship, he also delivered a stern rebuke—while not specifically citing black anti-Semitism—to those black leaders who have sought to bolster their own strength thorough division. Mr. Jackson and others have learned that we must not allow demagogues to turn the wellspring of memory into a renewable resource of enmity everlasting.

We must begin by recognizing what is new about the new anti-Semitism. Make no mistake: This is anti-Semitism from the top down, engineered and promoted by leaders who affect to be speaking for a larger resentment. This top-down anti-Semitism, in large part the province of the better educated classes, can thus be contrasted with the anti-Semitism from below common among African-American urban communities in the 1930's and 40's, which followed in many ways a familiar pattern of clientelistic hostility toward the neighborhood vendor or landlord. In our cities, hostility of this sort is now ceremoniously directed toward Korean shop owners. But "minority" traders and shopkeepers everywhere in the world—such as the Indians of East Africa and the Chinese of Southeast Asia—have experienced similar ethnic antagonism. Anti-Jewish sentiment can also be traced to Christian anti-Semitism, given the historic importance of Christianity in the black community.

Unfortunately, the old paradigms will not serve to explain the new bigotry and its role in black America. For one thing, its preferred currency is not the mumbled epithet or curse but the densely argued treatise; it belongs as much to the repertory of campus lecturers as community activists. And it comes in wildly different packages. A book popular with some in the "Afrocentric" movement, *The Iceman Inheritance: Prehistoric Sources of Western Man's Racism, Sexism, and Aggression,* by Michael Bradley, argues that white people are so vicious because they, unlike the rest of mankind, are descended from the brutish Neanderthals. More to the point, it speculates that the Jews may have been the "'purest' and oldest Neanderthal-Caucasoids," the iciest of the ice people; hence (he explains) the singularly odious character of ancient Jewish culture. Crackpot as it sounds, the book has lately been reissued with endorsements from two members of the Africana Studies Department of the City College of New York, as well as an introduction by Dr. John Henrik Clarke, professor emeritus of Hunter College and the great paterfamilias of the Afrocentric movement.

Dr. Clarke recently attacked multiculturalism as the product of what he called the "Jewish educational Mafia." And while Dr. Leonard Jeffries's views on supposed Jewish complicity in the subjection of blacks captured headlines, his intellectual cohorts such as Conrad Muhammad and Khallid Muhammad address community gatherings and college students across the country purveying a similar doctrine. College speakers and publications have played a disturbing role in legitimating the new creed. Last year, U.C.L.A.'s black newspaper, *Nommo*, defended the importance of *The Protocols of the Elders of Zion*, the notorious Czarist canard that portrays a Jewish conspiracy to rule the world. (Those who took issue were rebuked with an article headlined "Anti-Semitic? Ridiculous—Chill.") Speaking at Harvard University earlier this year, Conrad Muhammad, the New York representative of the Nation of Islam, neatly annexed environmentalism to anti-Semitism when he blamed the Jews for despoiling the environment and destroying the ozone layer.

But the bible of the new anti-Semitism is *The Secret Relationship Between Blacks and Jews*, an official publication of the Nation of Islam that boasts 1,275 footnotes in the course of 334 pages. Sober and scholarly looking, it may well be one of the most influential books published in the black community in the last 12 months. It is available in black-oriented shops across the nation, even those that specialize in Kente cloth and beads rather than books. It can also be ordered over the phone, by dialing 1-800-48-TRUTH. Meanwhile, the book's conclusions are, in many circles, increasingly treated as damning historical fact. The book, one of the most sophisticated instances of hate literature yet compiled, was prepared by the historical research department of the Nation of Islam. It charges that the Jews were "key operatives" in the historic crime of slavery, playing an "inordinate" and "disproportionate" role and "carv[ing] out for themselves a monumental culpability in slavery—and the black holocaust." Among significant sectors of the black community, this brief has become a credo of a new philosophy of black self-affirmation.

To be sure, the book massively misrepresents the historical record, largely through a process of cunningly selective quotation of often reputable sources. But its authors could be confident that few of its readers would go to the trouble of actually hunting down the works cited. For if readers actually did so, they might discover a rather different picture. They might find out—from the book's own vaunted authorities—that, for example, of all the African slaves imported into the New World, American Jewish merchants accounted for less than 2 percent, a finding sharply at odds with the Nation's of Islam's claim of Jewish "predominance" in this traffic. They might find out that in the domestic trade it appears that all of the Jewish traders combined bought and sold fewer slaves than the single gentile firm of Franklin and Armfield. In short, they might learn what the historian Harold Brackman has documented—that the book's repeated insistence that the Jews dominated the slave trade depends on an unscrupulous distortion of the historic record. But the most ominous words in the book are found on the cover: "Volume One." More have been promised, to carry on the saga of Jewish iniquity to the present day.

However shoddy the scholarship of works like *The Secret Relationship*, underlying it is something even more troubling: the tacit conviction that culpability is heritable. For it suggests a doctrine of racial continuity, in which the racial evil of a people is merely manifest (rather than constituted) by their historical misdeeds. The reported misdeeds are thus the signs of an essential nature that is evil.

How does this theology of guilt surface in our everyday moral discourse? In New York, earlier this spring, a forum was held at the Church of St. Paul and Andrew to provide an occasion for blacks and Jews to engage in dialogue on such issues as slavery and social injustice. Both Jewish and black panelists found common ground and common causes. But a tone-setting contingent of blacks in the audience took strong issue with the proceedings. Outraged, they demanded to know why the Jews, those historic malefactors, had not apologized to the "descendants of African kings and queens." And so the organizer of the event, Melanie Kaye/Kantrowitz, did. Her voice quavering with emotion, she said: "I think I speak for a lot of people in this room when I say 'I'm sorry.' We're ashamed of it, we hate it, and that's why we organized this event." Should the Melanie Kantrowitzes of the world, whose ancestors suffered Czarist pogroms and, latterly, the Nazi Holocaust, be the primary object of our wrath? And what is yielded by this hateful sport of victimology, save the conversion of a tragic past into a game of recrimination? Perhaps that was on the mind of another audience member. "I don't want an apology," a dreadlocked woman told her angrily. "I want reparations. Forty acres and a mule, plus interest."

These are times that try the spirit of liberal outreach. In fact, Louis Farrakhan, leader of the Nation of Islam, himself explained the real agenda behind his campaign, speaking before an audience of 15,000 at the University of Illinois last fall. The purpose of *The Secret Relationship*, he said, was to "rearrange a relationship" that "has been detrimental to us." "Rearrange" is a curiously elliptical term here: If a relationship with another group has been detrimental, it only makes sense to sever it as quickly as possible. In short, by "rearrange," he means to convert a relationship of friendship, alliance and uplift into one of enmity, distrust and hatred.

But why target the Jews? Using the same historical methodology, after all, the researchers of the book could have produced a damning treatise on the involvement of left-handers in the "black holocaust." The answer requires us to go beyond the usual shibboleths about bigotry and view the matter, from the demagogues' perspective, strategically: as the bid of one black elite to supplant another. It requires us, in short, to see anti-Semitism as a weapon in the raging battle of who will speak for black America—those who have sought common cause with others, or those who preach a barricaded withdrawal into racial authenticity. The strategy of these apostles of hate, I believe, is best understood as ethnic isolationism—they know that the more isolated black America becomes, the greater their power. And what's the most efficient way to sever black America from its allies? Bash the Jews, these demagogues apparently calculate, and you're halfway there.

I myself think that an aphorist put his finger on something germane when he observed, "We can rarely bring ourselves to forgive those who have helped us." For sometimes it seems that the trajectory of black-Jewish relations is a protracted enactment of this paradox.

Many Jews are puzzled by the recrudescence of black anti-Semitism, in view of the historic alliance. The brutal truth has escaped them: that the new anti-Semitism arises not in spite of the black-Jewish alliance but because of it. For precisely such trans-racial cooperation—epitomized by the historic partnership between blacks and Jews—is what poses the greatest threat to the isolationist movement. In short, for the tacticians of the new anti-Semitism, the original sin of American Jews was their involvement—truly "inordinate," truly "disproportionate"—not in slavery, but in the front ranks of the civil rights struggle.

For decent and principled reasons, many black intellectuals are loath to criticize "oppositional" black leaders. Yet it has become apparent that to continue to maintain a comradely silence may be, in effect, to capitulate to the isolationist agenda, to betray our charge and trust. And, to be sure, many black writers, intellectuals and religious leaders have taken an unequivocal stand on this issue. Cornel West aptly describes black anti-Semitism as "the bitter fruit of a profound self-destructive impulse, nurtured on the vines of hopelessness and concealed by empty gestures of black unity." After 12 years of conservative indifference, those political figures who acquiesced, by malign neglect, to the deepening crisis of black America should not feign surprise that we should prove so vulnerable to the demagogues' rousing messages of hate, their manipulation of past and present.

Bigotry, as a tragic century has taught us, is an opportunistic infection, attacking most virulently when the body politic is in a weakened state. Yet neither should those who care about black America gloss over what cannot be condoned: That much respect we owe to ourselves. For surely it falls to all of us to recapture the insight that Dr. King so insistently expounded. "We are caught in an inescapable network of mutuality," he told us. "Whatever affects one directly affects all indirectly." How easy to forget this—and how vital to remember.[10]

NOTES

1. Quoted in Murray Friedman, *What Went Wrong? The Creation and Collapse of the Black-Jewish Alliance* (New York: Free Press, 1995), 146.

2. Michael C. Kotzin, "Louis Farrakhan's Anti-Semitism: A Look at the Record," *Christian Century,* Mar. 2, 1994, 225-226.

3. Saul S. Friedman, *Jews and the American Slave Trade* (New Brunswick, N.J.: Transaction Publishers, 1998), 217-218.

4. David Brion Davis, "The Slave Trade and the Jews," *New York Review of Books,* Dec. 22, 1994, 15-16.

5. Rev. Matt Hale, *Facts That the Government and the Media Don't Want You to Know* (East Peoria, Ill.: Creativity Movement, n.d.), 9-10.

6. Most black Muslims are not members of Farrakhan's NOI, and there are five or so distinct groups that call themselves "The Nation of Islam" that have different leaders, practices, theological orientations, and so on.

7. Surinam's Jewish community and its slave-holding are much more objectively and illuminatingly presented in the forthcoming book by the distinguished historian Natalie Zemon Davis, tentatively titled *Braided Histories.*

8. From the Historical Research Department of the Nation of Islam, *The Secret Relationship Between Blacks and Jews* (Chicago: Nation of Islam/Latimer Associates, 1991), vi-viii, 11-13, 18-19, 88-91, 121, 139, 143, 177-178, 190-191, 213; the footnotes have been deleted.

9. From *The New York Times,* Jan. 14, 1994, 24.

10. Henry Louis Gates, Jr., "Black Demagogues and Pseudo-Scholars," *The New York Times,* July 20, 1992, A15. To facilitate reading, several paragraphs of the original have been consolidated.

THIRTY

Muslim Antisemitism: Recycling Old Myths

Parallels can readily be drawn between the demonization of the Jews by the Nazis and the current depiction of Jews in Muslim lands. Radical Islamists and even mainstream journalists, teachers, and intellectuals have dredged up long-discredited Christian and Nazi antisemitic myths and caricatures, including vile cartoons adapted from the bloodcurdling originals of Nazi propaganda. In particular they make wide use of the *Protocols of the Learned Elders of Zion*. Thus an article in the *Jihad Times* made the bizarre accusation that a "300-member apex Zionist body" of Elders launched the attacks on the World Trade Center and the Pentagon. The Elders issued a "secret directive" to four thousand Jews not to report to work on September 11 so "that not a single Israeli or American Jew working in the World Trade Center was reported killed or missing." (Actually some three hundred Jews perished.) The myths of ritual murder and Holocaust denial, among others, continue to circulate widely in the Arab world.

Islamism originated in Egypt with the founding of the Muslim Brotherhood in 1928. Apocalyptic and murderous from early on, it grew steadily until President Gamal Abdel Nasser turned against it and drove it underground and into exile all over the Muslim world (in the 1970s President Anwar El-Sadat tolerated the Brotherhood as a counterweight to Marxism). A great many of the fugitives fled to Saudi Arabia, where they were hospitably welcomed, for Islamism meshed readily with traditional Saudi Wahhabism, also a fundamentalist version of Islam. Despite some setbacks, Islamism forged ahead and gained a footing in almost every Muslim country and beyond. The events of September 11, 2001, showed that a murderous and irrational cult committed to terrorism and obsessed with death had emerged on the world stage. As one of its spokesmen said, "If a faith, a belief, is not watered and irrigated by blood, it does not grow. It does not live. Principles are reinforced by sacrifices, suicide operations, and martyrdom for Allah. Faith is propagated by counting up deaths everyday, by adding up massacres and charnel-houses. It hardly matters if the person who has been sacrificed is no longer there. He has won."[1] The ruthless regime established by radical Islamists in Afghanistan and Sudan reveal their political and ideological goals. To impose their vision of Islam, the fundamentalist leaders of Sudan launched jihad against

Christian and animist blacks in the south. Some two million people perished in the conflict that was marked by numerous atrocities and the proliferation of slavery. A similar campaign of ethnic cleansing has emerged more recently in the Darfur region of Sudan. In Afghanistan the radical Islamists, who ruled in the 1990s until overthrown by the invasion of largely American forces in 2001, transformed the country into a repressive theocratic regime based on a narrow interpretation of Islamic law. In particular, the Taliban imposed tyrannical rules for women, permitting beatings by male relatives, prohibiting females from working, barring them from schools, and requiring them to wear a garment, the burka, that covered them from head to toe. Violators were subject to severe beatings, imprisonment, or execution.

No doubt Islamist totalitarianism has local, national, and indigenous religious roots, but equally important is what has been grafted onto those roots from the West, notably antisemitism. Classic antisemitic texts—the *Protocols of the Learned Elders of Zion,* Ford's *International Jew,* Hitler's *Mein Kampf,* August Rohling's *Talmud Jew* (which usually appears as *Treasures of the Talmud* by Yusuf Hana Nasrallah but is actually a translation of Rohling), and others—circulate widely in the Muslim world. Interpreted and applied in the light of Qur'anic and other Muslim texts, antisemitism is rendered, in Ronald Nettler's phrase, "Islamically persuasive."[2]

Space constraints prevent including documents by Muslim scholars and religious leaders who explicitly reject jihadist terrorism, urge adopting those Western institutions and traditions that would promote freedom and tolerance in the Muslim world, and do not share in the demonization of Jews. In any event, these writings are rare and some of their authors live under threat. One of the most compelling is the distinguished Tunisian historian of medieval North Africa and Muslim religious thinker, Mohamed Talbi, in his essay "Unavoidable Dialogue in a Pluralist World: A Personal Account," *Encounters,* 1, 1 (1995): 56–69; or "Religious Liberty: A Muslim Perspective," in *Religious Liberty and Human Rights in Nations and Religions,* ed. Leonard Swidler (Philadelphia: Ecumenical Press, 1986), 175–187. Critical evaluation is the theme of Wafa Sultan's interview in 2006 on Al-Jazeera (available at http://www.memritv.org/Transcript.asp?P1=1050), in which she says that violence is ultimately self-defeating, that the present clash is "a battle between modernity and barbarism which Islam will lose"; and Irshad Manji, *The Trouble with Islam: A Muslim's Call for Reform in Her Faith* (New York: St. Martin's Press, 2003). Suggestive analysis will be found in Tariq Ramadan, *Western Muslims and the Future of Islam* (New York: Oxford University Press, 2004); and Ibn Warraq, ed., *Leaving Islam: Apostates Speak Out* (Amherst, N.Y.: Prometheus Books, 2003). In many ways *The Arab Human Development Report* by Arab scholars published by the UN in 2002 (available at www.undp.org) is a remarkably frank piece of self-examination and self-criticism that lays bare Arab xenophobia, intolerance, backwardness, and poverty, among much else, but concludes with the characteristic non-sequitur that Israel is "one of the most pervasive obstacles to security and progress" and damages "nearly all aspects of human development and human security directly for millions and indirectly for others."

Sayyid Qutb

"Our Struggle with the Jews . . . the Jews . . . the Jews!!" 1950s

The Egyptian fundamentalist Sayyid Qutb, 1906–1966, had a traditional religious education but branched out to study literature, was drawn to socialism, and worked for the education ministry, which sent him to the United States in 1948 to study its educational policy; he was incensed by its support of the new state of Israel, its prejudices against Arabs and Islam, and its racism. He returned to Egypt in 1951 and joined the Muslim Brotherhood and directed its publications. Sentenced to fifteen years imprisonment, he was released after serving ten, re-arrested, tried, and executed after the Muslim Brotherhood's abortive attempt to assassinate President Nasser. A prolific author, many of whose works were written in prison, Qutb is the fountainhead of radical Islam, now designated Islamism; he exalted martyrdom, called for theocratic rule over state and society and culture, and excoriated the West for its "hideous schizophrenia," by which he meant that the spiritual and divine are radically separated from the secular and physical. The United States and the West, in Qutb's view, are immoral and "mechanical," the East is "spiritual."

The "Struggle" first appeared in Saudi Arabia in 1970, apparently a compilation selected and redacted by Rukabi, a Saudi who attributed it to Qutb; while no original essay or chapter is traceable to Qutb, many sentences and paragraphs in the 1970 article appear verbatim in Qutb's writings as do its ideas. It argues that the "struggle" between Muslims and Jews has roots in the Qur'an and is sanctioned by Muhammad. Qutb conforms to a long tradition of Muslim commentators in interpreting selectively passages in the Qur'an concerning Jews—utilizing those passages that disparage Jews as enemies of Islam and nullifying favorable references to Jews by ignoring or explaining them away. During "the war of 1400 years," according to Qutb, the Jewish "menace" was contained and averted because as *dhimmis* (protected minority), Jews were repressed and humiliated; it was only with the incursions in the Middle East of the imperialist powers, the decline of the Ottoman Empire and abolition by Kemal Attatürk of the Caliphate in 1924, for which Qutb blames the Jews, and "traitorous" attempts to westernize or modernize Islam and Muslim states and societies that the Jews broke their Muslim-imposed restraints and inflicted harm and defeats on the Muslims, culminating in Israel reborn in 1948. He rails against Zionism and regards Marxism, another threat to Islam, as a Jewish invention. Qutb attributes to the Jews the satanic powers, infinite resources, and relentless persistence that one finds in the *Protocols,* a document with which he was closely familiar (he cites it as the Jews' master plan for world domination in his extensive commentary on the story of the biblical Joseph)[3] and paraphrases but does not quote it directly. Those who murdered President Anwar El-Sadat in Egypt appear to have been Qutb's disciples; they violated the Qur'an's prohibition of Muslims killing Muslims, asserting Qutb's principle (*takfir*) that "apostates" must be killed, and that Sadat was an "apostate" because he made peace with Israel. Those who brought Ruholloh Khomenei to power in Iran are also reported to have been disciples of Qutb; his younger brother Muhammad was a teacher of Osama bin Laden in Saudi Arabia.

What makes antisemitism so compelling in its appeal to the Arab-Muslim world is its native tradition of Judaeophobia rooted in the Qur'an on to which has been grafted Christian, European, and Nazi antisemitism. Thus antisemitism that is foreign and imported becomes acceptable to the Muslim in the street or in the basement making bombs as well as to the imam in the mosque or *madrassa* (religious school). Since the Six Day War of 1967 antisemitism has turned more radical, even genocidal. While Qutb indulged in what has been called "intellectual terrorism," he did not call for physical terrorism against Jews. The following part of Qutb's work was translated for this volume by Shlomo Daskal, a graduate student in the Department of Arab Language and Literature, the Hebrew University of Jerusalem. Asterisks and punctuation appear as in the Arabic text.

The Muslim nation [or community] (*Umma*) still suffers from the schemes and trickery of the Jews—the same trickery and schemes that [the *Umma's*] forefathers suffered from. It is unfortunate that the Muslim *Umma* does not take advantage of the Qur'an's guidance and its divine path of righteousness. . . .

The Muslim *Umma* does not take advantage of what its forefathers knew. For when they subdued the cunning and trickery of the Jews in [the city of] *al-Madina*, religion [Islam] sprang forth and the Muslim community was born [in the seventh century].

The Jews . . . with their wickedness and trickery . . . are still misleading the *Umma* away from its religion and turning it away from its Qur'an. . . . Whoever distracts the *Umma* from its religion and its Qur'an is no more than an agent of the Jews, whether he knows it or not, whether he does so [intentionally] or not. The Jews will stay in safety [only] so long as they divert the *Umma* away from the only single truth from which it draws its existence, power, and victory: the truth of the Islamic creed, the religious way of action, and the religious law (*Sharia*). This is the way and these are the milestones.

*   *   *

. . . The *Umma's* enemies will achieve nothing against it so long as the *Umma* holds firmly to the bond of the faith, leans on its [the faith's] base, walks according to its way, carries its flag, and takes pride alone in its lineage.

From here we can see that the worst enemy of the *Umma* is the one who distracts it from its Islamic creed and diverts the *Umma* away from the path of Allah and His way and misleads the *Umma* about the true character of its enemies and the true nature of their long term objects.

The struggle between the Muslim *Umma* and its enemies is first of all the struggle of this Islamic creed. Even when the *Umma's* enemies wanted to conquer it socio-economically through land, products, economy, and raw materials, they first tried to overcome the Islamic creed. For they knew from their long experience that they will achieve none of their goals, as long as the Muslim *Umma* maintains its Islamic creed, stays committed to its ways, and remains on guard against the cunning of its enemies. . . . Consequently, these enemies and their agents expend enormous amounts of energy to divert the *Umma* from the real struggle, in order to achieve the colonization and exploitation that they desire. [While they continue to mislead the *Umma*, they] are safe from the firmness of this Islamic creed. . . .

[The Qur'an] serves to warn of the conspirators' cunning and to expose the enemies' hidden intentions, impure techniques, and dangerous aims, and [it reveals the enemies'] hatred of Islam and Muslims because of their exclusive possession of mighty grace. . . .

. . . [The Qur'an] also made it clear for the Muslim *Umma* that Allah is with [the *Umma*] and He is the King of Kingship, the [one who] elevates and humbles, He alone with no copartner. He will make the infidel Jews suffer and punish them with exemplary punishment, the same way he did to the polytheists before.

* * *

And our *Umma* suffered from the deceptions and schemes of the Jews.

"Why do you confound the truth with falsehood and knowingly conceal the truth?" [Qur'an 3:71]. The Muslims must realize this characteristic of the [Jews] . . . their characteristic of fraud and scheming . . . and they must be aware of it.

And the thing that Allah . . . warns of among the acts of the People of the Book [Jews and Christians] at that time, is that they followed the [same evil] course from that time until now . . . this is their way throughout history.

The Jews started it . . . the [Christian] Crusaders followed in their footsteps. . . .

They schemed and corrupted Islamic history, its traditions and people, and corrupted the prophetic tradition [the *hadiths*, the corpus of theological and legal traditions originated by the first generation of Muslims and handed down orally for a century until they were committed to writing] until Allah had to send His people who examined and rectified it. . . .

They schemed against and corrupted Qur'anic exegesis.

And this is a seriously menacing plot.

They placed people and leaders [in the Muslim world] to conspire against the *Umma*.. . . .

* * *

The campaign by the Jews of [spreading] doubts in the Muslim *Umma* continues. . . .

This is the evil way of trickery. . . .

This deception still occurs today in various forms, which remain appropriate to the evaluation of environments and people in every generation. . . .

These forces in the Islamic world have a tremendous army of [Western-educated] cooperators who present themselves as teachers, philosophers, professors, and researchers . . . and sometimes writers, poets, artists and journalists . . . all of whom carry Muslim names because they are descendants of Muslims!! Some of them descend from Muslim "scholars"!!

This army of "scholarly authorities" is determined to convulse the creed in the souls [of Muslim believers] using various techniques: by research, science, culture, art, and journalism. . . . To undermine it to its foundations. . . . They weaken the creed and the Islamic law equally. . . . They distort the whole history [of Islam] and they corrupt it the way they corrupt texts!!

Thereby they are Muslims!! . . "They fulfill the ancient task of the Jews" that has not changed! . . .

The agents of Zionism are like this today. . . . They understand each other [in this matter] of . . . the ruination of this Islamic creed at the first good opportunity that may not return. . . . This understanding may not appear openly in an agreement or meeting, but this is the understanding one [Zionist] agent has with another concerning the basic task. . . .

*   *   *

The Qur'an spoke much about the Jews and interpreted their evil mentalities. It is not a coincidence that the Qur'an singled out the Jews; never before did a nation show such cruelty, ingratitude, and denial of righteous providence as the Israelites. For they have killed, slaughtered, and expelled their Prophets . . . which is the most repulsive thing that a nation can inflict on the honest preachers of truth. They committed the most horrible apostasy, they [showed sinful] hostility and repulsive disobedience. In each aspect [mentioned above] they [the Jews] performed abominable acts!!

We expect that creatures who kill prophets, slaughter them, and expel them, will indulge in the spilling of human blood and [will] exploit any filthy expedient, which will be consistent with their malice and viciousness.

*   *   *

The holy Qur'an expresses astonishment at the amazing ways of the Jews. . . .

. . . [Jewish egotism] prevents them from feeling themselves to be part of the grand human connection that binds the whole of humanity.

That is how the Jews lived . . . apart in segregation.

They feel they are a separate branch of the tree of life, and they are just waiting for humanity to suffer disaster, harboring animosity for people who suffer their malice, hatred, and rancor. They [the Jews] give humanity the taste of these hateful dissensions, which instigate troubles and hateful contentions between peoples. They ignite wars in order to draw spoils from them, showing again their inextinguishable hatred. They inflict destruction upon people and [as a consequence] people impose destruction upon them. . . .

The black hatred of the Jews for the Messenger of Allah, for the Qur'an, and for Islam made them prefer polytheism to Islam . . . and they [the Jews] are People of the Book.

Today they [the Jews] prefer communism to this religion [Islam]; it is another corrupting connection. They bring forth these apostate and heretical ideas to attack Islam! . . .

*   *   *

Allah almighty was right saying: "You will surely find the worst enemies of the Muslim to be the Jews and the idolaters. . . ." [Qur'an 5:82.] . . .

When a person in this sacred assignment [interpreting the Qur'anic passage 5:82] gathers information about the historical facts since the birth of Islam until today, he cannot hesitate but conclude that the enmity of the Jews towards the believers was always more vehement and cruel, and that it lasted longer than the enmity of the idolaters.

The Jews have faced Islam with enmity from the first minute when an Islamic state was established in *al-Madina*. They conspired against the Muslim *Umma* since the first day it became a nation. The Qur'an contains conformations and signs concerning this [Jewish] animosity and conspiracy, which alone are enough to demonstrate the tenacious war that the Jews launched against Islam and the Messenger of Allah . . . and against the Muslim *Umma* in its long history. [It is a war] that did not pause for a single moment over nearly 14 centuries and to this moment it blazes hotly over the whole world.

They [the Jews] treasured in their hearts their animosity towards Islam and Muslims from that day on which Allah united the [tribes] of *Aws* and *Hazraj* under Islam, and the Jews could not join them [but chose to oppose Islam]. Since the day on which the leadership of the Muslim *Umma* was established and Muhammad . . . assumed power over it, the opportunity to rule did not return to the Jews.

They [the Jews] used all the weapons and techniques that the Jewish genius for deception produced and employed since the Babylonian captivity, their slavery in Egypt . . . and humiliation under the Roman Empire. . . . Although Islam was generous to them . . . after religious communities and groups throughout history had subjected them . . . from the first day their reaction to Islam's [tolerant policy] was the most monstrous wiliness and nefarious deceitfulness.

They had incited all the idolatrous powers of the Arabian peninsula against Islam and the Muslims, and they set out to gather the scattered tribes to fight the Muslim community: "and they say to those who disbelieved [Islam]: 'These are more rightly guided than those who believe'" [Qur'an 4:51].

When Islam defeated them with the power of righteousness . . . in the days when the peoples became true Muslims . . . they [the Jews] went about harming it [Islam] by inserting falsities in its books . . . only the book of Allah [the Qur'an] which He . . . guaranteed and kept safe, was not damaged by this conspiracy. [The Jews] conspired against Islam by machinations in the ranks of the Muslims . . . and caused dissensions by using recently converted Muslims and those who have no understanding [of Islam] from among the Muslims of the whole world . . . conspiring against it by inciting its opponents against it everywhere . . . eventually in the most recent era they [the Jews] lead the struggle with Islam on every inch of the globe . . . and they are the ones who use the Crusaders [meaning Christians] and Paganism [meaning communism] in this total war . . . and they [the Jews] are the ones who determine the circumstances and create the "heroes" who are disguised by Muslim names . . . launching a Zionist crusade against the very foundations of this religion!![4]

Allah almighty was right in saying: "You will surely find the worst enemies of the Muslim to be the Jews and the idolaters. . . ." [Qur'an 5:82.]

The one who incited the parties against the rising Muslim empire in *al-Madina* and gathered up the Jews of *Banu Quraiza* and others with the *Quraish* [tribe] from Mecca and other tribes in the peninsula . . . [was] a Jew.

The one who incited the common people, gathered the gangs, and spread the rumors in the sectarian discord that led [in 656] to Caliph Uthman's murder . . . and the numerous catastrophes that proceeded from it . . . [was] a Jew.

The one who led the campaign of . . . falsehoods about the sayings of the Messenger of Allah . . . and in the biographical accounts [*hadiths*] about him . . . [was] a Jew.

Furthermore, the one behind the . . . total abolition of the [Ottoman] Caliphate by the "hero" [Mustapha Kemal] Atatürk, [the secularist, Westernizing president of the Republic of Turkey 1920-1938, was, Qutb claims falsely] a Jew.

From every corner of the world Jews stand behind the war declared against the pioneers of the Islamic revival!!

Moreover, behind apostasy and atheistic materialism [stands] "a Jew"; behind bestial sexual inclination [stands] a Jew; behind the destruction of the family and the wreckage of the sacred bonds of society . . . [stands] a Jew. . . .

The war that the Jews launched against Islam was longer, more widespread and brutal than the war that the idolaters and the pagans launched against Islam, today as in the past. For the struggle with the Arab idolaters, as a whole, did not last more than 20 years. This also happened in the struggle with the Persians in the first era [of Islam]. . . . As for the modern era, the ferocity of the struggle between Indian idolatry [Hinduism] and Islam [is] striking, but it does not attain the ferocity of world Zionism, of which Marxism is considered to be [one of its] spin-offs.

* * *

The story of the Israelites, which the Qur'an detailed, contains multifaceted lessons.

One of the phases of these lessons is that the Israelites are the first who countered the Islamic call with malice, cunning, and war in *al-Madina* and in the whole Arab peninsula. . . . They fought the Muslim community since the first day, they are the ones who embraced the hypocrisy and hypocrites in *al-Madina* and assisted them in their ways of deception. [The fight was] both against the Islamic creed and against the Muslims. . . . They are the ones who provoked the idolaters, arranged and plotted with them against the Muslim community. . . . They are the ones who engaged in the war of rumors, conspiracy, and cunning among the Muslims. They are also the ones who spread doubts, uncertainty, and forgeries concerning the articles of the creed and the [Muslim] leaders. . . . They did it all without exposing their true intentions in the war declared [against Islam]. It is necessary to expose them before the Muslim community in order that all shall know who are its enemies; what is their nature; what is their history; what are their techniques and what is the true [nature of the] struggle that they wage against [the *Umma*].

Allah . . . knew they [the Jews] are the ones who will be the enemies of this nation, in its whole history, the same as they were the enemies of Allah's guidance in their past. Therefore He presented to the *Umma* their [the Jews'] whole story, unmasked . . . and all their techniques revealed.

. . . [T]he Israelites' . . . history before [the birth] of Islam extended [over] a long period. . . . Deviations occurred in their religious doctrines and they repeatedly violated their covenant with Allah. . . . It was necessary for the Muslim *Umma* . . . to be acquainted with the history of the [Jewish] people. . . . And . . . to know their treacherous double-dealing and its effects, which are reflected in the life and morals of the Israelites. . . . [The *Umma*] will be aware . . . of the treacherous ways [of the Jews], their Satanic behavior, and the indications of [theological] deviations down the centuries. . . .

*   *   *

Accordingly, the struggle between Islam and the Jews continues and it will continue as it has because the Jews will be satisfied only with the destruction of the Muslim religion.

After Islam defeated them, they [the Jews] fought this religion using plots, schemes, and through their [the Jews'] agents operating in the darkness.

Today the struggle has grown in scale, intensity, and explicitness, after they [the Jews] came from everywhere and declared that they established the state of Israel. . . .

*   *   *

The Israelites will fight the Muslims over the inheritance of al-Aqsa mosque [on Jerusalem's Temple Mount]. And the struggle will go on. . . .

At first they [the Jews] will arrive in the sacred land. They will have power and might. They will corrupt it, so Allah will send against them His servants of great might, and of great strength and force. . . .

The story of corruption will recur. . . . And [the story of] humiliation and expulsion will recur.

Whenever the Israelites return to corrupt the land, the repayment is ready and the customary procedure will be: "If you return (*to do evil*), we shall return (*to inflict punishment*)."

Allah imposed on them the Muslims who expelled them from the whole Arabian peninsula. . . . He imposed on them other [harsh] servants, until in the modern era He imposed on them Hitler, but they returned to do evil in the form of [the state of] Israel, which gave the Arabs, the owners of the land, the taste of disaster. Allah will impose on them one of the worst punishments, according to His definite promise: "If you return (*to do evil*) we shall return (*to impose punishment*)" [Qur'an 17: 8], and [will do so] according to His customary course of action, which will not differ [from the past]; tomorrow [the day of reckoning] is close.[5]

Arab Theologians on Jews and Israel

"Their evil nature is transmitted by their repugnant culture," 1968

A conference in the autumn of 1968 sponsored by the Al-Azar Academy of Islamic Research was a month-long chorus of hatred and vituperation, its animosity reflecting the decisive Arab defeat by Israel in the June War of 1967. The academy, founded in 1961, was attached to the venerable University of Cairo. The participants, eminent imams, professors, physicians, muftis, and sheiks, came from almost every Arab state and from several African and Asian lands. These leading intellectuals and theologians assembled with the purpose of elucidating Islam's doctrines and teachings on the Jews and Judaism, Israel and Zionism.

The leitmotifs that emerged over and over will be recognizable to anyone familiar with European antisemitism in its lethal guise. The Jews are "enemies of God," the "sworn enemies of humanity" (62), indeed, are the "dogs of humanity" (65). By nature and culture, and inescapably, the Jews are an evil, criminal people, have always been so and will always be so, for nothing can induce them to become a normal, moral, or civilized people. It is the Hebrew Bible and the Talmud that corrupt the Jews, because they themselves corrupted scripture by forgeries counterfeiting and falsifying the divine message. Moreover, the Jews, "a people of liars and slanderers," were "cunning in inserting narratives that blemish Islamic texts," infecting those works of exegesis and commentary with superstitions and forgeries that ignited heresies and sedition among the Muslims (58). Appropriating Christian antisemitism to underscore Jewish evil, the story of Jesus, "the last of a series of the Israelitic Prophets," is told. "They killed their Prophet"; therefore, God doomed them to eternal humiliation, taking away the kingship, dispersing them, compelling them to pay tribute to foreign rulers, and inflicting degradation and poverty on them to the end of time (70). In the same vein, "among the foremost friends of Satan in our present age are the Jews," who "fight truth and justice and try to impede the struggle against evil and aggression. . . . fighting in the path of Satan. Allah commands the Muslims to fight the friends of Satan wherever they are found" (95). With equal conviction, the conference participants denied the Holocaust. The Jews, we are also told, are a mongrel people—"a gang of adventurers from diverse parts of the globe" (54)—who cannot become a people or nation, cannot constitute a nationality. Their evil nature is transmitted by their repugnant culture and infects all who come into contact with them or are converted to Judaism. From the dawn of history their evil nature and evil culture resulted in evil behavior, which has brought them the hatred of mankind and the persecution they deserve. In 1948 Israel was established through aggression, the culmination of Jewish depravity—"They fight a dishonest war without using known conventional weapons" (95)—since the seventh century. The "very perilous cancer" of Zionism must be cut out by jihad so as to "chase it [Israel] and throw it into the sea" (66, 54). Islam is repeatedly asserted to be superior to all other religions. The entire world must be brought to Islam, by war or persuasion, because "We believe, as commanded by Allah, that we are a nation elected above all nations" (89). Once a people or land has become Muslim and enters "the abode of Islam," it must remain there or be restored by jihad, and not allowed to relapse to "the abode of war." The proper status for Jews is *dhimmis,* the legal-socio-economic category to which they were relegated for centuries under Muslim rule: oppressed, humiliated, segregated, impoverished, inferior, barely tolerated, and subject to occasional pogroms. (The Ottoman Empire was a partial exception to this generalization: in 1992 Jews marked the quincentennial of the expulsion from Spain and celebrated the refuge—though marred occasionally—they continue to enjoy under Turkish rule.) Throughout the proceedings the Jews are referred to as worshippers of money, grasping materialists, baneful usurers who employ their criminally gotten wealth to conspire at the destruction of Islam, now as in the time of Muhammad.

The logical inference of the conference's ideas and claims is the liquidation of Israel and genocide of the Jews. As the editor of the conference's transactions, D. F. Green, indicates, "If the evil of the Jews is immutable and permanent, transcending time and circumstances, and impervious to all hopes of reform, there is only one way to cleanse the world of them . . . by their complete annihilation" (9). The conferees fall into line as Qutb's heirs and disciples (for example, both parties discount passages in the Qur'an that are favorable to Jews, and treat the conflict in Medina with Muhammad and the conspiratorial penchants of seventh-century Jews as cosmic and eternal, broadcasting with state sanction and over a much wider area than Qutb could, a destructive, totalitarian, fundamentalist version of Islam–Islamism). The excerpts below were compiled from speeches given at the conference and published as part of its transactions.

[This] conference is an Arab, Islamic, and patriotic necessity in view of the present circumstances in which the Arabs and Muslims face the most serious difficulties. . . . [No] Muslim or Arab [is absolved] from *Jihad,* which has now become a duty incumbent upon the Arabs and Muslims to liberate the land . . . from the hands of Zionism . . . the enemy of man, of truth, of justice, and the enemy of Allah.

. . . May your decisive word rise to the occasion and enlighten the Arab and Muslim world, so that it may be a battle-cry, urging millions of Muslims and Arabs on to the field of *Jihad* which will lead us to the place that once was ours.

Evil, wickedness, breach of vows, and money-worship are inherent qualities in them [the Jews]. Many a time were they punished for their evil, but they never repented or gave up their sinfulness. They have usurped Palestine from its rightful owners, doing evil, shedding blood, ripping up pregnant women, blowing up villages, and disregarding and defying world opinion.

[F]rom a survey of the Old Testament, which is a Jewish historical document full of contradictions. . . . we learn . . . that the Jews' wicked nature and inherent sinfulness account for the disasters, the afflictions, and persecutions that befell them throughout their history. We learn also that the Jews never change. Their nature, habits, and customs have remained unchanged since the dawn of their history. Modern civilization has only increased their hypocrisy, power, wealth, and their penetration into the social life of nations from behind the scenes. . . .

From those studies and comparisons I have come to this decisive conclusion that worldly avarice, obstinate contention, and cruelty are deeply ingrained in the innermost being of the Jews, who try to achieve their individual and social ambitions by fair means or foul. They are so obstinate as to reject even the teachings of Allah's prophets and apostles, so cruel as to exact severe retribution for an injury, so aggressive as to flout all positive and religious laws and human feelings. With them, the end justifies the means, for arrogance and evil doing are inherent qualities of their nature. . . .

. . . [I]t behooves us to refer to the distortion of the Jewish creed that filled the life of Jews with perfidy and evil.

From the very beginning Jews declared their hostility to Islam and even to all the other religions, and have not ceased to do so ever since.

Islamic tolerance is in complete contrast to Jewish intolerance and cruelty.

. . . I have thoroughly scrutinized the nature of the Jews. They are avaricious, ruthless, cruel, hypocritical, and revengeful. These traits govern their lives. They never change nor are they inclined to change.

They always try to seize any opportunity to take revenge on Islam and Muslims. . . .

The Jews harmed the Muslims economically [in Muhammad's time], because they had possessed most of the wealth in Medina and thus controlled the economic position. They used to adopt the same policy at all times. They dealt with loans, usury, and monopolised foods. They are characterized by avarice and many other vices, which arose from selfishness, love of worldly life, and envy. The Jews colluded with every hostile movement against the Islamic Call [to conversion] and the Muslims. . . .

It is deduced and inspired from the verses [in the Qur'an] that the Jews did not say the truth and they coated what was right with what was wrong. The Jews were also stubborn in telling lies and contradicting the truth. They preferred the pleasures of the world. They enjoined the good although they were not good people. They deceived the people. They did not cooperate with others. They put their heads together and secretly agreed among themselves to deceive the people, and to be hypocrites. The Jews did not help others or teach them. They told lies about Allah and let people suspect their religion. They broke their promises and practised malice and harmful activities against the people. They misled them. They resorted to foul means to usurp people and embezzle their money. The Jews stirred up sedition and scattered the seeds of corruption among the people. They were not good neighbours to the Arabs and they did not co-exist with the Arabs. They rejoiced when others were molested or suffered from catastrophes. The Jews were notorious for covetousness, avarice, and bad manners. They were not ashamed of embracing polytheism or performing the rites of paganism. They sometimes praised the idols and were in collusion with idolaters against monotheists. They displaced the words of Allah and disfigured the laws of Heaven and God's advice. They were hard-hearted and sinful, they committed unlawful and forbidden crimes. The Jews indulged deeply in the pleasures and lusts of the world neglecting the Laws of Allah. They sowed the seeds of suspicion and doubt among the people.

Thus the Jews rightfully deserved the wrath and the curse of Allah, recorded throughout many verses [of the Qur'an]. God branded them with the stigma of humiliation and meanness. Allah has sent among them those who torture them severely and will keep on persecuting them up to the Last Day. It has been prescribed for them to be thus dispersed upon the Earth. . . .

They [the Arabs and Muslims] formerly treated the Jews [as *dhimmis*] kindly and graciously. The Arabs and the Muslims housed and protected the Jews. They gave them their religious freedom inside their temples to perform their rites. They let the Jews trade and even live freely. . . . In [non-Muslim] countries the Jews were cruelly molested and they suffered from privation and atrocious oppression. However, the Jews treated the Arabs and the Muslims evilly, unjustly, treacherously, and mercilessly. The Jews followed the attitudes of their ancestors towards the Prophet and the Muslims. The Jews kept on sticking to their corrupt, demoralized instinct, and their vicious wicked prejudice. They committed their treacherous, oppressive atrocities in Palestine and they paid no heed to honour, manliness or truth.

The atrocities of the Jews are so terrific that they curdle one's blood. Their wicked intentions towards all the Arabs and their countries are quite evident. They attacked their countries several times and occupied some areas of the Arab world in addition to all parts of Palestine.

The Jews slaughtered, tortured, and expatriated the inhabitants from those occupied Arab areas. They ruined and damaged the land, possessions, and property of the Arabs. The Jews were backed by their friends all over the world. They instigated some states, especially the imperialist ones [Britain, France, and the United States], to stand against the Arabs. The imperialist states supported the Jews and secured their mastery and superiority.

It is essentially necessary to resort to seriousness in this respect from the religious and national viewpoints. The Arabs should take all measures and do their best to eradicate the state of the Jews in order to get rid of them, as the Prophet did before [by expelling the Jews from Arabia]. . . .

The Muslims and the Arabs cannot agree to [a compromise settlement for Palestine] even if the Jews leave some parts of what they have usurped and remain in the sections that the U. N. has allotted to the Jews. It is the homeland of the Muslims and the Arabs and thus the U. N. has no right at all to permit the Jews to possess any small part of it. None of the Muslims or Arabs has the right to accept that matter. Any pliancy or submission in this matter is treachery to Allah, His Apostle, and the Muslims.

It is incumbent on the Muslims to strain every nerve and make all efforts in order to be well equipped by all means to fight the Jews. The Muslims should corner the Jews without feeling exhausted or tired as Allah enjoins upon them. The Muslims should spare no effort to exterminate their state and deliver every place of the Muslims' homeland from the Jews' desecration and keep it under the control of the Islamic authorities as it was. Any slight indifference to this matter is indeed a shameful sin against religion.

[Many people] have been plagued by the Jews as individuals or as groups. For the Jews are like evil which has the same effect whether it were big or small, or like germs of a malignant disease where only one germ is sufficient to eliminate an entire nation. . . .

We are fortunate enough to have an available document that tells the truth about the Jews, and reveals their nature, life, and the inherent poison they carry as well as the remedy for such poison. This document is represented in the Holy Qur'an, which provides the real description of the Jews and constitutes the microscope through which we can see the pests and poisons that reside in their minds and hearts.

Verses [in the Qur'an] were subjects of controversy [because they spoke positively of the Jews]. Taken literally out of their context with other verses that were expressive of God's wrath against the Jews, such controversial verses might provide an argument for some people who say that if God had cursed the Jews in some verses, He however glorified them in other verses, and conferred His blessings on them. The [seeming] favours of God on the Children of Israel and the revelations which He made to them were therefore a mere introduction to this hardship that God incurred on them. These favours only . . . constituted reasons leading to their expulsion by God from the community of human beings, and rendering them strangers in the society of men. The many messengers which God sent the Jews stand as a testimony that they were of a different nature than human nature, and that they were carriers of diseases and pests. Therefore, God sent them numerous messengers to try and treat such diseases and to alleviate the effect of such pests which could spread to corrupt the entire world. . . .

Such commands turned the life of the Jews into a devastating danger and an obnoxious evil, both to themselves and to those people who have been unfortunate enough to be their neighbours. According to those "heavenly" commands, the Jews are required to stir up war with their neighbours once they have the opportunity to do so. Again they are required to eliminate and uproot the neighbouring peoples, so that no man or animal would exist therein. Such action would, in the opinion of the Jews, bring them security. It is [only] amidst the totally waste lands and wilderness that they can live in peace.

Such has been the tradition of the Jews with their neighbours throughout history. Time could not change those rules since the Jews themselves have not changed and so long as their false Torah from which they derived their teaching also existed. . . .

But Jews could never give up their love for money. When given the choice between God and money, they chose money because it was the essence of their life and earthly pleasure. . . . You cannot serve God and money! Jews did not like this talk. They "heard all this and loved money and insulted him [Christ]." Thus the Jews called for the crucifixion of Christ, and events followed.

[The idea of the Holocaust of European Jewry] cannot stand the test of logic and established facts. The various forms of persecution to which the Jews were exposed in some countries of Eastern Europe and in Nazist Germany were due to secret movements led by Jewish magnates against the established authorities and system of government; to their domination, through financial influence and crafty methods, of the social classes in the countries where they lived; and to their adherence to religious racialism. . . .

Curiously enough, the Jews who claim to be the victims of Nazist atrocities have exceeded the Nazis in their massacres and brutal acts perpetrated against the Arabs of Palestine. On the ruins of Hitlerian Nazism, the Jews have established a Zionist Nazism more horrible and monstrous, and more disregardful of human rights. . . .[6]

Egyptian Soldiers' Handbook

Our Faith—Our Way to Victory, *1973*

Excerpts follow from *Our Faith—Our Way to Victory,* the soldiers' handbook issued to the Egyptian armed forces shortly before the Yom Kippur War of October 1973.

The Jews have overstepped their bounds in injustice and conceit. And we sons of Egypt have determined to set them back on their heels, and to pry round their positions, killing and destroying, so as to wash away the shame of the 1967 defeat and to restore our honour and pride. Kill them wherever you find them [paraphrasing the Qur'an 2:191, 4:91], and take heed that they do not deceive you, for they are a treacherous people. They may feign surrender in order to gain power over you, and kill you vilely. Kill them and let not compassion or mercy for them seize you! . . . Avenge yourselves and the souls of the sons of Egypt! We must enter the battle with the motto, 'Victory or Martyrdom.' If this be our motto, victory is at our heels, by Allah's grace.[7]

Covenant of the Islamic Resistance Movement (Hamas)

"Their plan is the Protocols of the Elders of Zion,*" April 18, 1988*

The Islamic Resistance Movement, known as Hamas, initially gained ground partly from Israeli tolerance of it as a counterweight to the secular, leftist Palestine Liberation Organization led by Yasser Arafat, which had links to the Soviet Union from which it received material and diplomatic support. Radical Islamists organized Hamas as the fighting branch of the Muslim Brotherhood; it soon began to plant bombs that killed many people randomly and indiscriminately, often Jews and Palestinians being victims together. Hamas recruits children of both sexes to commit numerous homicide bombings and suicide terror, an obvious violation of normative Islam. Kindergartens and charitable institutions display mottoes like, "The children of today are the holy martyrs of tomorrow," and Palestinian parents tell reporters how proud they are that their children are holy martyrs or that they hope their children will die as martyrs for the cause; that is, that they will kill and maim Israeli men, women, and children, deliberately targeting popular restaurants, shopping areas, and buses. As an Islamist organization, Hamas calls for the destruction of the Jewish state through jihad. Employing themes from the *Protocols of the Learned Elders of Zion* and many other European and Christian antisemitic texts, Hamas' covenant, excerpted below, designates Jews as a conspiratorial people responsible for the French Revolution, communism, the two world wars, and many more calamities. Central to Hamas' perception of the Jew is the image of the Shylockian money-wizard and fiendish exploiter. It exhibits all the characteristics of the international Islamist movement. In addition to its antisemitism, Hamas is anti-Western, anti-liberal, and totalitarian in its claims to authority and power, use of terror, commitment to any sacrifice of blood and treasure to attain its ideological goal to the point of a cult of death and destruction. Islamic Jihad is a smaller group sharing essentially the same outlook, the same aims, and the same methods; their inroads in Palestinian society indicate a progressive Islamization of the Palestinian question. Hamas' "assertions lack any continuity with traditional Islamic thought," writes Andrea Nüsse, and so it turns for justification to radicals like Sayyid Qutb and the extreme forms of European, Christian, Nazi Judaeophobia.[8] The following excerpts from Hamas' covenant reveal the organization's descent into the murky world of antisemitic myths.

Our enemies [the Jews] have planned from time immemorial in order to reach the position they've obtained now. They strive to collect enormous material riches to be used in the realization of their dreams. With money, they've gained control of the international media beginning with news agencies, newspapers and publishing houses, broadcasting stations . . . with their money they have detonated revolutions in different parts of the world to obtain their interests and reap their fruits. They were behind the French Revolution and the Communist Revolution and were responsible for most of the revolutions we've heard about elsewhere. With their money, they've created secret organizations which spread throughout the world in order to destroy societies, and to achieve the Zionist interest such as the Free Masons, the Rotary and the Lions Club. All these are destructive espionage organizations. With their money, they've been able to take control over the imperialist countries and spread corruption there. The same goes for international and local wars. They were behind World War I in order to destroy the Islamic Caliphate (Turkey) and make material profit. Then they obtained the Balfour Declaration [of November 2,

1917, by which the British government committed itself to facilitate the restoration of a Jewish homeland in Palestine] and established the League of Nations in order to rule the world through this organization.

They were also behind World War II where they made enormous profits from speculation in war material; paved the way for the creation of their state and inspired the establishment of the United Nations and Security Council to replace the League of Nations in order to rule the world through them. There is no war anywhere in which their fingers do not play. . . . The Imperialist powers in the capitalist West and the Communist East support the enemy with everything they can. And they switch roles. . . . In the day that Islam will appear, the powers of heresy will unite to confront it because the nation of heresy is one. . . . [Article 22.]

World Zionism and the imperialist powers are trying through wise movement and careful planning to get Arab countries one-by-one out of the circle of struggle with Zionism so that finally they will face only one Palestinian people. . . . [T]oday it will be Palestine, but tomorrow it will be some other country since the Zionist plan has no limits. After Palestine, they aspire to the destruction of the area they reach, they will still aspire to further expansion. Their plan is the *Protocols of the Elders of Zion* and their present [conduct] testifies to the truth of what we say. [Article 32.][9]

Hassan Sweilem

"The Jewish Personality and the Israeli Actions," 2000

Antisemitic articles and books, including school texts, proliferate in the Arab world; these works employ traditional myths about Jews that originated in Europe. A good example of this is found in a two-part series published in December 2000 in a weekly sponsored by the Egyptian government. Written by Gen. (Res.) Hassan Sweilem, the series, entitled "The Jewish Personality and the Israeli Actions," is replete with utterly false history and antisemltic delusions. It accepts discredited canards at face value and makes use of crude forgeries. For example, the statement denouncing Jews that Sweilem attributes to George Washington was never said by him. Indeed, in his famous letter "To the Hebrew Congregation in Newport Rhode Island," President Washington declared that the United States will not tolerate bigotry or persecution. The passage attributed to President (!) Benjamin Franklin is another forgery that is much used in post-1945 Muslim writings and first appeared in 1935 in a Nazi publication, *Handbook on the Jewish Question,* compiled through many editions by Theodor Fritsch, a notorious antisemite (see page 114); Franklin never gave such a speech as "The Jewish Danger," nor espoused such sentiments as are here attributed to him. Excerpts from these articles follow.

Historians, race-studies professors [?] and sociologists agree that humanity, throughout its long history, has never known a race such as the Jewish race in which so many bad qualities—base and loathsome—have been gathered.

The Jews had a quality which distinguished them from others: whenever they gathered in a particular place and felt comfortable there, they turned the place into a den of evil, corruption, incitement to internal strife and the spreading of wars. The Jews took advantage of the lack of attention by the people and rulers to the plots and traps designed by the Jews.

Ancient History

When the peoples felt endangered by the Jews' plots and traps, they took revenge and punished them in different ways, like annihilation, expulsion, captivity, and exile. The situation came to a point where Diaspora became a characteristic of Jewish history to this very day. This can be clearly seen in ancient history from the punishments meted out to the Jews by the Babylonians, the Assyrians, the Ancient Egyptians, the Romans, the Greeks and the Persians since the 8th century BC, let alone what came to be known as "the Babylonian Exile," which lasted one hundred years.

The Middle Ages

In the Middle Ages this phenomenon reoccurred, when the Jews tried to control the Byzantine State, and in the year of 483, Caesar Justinianus committed many massacres of Jews throughout the Empire.

The Modern Age

The phenomenon reoccurred in Europe: the king of France expelled the Jews to England in 1253, when he discovered their dangerous plots against France. In England, the Jews built an immense financial empire that controlled the British economy, but when King Edward I understood the danger in this situation, he enacted "special laws" for the Jews in order to limit their influence. They rebelled against these rules and he had to expel them. In 1306 all European countries, without exception, followed suit. This came to be known as "The great exile of the Jews of Europe." In 1492, Spanish courts of Inquisition were established to try the Jews. When the Jews returned to Europe in the fifteenth century, they resumed their plots and attempts to take control of these countries' economies. In 1744, a decision was made to expel them once again. They gathered in the Baltic region—as for the Jews who remained in the European states, the local authorities gathered them into special ghettos to protect themselves from the Jews' bad conduct.

A reexamination of the Crusades reveals that the crusader-armies that advanced along the basin of the Rhine River, searched for Jewish communities and exterminated them (to become closer to God). When they entered Jerusalem on July 14, 1099, the first thing they did was to gather the Jews of Jerusalem in one of the churches and burn them. When the Muslims, headed by Omar Ibn Al-Khattab, conquered Jerusalem in 636, the Patriarch Sofronius asked only one thing from our master Ibn Al-Khattab: that no Jews remain in Jerusalem and that none enter the city. The Caliph Omar fulfilled this request, and it entered history as "The Pact of Omar."

US Jewry

The first American presidents warned against the danger of Jewish hegemony over American life. First and foremost was President George Washington who warned in 1788: "It is troubling that the [American] nation has not purified its land from these pests. The Jews are the enemies of America's well-being and the corrupters of its prosperity." Further, Washington writes about the Jews: "They operate against us in a way much more effective than the enemy's armies. They endanger our liberty and our interests one hundred times more than the enemy. It is most troubling that the states have not begun long ago to follow them, because they are a plague [threatening] society."

American President Benjamin Franklin said in his speech to the 1789 Constitutional Convention in Philadelphia: "A great danger threatens the United States—the Jewish danger. When the Jews settle down [in the United States], we will discover that they are weakening the determination of the people, shaking up the ethics of trade and establishing a government within a government. When they meet resistance, they will suffocate the nation economically."

Thus, Franklin pointed to the attempts by the Jewish moneylenders to subjugate the Bank of America to the Bank of England, that was directed by Meir Rothschild. Later, Franklin continued his warnings to members of the Convention: "If constitutional law does not deny the Jews the right to immigrate to the US, they will, in less than one hundred years, pour into the nation in immense numbers, like locusts. They will take control and destroy us. In less than 200 years, our sons will be made field-workers in order to provide food for the Jews, who will sit in their mansions and rub their hands with glee." Franklin recalled an important fact, that the Jews' morals and character cannot be changed: "Their mentality will continue to be different from ours even if they live among us for ten generations. A leopard cannot change its spots. They are a danger to this country, and they must be removed through this Constitutional Convention."

Colonialist Judaism

Many are the bad and loathsome traits in the Jewish personality. There is no difference between yesterday's few and those of today, or between the Jewish and the Israeli personality, as some claim. This is because Israel, as a state, is nothing but a receiving vessel for all of the Jews in the world—Zionism is the political and colonialist aspect of the Jewish faith. Therefore, an investigation of the traits of the Jewish personality, in order to defend ourselves from it, is a fundamental step in our war against it, in the defense of our existence, and for future generations.

Jewish Holocaust Lies

One of the characteristics that is deeply-rooted in the Jewish personality is manifested in the rule "lie, lie and lie again, until people believe you, and then you will believe it yourself." This characteristic is revealed in their lie regarding the Holocaust, which they claim was carried out by Nazi Germans during WWII against six million Jews. This is a huge lie which they managed to market around the world. Through this lie, they extorted most of the world's countries, even though many have proved that [the Holocaust] was not practically possible. Today, nobody in Europe may doubt the Holocaust or accuse the Jews of extortion, without *finding* himself *in* jail, according to the law that was imposed by the Zionist organizations.[10]

Fiamma Nirenstein

"Observations: How Suicide Bombers Are Made," 2001

By September 2001, the intifada, "Arafat's war," had run for a year and thoroughly disrupted the Oslo peace process in the Middle East; a UN-sponsored conference on racism in Durban, South Africa, had been turned by Arab states into an anti-Israel and antisemitic jamboree; and Muslim terrorists had hijacked commercial airliners that were used as suicide weapons to destroy the World Trade Center in New York City and part of the Pentagon in Washington, D.C. That year saw an upsurge of antisemitic propaganda, centering in the Middle East but echoed worldwide. Elie Wiesel, who was invited to participate in the Durban conference, withdrew on the grounds that it had been turned into a "circus of calumny . . . a meeting of hatred characterized by wickedness," which would "go down in history as a moral catastrophe." Wiesel continues,

> The fact that militant Palestinians hate Jews—that is known already. One need only hear the various Islamic leaders and read the books printed by the Palestinian Authority: They preach hatred and violence, not against Zionists but against Jews. Their slogan, naked and brutal and identical everywhere, was keenly felt and even heard in Durban: "Kill the Jews." What is painful is not that the Palestinians and the Arabs voiced their hatred, but the fact that so few delegates had the courage to combat them [or walk out as the US delegation did]. It is as if in a strange and frightening moment of collective catharsis, everyone removed their masks and revealed their true faces. By means of the disgraceful conference in Durban, history has given us, the Jews, a sign. And we had better learn how to decipher it.[11]

All the elements of the anti-Jewish myths dealt with in this book reappear in the propaganda and justifications that have been issued in the last few years, the most salient of which have been the conspiratorial motifs that derive from the *Protocols of the Learned Elders of Zion*. The most notorious terrorist leader, Osama bin Laden, for example, asserts in his recruiting videos that he is engaged in "the religious-cultural-historical struggle of Islam with the Judeo-Crusader conspiratorial alliance, which aims at defeating Islam and conquering its sacred lands." In the media, schools, and mosques, Arab states employ the libelous myth of ritual murder as propaganda in their struggle against Israel. In 1972 King Faisal of Saudi Arabia shamelessly asserted that "while I was in Paris on a visit, the police discovered five murdered children. Their blood had been drained, and it turned out that some Jews had murdered them in order to take their blood and mix it with the bread they eat on that day."[12] In *The Matza of Zion* (1983, second "more scientific" edition 1986), Mustafa Tlas, defense minister and deputy prime minister of Syria, who had been a doctoral candidate at the Sorbonne in Paris, propagated and embellished the libelous myth. Referring to the Damascus incident of 1840, Tlas wrote, "The investigators uncovered not just the objective facts of the crime but also the religious motive behind it. . . . [And so] from that moment on every mother was warning her child: 'Do not stray far from home. The Jew may come by and put you in his sack to kill you and suck your blood for the matza of Zion.'"[13] Vicious ritual murder cartoons are copied from *Der Stürmer* (see page 183) and nineteenth-century Russian sources. As with all ritual murder accusations, no convincing evidence is produced; indeed, none can be, for they are lies or fairy tales.

The following article, "Observations: How Suicide Bombers Are Made", shows how the Palestinian Authority has used historic antisemitism and how it is translated, as it has been for two millennia, into murderous violence against Jews. Fiamma Nirenstein is an Italian journalist who writes from Israel for the daily *La Stampa* and the weekly *Panorama;* she is the author of *Israel: Peace in War* (1996).

During his historic visit to Syria last May [2001], Pope John Paul II was unexpectedly upstaged by the country's young new president, Bashar al-Assad. Greeting the pontiff at the airport in Damascus, Assad used the occasion not to declare his own hopes for mutual understanding among the world's great faiths but—rather less in keeping with the spirit of the moment—to mount a vicious attack on the Jews. They have "tried," he inveighed in the presence of the Pope, "to kill the principles of all religions with the same mentality with which they betrayed Jesus Christ," and in "the same way they tried to betray and kill the prophet Muhammad."

So spectacular a venting of hate could hardly pass unnoted, and thus, for the duration of a news cycle, the usual fare of Middle East reporting—rock-throwers and settlers, bombings and retaliatory strikes, ceasefires and "confidence-building" measures—gave way to tongue-clucking over the charged words of the Syrian president. As *The New York Times* lamented, Assad had not only "marred" the Pope's visit but had reinforced his own "growing reputation for irresponsible leadership." So the coverage generally went, admonishing a new leader whose inexperience and immaturity had seemingly led him to embrace, as the *Times* put it, "bigotry."

Largely ignored amid all this was a far bigger story—a story not about a petty tyrant but about the poison that rose so readily to his lips. As few journalists either knew or thought it worthwhile to relate, such sentiments as Assad expressed are hardly uncommon in today's Arab world. Wherever one looks, from Cairo and Gaza to Damascus and Baghdad, from political and religious figures to writers and educators, from lawyers to pop stars, and in every organ of the media, the very people with whom the state of Israel is expected to live in peace have devoted themselves with ever greater ingenuity to slandering and demonizing the Jewish state, the Jewish people, and Judaism itself—and calling openly for their annihilation. Only by turning a determinedly blind eye to this river of hatred is it possible to be persuaded that, after all, "everybody" in the Middle East really wants the same thing.

The anti-Semitic propaganda that circulates in such abundance in the Arab world draws its energy in large part from the technique of the "big lie"— that is, the insistent assertion of outrageous falsehoods about Israel or the Jews, the more outrageous the better. The examples are truly numberless. In Egypt and Jordan, news sources have repeatedly warned that Israel has distributed drug-laced chewing gum and candy, intended (it is said) to kill children and make women sexually corrupt. When foot-and-mouth disease broke out recently among cattle in the Palestinian Authority (PA), the Israelis were quickly accused of intentionally spreading the illness (despite the immediate mobilization of Israeli veterinary groups to treat the animals).

Especially garish have been the fabrications directed at Israel's response to the now year-old *intifada*. Earlier this year, at the world economic forum in Davos, Switzerland, a thunderstruck audience heard Yasir Arafat himself declare that Israel was using depleted uranium and nerve gas against Palestinian civilians. Official PA television obligingly furnished "evidence" for this charge, broadcasting scenes of hapless victims racked by vomiting and convulsions. Another recent film clip from Palestinian television offered a "re-enactment" of an assault by the Israeli army on a Palestinian house, culminating in the staged rape and murder of a little girl in front of her horrified parents. As for Israeli victims of Arab terrorists, the PA's Voice of Palestine radio assured its listeners in April that Israel was lying about the assassination of a ten-month-old girl by a Palestinian sniper in Hebron; in fact, the commentator explained, the baby was retarded and had been smothered by her own mother.

The Arab press has also helped itself to the rich trove of classical European anti-Semitism. Outstanding in this regard has been *Al-Ahram*, Egypt's leading government-sponsored daily. One recent series related in great detail how Jews use the blood of Gentiles to make matzah for Passover. Not to be outdone, columnist Mustafa Mahmud informed his readers that, to understand the true intentions of the Jews, one must consult *The Protocols of the Elders of Zion*, in which the leaders of the international Jewish conspiracy acknowledge openly their "limitless ambitions, inexhaustible greed, merciless vengeance, and hatred beyond imagination. . . . Cunning," it allegedly declares, "is our approach, mystery is our way."

In a class of its own is the effort of Arab and Islamic spokesmen to distort or dismiss the record of Nazi genocide. Indeed, nowhere else in the world is Holocaust denial more warmly or widely espoused. A conference of "scholars" held in Amman in mid-May concluded that the scope of the Nazi war against the Jews had been greatly exaggerated, a claim enthusiastically parroted by the *Jordan Times*. On Palestinian television, Issam Sissalem of the Islamic University of Gaza recently asserted that, far from being extermination camps, Chelmo, Dachau, and Auschwitz were in fact mere "places of disinfection."

On April 13—observed in Israel as Holocaust Remembrance Day—the official Palestinian newspaper *Al-Hayat al-Jadida* featured a column by Hiri Manzour titled "The Fable of the Holocaust." Among his claims: that "the figure of 6 million Jews cremated in the Nazi Auschwitz camps is a lie," promulgated by Jews in order to carry out their "operation of international marketing." A few weeks later, at a well-attended pan-Islamic conference in Teheran, Iran's supreme leader, the Ayatollah Khamenei, used his opening remarks to make a similar point. "There is proof," he declared, "that the Zionists had close ties with the German Nazis, and exaggerated all the data regarding the killing of the Jews . . . as an expedient to attract the solidarity of public opinion and smooth the way for the occupation of Palestine and the justification of Zionist crimes."

Occasionally, to be sure, the same organs of anti-Semitic opinion that deny the Holocaust do find it necessary to affirm that it took place but only so that they can laud its perpetrators. A columnist in Egypt's government-sponsored *Al-Akhbar* thus expressed his "thanks to Hitler, of blessed memory, who on behalf of the Palestinians took revenge in advance on the most vile criminals on the face of the earth. Still, we do have a complaint against [Hitler], for his revenge on them was not enough."

Another variation on this theme is the now incessant comparison of Israel itself to Hitlerite Germany. In the eyes of *Al-Ahram*, "the atrocities committed by the Israeli army show . . . how those who complain about Nazi practices use the same methods against the Palestinians." For its sister Egyptian paper, *Al-Akhbar*, the ostensibly dovish Israeli foreign minister Shimon Peres is in actuality "a bird of prey, a master in the killing of the innocents," and a man responsible for deeds that "make Israel worse than the Nazis." In May, a columnist for Egypt's *Al-Arabi* wrote, "Zionism is not only another face of Nazism, but rather a double Nazism." Unsurprisingly, President Assad of Syria also favors such language, recently asserting that "Israel is racist, [Prime Minister] Sharon is racist, the Israelis are racist. They are more racist than the Nazis."

The effect of this relentless vilification is not difficult to discern. In the Arab world, where countervailing sources of information about Jews and the Jewish state are rare to non-existent, Israel has been transformed into little more than a diabolical abstraction, not a country at all but a malignant force embodying every possible negative attribute—aggressor, usurper, sinner, occupier, corrupter, infidel, murderer, barbarian. As for Israelis themselves, they are seen not as citizens, workers, students, or parents but as the uniformed foot soldiers of that same dark force. The uncomplicated sentiment produced by these caricatures is neatly captured by the latest hit song in Cairo, Damascus, and East Jerusalem. Its title: "I Hate Israel."

From such hatred it is but a short step to incitement and acts of violence. Arab schools teach not just that Israel is evil, but that extirpating this evil is the noblest of callings. As a text for Syrian tenth graders puts it, "The logic of justice obligates the application of the single verdict [on the Jews] from which there is no escape: namely, that their criminal intentions be turned against them and that they be *exterminated*" (emphasis added). In Gaza and the West

Bank, textbooks at every grade level praise the young man who elects to become a *shahid*, a martyr for the cause of Palestine and Islam.

The lessons hardly stop at the classroom door. Palestinian television openly urges children to sacrifice themselves. In one much-aired film clip, an image of twelve-year-old Mohammed al-Dura—the boy killed last September in an exchange of fire between Israeli soldiers and Palestinian gunmen—appears in front of a landscape of paradise, replete with fountains and flowers, beckoning his peers to follow.

In early June, just two weeks after the fatal collapse of a Jerusalem wedding hall, PA television broadcast a sermon by Sheikh Ibrahim Madhi praying that "this oppressive Knesset will [similarly] collapse over the heads of the Jews" and calling down blessings upon "whoever has put a belt of explosives on his body or on his son's and plunged into the midst of the Jews." Slogan-chanting mass demonstrations, with Israeli and American flags aflame and masked gunmen firing shots into the air, reinforce the message. One need look no further to understand how children grow up wanting to be suicide bombers—a pursuit that won a fresh wave of media acclaim after a bombing at a Tel Aviv discothèque took 21 Israeli lives and that according to a recent poll has the approval of over three-quarters of Palestinians. "This missile," wrote an ecstatic Palestinian columnist, meaning the bomber himself, "carried a soul striving for martyrdom, a heart that embraces Palestine, and a body that treads over all the Zionist invaders."

Virulent anti-Semitism is no less essential in maintaining the region's most militant and totalitarian-minded regimes. Such standing as Syria's Bashar Assad now enjoys in the wider Arab world derives in large part from his unceasing denunciations of Israel and the Jews. For his part, Iraq's Saddam Hussein has repeatedly made known his readiness to destroy the "criminal Zionist entity." Should his own efforts not suffice, he has even sought divine aid, ending his speech at the recent Arab summit with the pithy entreaty, "God damn the Jews."

As for "moderates" like King Abdullah of Jordan and President Mubarak of Egypt, offering wide latitude to anti-Semitic vituperation enables them to demonstrate their own populist *bona fides*, to show their sympathy with the Arab "street." Do they themselves endorse such views? Of course not, they hasten to declare, disingenuously suggesting that nothing can be done about it since under their regimes even government-owned newspapers and television stations possess the right to speak their mind.

That moderate Arab leaders have remained mum in the face of rising anti-Semitism may be all too understandable, considering their overall records as statesmen. The West's moral and political leaders should be another matter, but they are not. In the days after Assad's anti-Semitic diatribe in Damascus, one waited in vain for the Pope, the same Pope who has recognized the state of Israel and visited the Holocaust memorial in Jerusalem, to utter a word of protest. . . .

One source of the general silence may be a subtle form of racism, or what

George W. Bush in another context called "the soft bigotry of low expectations." The Arabs, it is implicitly suggested, are a backward people, not to be held to the civilized standards of the West. In this reading, rabid anti-Semitism is just another feature of Arab culture—the same ancient culture that is often also portrayed, with reason, as one of the world's most civilized and sophisticated.

Many Westerners who fastidiously ignore the Arabs' outrageous lies and insults about Jews also believe that the Arabs do, after all, have a legitimate grievance against Israel, however excessively they may at times express it. Once the substantive demands of the Palestinians or the Syrians are met, this line of thought goes, their hatred of Israel and the Jews will likewise subside, it being just a form of politics by other means. Throughout the Oslo years, the government of Israel itself seemed to share this attitude, systematically ignoring or explaining away the Arabs' unremitting verbal incitement.

But if we have learned nothing else from the latest *intifada*, it is that the Arab world's grievance against Israel has little to do with the minutiae of dividing up territory and political authority. It has to do instead with the entire Zionist project, with the very existence of a Jewish state in the Middle East. What Westerners (including some Israelis) dismiss as so much unfortunate rhetoric is an exact articulation of that grievance, whose goal is not to achieve but to prevent accommodation. For how can one accommodate a people who are nothing but murderers of children, instruments of world conspiracy, sworn enemies of religious and historical truth, and perfecters of Nazi brutality—a people who according to Islamic authorities must be driven out and killed, their body parts "spread all over the trees and electricity poles"? No, anti-Semitism in the Middle East is not just politics by other means; it is an end in itself.[14]

From Matzos to Purim Pastries:
A Saudi Variant of Ritual Murder

"Jews Use Teenagers' Blood for 'Purim' Pastries," 2002

Calumniation of Jews and Judaism goes on relentlessly in the Muslim world, characteristically in official publications and government newspapers and journals, nowhere more voluminously and venomously that in Saudi Arabia. The government both initiates through its own publishing apparatus and condones privately produced antisemitic propaganda of the most extreme and baseless kind, whether of Western-Christian origin or intrinsic to fundamentalist interpretation of the Qur'an. Its website is saturated with the same bizarre and outrageous assertions.

In an article published by the Saudi government daily *Al-Riyadh,* March 10, 2002, columnist Dr. Umayma Ahmad Al-Jalahma of King Faysal University in Al-Dammam wrote on the Jewish Holiday of Purim. Unsurprisingly, this Saudi variant on ritual murder is plagiarized from European sources, such as an obscure booklet of the early nineteenth century by a "Moldavian Jew," supposedly ex-rabbi, convert, and orthodox Christian monk, or Édouard Drumont, who spoke of "the Jew-boys with corkscrew curls from Galicia, who, met together for some ritual murder, look at each other with merry glances while, from the open wound of their victim, issues pure and scarlet the Christian blood destined for their sweet bread of Purim."[15] An uproar abroad ensued, which induced the Saudi editor, who seems not to know what appears in his own newspaper, to repudiate the article as nonsense, averring that it should not have been published. Such retractions are typically for foreign consumption but are not set forth in Arabic for the enlightenment of Muslims. Following are excerpts from the article entitled "Jews Use Teenagers' Blood for 'Purim' Pastries."

Special Ingredient for Jewish Holidays Is Human Blood from Non-Jewish Youth

I chose to [speak] about the Jewish holiday of Purim, because it is connected to the month of March. This holiday has some dangerous customs that will, no doubt, horrify you, and I apologize if any reader is harmed because of this.

During this holiday, the Jew must prepare very special pastries, the filling of which is not only costly and rare—it cannot be found at all on the local and international markets.

Unfortunately, this filling cannot be left out, or substituted with any alternative serving the same purpose. For this holiday, the Jewish people must obtain human blood so that their clerics can prepare the holiday pastries: In other words, the practice cannot be carried out as required if human blood is not spilled!!

Before I go into the details, I would like to clarify that the Jews' spilling human blood to prepare pastry for their holidays is a well-established fact, historically and legally, all throughout history. This was one of the main reasons for the persecution and exile that were their lot in Europe and Asia at various times.

This holiday [Purim] begins with a fast, on March 13, like the Jewess Esther who vowed to fast. The holiday continues on March 14; during the holiday, the Jews wear carnival-style masks and costumes and overindulge in drinking alcohol, prostitution, and adultery.

This holiday has become known among Muslim historians as the "Holiday of Masks."

How the Jews Drain the Blood from Their Young Victims

Who was Esther, and why the Jews sanctify her and act as she did, I will clarify in my article next Tuesday,[16] Allah willing. Today, I would like to tell you how human blood is spilled so it can be used for their holiday pastries. The blood is spilled in a special way. How is it done?

For this holiday, the victim must be a mature adolescent who is, of course, a non-Jew—that is, a Christian or a Muslim. His blood is taken and dried into granules. The cleric blends these granules into the pastry dough; they can also be saved for the next holiday. In contrast, for the Passover slaughtering, about which I intend to write one of these days, the blood of Christian and Muslim children under the age of 10 must be used, and the cleric can mix the blood [into the dough] before or after dehydration.

The Actions of the Jewish Vampires Cause Them Pleasure

Let us now examine how the victims' blood is spilled. For this, a needle-studded barrel is used; this is a kind of barrel, about the size of the human body, with extremely sharp needles set in it on all sides. [These needles] pierce the victim's body, from the moment he is placed in the barrel.

These needles do the job, and the victim's blood drips from him very slowly. Thus, the victim suffers dreadful torment—torment that affords the Jewish vampires great delight as they carefully monitor every detail of the blood-shedding with pleasure and love that are difficult to comprehend.

After this barbaric display, the Jews take the spilled blood, in the bottle set in the bottom [of the needle-studded barrel], and the Jewish cleric makes his co-religionists completely happy on their holiday when he serves them the pastries in which human blood is mixed.

There is another way to spill the blood: The victim can be slaughtered as a sheep is slaughtered, and his blood collected in a container. Or, the victim's veins can be slit in several places, letting his blood drain from his body.

This blood is very carefully collected—as I have already noted—by the "rabbi," the Jewish cleric, the chef who specializes in preparing these kinds of pastries.

The human race refuses even to look at the Jewish pastries, let alone prepare them or consume them![17]

Mahathir Mohamad

Farewell Address to the Organization of the Islamic Conference, 2003

Mahathir Mohamad, the autocratic prime minister of Malaysia, 1981–2003, was notable for modernizing the country through sustained economic growth, improving education, and raising the standard of living by conversion from exporting raw materials to high-tech products. Mahathir has been called "pugnacious," "clever" but "loathsome," and "forward-looking" but "guilty of serious abuses of power." Throughout his career, Mahathir has indulged in attacks on Jews as "monsters" and the like. In the 1970s he wrote that "The Jews . . . are not merely hook-nosed but understand money instinctively." During the 1997–1998 Asian economic crisis, he proclaimed "that this is a plot by the Jews," engineered in particular by the Holocaust survivor and financier George Soros. Most of his farewell speech of October 16, 2003, delivered before the assembled presidents, kings, sheiks, and emirs representing the fifty-seven members of the Organization of the Islamic Conference, was devoted to criticism of Muslim society and governments, and especially Muslim clergy. His critique is consistent with recent searching and wide-ranging analysis and evaluation by some Muslim intellectuals and moderates, as it contrasts with the extremism of the1968 Cairo Conference. However, Mahathir could not refrain from nastily attacking Jews. While he seemed to be saying that Muslims should study Jewish successes, Mahathir later appeared to assume an apocalyptic struggle, declaring that "1.3 billion Muslims cannot be defeated by a few million Jews." In response to widespread criticisms, Mahathir repeated his assertion "that they control the world." Far from denying the Holocaust, he said, "We sympathize with them, we were very sad to see how the Jews were so ill treated by the Europeans," yet nullified that positive feeling with the false assertion that "Muslims have never ill treated the Jews" and the even falser claim that "now they are behaving [against Palestinians] exactly in the way the Europeans behaved toward them." Mahathir insists that he is not antisemitic, that he has Jewish friends, that he urges Muslims to renounce violence, and that he wants a peaceful resolution of the Israeli-Palestinian conflict. But, as the following speech indicates, he perpetuates the myth, among others, that the Jews are a conspiratorial people seeking world domination.

To begin with, the Governments of all the Muslim countries can close ranks and have a common stand if not on all issues, at least on some major ones, such as on Palestine. We are all Muslims. We are all oppressed. We are all being humiliated. . . .

The early Muslims produced great mathematicians and scientists, scholar physicians and astronomers etc., and they excelled in all the fields of knowledge of their times, besides studying and practicing their own religion of Islam. As a result the Muslims were able to develop and extract wealth from their lands and through their world trade, able to strengthen their defenses, protect their people and give them the Islamic way of life. . . . At the time the Europeans of the Middle Ages were still superstitious and backward, the enlightened Muslims had already built a great Muslim civilisation, respected and powerful, more than able to compete with the rest of the world and able to protect the *ummah* [the Muslim community] from foreign aggression. The Europeans had to kneel at the feet of Muslim scholars in order to access their own scholastic heritage [of classical Greece]. . . .

But halfway through the building of the great Islamic civilisation came new interpreters of Islam who taught that acquisition of knowledge by Muslims meant only the study of Islamic theology. The study of science, medicine, etc. was discouraged.

Intellectually the Muslims began to regress. With intellectual regression the great Muslim civilisation began to falter and wither. But for the emergence of the Ottoman warriors, Muslim civilisation would have disappeared with the fall of Granada [to Spain] in 1492.

The early successes of the Ottomans were not accompanied by an intellectual renaissance. . . . The Industrial Revolution was totally missed by the Muslims. And the regression continued until the British and French instigated rebellion against Turkish rule brought about the downfall of the Ottomans [in World War I]. . . .

. . . The Europeans could do what they liked with Muslim territories. It is not surprising that they should excise Muslim land to create the state of Israel to solve their Jewish problem. Divided, the Muslims could do nothing effective to stop the Balfour [Declaration of 1917] and Zionist transgression. . . .

There is a feeling of hopelessness among the Muslim countries and their people. They feel that they can do nothing right. They believe that things can only get worse. The Muslims will forever be oppressed and dominated by the Europeans and the Jews. . . .

But is it true that we should do and can do nothing for ourselves? Is it true that 1.3 billion people can exert no power to save themselves from the humiliation and oppression inflicted upon them by [Israel] a much smaller enemy? Can they only lash back blindly in anger? Is there no other way than to ask of young people to blow themselves up and kill people and invite the massacre of more of our own people?

It cannot be that there is no other way. 1.3 billion Muslims cannot be defeated by a few million Jews. There must be a way. And we can only find a way if we stop to think, to assess our weaknesses and our strength, to plan, to strategise and then to counterattack. . . .

We are actually very strong. 1.3 billion people cannot be simply wiped out. The Europeans killed 6 million Jews out of 12 million. But today the Jews run this world by proxy. They get others to fight and die for them. . . .

We also know that not all non-Muslims are against us. Some are well disposed towards us. Some even see our enemies as their enemies. Even among the Jews there are many who do not approve of what the Israelis are doing. . . .

Over the past 50 years of fighting in Palestine we have not achieved any result. We have in fact worsened our situation. . . . But think. We are up against a people who think. They survived 2000 years of pogroms not by hitting back, but by thinking. They invented and successfully promoted Socialism, Communism, human rights and democracy so that persecuting them would appear to be wrong, so they may enjoy equal rights with others. With these they have now gained control of the most powerful countries and they, this tiny community, have become a world power. We cannot fight them through brawn alone. We must use our brains also.

Of late because of their power and their apparent success they have become arrogant. And arrogant people, like angry people, will make mistakes, will forget to think.

They are already beginning to make mistakes. And they will make more mistakes. There may be windows of opportunity for us now and in the future. We must seize these opportunities.[18]

NOTES

1. Quoted in Paul Berman, *Terror and Liberalism* (New York: Norton, 2003), 119–120; terrorism in quest of a political or ideological ideal has a compelling precedent in

practice in Robespierre, the Committee of Public Safety, and the terror of the French Revolution; in theory in the numerous Christian movements of the late Middle Ages that would redeem humanity and inaugurate the millennium by mass slaughter, especially of Jews; such ideas stem from the biblical books Daniel and Revelation.

2. Ronald L. Nettler, *Past Trials and Present Tribulations: A Muslim Fundamentalist's View of the Jews* (Oxford: Pergamon Press, 1987), 54.

3. Hugh S. Galford, "Sayyid Qutb and the Qur'anic Story of Joseph," in *Muslim-Jewish Encounters, Intellectual Traditions and Modern Politics*, ed. Ronald L. Nettler and Suha Taji-Farouki (Amsterdam: Harwood Academic Publishers, 1998), 48.

4. Qutb's exposition in Arabic is extremely sarcastic and demeaning.

5. From "Our Struggle with the Jews" [*Maa'rakatuna ma' al-Yahud*], ed. Zein al-Din al-Rukabi (Jeda, a-Dar a-Sau'diyya: li-Nashr wa-a-Tawzi', 1970), 41-64, trans. Shlomo Daskal for this volume, 2003.

6. From D. F. Green, ed., *Arab Theologians on Jews and Israel; Extracts from the Proceedings of the Fourth Conference of the Academy of Islamic Research*, 3rd ed. (Genève: Éditions de l'avenir, 1976), 18, 23-25, 27, 33, 36-38, 42-43, 46, 58, 60; minor errors of grammar and spelling have been corrected but without changing the meaning; the speakers, unidentified here, are representative of the conference and spoke, as it were, with one voice.

7. From D. F. Green, *Arab Theologians on Jews and Israel*, 94.

8. Andrea Nüsse, "The Ideology of Hamas," in *Studies in Muslim-Jewish Relations*, 2 vols., ed. Ronald L. Nettler (Philadelphia: Harwood Academic Publishers, 1993), 1: 109.

9. From "Charter of Islamic Resistance Movement," Hamas, Gaza, *Selected Translations and Analysis* (Simon Wiesenthal Center, Fall 1988).

10. From Special Dispatch No. 166, Egypt, Dec. 16, 2000, www.memri.org, website of the Middle East Media & Research Institute (MEMRI), the best source for Middle Eastern press material translated from the Arabic.

11. "Elie Wiesel on Durban," *Yedioth Ahronoth*, Sept. 2001, p. 14.

12. Quoted by Efraim Karsh, "Intifada II: The Long Trail of Arab Anti-Semitism," *Commentary*, 110 (Dec. 2000): 51.

13. From www.memri.org (MEMRI).

14. From Fiamma Nirenstein, "Observations: How Suicide Bombers are Made," *Commentary*, 112 (Sept. 2001): 52-55; translations from the Arab press are from MEMRI, on its website at www.memri.org.

15. David I. Kertzer, *The Popes against the Jews* (New York: Knopf, 2001), 92-93, a screed long accepted by popes and touted as authoritative by the Nazi Julius Streicher; Drumont as quoted in Malcolm Hay, *The Foot of Pride* (Boston: Beacon Press, 1950), 191.

16. In the article's sequel (March 12), the columnist tells the story of the Book of Esther and concludes, "Since then, the Old Testament, the Jewish holy book, requires the Jews to glorify this holiday and show their joy. This joy can only be complete with the consumption of pastries mixed with human blood."

17. From Special Dispatch No. 354, Saudi Arabia/Arab Antisemitism, 3/13/02, from the Saudi government daily, *Al-Riyadh*, March 10, 2002, www.memri.org (MEMRI).

18. From Google, oicsummit2003.org.my/speech; *The New York Times*, Oct. 20, 2003, A1-13; see also Paul Krugman, "Listening to Mahathir," *The New York Times*, Oct. 21, 2003, A27.

BIBLIOGRAPHY

General

Baron, Salo Wittmayer. *A Social and Religious History of the Jews.* 2nd ed. 18 vols. New York: Columbia University Press, 1952-1983.

Carmichael, Joel. *The Satanizing of the Jews: The Origin and Development of Mystical Anti-Semitism.* New York: Fromm, 1992.

Carroll, James. *Constantine's Sword: The Church and the Jews: A History.* Boston: Houghton Mifflin, 2000.

Flannery, Edward H. *The Anguish of the Jews: Twenty-Three Centuries of Antisemitism.* Rev. and updated. New York: Paulist Press, 1985.

Katz, Jacob. *Exclusiveness and Tolerance.* Oxford: Oxford University Press, 1961.

Langmuir, Gavin I. *History, Religion, and Antisemitism.* Berkeley: University of California Press, 1990.

Laqueur, Walter. *The Changing Face of Anti-Semitism: From Ancient Times to the Present Day.* Oxford: Oxford University Press, 2006.

Levy, Richard S., ed. *Antisemitism: A Historical Encyclopedia of Prejudice and Persecution.* 2 vols. Denver: ABC-CLIO, 2005.

———, ed. *Antisemitism in the Modern World: An Anthology of Texts.* Lexington, Mass.: D. C. Heath, 1991.

Michael, Robert, and Philip Rosen. *Dictionary of Antisemitism from the Earliest Times to the Present.* Lanham, Md.: Scarecrow Press, 2006.

Nicholls, William. *Christian Antisemitism: A History of Hate.* London: Jason Aronson, 1993.

Perry, Marvin, and Frederick M. Schweitzer. *Antisemitism: Myth and Hate from Antiquity to the Present.* 2002; paperback, New York: Palgrave Macmillan, 2005.

———, eds. *Jewish-Christian Encounters over the Centuries: Symbiosis, Prejudice, Holocaust, Dialogue.* New York: Peter Lang, 1994.

Poliakov, Léon. *The History of Anti-Semitism.* 4 vols. New York: Vanguard, 1965-1986.

Wistrich, Robert S. *Antisemitism: The Longest Hatred.* New York: Pantheon, 1991.

Part 1

Chazan, Robert. *Medieval Stereotypes and Modern Antisemitism.* Los Angeles: University of California Press, 1997.

Cohn, Norman. *Pursuit of the Millennium: Revolutionary Millenarians and Mystical Anarchists of the Middle Ages.* London: Palidin, 1970.

Crossan, John Dominic. *Who Killed Jesus? Exposing the Roots of Anti-Semitism in the Gospel Story of the Death of Jesus.* New York: HarperCollins, 1995.

Dundes, Alan, ed. *The Blood Libel Legend: A Casebook in Anti-Semitic Folklore.* Madison: University of Wisconsin Press, 1991.

Edwards, John, ed. and trans. *The Jews in Western Europe 1400-1600.* Manchester, England: Manchester University Press, 1994.

Frankel, Jonathan. *The Damascus Affair: "Ritual Murder," Politics, and the Jews in 1840.* Cambridge: Cambridge University Press, 1997.

Gager, John. G. *The Origins of Anti-Semitism.* New York: Oxford University Press, 1985.

Hsia, R. Po-Chia. *The Myth of Ritual Murder.* New Haven, Conn.: Yale University Press, 1989.

Jones, Norman. *God and the Moneylenders: Usury and Law in Early Modern England.* Oxford: Blackwell, 1989.

Kamen, Henry. *Inquisition and Society in Spain in the Sixteenth and Seventeenth Centuries.* Bloomington: Indiana University Press, 1985.

Langmuir, Gavin I. *Toward a Definition of Antisemitism.* Berkeley: University of California Press, 1990.

Marcus, Jacob R. *The Jew in the Medieval World: A Source Book: 315-1791.* 1938. Reprint, New York: Harper and Row, 1965.

Michael, Robert. *Holy Hatred: Christianity, Antisemitism, and the Holocaust.* New York: Palgrave Macmillan, 2006.

Netanyahu, Benzion. *The Marranos of Spain from the Late Fourteenth to the Early Sixteenth Century.* Ithaca: Cornell University Press, 1999.

Parkes, James. *The Conflict of the Church and the Synagogue: A Study in the Origins of Antisemitism.* New York: Atheneum, 1969.

——. *The Jew in the Medieval Community.* 2nd ed. New York: Hermon Press, 1976.

Roth, Cecil. *A History of the Marranos.* Philadelphia: Jewish Publication Society, 1932.

Rubin, Miri. *Gentile Tales: The Narrative Assault on Late Medieval Jews.* New Haven, Conn.: Yale University Press, 1999.

Sanders, E. P. *Jesus and Judaism.* Philadelphia: Fortress Press, 1985.

Shapiro, James. *Oberammergau: The Troubling Story of the World's Most Famous Passion Play.* New York: Pantheon, 2000.

Tomson, Peter J. *Presumed Guilty: How the Jews Were Blamed for the Death of Jesus.* Trans. Janet Dyk. Minneapolis: Fortress Press, 2005.

Trachtenberg, Joshua. *The Devil and the Jews: The Medieval Conception of the Jew and Its Relationship to Modern Anti-Semitism.* Philadelphia: Jewish Publication Society, 1943.

Part 2

Bartov, Omer. *The Eastern Front, 1941-45, German Troops and the Barbarisation of Warfare.* New York: St. Martin's Press, 1986.

——. *Germany's War and the Holocaust: Disputed Histories.* Ithaca: Cornell University Press, 2003.

——. *Murder in Our Midst: The Holocaust, Industrial Killing, and Representation.* Oxford: Oxford University Press, 1996.

Bauer, Yehuda. *Rethinking the Holocaust.* New Haven, Conn.: Yale University Press, 2001.

Birnbaum, Pierre. *The Anti-Semitic Moment: A Tour of France in 1898.* Trans. Jane Marie Todd. New York: Hill and Wang, 2003.

——. *Anti-Semitism in France: A Political History from Léon Blum to the Present.* Trans. Miriam Kochan. Oxford: Blackwell, 1992.

Browning, Christopher. *Ordinary Men: Reserve Battalion 101 and the Final Solution.* New York: HarperCollins, 1992.

Brustein, William I. *Roots of Hate: Anti-Semitism in Europe before the Holocaust.* Cambridge: Cambridge University Press, 2003.

Busi, Frederick. *The Pope of Antisemitism: The Career and Legacy of Edouard-Adolphe Drumont.* New York: University Press of America, 1986.

Byrnes, Robert F. *Anti-Semitism in Modern France.* New York: Howard Fertig, 1969.

Carlebach, Julius. *Karl Marx and the Radical Critique of Judaism.* London: Routledge and Kegan Paul, 1978.

Cohn, Norman. *Warrant for Genocide: The Myth of the Jewish World-Conspiracy and the Protocols of the Elders of Zion.* 3rd ed. Chico, Calif.: Scholars Press, 1981.

De Felici, Renzo. *The Jews in Fascist Italy: A History.* Trans. Michael A. Ledeen. New York: Enigma Books. 2001.

Dwork, Debórah, and Robert Jan van Pelt. *Auschwitz: 1270 to the Present.* New York: Norton, 1996.

Feingold, Henry. *The Politics of Rescue: The Roosevelt Administration and the Holocaust, 1938-1945.* New Brunswick, N.J.: Rutgers University Press, 1970.

Fischer, Klaus P. *The History of an Obsession: German Judeophobia and the Holocaust.* New York: Continuum, 1998.

Friedländer, Saul. *Nazi Germany and the Jews,* 2 vols. New York: HarperCollins, 1997, 2007.

Gutman, Yisrael, and Michael Berenbaum, eds. *Anatomy of the Auschwitz Camp.* Bloomington: Indiana University Press, 1994.

Hertzberg, Arthur. *The French Enlightenment and the Jews.* New York: Columbia University Press, 1968.

Hilberg, Raul. *The Destruction of the European Jews.* 3rd ed. New Haven, Conn.: Yale University Press, 2003.

Hofstadter, Richard. *The Paranoid Style in American Politics and Other Essays.* New York: Knopf, 1966.

Jacobs, Steven L., and Mark Weitzman. *Dismantling the Big Lie: The Protocols of the Elders of Zion.* Jersey City: Ktav, 2004.

Judge, Edward H. *Easter in Kishinev: Anatomy of a Pogrom.* New York: New York University Press, 1992.

Katz, Jacob. *From Prejudice to Destruction: Anti-Semitism, 1700-1933.* Cambridge, Mass.: Harvard University Press, 1980.

Kertzer, David I. *The Popes against the Jews: The Vatican's Role in the Rise of Modern Anti Semitism.* New York: Knopf, 2001.

Klier, John D., and Shlomo Lambroza, eds. *Pogroms: Anti-Jewish Violence in Modern Russian History.* Cambridge: Cambridge University Press, 1992.

Marrus, Michael R. *The Holocaust in History.* New York: New American Library, 1989.

Mosse, George L. *The Crisis of German Ideology: The Intellectual Origins of the Third Reich.* New York: Grosset and Dunlap, 1964.

Pauley, Bruce F. *From Prejudice to Persecution: A History of Austrian Anti-Semitism.* Chapel Hill: University of North Carolina Press, 1992.

Penslar, Derek J. *Shylock's Children: Economics and Jewish Identity in Modern Europe.* Berkeley: University of California Press, 2001.

Phayer, Michael. *The Catholic Church and the Holocaust, 1930-1965.* Bloomington: Indiana University Press, 2000.

Pulzer, Peter G. J. *The Rise of Political Anti-Semitism in Germany and Austria.* New York: Wiley, 1964.

Rose, Paul Lawrence. *German Question/Jewish Question: Revolutionary Antisemitism from Kant to Wagner.* Princeton: Princeton University Press, 1990.

Rosenberg, Alan, and Gerald E. Meyers, eds. *Echoes from the Holocaust.* Philadelphia: Temple University Press, 1988.

Rummel, Rudolph J. *Democide: Nazi Genocide and Mass Murder.* New Brunswick, N.J.: Transaction Press, 1992.

Sereny, Gitta. *Into That Darkness: From Mercy Killing to Mass Murder.* New York: McGraw-Hill, 1974.

Weber, Max. *The Protestant Ethic and the Spirit of Capitalism.* Trans. Talcott Parsons. New York: Scribner's, 1958.

Wegner, Gregory Paul. *Anti-Semitism and Schooling under the Third Reich*. London: Routledge Falmer, 2002.

Weiss, John, *Ideology of Death: Why the Holocaust Happened in Germany*. Chicago: Ivan R. Dee, 1996.

———. *The Politics of Hate: Anti-Semitism, History, and the Holocaust in Modern Europe*. Chicago: Ivan R. Dee, 2003.

Yahil, Leni. *The Holocaust*. Oxford: Oxford University Press, 1987.

Part 3

Banki, Judith H., and John T. Pawlikowski, eds. *Ethics in the Shadow of the Holocaust: Christian and Jewish Perspectives*. Chicago: Sheed and Ward, 2001.

Canto, David. *The Religious Right*. New York: Anti-Defamation League, 1994.

Cohen, Mark R. *Under Crescent and Cross: The Jews in the Middle Ages*. Princeton: Princeton University Press, 1994.

Dinnerstein, Leonard. *Antisemitism in America*. New York: Oxford University Press, 1994.

Evans, Richard. *Lying about Hitler: History, Holocaust and the David Irving Trial*. New York: Basic Books, 2001.

Faber, Eli. *Jews, Slaves, and the Slave Trade: Setting the Record Straight*. New York: New York University Press, 1998.

Friedman, Murray. *What Went Wrong? The Creation & Collapse of the Black-Jewish Alliance*. New York: Free Press, 1995.

Friedman, Saul S. *Jews and the American Slave Trade*. New Brunswick, N.J.: Transaction Press, 1998.

Goldberg, Robert Alan. *Enemies Within: The Culture of Conspiracy in Modern America*. New Haven, Conn.: Yale University Press, 2001.

Guttenplan, D. D. *The Holocaust on Trial*. New York: Norton, 2001.

Hockenos, Matthew D. *A Church Divided: German Protestants Confront the Nazi Past*. Bloomington: Indiana University Press, 2004.

Iganski, Paul, and Barry Kosmin, eds. *A New Antisemitism? Debating Judeophobia in 21st-Century Britain*. London: Profile Books, 2003.

Lewis, Bernard. *The Jews of Islam*. Princeton: Princeton University Press, 1984.

———. *Race and Slavery in the Middle East: An Historical Inquiry*. New York: Oxford University Press, 1990.

———. *Semites and Antisemites*. New York: Norton, 1986.

Lifton, Robert Jay. *The Nazi Doctors: Medical Killing and the Psychology of Genocide*. New York: Basic Books, 1986.

Lipstadt, Deborah E. *Denying the Holocaust: The Growing Assault on Truth and Memory*. New York: Free Press, 1993.

Marcus, Jacob R., ed. *The Jew in the American World, A Source Book*. Detroit: Wayne State University Press, 1996.

Michael, Robert. *A Concise History of American Antisemitism*. New York: Bowman and Littlefield, 2005.

Passelecq, Georges, and Bernard Suchecky. *The Hidden Encyclical*. Trans. Steven Rendall. New York: Harcourt Brace, 1997.

Rittner, Carol, and John K. Roth, eds. *Pope Pius XII and the Holocaust*. London: Leicester University Press, 2002.

Shermer, Michael, and Alex Grobman. *Denying History: Who Says the Holocaust Never Happened and Why Do They Say It?* Berkeley: University of California Press, 2000.

Stillman, Norman A. *The Jews of Arab Lands: A History and Source Book*. Philadelphia: Jewish Publication Society of America, 1979.

———. *The Jews of Arab Lands in Modern Times*. Philadelphia: Jewish Publication Society of America, 1991.

Taguieff, Pierre-André. *Rising from the Muck: The New Anti-Semitism in Europe*. Trans. Patrick Camiller. Chicago: Ivan R. Dee, 2004.

Wasserstein, Bernard. *Vanishing Diaspora: The Jews in Europe since 1945*. Cambridge, Mass.: Harvard University Press, 1996.

West, Cornel. *Race Matters*. Boston: Beacon Press, 1993.

Wistrich, Robert S. *Muslim Anti-Semitism: A Clear and Present Danger*. New York: American Jewish Committee, 2002.

DETAILED TABLE
OF CONTENTS

PART 2. MODERN

INDEX

DR. MARVIN PERRY taught history at Baruch College, City University of New York, for many years. His books include *An Intellectual History of Modern Europe; Arnold Toynbee and the Western Tradition; Antisemitism: Myth and Hate from Antiquity to the Present* (co-author with Frederick M. Schweitzer); *Jewish-Christian Encounters over the Centuries: Symbiosis, Prejudice, Holocaust, Dialogue* (co-editor with Frederick M. Schweitzer); and *Western Civilization: A Brief History.*

DR. FREDERICK M. SCHWEITZER taught modern European and world history for forty years at Manhattan College. He has worked for forty-plus years in Jewish-Christian relations and Jewish history. He is a legally certified expert on antisemitism and his testimony in behalf of the Canadian Human Rights Commission was instrumental in a landmark decision barring a Holocaust denier and antisemite from the Internet. Schweitzer contributes reviews and articles to scholarly journals and encyclopedias, and he has co-authored several works with Marvin Perry.

- eugenics
- the killing of children/disabled people

CPSIA information can be obtained
at www.ICGtesting.com
Printed in the USA
LVHW022105131122
733046LV00003B/14